ROGUE FORCES

AN EXPLOSIVE INSIDERS' ACCOUNT OF AUSTRALIAN SAS WAR CRIMES IN AFGHANISTAN

MARK WILLACY

SIMON &
SCHUSTER

London · New York · Sydney · Toronto · New Delhi

ROGUE FORCES
First published in Australia in 2021 by
Simon & Schuster (Australia) Pty Limited
Suite 19A, Level 1, Building C, 450 Miller Street, Cammeray, NSW 2062

10 9 8 7 6 5 4 3 2 1

Sydney New York London Toronto New Delhi
Visit our website at www.simonandschuster.com.au

A catalogue record for this
book is available from the
National Library of Australia

ISBN: 9781761101786

Images on pages 4 (top), 6 (top) and 8 (top) of the first photo insert, and pages 2 (bottom)
and 5 (top) of the second photo insert, supplied courtesy of Dusty Miller. Images on pages 6
(bottom) and 7 (top) of the first photo insert supplied courtesy of Braden Chapman.
Images on pages 12 (top & bottom), 13 (top), 15 (bottom) of the first photo insert, and
page 3 (centre & bottom) of the second photo insert, supplied courtesy of an Afghan
journalist employed by the ABC. Image on page 21 (bottom) supplied courtesy of
Jeremy Ross. Images on page 22 (top & bottom) supplied courtesy of Andrew Hastie.
Image on page 23 supplied courtesy of Fergus McLachlan.
Extracts from the *No Limitations* podcast in Chapter 18 reproduced with permission
from Blenheim Partners Executive Search and Board Advisory Firm.

Cover design: Luke Causby/Blue Cork
Typeset by Midland Typesetters, Australia
Printed and bound in Australia by Griffin Press

We are the Pilgrims, master; we shall go
Always a little further; it may be
Beyond that last blue mountain barred with snow
Across that angry or that glimmering sea.

James Elroy Flecker, *Hassan: The Story of Hassan of Baghdad and How he Came to Make the Golden Journey to Samarkand: A Play in Five Acts*

(As inscribed on the clock tower of the Hereford barracks of the British SAS)

CONTENTS

For Braden, Christina, Dusty and Tom

INTRODUCTION

Peruse the shelves of any bookstore or browse online and you will find an almost inexhaustible array of titles espousing the derring-do of the Special Forces. No unit has been written about or lauded more in print than the Special Air Service, better known as the SAS. From the British SAS's beginnings in the deserts of North Africa as a ramshackle congregation of oddball aristocrats, cut throat reprobates and men of simmering violence, readers have been captivated by the exploits of these undeniably brave and remarkable soldiers. In Australia too, much has been written about our own Special Air Service Regiment and its feats behind enemy lines in places like Vietnam, Iraq and Afghanistan. These deeds, and the men who perform them, deserve recognition and acclaim, though most shun it, preferring to remain true to the secretive ethos of the Regiment. But maybe there is a murkier reason some of these men prefer secrets. Operational cloak and dagger is critical to the work the SAS does, but it can also mask mistakes, misconduct and misdemeanours. Until very recently, little has been written about the truly nasty business that has occurred in the shadows, acts that violate not only the Australian military's Rules of Engagement, but the very morality, standards and professionalism upon which the SAS has built its name.

No conflict has tested the SAS like Afghanistan. A land of seemingly intractable conflict, its soaring peaks and deep valleys make it a place of natural shadows. For centuries, the laws of war here were dismissed as a rather quaint notion propagated by invading Western armies brandishing technologically superior weaponry. But those same Western armies often dispensed with those rules the moment they were confronted by a hostile landscape and a cunning, ruthless and relentless Afghan resistance. Massacre and murder became necessary and convenient substitutes for the more confining laws of war.

This book is not an historian's account of what Australia's Special Forces did in Afghanistan. It certainly is not a hagiographical potboiler like many of those that litter the military and history sections of our bookshops. This book is an attempt at a nuanced investigation into what some – I repeat, *some* – of our SAS soldiers did in Afghanistan. It explores in detail how those soldiers visited needless and terrible violence on Afghan civilians, prisoners and combatants who had surrendered from the fight. It delves into the circumstances of these crimes – the perpetrators, the victims, the enablers, the possible motives, the methods, the cover ups, and the code of silence that allowed this deviance to perpetuate. But at its core, this is a book about good people – men and women who were drawn into these dark events by virtue of their service, and who, driven by good conscience and a desire for justice, have emerged to stand on the right side of history. They have done this at great cost. Some have had their careers destroyed, while others remain riven by guilt and shame over what they have seen or been forced to do. Almost all of them still suffer from the moral injuries and bear the psychological scars inflicted by what they have witnessed. To me, these people represent the true ethos of the SAS because, despite it all, they want to see things made right.

I have spent more than two years investigating allegations of Australian Special Forces war crimes in Afghanistan, producing more than 20 separate stories for the ABC on alleged unlawful killings, cover ups, bashings and cultural deviance. The most memorable and devastating of these stories was 'Killing Field', a *Four Corners* program that broadcast – for the first time – the killing of an unarmed and frightened Afghan man in a field by an SAS operator. Caught on the helmet camera of a patrol member, this horrific killing shocked many SAS members past and present and resulted in an Australian Federal Police war crimes investigation. It also sparked a new line of investigation by the Inspector-General of the Australian Defence Force's Brereton war crimes inquiry. As one senior Defence officer told me after the program went to air, 'Killing Field' was a game-changer. For me, it was the beginning of the journey to this book. After the *Four Corners* program was broadcast I was contacted by other former Special Forces soldiers and support staff with their own gut-wrenching stories. Their consciences jarred by 'Killing Field', or simply realising that the time was right to tell what they knew, they trusted me with their stories. They helped me uncover new killings. They gave me undeniable evidence and eyewitness testimony about senseless atrocities. They led me to the doorsteps of the alleged killers, men they served alongside. One SAS operator accused of war crimes even invited me to come and sit with him and listen to why he killed the Afghans he killed. 'We just go in there and just do the job, because it takes bad men to do bad work in the end,' he told me. Consequently, I was left with hundreds of hours of interviews, thousands of photos, dozens of video files, and a series of stories that are being told for the first time in this book.

Rogue Forces attempts to tell the story of what went wrong in Afghanistan through the lens of one SAS squadron during one deployment in one given year. It is an attempt to explain the macro through the micro. I hope it provides the reader with an understanding of how one of the world's most elite and honourable Special Forces units could normalise deviance.

I will no doubt be charged by some with besmirching the great and venerable Regiment, and along with it the daring soldiers who for years fought valiantly and tirelessly in Afghanistan against a callous and miscreant enemy. I know this because I have already been accused of capital crime-level treachery for having the impudence to report on allegations of Australian war crimes for the ABC. However, I hope these critics read this book and understand that, at its heart, it celebrates true grit and raw courage of the type these same self-declared patriots supposedly defend and espouse.

To me, the most courageous people are those soldiers who agreed to go on the record for this book, thereby risking ostracism, recrimination, and even physical reprisal. Dozens more spoke to me on the condition of anonymity, many of them desperate to see the honour of their beloved Regiment restored through a sustained blast of journalistic sunlight.

While these good people have often bared their souls, shared their dark stories and strived to expose the terrible things they witnessed, the Australian Defence Force wanted nothing to do with this book. In this, I was not surprised. Despite knowing that the ADF would decline my overtures, I formally asked for interviews with the Chief of Defence, Angus Campbell, and with the Chief of Army, Rick Burr, both men who came up through the ranks of the SAS and who both held key positions during the Afghanistan war. Six weeks after my approach I received an email from Defence Media 'politely' declining the opportunity to participate. No reasons were given for this.

Maybe it is for the best because it has provided more space in the book for those who made up the so-called tip of the spear – the medics who patched up the wounded, the signals intelligence officers who tracked the targets, and the soldiers who squeezed the triggers, not to mention the Afghans whose villages or compounds were raided or destroyed and whose family members were taken prisoner or left dead and bleeding. Paradoxically, the Afghan people are an often forgotten part of the Afghanistan War. For years they complained about killings by Australian soldiers and their allies, only to be dismissed as liars, money-seekers, or Taliban stooges. This book aims to correct that injustice, at least as best it can. From the Kuchi nomad camps of Deh Rawood, to the wheat fields of Deh Jawz-e Hasanzai, to the mud compounds of Shah Wali Kot, these people have recounted their stories. Their courage, honour and endurance is equal to that of the Australian Special Forces soldiers who have also helped me to try to understand what happened and why.

PROLOGUE

GETTING AWAY WITH IT
(ALL MESSED UP)

'Once the killing starts, it is difficult to draw the line'
Tacitus

'We were crossing a field.'

Tom is staring at the fireplace. We are sitting in his lounge, high up on a hill among the ghost gums. It is winter, and a mist has settled in the valley below us. Wood ducks glide across the dam next to the house.

Tom's 50-kilogram South African mastiff is lying across his lap snoring.

He is taking me back to 2012. The field Tom is crossing is in the Shah Wali Kot district, a Taliban stronghold in Afghanistan's Kandahar Province. A world away from rural Victoria.

Tom's SAS patrol has been dropped in the field by helicopter. They sprint from underneath its whirling blades. They are at their most vulnerable here, easy targets out in the open.

Tom is an 'operator', a trigger puller. If there is killing to be done, the operators do it. They wear the coveted sandy beret of the Special Air Service Regiment, the SAS. On the beret is a badge depicting the sword Excalibur wreathed in flames. It is also inscribed with the regimental motto 'Who Dares Wins'. Only operators get the beret. The other SAS staff – the signal intelligence officers, the radio operators, the medics – don't qualify.

As the former British commander Sir Robert Fry once put it, SAS soldiers must have a capacity for 'elegant unpleasantness'.

What is about to happen is extremely unpleasant. There is nothing elegant about it.

Tom is a trooper in 3 Squadron SAS, the equivalent to an Australian Army private. It is one of the Regiment's three 'sabre' or combat squadrons. Known as the 'Third Herd', the men of 3 Squadron wear patches on their shoulders depicting a fearsome long-horned bull with demonic red eyes.

Other patches serve a more practical and potentially life-saving purpose. Operators velcro their blood type to their shoulders or helmets. 'B NEG', 'O POS', 'B POS'.

A few of the men wear another patch too, one that they know could cause deep offence in the Islamic Republic of Afghanistan. It is not an Australian Defence Force approved insignia, but these SAS operators wear this symbol proudly. It is in the shape of a shield, and a Christian cross lies within it. It is the cross of the Knights Templar, one of the most skilled military units of the Crusades. In the 12th century, the Templars were often used as heavily armoured shock troops, the first into battle against the Muslim enemy.

Those who wear the cross patch are sending a message – one of pure intimidation.

'If you're waking people up in the middle of the night and you wanted an effect, I think there was a place for it,' says an SAS operator. 'We used to walk out on jobs and give ourselves the white hand of Saruman like *Lord of the Rings*, [camouflage] on our faces because you wanted that intimidating, scary effect. You're chasing a bad guy. You're not there for hearts and minds. You're hunting someone.'

The Third Herd has only been in Afghanistan for a month. But like most of his 3 Squadron comrades, Tom has been here before.

He has been an operator for four years. He did the gruelling three-week SAS selection process twice and finished it both times. But the first time he is told he hasn't demonstrated enough 'resolve'. He has passed and failed at the same time.

'The rhetoric has always been that you are really looking for similar features to a psychopath,' says a psychologist who was involved in screening Special Forces candidates.

But they don't really want psychopaths. Just men who exhibit a few of their traits.

'What we're looking for is someone who has high sensation-seeking attributes. They want to and are happy to take risks. But they may also have lower scores on something called warmth,' says the psychologist.

Tom trains, waits two years and does selection again.

'I was prepared to die on that course to get in.'

Out of more than 300 applicants who start, only about a dozen will be chosen. One test involves dropping them in the middle of the West Australian desert to fend for themselves. For 'Exercise Happy Wanderer', the men will traverse about 150 kilometres of the toughest terrain in the country carrying a 50-kilogram pack for five days and nights.

'One guy lost 17 kilograms,' says Tom. 'You're all emaciated.'

Those lucky enough to make it through selection, like Tom, must then spend about a year and a half on the 'Reinforcement Cycle'. On the REO cycle they learn how to become a fully-fledged SAS operator. One of the courses they are put through is 'Resistance to Interrogation'. As soldiers in the SAS, they are the most at risk of any Australian military personnel of falling into the hands of the enemy. To prepare them, they are 'put into the bag'. That is, they are subjected to exactly what they might have to endure if they are captured.

One SAS operator will later describe being put into the bag as the worst three days of his life.

'They strip you naked,' says Trooper Jim, a veteran SAS operator. 'Then they handcuff you and you're sitting there naked on a plastic bathmat, cross-legged. You've got to sit up straight, and you sit like that for three days.'

7

Tom remembers being kept naked on his bathmat for even longer.

'They keep you up for 96 hours, with no food. Just water,' he recalls.

It is full sensory deprivation. They put earmuffs and blacked out ski goggles on the men. Then they play deafeningly loud music.

'They play a song by the White Stripes which is just someone screaming into a microphone. It just thumps through your skull. They just put it on endless loop,' says Tom.

The song is 'Aluminium', whose sole lyric is 'Ahhhhhhhhhh'.

'I used to like the White Stripes,' says Trooper Jim. 'Not anymore.'

Occasionally they haul candidates away for questioning. Most times the interrogators try to scare them or trick them. But Trooper Jim remembers them trying a different tactic during one grilling.

'They bring in women, like female intelligence staff,' he says.

He is naked, and they have uncuffed his hands from his front and re-cuffed them behind his back. They take off his blindfold. Trooper Jim is in the room with the 'guards' and an attractive female nurse.

'To the guards, she says, "Leave the room please." So they leave. Then she comes over and starts sweet talking to me. I'm in the nude. And then she starts talking dirty to me … and I'm thinking, "Now I know why you handcuffed me from behind!" And I'm going, "Oh, no. Things are moving".'

Trooper Jim doesn't wilt, physically or mentally. He has passed another test. They grab him to take him back to his bathmat.

'As I'm walking out, I'm going, "Hey, call me". She's trying not to smile,' he says.

Cut off from the world for hour after hour, some of the men begin to hallucinate.

'I remember one. I was playing cards with World War Two soldiers in an antique store,' says Trooper Jim. 'The guy next to me, he started screaming, *Get them off me! Get them off me!*'

The bloke next to him explains later that he thought burning squirrels were trying to eat his tongue.

'We had one guy who wanted to jump up and catch the number 89 bus to Sydney,' says Tom.

On his couch this day above the mist, Tom is about to recount a scene that could well have been a hallucination. Except he saw it. So too did everyone else on the patrol.

It is 28 March 2012 and India Three patrol of 3 Squadron SAS has just been dropped in the field in Shah Wali Kot.

Like other SAS patrols, India Three is made up of four to five operators and a signaller. The signaller's job is to trace and track a target's communications device, to analyse data from enemy communications, and to provide threat detection and intelligence to ground forces. One of the operators is a sergeant who is the patrol commander.

With India Three on today's mission is combat medic, Dusty Miller. Dusty and Tom are great mates. But there is little mateship between Tom and a couple of his fellow operators in India Three.

The patrol commander and another trooper – 'Soldier C' – have made it clear they don't think Tom is much of an operator. Tom doesn't know what he's done, why he's being singled out. Before they deployed, the patrol commander had pulled Tom aside.

'Mate, I don't want you on this trip. I don't want you with me,' he tells Tom.

Fucking brilliant, thinks Tom. I'm in your patrol and this is where I stand.

Soldier C is junior to Tom. Tom has been in the Regiment longer. But that doesn't stop Soldier C from giving Tom a frank assessment of his soldiering skills.

'I just don't think you should be a fucking operator,' Soldier C tells him one day while a group of them are drinking up at their boozer on their base in Perth.

9

'Well, mate, fortunately the decision isn't up to you,' replies Tom. 'I'm here to stay.'

Now Tom is walking across the field in southern Afghanistan looking for Taliban insurgents right alongside the patrol commander who doesn't want him, and Soldier C who thinks he isn't up to being an operator.

Dusty Miller is in the formation behind Tom. Dusty knows there is tension in the patrol and that Tom is its focal point.

'Tom, in my opinion, was the perfect SAS operator. He was intelligent, spoke other languages, didn't look like a fucking clone like the rest of them,' says Dusty. 'These guys are fucking thugs.'

Dusty Miller regards Soldier C as an insubordinate upstart.

'No time up. No fucking scores on the board,' says Dusty.

Even though Dusty is a sergeant and outranks him, Soldier C talks down to the veteran medic.

'Who the fuck do you think you're talking to?' snaps Dusty one day. 'Just back up.'

The patrol crosses an irrigation channel into a newly ploughed field. They have only been on the ground for a matter of minutes, having flown in on a United States Black Hawk from their base at Tarin Kowt, in the neighbouring Uruzgan Province.

It is here, in the bare field, that they all spot the figure. He is wearing what the soldiers like to call a 'man dress'. It is dark brown. They can see him clearly in the open. The young man has spotted the Australians too. He wants nothing to do with them and is walking away.

But there is something in the man's walk that troubles Tom. There is something about him that is obvious to all of them.

This guy's not fucking right, thinks Dusty.

He is disabled, thinks Tom. He is physically and intellectually disabled.

The man is running now. More like limping, thinks Tom. As fast as he can.

He is clearly not a threat.

To Tom's left is Soldier C.

Tom watches as Soldier C raises his weapon. Nothing unusual in that. Operators often raise their weapon to get a clearer view of a possible target through the sight picture of their rifle scope.

But Tom thinks this is strange. By now, the Afghan is only about 20 metres away from them, not that far at all. You don't need to look through your scope at this range. The Afghan isn't a threat anyway.

The guy isn't tactically manoeuvring either. 'Tactically manoeuvring' is a military term. It means that an enemy is moving to gain a tactical advantage. During the war in Afghanistan, Special Forces soldiers killed many alleged insurgents on the basis that their targets were tactically manoeuvring to a better firing position or to a suspected weapons cache. Under these circumstances the SAS is permitted to kill them under the Rules of Engagement. 'Tactically manoeuvring' will become a catch all, a convenient justification for using lethal force.

But the Afghan in the field is not doing this. He is trying to limp away. It is clear to Tom and Dusty that the young Afghan man is scared and confused and only wants to get away from these strange men with their alien weapons, wraparound sunglasses and their black and green painted faces.

Why wouldn't you run, thinks Dusty. I fucking would. We are bloody intimidating.

'It's all about shock and awe,' says another member of the 3 Squadron rotation. 'That's why I used to wear camouflage cream all the time, [to] scare the fucking bejesus out of them.'

It is working with the Afghan in the field. He is frightened to death. It is abundantly clear to the patrol that this guy isn't Taliban. Nowhere near it. In the days to come, he will become known derisively by 3 Squadron SAS as 'the village idiot'.

There are no words or warnings, just two pops. They are bullets leaving the barrel of Soldier C's suppressed M4 assault rifle.

Tom watches as the Afghan's head explodes.

'Emptied his skull,' says Tom. He is on his couch looking out over the mist-filled valley, but he is back in Afghanistan.

'I was in shock … why would you do that? The guy just took a life, and he didn't need to take a life. Why?'

Frozen in the field, Dusty Miller watches the Afghan fall.

'I remember it so clearly because his fucking brain literally hit the ground before he did,' he says. 'If somebody's running away unarmed, why would you shoot them? Why? It didn't make sense to me.'

The men of the patrol gather around the dead man. For a while no one says anything.

The silence is broken by the patrol commander. He orders his 2-I-C to dress the body in a 'battle bra' chest rig containing assault rifle magazines. The 2-I-C isn't happy, but he will do as he is told.

This is the beginning of the cover up.

They roll the Afghan over. As the 2-I-C slips the lifeless man into the battle bra, Tom is ordered to take his fingerprints and to scan his irises. But there are no irises left to scan.

'His skull was completely pulverised,' says Tom. There are bits of brain and scalp everywhere.

The dead man's hands are covered in blood. Tom pulls out an alcohol swab and wipes them down and takes the prints using a Secure Electronic Enrolment Kit or SEEK machine. The size of a house brick, the SEEK electronically captures iris scans, facial images and fingerprints. Later, the dead man's prints will be sent to the Special Operations database, but there is no match. He is not Taliban or a target of any kind.

Photos are taken of the disabled man wearing the battle bra and the magazines.

'That enables him to be identified as a combatant,' says Tom. 'And you can engage him using lethal force.'

The battle bra, and the fact he was 'tactically manoeuvring', will be used to justify the kill. They are creating their own narrative, one that will be reflected in the official patrol report.

They strip the dead man of the battle bra and the magazines.

'Move on,' says the patrol commander. They move on. The Afghan with the emptied head is left in the field.

Later, back in their patrol room at Camp Russell, the SAS base in Tarin Kowt, the patrol commander gathers his men together. It is a standard debrief. He praises Soldier C for taking out a 'high value target'.

'We got the guy we were after,' the patrol commander tells his men.

Tom is stunned. You've got to be fucking joking, he thinks. This was an execution of an unarmed man.

'I knew that was a lie. Everyone knew that was a lie,' he says. 'It was an execution.'

Everyone in the room knows the Afghan was a civilian. They know because he wasn't right, there was something wrong with the bloke. They know, because afterwards some of them will joke about the killing of the 'village idiot'.

'Clearly it was a cover up,' says Tom. 'He was just saying that to try and cover it up within the patrol dynamics.'

Tom stands up and walks out. It is an act of defiance, a direct challenge to the authority of the patrol commander. It can be career ending. But no one says a word. No one tries to stop him. The patrol commander and Soldier C will deal with Tom later.

Thirteen days after the 'village idiot' killing, Soldier C will write home from his personal email account. He will describe how a fortnight before he had a 'particularly good day down south'. He goes on to explain that the reason for this good day was that he 'was able to drop the hammer on a cunt'.

Drop the hammer on a cunt. He means he has killed an Afghan. He is writing about the 'village idiot' killing.

Eight years later I am sitting with Tom in his home high up on the hill among the ghost gums. This is the first time he has talked about this killing with anyone other than Dusty. For eight years this secret has been kept hidden, known only to the men who were in that bare field that day. Here, above the mist in the valley, Tom still can't get the killing out of his head.

'Clearly, there's a sense of getting away with it all, with what they were doing over there,' he says. 'They were rogue.'

———

Are you aching for the blade?
That's okay
We're insured

The stereo at The Gratto is cranking with 'Getting Away With It (All Messed Up)' by the British rock band James. The mood is exuberant, and the guys are singing at the top of their lungs. Some dance about virtually naked, wearing only Speedos and thongs. One of them is playing air guitar.

Are you aching for the grave?
That's okay
We're insured

As the lyrics suggest, these men regard themselves as invulnerable, both on the battlefield and in the bar. Reaching into a giant esky a guy wearing only red Speedos and a cowboy hat is singing along and serving up cans of rum and Coke. A shirtless operator in board shorts shuffles in front of the bar and raises his arms in triumph. He tilts his head back and sings at the ceiling.

Getting away with it all messed up
Getting away with it all messed up
That's the living . . .

14

It is December 2013 and these soldiers are celebrating. They have gotten away with it, they have survived another tour of Afghanistan, this war without end.

Four SAS operators are arm in arm in their own private huddle, singing along. Everyone knows the words. This song is their unofficial anthem. It has been played at wakes, at parties, at their bar in Afghanistan. They like to play it here too, at their boozer next to their base in Perth.

> *Daniel drinks his weight*
> *Drinks like Richard Burton*
> *Dance like John Travolta, now*

Few understand what these men have been through, or what they have seen and done.

They are part of the most elite and lethal fighting force in the Australian military. Men of exquisite violence and elegant unpleasant-ness. They have skills few soldiers anywhere in the world can match.

Like ghosts, they can go out on reconnaissance for weeks and not be seen. Even drink their own piss if they have to. Drop them into the silent gloom of an Afghan night and they will find the target. Kill him if they have to. They can scuba, parachute, abseil.

They can survive for as long as it takes behind enemy lines. They can thrive in wars that have no battlelines at all. Wars like Afghanistan.

Based on the British SAS, the Australian Special Air Service Regiment was formed in 1957. Men of the Regiment have fought in Borneo, Vietnam, Somalia, East Timor and Iraq. In conflicts like these there are dozens of ways to die. In 1965, the SAS lost its first soldier in action when Lance Corporal Paul Denehey was gored by a wild elephant during a reconnaissance patrol in Borneo. In Vietnam, where SAS patrols conducted hundreds of raids deep behind enemy lines, the Viet Cong called them 'Ma Rung', or phantoms of the jungle. But never have the men of the Regiment seen such relentless fighting as in Afghanistan.

The soldiers produced by the Regiment are the embodiment of physical endurance, cold-blooded rationality and rat cunning. They possess a skill set of preternatural lethality. They have survived a Darwinian selection process to join the Regiment.

The SAS is part of a global Special Forces network capable of everything from counterterrorism to pinpoint assassination to surveillance and long-range reconnaissance to raids and sabotage behind enemy lines.

Think of British SAS soldiers abseiling down the outside of the Iranian Embassy in London in 1980 before freeing all but one of the hostages besieged inside. Or the US Navy SEALs and their audacious operation to kill Osama bin Laden.

Since 9/11 the Special Forces have come into their own.

The 21st century world order has thrown up a range of unconventional battlefields that suit their capacity for versatility, ingenuity and lethality.

As Vietnam, Iraq and Afghanistan proved, industrial scale warfare with conventional forces only gets you so far. When the battlefields are mud compounds or pomegranate groves or rubbish-strewn slums, and the enemy is a farmer by day and an insurgent by night, big battalions are all but ineffectual. These modern-day kinetic battlegrounds are just what the Special Forces have trained for. It suits their ability to deliver focused, discriminate violence.

And they can party hard.

Daniel's saving grace
He was all but drowning
Now they live like dolphins

At its core, this is a song about redemption, about a man who saves himself by saving a woman. But the men of the SAS who scream out these lyrics have perverted that meaning. It doesn't matter here. At The Gratto they can sing what they want. This is the SAS boozer next to the Regiment's base at Campbell Barracks in Perth. It is their private place.

It is named for Percy Gratwick who won a Victoria Cross for charging a German machine gun position during a battle in Egypt in World War Two. Gratwick killed the machine gun crew with hand grenades. Armed with his rifle and bayonet, he then charged another German position under heavy fire, only to be cut down.

A framed photograph of Percy Gratwick VC now hangs on the wall of the SAS boozer.

The Gratto is where operators can play hard away from the prying eyes of the brass. It has been the scene of some wild parties. There was the time they even had a game of nude Twister here with a couple of strippers. Dozens watched that show.

Who knows what Percy Gratwick would have thought of some of the antics that go on in the club named in his honour.

'Naked chin ups on the chin up bars,' says a former SAS operator. 'They come up and talk to you and their penises are hanging out,' says the partner of an SAS sergeant.

I have seen the photos from inside The Gratto. One shows a shirtless operator standing under the chin up bar, his pants pulled down around his sneakers. He has his arm around another operator in a singlet who has no pants to pull down. Between them they almost have an outfit. They are smiling and posing for the photo with their cocks and balls on full display. They are surrounded by fellow SAS soldiers, who are too busy drinking to pay them a glance. Another operator swerves wildly about the bar in a wheelchair until he tips it over and falls out. He is so smashed he struggles to regain his feet.

These men are alpha males. And sometimes when they have had too much booze it can get willing. Like the time two of the blokes got stuck into each other.

'Now these guys are amicable colleagues,' says an operator. 'This guy hit him so hard he broke a couple of bones in his hand.'

He might have broken his hand, but the other bloke came off second best.

'I said, "You'll need an excuse, mate, because you've got black eyes. I think you have to take a motorbike for a spin and pretend to fall off it. You need a cover story."'

Getting away with it all messed up
Getting away with it all messed up
That's the living . . .

Things are starting to get very messy. On this night, an operator from 3 Squadron ends up with a nasty gash that runs the whole way along the underside of his chin. Blood drips from it as he guzzles from his stubbie of beer.

It is 18 months after the killing of the 'village idiot' in that field in Shah Wali Kot.

In faraway Afghanistan a secret war has been raging for years. The Australian public knows very little about what these men – our Special Forces – have been doing in the valleys, fields and mud compounds of this war-weary country.

This graveyard of empires.

This gateway for invaders.

All the greats have been through Afghanistan. Cyrus the Great, Alexander the Great, Genghis Khan, Tamerlane. The British and the Soviets, both at the height of their power and reach, tasted bitter defeat in Afghanistan. How do you tame a country like this?

We're getting away with it
All messed up
That's the living

'We're getting away with it.' These men delight in the literal message conveyed by these lyrics. But they have misinterpreted the song's theme of redemption through saving life, not taking it. There is something

18

about the way they have twisted the words, and the way they play this song over and over. Is it a wink and a nod? Or just a tasteless joke? Or does it hint at something darker?

'You had the culture of there was no consequence. You could get away with it,' says a former SAS operator. 'So if you're getting away with it, then what's to stop you from doing it again?'

'It certainly was like a theme song and I think that a lot of them really identified with that song,' says another former Special Operations member. 'In relation to Afghanistan [it has] more sinister undertones ... they could get away with whatever they wanted to get away with.'

1

KILO

'Even the air of this country has a story to tell about warfare.
It is possible here to lift a piece of bread from a plate
and following it back to its origins, collect a dozen stories
concerning war – how it affected the hand that pulled it
out of the oven, the hand that kneaded the dough, how war
impinged upon the field where wheat was grown'
Nadeem Aslam, *The Wasted Vigil*

The rules of the Drip Mile are simple. Kit up with a full combat load of pack, rifle, medical gear. Total weight: 30 kilograms. Run 400 metres and insert a cannula into a live patient.

'So we had to establish a drip into someone and then run another 400, do the same,' says Dan Pronk, the SAS Regimental Medical Officer. 'It was four lots of 400 completing the mile, and four successful intravenous cannulations.'

The Drip Mile is Dan's idea. He is something of a rarity. A qualified doctor, Dan has passed SAS selection. He did what is called Category B selection. He is not a fully-fledged operator and he does not qualify for the sandy beret. But he is part of the Regiment.

Dan has already done a tour of Afghanistan. He was the Special Operations Task Group doctor, overseeing everything from medical support planning for missions to dealing with casualties.

'By far it was blast and high velocity gunshot wounds. Penetrating trauma.'

Then there were the improvised explosive devices, or IEDs.

'So severe lower limb injuries, often losing both their legs,' says Dan.

Dan trains his SAS medics hard. They must be fit, fast and agile. They must be able to work under extreme pressure and under fire. If they can't, wounded soldiers could die.

The Drip Mile is just one of the gut-busting training programs Dan has designed to simulate what his medics could face on the battlefields of Afghanistan.

'The aim is to replicate that ability to have your fine motor skills and your co-ordination and concentration intact to be able to do a procedure like an intravenous cannulation when your heart rate is up and your adrenalin is pumping.'

Dusty Miller is kitted up and ready to race.

Dusty is one of Dan's medics and is preparing for a deployment to Afghanistan with 3 Squadron SAS beginning in February 2012. He looks up to Dan as a mentor and a friend. But Dusty sometimes bristles at Dan's uncompromising standards.

'He trained me to the point where sometimes I wanted to knock him out because he pushed me that hard,' says Dusty. 'I'm serious. I wanted to come to blows a couple of times because he really pushed me past it.'

'I, on reflection, might have taken it all a bit seriously,' Dan concedes.

Dusty Miller is no greenhorn. The native of South East Anglia in Cambridgeshire joined the British army at 17.

'I was always looking for a father figure,' he says. 'I don't remember having a dad.'

That is because Dusty's old man left when he was six. His mum brought him and his two sisters up on her own.

'Strong woman. Did as good as she could.'

The army gives him structure, and a sense of purpose. He is trained as a medic in the Royal Anglian Regiment. 'The Poachers', as Dusty's battalion is known, have done many tours of duty to Northern Ireland during 'The Troubles'. In 1989, they are over there again and Dusty is with them when one of the Regiment is killed in a bombing.

'His name was Dusty, which I thought was weird,' he says.

In the early nineties a mate rings Dusty and tells him to come out to Australia. He is up for a change of scenery so he quits the Poachers. In Australia he travels and works for a few years as a fitness instructor. He fancies himself as a DJ too.

But he misses the military. In 2001 he joins the Australian Army. He goes to Iraq in 2006 as part of an army security detachment or SECDET team.

'That's the year they hung Saddam. So it was pretty crazy.'

The job of Dusty's SECDET team was to escort diplomats and government officials to meetings in Baghdad. Their mission was to keep them safe from everything from roadside bombs to insurgent ambushes to rocket attacks.

'It was pretty risky,' says Dusty.

That is an understatement. In 2006 Iraq is blood-spattered chaos. In February, Sunni insurgents blow up the Al-Askari Mosque in Samarra. It has stood for more than a thousand years. It sets off sectarian bloodshed that Iraq has not experienced before. Sunni and Shi'ite death squads roam the streets. More than 100 people a day are turning up dead in the streets of the capital alone. The country is on the verge of civil war.

'I saw a lot of dead people on that trip and I saw people killed,' says Dusty.

In 2010 Dusty is attached to the SAS. It is his dream posting. He is a 'Kilo', a combat medic. But Dusty is older than just about everyone he is serving alongside. He is now 40 years old. What he gives away in age, he must make up in sheer commitment and determination.

'Dusty was hands down the fittest medic I ever served with and tirelessly maintained a physical training regime that would shame most professional athletes,' says Dan Pronk.

He may have the sinewy physique of a triathlete, but pound for pound, the 'Kilo' is one of the strongest men in the Regiment. He has to be.

For Dan's dreaded Drip Mile, Dusty will have to be able to lug 30 kilograms of kit 1600 metres while cannulating four blokes at 400-metre intervals along the way. It is a race against the clock. It is clear from the start that Dusty is up to the challenge. He sprints the first 400 metres and gets the cannula neatly into the 'patient'. He repeats the process three times and when he is done they check the stopwatch. His time has smashed the old record. Not bad for an old bloke.

Dan presents him with a massive 'piss take' trophy with a sprinting and armed figurine mounted on the top. Dusty cherishes it.

'It was such a competitive environment,' says Dusty. 'So much rides on those small challenges. I would make sure I could beat a whole squadron of SAS guys on a run. I'd fucking run them out of their skins.'

Dusty's incredible fitness doesn't mean he is accepted by the SAS operators. He soon discovers that the operators aren't called 'Cats' for nothing. They are a cliquey and caustic bunch, ultra-macho types who look down their noses at support staffers like Dusty. He doesn't have the sandy beret. To the operators, he is just a 'crap hat'.

'It's a real dog-eat-dog world. If you play your cards wrong, you'll be immediately ostracised,' says Dan. 'Often it could be fairly humiliating to be honest, being a support element with an SAS unit. On occasions we were treated very much like second-rate citizens.'

Other professionally competent medics, men capable of doing the job in Afghanistan, are 'binned'. Their only sin is that they don't fit in, they are not liked.

'They were pretty much classed as lemons and they would get sent back to med troop,' says Dusty. 'It's the harshest environment.'

Dusty quickly works out that medics must have three key attributes if they are going to cut it in the SAS.

'You've got to be as fit as fuck. Next, you've got to be great at your job. And the third thing is – I'll use profanity here – you've got to be a good cunt. You've got to fit in.'

Fitting in proves hard. For a while Dusty sits in the mess on his own. He eats on his own, trains on his own. No one comes near him.

'I got treated like a fucking leper,' says Dusty.

He finds it a bit depressing. He thinks he is great at his job and that he is a good cunt.

Dusty keeps kicking everyone's arse at training, and after a while a couple of the operators in 3 Squadron come over to say hello or to share a meal. One of them is Victoria Cross winner Mark 'Donno' Donaldson. Another is Tom.

'Tom was different,' says Dusty. 'He didn't get involved in that mob culture or that wolf pack. He's more of a thinker.'

But Tom is still an operator. He is not supposed to get pally with a support staffer like Dusty. Another operator – a corporal – pulls Tom aside.

'I was given an absolute face ripping. He just tore shreds off me for engaging and talking to support staff,' says Tom.

3 Squadron SAS deploys to Afghanistan in February 2012. The war in Afghanistan is well into its eleventh year. By this point, 32 Australian soldiers have lost their lives in the conflict. But back home in lounge rooms, in workplaces, at the footy and in pubs, the war is largely forgotten. It only intrudes into the public consciousness every time there is the solemn announcement of another Australian death. TV news bulletins show a flag-draped coffin and a guard of honour, and another bereaved family. The prime minister will read another tribute to the fallen in parliament, while vowing that Australia will stay true to the cause of not allowing Afghanistan to yet again become a safe haven for terrorists who present a threat to our security and way of life, both abroad and at home. This is about as close as the public will get to the conflict in Afghanistan because the war has become a counterinsurgency fought under the guise of operational secrecy by the Special Forces, by men who never leave the shadows. What they do over there we are never meant to know.

3 Squadron is part of the 17th Australian Special Forces rotation through the country in less than seven years. Dusty and his comrades are members of the Special Operations Task Group or SOTG – a joint unit made up of about 320 personnel. It is a mix of 3 Squadron SAS and Delta Company from the 2nd Commando Regiment. The men of the Special Operations Engineer Regiment are also part of Rotation 17.

There is a bitter rivalry, bordering on hatred, between the SAS and Commandos. A toxic caste system has developed in which the SAS regard the green beret Commandos as inferior. The men with the sandy berets are also better paid than the Commandos. The soldiers of 2nd Commando Regiment, formed more than 50 years after the SAS, are seen as the new boys on the block.

'Despite coming under the [Special Operations Command] umbrella, we always thought someone forgot to tell the Commandos that they actually weren't Special Forces in the true sense of the word,' says one veteran SAS operator. 'They are actually an "Elite Conventional" force … the widely accepted definition of a "Commando" is a soldier specifically trained for carrying out raids, whereas an SASR soldier is a "Commando" and more. In other words, we can do their job and more. They can't do ours.'

One SAS operator writes home in 2010 describing the Commandos as over-paid, under-trained and 'our little retarded brother unit'.

But in Afghanistan there is mission overlap between these two brother regiments and that is a source of ongoing friction on base, a base they share but rarely mix on. On one Afghanistan rotation, the SAS sergeants bring in a rule. Any SAS member seen speaking to a Commando is told they must shout their comrades a carton of beer.

'You had that whole, "We're like fucking rock stars",' says Dusty of the SAS.

'It's almost like the psyche of a motorcycle gang,' says Tom.

The SAS is based at Camp Russell on the outskirts of Uruzgan's capital Tarin Kowt. The camp is named for SAS sergeant Andrew Russell, the first Australian to be killed in Afghanistan. The 33-year-old SAS veteran died in February 2002 when the patrol vehicle he was in hit what was suspected to be an anti-tank mine left over from the Soviet occupation.

Uruzgan is a wild place. It is a landscape of razor-like peaks, writhing river deltas, moonscape deserts and cultivated quilts of bronze, yellow and green. While its natural beauty is breathtaking, life here is brutal and short. Under the Taliban, life expectancy was one of the lowest in the world at just 44. Even by Afghan standards, Uruzgan is considered isolated, tribal and backward. Only 10 per cent of men can read. For women, the literacy rate is zero. Despite the overthrow of the Taliban and the Australian presence, this Pashtun-dominated province is teeming with insurgents. Uruzgan is one of Afghanistan's main opium smuggling routes. This makes it important to the Taliban because opium is one of its main sources of revenue.

The SAS has a delicate mission, one that involves walking a tightrope between taking out high-value Taliban targets while ensuring that Afghans can go about their lives peacefully. They are both door-kickers and protectors. Hearts and minds are their mission – winning some, putting bullets into others. Their operations are often heart-racing affairs involving lightning raids in rabbit warren compounds, operating in pitch black windowless rooms, where their targets sometimes hide among women and children. The enemy does not subscribe to the laws of armed conflict, like the SAS. The Taliban uses civilians as human shields, brutalises those it sees as aiding its adversaries, employs IEDs and suicide bombers to terrifying effect, and often dispatches prisoners after horrendous torture. The Australian Special Forces are expected to play by the rules against an enemy that flouts them.

It is snowing the day Dusty sets foot in Tarin Kowt. Members of 3 Squadron SAS dub their deployment to Afghanistan 'Strandhögg'.

'It's Viking for pillage, rape, burn, loosely translated,' says Dusty. 'Stick that in your fucking book.'

Strandhögg is still used in Iceland as a term to describe hostile takeovers in business. But in Afghanistan, the Australians will employ Strandhögg like the fearsome Norsemen once did.

'They did pillage, I guess. They just didn't do the raping,' jokes a 3 Squadron operator.

The men of the squadron will later have Strandhögg T-shirts made up bearing a fearsome Viking in a horned helmet on the left breast. On the right is the word *Valhöll*, the old Norse word for Valhalla, the mythical hall ruled by the god Odin. The Vikings believed that warriors slain in combat would live on blissfully in Valhalla, feasting, drinking and fighting.

Dusty has been told by Dan Pronk what to expect when it comes to some of the injuries he might have to deal with out in the field. It is a grisly shopping list: Massive bleeding. Traumatic amputation. Evisceration. Arterial bleeds. Blast lung caused by IEDs. Fractures.

'You name it, we have to be able to deal with it,' says Dusty.

But as a 'Kilo' or combat medic, Dusty isn't just in Afghanistan to save people. First and foremost he is a soldier, exquisitely trained in the art of war. He carries a medical kit and an assault rifle. He will have to shoot and suture.

'What you don't realise is once the chopper hits the ground, there's no delineation. You are front line,' says Dusty. 'You're going through doors with them. So whatever you encounter you need to be able to deal with that.'

At its heart, being a combat medic is a paradox, says Dan Pronk.

'So it is odd, maybe to someone looking at it from the outside, that someone would have those somewhat conflicting ambitions to be able to save a life, but then also go and train to potentially take a life if required,' says Dan. 'If required, you shoot. If required, you patch someone up. And you didn't care who that someone was.'

Within a few weeks of the deployment, Dusty will be in the thick of the shooting and the patching.

——

'Fuck me!'

The Black Hawk hits the ground hard, snapping Dusty's head forward. He has already unhooked his wire safety cable and is in the open doorway of the aircraft ready to jump out when it slams into dusty earth. He grabs for something to stop him being thrown out as the chopper bounces back into the air. The pilots wrestle the Black Hawk under control and ease it down. It is the scariest landing Dusty has had so far in his first month of going out on operations.

'I'm surprised any of us got out of that chopper,' he says. 'It was bad.'

The Black Hawk finally settles on the ridge, blowing up plumes of fine dust. It gets up everyone's noses, even the soldiers wearing coverings across their faces.

They are not even on target. They have been dropped about half a kilometre from where they are supposed to be.

It is 4 April 2012 and several patrols from 3 Squadron SAS, along with their Wakunish allies, are hunting a Taliban bombmaker in Deh Rawood. The insurgent target has recently led an attack on an Afghan police checkpoint. He is a dangerous foe, and heavily armed. If cornered, he will fight.

For Dusty Miller, this will be a traumatic day, one that will remind him of the terrible carnage modern weapons can wreak on a human body.

The Wakunish, or 'Wakas' as the Australians call them, are the Afghan special forces. They wear a darker green camouflage uniform and are embedded with SAS patrols. The Wakas are mainly Hazaras from the country's north. Mostly Shi'a Muslims, the Hazaras have a special hatred for the Pashtun-dominated Sunni Muslim Taliban, and some are motivated by a burning desire for vengeance.

'I remember speaking to one of the Wakas and he was saying that when he was a kid [the Taliban] came into his village,' says Dusty. 'They killed all the blokes in the village, all of them. Because they were having a soccer match. [The Wakas] were highly motivated to kill bloody bad guys.'

The Wakas are not the only ones feared by the enemy. With their facial hair and camouflaged faces, the SAS are called 'red beards' by the Taliban.

'I think most of us are Anglo descent. Brown hair, and most have a bit of ginger or red in our beards,' says Dusty. Along with Mark Donaldson, Dusty is one of the reddest of red beards in 3 Squadron.

According to communications intercepts, the Taliban has sometimes told their fighters that when the red beards land they should hide their weapons and pick up ploughs and go back to being farmers.

'We kind of loved that. It was a good thing. It means our reputation was preceding us,' says Dusty.

The insurgent bombmaker is believed to be holed up in a Kuchi camp in Deh Rawood. The Kuchis are Pashtuns who herd sheep and goats. Conservative and traditionally nomadic, the Kuchis are a powerful tribe. A leaked secret cable based on Afghan intelligence from the US Ambassador to Afghanistan, Karl Eikenberry, suggests up to half of the Taliban are Kuchis. They despise the northern Hazaras. Of course, the feeling is mutual.

From the ridgeline Dusty can see the valley below. A dry creek bed seems to be its only feature. Even goats find it tough to survive in Deh Rawood.

Dusty trudges over the shaley ground which slips and slides under his feet. He can now see the Kuchi camp. It is 150 metres away, down the hill on his left. To his right, over the creek bed, is another SAS patrol. One of the Kuchi structures ahead looks like a mud igloo. Another looks like it hasn't been finished. Sticks form arches over the dirt base like a primitive cathedral.

Doop, doop, doop.

The low, guttural crump of machine gun fire echoes down the creek bed and up the ridge. Puffs of dust appear on the hill opposite the igloo.

'Contact!' shouts the sergeant next to Dusty. 'Kilo, with me!'

More machine gun fire. A longer burst this time. The veterans among the SAS patrols know immediately it is from a PKM, a Soviet-era weapon that can fire at a rate of more than 600 rounds a minute.

Dusty's patrol and the one in front are running now towards the igloo. Another patrol is already there, a few men swarming around the mud structure. The machine gun fire is coming from its entrance. A call comes over the radio.

'Man down! Medic!'

Dusty is now behind the igloo and can see one of the senior operators, Soldier A, creeping around it towards the entrance. He throws something inside. A couple of seconds pass.

BOOM.

It is a fragmentation grenade. There is a pause.

Doop, doop, doop.

The PKM inside is still firing out. Whoever is inside is still alive.

Soldier A is taking command. The men wait for his orders and let him take the lead. Soldier A is in charge of a patrol of Wakas. He is what is called the 'partner force handler', meaning the Wakas are his responsibility, they answer to him. Everyone respects Soldier A. He is a veteran of Iraq and Somalia and multiple tours of Afghanistan. He is a good operator and many of the younger guys look up to him as a leader.

Dusty also admires Soldier A. He reckons he is brave, but a little crazy too.

The medic cannot see who is wounded. Whoever it is must be on the other side of the igloo in front of the entrance. Maybe it is one of Soldier A's Wakas who has been hit, thinks Dusty.

'Thermo the cunt!'

One of the operators wants to drop in a thermobaric grenade. These use oxygen from the surrounding air to generate a high-temperature explosion. 'They turn your insides to jelly,' one SAS soldier tells me.

'Thermo it!'

'Dusty, get the fuck out of the way, cunt!'

Soldier A is signalling an operator to get out of the way. But it isn't Dusty. It is Mark Donaldson. Dusty is just up the hill behind the igloo. In the frenzy, and almost blinded by the dust billowing from the structure's entrance, Soldier A has gotten him mixed up with Donaldson. They are a similar height and both have red beards.

'You want a thermo?' asks another operator.

'We're right, we're right, we're right,' shouts Soldier A. 'Dusty, get the fuck out of the way, cunt!'

Donaldson, realising Soldier A thinks he's the medic, steps back.

'Get out of there!' screams another.

Soldier A throws in another fragmentation grenade. The men near the igloo retreat a few steps.

BOOM.

Dust and smoke flies out of the entrance to the igloo. Soldier A races back around to the front and pokes his rifle in. He lets off a two second burst.

There is no more fire coming from the igloo.

'We can pull back and fucking Hellfire it,' yells one of the patrol from up the hill. He wants an Apache helicopter to put a Hellfire missile into the igloo and finish this once and for all. The Hellfire is a pinpoint weapon, designed to plunge deep into a target without damaging nearby property.

'Steady,' says an operator next to Soldier A. He raises his hand at the others. We aren't going anywhere is the message. Calm the fuck down.

Soldier A is now leaning across the front of the igloo, his face nearly in the entrance. He throws in another grenade and they pull back a few metres.

BOOM.

More dust and smoke billows out. Some escapes from a hole in the top of the igloo. Three fragmentation grenades have been thrown inside it. Somehow the mud hut is still intact.

'One KIA here. Friendly.' It is one of the operators on the radio.

Whoever was hit by the PKM fire must be dead, killed in action. A friendly confirms it is one of theirs. Dusty still can't see who it is lying in front of the igloo.

'We can pull back and Hellfire it,' says someone.

'Everybody just pull back,' orders another.

But Soldier A is going nowhere. He is walking counter-clockwise around the igloo. He has spotted the hole in the roof. He pokes the barrel of his assault rifle through it and squeezes the trigger. He rotates the end of the weapon as he fires three bursts.

He pulls back, points to the hole and orders Donaldson to come around and drop a grenade in.

'Let's get him out of here,' says another operator. He is talking about the dead or wounded soldier in front of the igloo.

'I got him, mate. Go!' shouts Soldier A. He pulls out the empty magazine from his rifle and slots a full one in.

'Thermo in!' says Donaldson as he jogs away from the igloo. The men pull back, further this time.

KABOOM.

There is a flash of flame and then the thermobaric grenade tears the igloo apart. Lumps of mud hurtle into the air. Dust rises 10 metres.

'Fuck yeah!'

The men approach the igloo which no longer has a roof and is oozing powdery dust and smoke.

'Watch out! Watch out!' shouts one.

Soldier A raises his rifle and bends his knees. The burst lasts four seconds this time. He has emptied another magazine.

33

The dust is clearing. The men can see two Afghans inside. They are somehow still alive. They are finished off with several shots.

The SAS can now get to the soldier in front of the igloo. Soldier A already knows he is dead. Now everyone can see. It is one of the Wakas. He is face down and covered in dust.

A snaking rivulet of blood has trickled from his torso into the dirt.

'Hey, he's fuckin' dead!' says one of the operators.

Soldier A steps out of the igloo crater and walks over to the Waka's body. He looks down and then walks off. The Waka was one of his team. His name was Rahul.

'Dusty, here!' screams another SAS operator. Not everyone has given up hope, it seems.

Dusty sprints over. A Waka is leaning over Rahul, his hand on the dead man's back. The gesture is gentle, tender even.

An operator in the ruins of the igloo a couple of metres away lets off two shots. They are making sure whoever is inside it is well and truly dead.

Dusty has reached Rahul, whose body is shrouded in dust from the grenade blasts. He knows instantly that he is gone. But two of Rahul's Afghan comrades are watching, so the medic decides to look over the body. He will do what is called a primary survey. Dusty wants to show the same respect and care for Rahul as he would for a fallen Digger.

Dusty rolls the body over. For the first time he recognises who it is. Rahul. The big kid. Just 20 or 21 years old. He was a good lad, thinks Dusty.

He unstraps Rahul's helmet. Blood and brains leak onto Dusty's lap. PKM rounds have gone through the Waka's eye and his mouth. Other rounds have struck him along his side.

'What do you need, Dusty?' asks an operator.

Dusty doesn't answer. He doesn't need anything because there is nothing he can do.

'It was pretty traumatic. It was pretty bad,' he says.

The patrol knows that the body lying in the dirt, covered in dust with his head peeled open, could have been any one of them. It was just Rahul's bad luck that he had been told by Soldier A to look inside the igloo to see if anyone was in it. He had bent down and peered inside, an easy target. That was the first burst of machine gun fire Dusty and the others had heard.

'There was no way you were going to get in that door without 'em getting a burst on you,' says one operator to another. They are standing nearby watching Dusty inspect Rahul's lifeless body.

'Whoever went in that door was a dead man,' replies the other.

'Fucking oath.'

'Lucky it wasn't one of us,' says a third operator squatting nearby.

Up on the ridgeline an operator is joined by one of his patrol who had been close to the battle. They watch as Dusty crouches over Rahul near the mud igloo in the gully below. A helicopter is approaching to medevac the Waka out.

'How'd that Waka look?' asks the first operator.

'He's dead.'

'Where'd he cop it?'

'All up his side. Machine gun burst.'

'Yuck. Which Waka was it? Could you tell?'

'Nah. Kind of bigger guy, chubby guy … chubbier cunt. One of [Soldier A's] ones. [He's] pissed.'

'Fortunes of war,' says a third operator standing nearby.

'It's their fucking country. It's unfortunate, but it's their fucking country. You go through the door first, cunt,' says the first operator. He is talking about Rahul. This is his country, so he should go through the door first.

The two Taliban fighters aren't the only ones found inside the hut.

'Digging through the rubble, we found four AK-47s, chest rigs, grenades, a PKM machine gun, a G3 automatic rifle and a lot of ammo,' wrote Mark Donaldson in his book *The Crossroad*. 'The [enemy killed in action] included the target plus three younger boys, most likely suicide bombers who'd come straight out of a training camp in Pakistan.'

Down near the igloo one of the patrol is ordered to guard about half a dozen Afghans from the camp. They have been rounded up and told to sit. But Rahul's comrades are out for blood.

One storms over to the detainees. He wants to kill them. Fucking Pashtuns.

'No, no, no,' says the SAS soldier. He is standing between the Waka and the prisoners.

The Waka lowers his rifle, walks around the soldier and kicks one of the bound men. His anger sated, he walks away.

'Hard pressed not letting them drop them,' says an operator.

Nearby, Dusty, Mark Donaldson and two Wakas load Rahul's body onto a stretcher and they carry it to the chopper.

With the body loaded onto the Black Hawk, Dusty watches Donaldson tap Rahul's foot and say something. He can't hear Donaldson's words over the sound of the chopper, but this display of camaraderie and respect will linger with Dusty for years.

Donno really gives a fuck, he thinks.

Dusty is told to escort Rahul's body back to Tarin Kowt. He thinks it is better if he stays with the patrol. But an order is an order.

On the way back the Role 2 medical facility at base radios in. The Role 2 has some of the capabilities of a hospital, including surgery and advanced life support, and is a step up from the more mobile Role 1 units whose immediate focus is triage and first aid. The Role 2 asks Dusty for an updated M-I-S-T: Mechanism of injury. Injury sustained. Signs and symptoms. Treatment given.

'Nil signs of life,' reports Dusty. 'It's over.'

They land at base. But there is no one there to meet them. Rahul is dead, there is no urgency. They are a long way from the Role 2.

So Dusty and two Wakas haul the flimsy cloth stretcher holding the Afghan across the tarmac.

Rahul is big. The three men are struggling to carry him. His hand is dragging on the ground. Dusty is covered in brains and blood, and the body is leaking.

'Fuck this. This is bullshit,' mutters Dusty. He is livid.

A US fire brigade team based at the air base spots them and gives them a lift.

At the Role 2 Dusty's job is to clean up the body and get Rahul ready for burial. Like most of the other Wakas, he is a Hazara. The plan is to fly him home to northern Afghanistan so he can be buried before sunset in accordance with Islamic tradition.

It is a tough assignment. Other than the bullet through his eye, Rahul's face is intact. But the back of his head is missing and there are large bullet holes along his side that must be stuffed with towels.

Fucking horrific, thinks Dusty.

They strip the body. In the Waka's pouches Dusty finds some muffins that Rahul had taken at breakfast time from the mess. He smiles. Rahul did love his tucker.

'He was a scallywag. He was a really good lad,' says Dusty. 'To have him taken away so violently ...' He pauses. 'It was just horrific. It bothered me. As far as I was concerned, it was no different than [losing] any of the other boys.'

The body is wrapped in a white shroud and placed on a clean stretcher. Rahul's Wakunish comrades then carry the body away so he can be buried in his home district.

The men of 3 Squadron who were on the job at Deh Rawood have now returned. They form two lines as the body is carried past to be loaded onto a helicopter. Some give Rahul a final salute.

Later, one of the SAS soldiers who knew Rahul will send the dead man's father $250 and a note translated for him by one of the military's Afghan interpreters.

'I worked closely with your son for the last number of months. He was attached to our unit. You should be very proud. You should be very proud of your son who fought to stabilise Afghanistan's future,' writes Tom.

2
BEAR

'It's not a tickling competition you know, mate.
People die. There were definitely fucking things that
were completely wrong and there were executions'
**Special Forces member of Rotation 17
(February – July 2012) speaking to the author**

Rahul has been taken home to northern Afghanistan to lie in the earth of his forebears.

Two days earlier Braden Chapman had been one of the SAS patrol members who had watched as Dusty Miller ran over to try to save the big Waka as he lay in his own blood, face down, his body shrouded in dust, in front of the mud igloo.

Rahul is the first member of the team – Afghan or Australian – to die on this rotation. Braden didn't know Rahul, but he felt sorry for his comrades who were watching as the Waka's brains fell out onto Dusty's lap.

Forty-eight hours later Braden Chapman is in the Ready Room at base kitting up for another raid. This is where everyone stores their weapons and gear and, as the name suggests, where everyone gets ready before they head out. Packing ammunition, slapping on camouflage paint, loading weapons, rigging up their communications, stocking up on energy bars and water.

This is Braden's first deployment to Afghanistan. The son of a pest controller, Braden grew up in western New South Wales, the eldest of five kids.

The family might live out bush, but they are townies. Braden was born in Coonamble and spent his early years in Moree before the family packed up and moved back to Coonamble.

He isn't exactly a straight-A student at high school. But he is not bad at maths. After Braden graduates, he finds himself bouncing from job to job – stacking bottle shop shelves, doing farm work, renovating swimming pools, sweating his arse off as a brickie's labourer.

He needs focus. He wants to join the army as an aircraft technician, but they aren't hiring for that job. Braden asks Defence recruitment what jobs they do have.

'And they said, "Oh, there's this electronic warfare job". And I was like, "What's that?"'

Within a week he is on the bus heading for army training to become an electronic warfare specialist.

His father, also a man of few words, drops him at the bus stop.

'He's like, "All right, good luck". Off he went.'

Braden's training takes him from Kapooka to Melbourne to Cabarlah near Toowoomba to Canberra. In the national capital he is posted to the secretive Defence Signals Directorate.

'It's a bit overwhelming when you first get there. They're scanning your retinas to get into the building.'

He is given a top-secret security clearance. But Braden doesn't like working in a hermetically sealed building in Canberra. He wants to work in the most elite fighting unit in the country.

After 12 months his application to be attached to the SAS is accepted. He is off to Perth.

'You're blown away. I'd grown up reading SAS books and that kind of stuff,' says Braden. 'There's that myth about them and who they are.'

Braden is what the SAS calls a 'Bear'. His official title is 'Electronic Warfare Operator'. To the traditionalists, he is a 'Sig' or signals intelligence operator.

The SAS operators may kick in the doors and capture or kill the targets, but it is the Bears who help find the doors and track the targets. If the operators are the trigger pullers, then the Bears are the tech heads.

Braden's initial posting to SAS is with 4 Squadron. This is the Regiment's secret squadron. It has never been officially acknowledged by government or the military that 4 Squadron even exists. Its symbol is a gecko with a scorpion's tail, meaning – according to one former 4 Squadron member – that the squadron possesses both sticky fingers and a sting. The 'gorpians', as some have nicknamed them, are the closest thing the military has to soldier spies. The squadron's Latin motto is *oleo tranquillior* or 'smoother than oil'.

'They're not your typical door kickers,' says Braden of the 4 Squadron soldiers. 'They're not your typical six foot three, built like a brick shithouse. That ain't going to fit in in most places.'

Operatives from 4 Squadron must blend in. One media report claims they don't wear uniforms, that they are undercover soldiers. That they have been carrying out operations in far-flung places such as Zimbabwe, Kenya and Nigeria. Countries Australia is not at war with. That they have been involved in gathering intelligence on terrorism operations and assessing rescue strategies for kidnapped Australians or those caught up in civil wars.

Braden can't talk in detail about the classified work that 4 Squadron does, except to say that his training there prepares him for being a Bear in Afghanistan.

'You get taught how to monitor communications and to find technical devices and that kind of stuff. Pretty much every technical device, electronic device you have that transmits a signal.'

For the 2012 deployment Braden has been attached to 3 Squadron. He is a greenhorn and only knows a few of the guys. Being a support staffer, some of the old hands barely acknowledge him. Some operators make a show of ignoring him. One thinks Braden is a fuckwit because he is a Bear and because he is quiet.

But the shy guy is as gung-ho as everyone else.

'You've got it in your head that the people we're going after, everyone we're going to shoot, they're a bad guy.'

In February 2012 Private Chapman – Electronic Warfare Operator in India Troop of 3 Squadron SAS – arrives in Afghanistan, a place he knows nothing about. Except for what he has seen in the Sylvester Stallone film *Rambo III*.

'You're kind of looking around thinking, How the fuck have we not won this war?' says Braden. 'They're goat herders. How the hell are we not beating these people?'

One of the few operators in the squadron who will talk to him is Tom.

'Tom didn't really fit in with his patrol,' says Braden. 'Tom was really intelligent. He was compassionate towards Afghanis.'

Among the support staff Braden will be bunking in with is Dusty Miller. The older man takes the rookie under his wing.

In Afghanistan, their training continues. There are operational, intelligence, mission and legal briefings. The military loves briefings.

They are drilled on the Rules of Engagement. The ROE spells out the mission, defines what hostile intent is, explains who soldiers can and can't target, and in what circumstances they are required to give a warning. They are all given a 'Red Card' listing all the rules.

'You are permitted to engage all persons taking an active or direct part in hostilities ... there is no need to await a hostile act or hostile intent ...'

'Attacks on civilians not taking an active or direct part in hostilities or persons who are not targetable members of organised groups are **PROHIBITED.***'*

'Do not engage anyone who has surrendered or is incapacitated by wounds or injury.'

As a Bear, Braden is told he will have two primary roles outside the wire.

Sometimes he will be put with an overwatch patrol and dropped with them on a rise, ridgeline or mountain. They will sit there overlooking the target area, acting as the eyes and ears of the patrols below.

The overwatch teams are armed with high-powered sniper rifles. But Braden's role isn't shooting. It's threat detection. Together with an Afghan translator he monitors the enemy's communications and passes on information to the patrols.

'I would often sit with either a sniper or machine gunner and give them the line of bearing so they could target the person talking on the radio,' says Braden.

Other times, Braden would be with the patrols on the ground, heading to the target area. Mostly, their targets are residential compounds that are often home to several generations of the one Afghan family.

A common method of approaching a target is for patrol teams to be dropped at each corner of a village and to converge on the target building.

Afghans captured or killed during operations are searched. Everything is taken out of their pockets and laid out on the ground. This is a Sensitive Site Exploitation, or SSE. If any Afghan has an electronic device Braden is called in to 'process' it and see if it matches the target device.

Standing at his workstation in the Ready Room, Braden loads, straps on, stuffs and packs all the usual gear: M4 assault rifle, ammunition, water, food and ICOMs (two-way radios).

He has a special bit of kit that is crucial to his role as a Bear. It is a device that gives him a 'line of bearing' to phones and ICOMs used by the insurgents to communicate. The device, plus spare batteries and the antenna and all of his other gear, pushes the load Braden has to carry to well past 30 kilograms.

On today's operation Braden will be down on the ground with one of the patrols.

In the briefing they are told their target is an insurgent bomb-maker, code-named Objective Yakuza Assassin. They have been given a card with his real name, approximate age, and physical description. Objective Yakuza Assassin has links to the Taliban fighter who killed Rahul. The SAS and their Waka partner force are itching to capture or kill him.

Their destination is about a kilometre south of the village of Fasil, which is south-east of the SAS base at Camp Russell in Tarin Kowt.

It is another Kuchi camp.

Braden will be attached to Soldier A's patrol. Wiry and barely average height, Soldier A does not look like the Hollywood version of a Special Forces warrior. But his courage is not questioned by anyone. It was Soldier A who was in charge of Rahul and the other Wakas at the battle of the mud igloo. It was Soldier A who led the assault on the igloo after Rahul was shot, and it was Soldier A who killed most of those inside. He is an experienced sergeant who has survived many close calls during his deployments to Afghanistan. Soldier A leads from the front. He doesn't care about the broad strategic aims of the counterinsurgency the SAS and the Australian military are prosecuting. Soldier A's only concern is making sure all his comrades make it through the rotation and that they get home safe to their families.

Braden looks up to the older man.

'He's the guy if you're going to hold any SAS operator on a pedestal ... super cool, calm and collected.'

After Rahul was killed Soldier A pulled aside all of the SAS rookies, all of those who had never deployed before. He wanted to talk to them about trauma.

'It wasn't formal. Just sitting around. He was talking about dealing with death and killing,' says Braden. 'He was saying that the only time he's ever had issues with trauma was when ... he had to deal with flood victims dying right in front of [him] he was trying to save.'

But Braden senses that while Soldier A is distressed by Australians dying, he is not so concerned about Afghans.

'He was saying, "I don't even see them as people, I don't give a shit",' says Braden.

Braden is unsure if Soldier A is talking about Taliban or Afghans in general.

There is no doubt about Soldier A's loyalty to his men, his skills as an operator, or his leadership in the field.

'Brave,' Dusty says of him. What of his other attributes? 'He's got crazy, crazy eyes, man.'

The medic isn't the only one who finds Soldier A's piercing gaze unnerving.

'He's got these mad eyes. Fucking mad, psycho eyes,' says another patrol member. 'He's a nice bloke. But he'll just sit there and stare at you. Mate, you will fucking shit your pants. He's just menacing.'

On a previous raid Soldier A had ordered all the men of a village to be rounded up. The SAS was deep in Taliban country and they suspected the villagers were hiding weapons and sheltering fighters.

'Regular forces had kept getting fucking smashed [there]. They couldn't get past the area,' says Dusty. 'They couldn't keep moving forward because they kept getting hit by the Taliban.'

Dusty and a special operations engineer watched on as Soldier A eyeballed the villagers and delivered a chilling ultimatum.

'He got all these men and boys, and he's standing up on this box with his weapon on his hip. And he's just laying into them,' says Dusty.

'He goes to the interpreter, "Tell these fuckwits that I know they're all Taliban. Tell 'em if they don't tell us what's fucking going on, I will come back and I'll shoot every fucking one of them in the face",' says a Special Forces engineer who was there. 'They were like, "My god, this bloke is going to kill us all".'

It was straight out of a war movie. Dusty thought it was hilarious.

'He meant it and they were fucking terrified,' he says. 'It was pretty full on.'

The flight on the Black Hawk to the Kuchi camp takes less than half an hour. They pass over a narrow ribbon of green running along a creek. The camp is further up the valley in the brown. There is not a blade of grass or even a withered bush. There are just half a dozen tents, some mud-fence stock yards, a few dozen sinewy goats, and dust as far as the eye can see.

A small team with sniper rifles sets up an overwatch position on the steep hills that hem in the valley. With them is the troop commander, a captain. It is standard operating procedure for the troop commander to be in overwatch, away from the target or objective on the ground below. It allows him to coordinate air support if needed. But it also means the highest-ranking soldier on the mission is out of the immediate fight and has little visibility or control of events on the ground. Running the actual operation is left to the patrol commanders, the battle-hardened sergeants, like Soldier A, who are the real power within the Regiment. Their word is law. No one questions their orders. This will have profound consequences for 3 Squadron's deployment in 2012.

One patrol is dropped at one end of the camp, Braden's at the other. The patrols walk towards each other, clearing the camp as they go. They detain what they call FAMs, fighting age males. An assault rifle is found. They are a dime a dozen in Afghanistan and are used for protecting hearth and home from any number of threats – bandits, insurgents, blood feuds, and occasionally foreign red beards.

The women stand apart in a group near a tent, pulling children into the folds of their clothes. There are about half a dozen men. They are huddled together by the SAS patrols, cuffed and questioned.

Braden's job is to process the mobile phones found on the men. Sometimes he sends the phone's details back over the radio to operations and they tell him if the device is of interest. Other times Braden has the details of the target with him and he can confirm a match straight away. Today he has those details.

Braden pulls the SIM cards from the phones of each of the men they have rounded up. From their SIM cards he checks what is called the International Mobile Subscriber Identity or IMSI. The IMSI is a 15-digit number that uniquely identifies every user of a mobile network.

There is a match. One of the men is their target: Objective Yakuza Assassin. He is the man in dark clothes. He fits the age and physical description of their objective. Then there is the final confirmation that seals it. When asked, he tells them his name.

We have him, thinks Braden. Confirmed match.

Years later I will find a series of photographs of the raid that day. It is from the SAS overwatch position high up on the hill. If you zoom in you can see three figures lined up, sitting on the ground with their legs outstretched and their hands cuffed behind their backs. There is Objective Yakuza Assassin in dark clothes, seated between the other two Afghans. He is alive.

The time on the picture is 10.52 am.

About this time, the SAS captain in the overwatch radios back to operations that they have a 'Touchdown'.

'Touchdown is like you've confirmed the phone,' says Braden.

In this case, the SAS have the phone and the target it belongs to. They have Objective Yakuza Assassin alive.

But then, just a few minutes later, Objective Yakuza Assassin is ordered up by Soldier A. Braden thinks they are preparing for the chopper to come to take him away.

Instead, he is led away by Soldier A and a Waka to a spot behind a small hill about 50 metres away.

'[They] went around the corner so that the people couldn't see,' says Braden.

They don't want the women and children standing nearby in a huddle to witness what is about to happen. From where he is standing,

Braden can clearly see the three men behind the little hill and the women and children. What happens next stuns him.

'[Soldier A] ordered the prisoner to kneel back on the ground. He then motioned for the Wakunish soldier to shoot him,' says Braden.

Braden sees Soldier A point his weapon at the kneeling prisoner and shake it, simulating the recoil of it firing.

The Waka is confused. He doesn't know what Soldier A wants him to do. Braden sees the Australian motion with his weapon again, pointing it at Objective Yakuza Assassin. Now the Waka understands. He wants me to kill him.

Braden hears a couple of shots and watches as the prisoner slumps to the ground.

Oh fuck, he thinks. They've executed him. We shouldn't be doing this.

Soldier A walks back past Braden.

'I had to give 'em a win,' Braden recalls him saying.

He understands. This is about vengeance. The Wakas lost Rahul, now Soldier A has helped them even the ledger.

Has the troop commander in the overwatch position up on the hill seen the killing? He has called in a 'Touchdown'. The target was secure. He was being brought back, alive. No contact with any enemy was reported. How will he explain that the prisoner is now dead? That the target is now a bloodied mess in the dirt behind a little hill.

Back down in the valley an AK-47 is placed with the dead man and a photo taken.

A while later the Black Hawks return, whipping up whirlwinds in this godforsaken dustbowl. The SAS soldiers load up some prisoners, all blindfolded and cuffed, and fly away. Objective Yakuza Assassin is left where he fell.

They return to base at Camp Russell and Braden speaks with one of the patrol members who was with the troop commander up on the overwatch position.

'We had a quick chat about it. I remember them asking me why it happened and enquiring about what [Soldier A] said about it,' he says. 'I remember [one of the soldiers] said that [the troop commander] said, "How am I going to explain this?" He was like, "We've said that the village is secure and suddenly we have another EKIA [Enemy Killed in Action]",' says Braden.

The patrol takes it to a 'hotwash'. This is a debrief run back at base where the mission is discussed, and any problems sorted. Sometimes grievances are aired and differences settled. But hotwashes can provide an opportunity to fabricate a story about what happened out on the operation, to create a false narrative that can then be inserted into post-mission reports that are required up the chain of command. Hotwashes can be a forum where criminal cover ups are concocted, like with the 'village idiot' killing where the disabled victim was redesignated a 'high value target' and this was inserted into the patrol report.

Hotwashes are '353s' only. A 353 is the Army's Employment Category Number for SAS operators. This means the hotwashes are operators-only. No Bears or Kilos or other support staff are allowed.

'I'm not sure if they said shit about these events or whether they are just like, "All right, let's get our fucking story straight",' says Braden.

It is early on in the deployment and Braden has witnessed his first unlawful killing. To the greenhorn, it has all the features of a cold-blooded execution. The prisoner was bound, and he was on his knees.

Braden starts to wonder if Soldier A is the cool, calm and collected operator he thought he was. He has fallen from Braden's pedestal. But he had been warned about what to expect out on operations.

In the first week of his Afghanistan deployment, the Bear had been prepping his gear in the Ready Room. A senior sergeant, Soldier B, had walked in and started chatting to him. Soldier B is a veteran of several Afghanistan tours, and a physically imposing man. He knows how to use his fists.

'Built like a brick shithouse. He's a triangle,' one of his SAS colleagues will tell me. He sees Soldier B one day in the gym. 'There wasn't an ounce of fat on him. I was like, "Fuck me".'

Braden was stunned. Soldier B didn't usually talk to Bears, or to any support staff for that matter. He usually just grunted at them.

'Other Bears from previous rotations warned me about him,' says Braden. 'They said he was wild and a bit out there.'

Another support staffer remembers how even the operators were fearful of this battle-hardened veteran. One morning the men assembled for orders to discover there were no targets. Everyone was looking forward to a rare day off. But Soldier B had other ideas.

'You, you, you, you, and you are going to clean the fucking toilets,' he said.

He was talking to operators, not support staff. He was ordering beret-qualified Special Forces soldiers to clean the toilets.

'I'm going, "Fuck me, we have the SAS cleaning fucking toilets". And they'd do it,' says the SAS support staffer. 'They were scared shitless of him.'

It did not take long for Braden's chitchat in the Ready Room with Soldier B to end. That was because this little talk had nothing to do with *esprit de corps*. Soldier B leaned towards Braden.

'I hope you're ready and prepared for this deployment because you need to be,' he said. 'You need to make sure that you're okay with me putting a gun to someone's head and pulling the trigger 'cause I don't want to read about it in ten or so years.'

Braden nodded.

'I'm good to go,' he said.

He has the social skills of an ape throwing shit, thought Braden. But he took the warning onboard. Soldier B has a reputation for indiscriminate and explosive violence.

3

ANGELA

'Inside Paddy Mayne there was a deep reservoir of anger
that welled up in violence; it had found one channel on
the rugby field, and another in alcoholic post-match
mayhem. On the battlefield, it would produce heroics;
off it, Paddy Mayne's destructive demon could erupt
without warning, and with terrifying force'
**Ben Macintyre on British SAS founding member,
Paddy Mayne, in** *SAS: Rogue Heroes*

'Go to your room. Whatever happens, don't come out.'

Angela is frightened. She knows Soldier B has been holding court
up at The Gratto and will come home wanting to confront her son
about writing off her car. There is no drinking limit up at The Gratto
and the veteran operator has been at the SAS boozer for hours. Angela
knows he is going to be drunk. And angry.

Nick knows that too. He listens to his mum and retreats to his
room.

Months have passed since Nick smashed up an old woman's fence
and wrote off Angela's car. The teenager visited the woman twice a
week, did her gardening and shared pots of tea with her. He paid for
the fence.

'He more than returned what he did wrong,' says Angela.

But Soldier B is still carrying on about it.

'He wrote off my car. He needs to be punished for what he did,'
he keeps saying.

'It was my car,' Angela keeps reminding him. 'Not yours.'

Angela feels sick in the stomach. She has a premonition that it will all come to a head when Soldier B stumbles home from The Gratto.

They have been together for six years. Angela met him after escaping an abusive marriage.

He looked exactly like she thought a Special Forces soldier would. Rippling with muscle, fit, chiselled. Angela thought he had the body of Arnold Schwarzenegger.

Soldier B was respectful too. He was kind, considerate, tender. Nothing like her abusive ex.

Angela was working in retail in Sydney, a single mum, struggling to make ends meet when Soldier B walked into her life.

She quit her job, sold all her furniture, and pulled her son out of school. Angela and Nick crossed the continent to Perth to live with Soldier B in the army housing next to Campbell Barracks, the SAS base in the suburb of Swanbourne. An estate of about 150 homes, Seaward Village is also known as 'the marriage patch'. There Angela would have to mix and socialise with what some of the operators derisively call the 'patch monsters'.

'They are the bogan army wives, who think their husband's rank and role in the Regiment is vicariously bestowed upon them as well,' says one SAS operator.

'The social pecking order of the wives and partners depended very much on who their husband was – his rank and standing in the Regiment,' says another operator. 'It was a very incestuous and closed environment.'

In 2015, the federal government's Defence Housing Authority announces that Seaward Village will undergo a redevelopment that involves selling off about a third of the estate.

The women of the marriage patch mobilise and a meeting is called.

'One of the wives got up and virtually chest-poked the [official] leading the sale of the patch,' says an SAS operator. 'She told him, "The patch is ours."'

The sell-off plan is shelved.

Angela was excited by the prospect of her new life, of being the partner of an SAS soldier, of her and her son being loved. Most of all she wanted to be protected.

But from the start, Angela found life in Perth lonely. It was hard to make friends among the established cliques of the wives and girl-friends. Being a teetotaller didn't help, though some of the girls took advantage of it up at The Gratto.

'They loved me when they were drunk because I would look after their kids. That's what I was good for.'

Less than two months after arriving in Perth, Angela's dream of a perfect home and family life started to unravel. Soldier B began to reveal his controlling side. He began demanding that she train every day.

'No one would mind training a little bit. But it had to be part of my daily ritual,' she says. 'He'd take me to the work gym and train me.'

He had sexual demands, things that Angela refused to do.

'He likes bondage . . . and shit like that,' she says. 'I was like, "No." And we would fight.'

Then there were his jealous rages. One night up at The Gratto he exploded when he saw Angela talking to another SAS guy. Soldier B was drunk, stark naked, and seething.

'Are you serious? Look at you,' she replied. 'If anyone should be worried it's me. You don't have any clothes on.'

For Soldier B clothes might have been optional up at The Gratto but he was very particular about what he wanted Angela to wear and to look like. She had to conform to his concept of the perfect SAS partner.

One day they went shopping at an upmarket Perth boutique for a dress for Angela for a regimental ball. Soldier B picked one.

'Try it on,' he said.

Angela looked at the price tag. It was a thousand dollars. She did what he said and took it into the change room. Then she started hyperventilating. It cost too much and she didn't even like it. Soldier B was waiting outside the door.

'What are you doing?' he asked.

'I don't want this,' said Angela through the door. 'It's too expensive. I know you want me to look good. But let me buy my own dress.'

Angela bought a consignment dress for $30. At the function she was complimented all night.

'You've got to let me do my own thing,' she told Soldier B. 'Don't make me someone I'm not.'

But he would not let up. Soldier B accused Angela of sleeping around, of wasting money. Then there were his bizarre outbursts.

'I'm not human. I don't have the same blood running through my veins as you. I'm indestructible,' Angela recalls him saying one time.

'Is that what you think? You're a fucking human. You're just like everybody,' she said.

'No, I'm not.'

Then there was his love of hunting. Soldier B was an avid big game seeker and liked showing off trophies of his kills.

'There were zebra skins around the house. There were antlers,' says Angela. 'He loves killing things.'

One day he told her about the close call he had in Canada while stalking a true apex predator.

'He was hunting this bear and he couldn't find it. He turned around and saw it charging at him, like in a movie scene, he reckons it sort of charged at him and he just shot it,' she recalls him telling her.

When they met, Angela had told him she didn't date drinkers. She had married one and she had suffered for it. Soldier B told her he didn't drink. But it later turned out that he drank more than her ex-husband. He was a guzzler.

Tonight, up at The Gratto, he has been drinking again.

It is late when Soldier B comes home, and Angela can see he is spoiling for a fight.

'Where's that kid?' he asks.

Here we go, thinks Angela. That bloody car again.

'It was months ago. It's been sorted,' she says.

But he is walking towards Nick's room now. Angela is frantic.

'You don't need to speak to him. Come to me,' she says.

He turns and walks towards her.

'You just want to take my money.'

This starts another argument and their raised voices eventually lure Nick from his room. He fears for his mum.

'Hey, what's going on?' he asks.

In a flash Soldier B is in the young man's face, complaining about the accident, how Nick hasn't paid for it, how he hasn't taken responsibility, how he fucked up.

'We've talked about this. I've done everything I can,' says Nick.

Angela manoeuvres her slight 157-centimetre frame between them.

'Fuck you both,' says Soldier B. He turns and walks out of the house.

Angela goes to follow him but her son takes her arm.

'Mum, let him go. Don't chase him. Let him cool off.'

In her room, Angela lies in bed thinking about what she has gotten herself and her son into. He isn't the man she thought he was. Nothing like it.

She has got nowhere to go. She can't go back to Sydney.

My dad is going to think I'm a loser, she thinks. He already thinks I'm a loser.

There is some rustling outside the window. It sounds like someone running up the driveway. Angela gets up and goes to the front door and opens it. Soldier B charges past her.

Nick has come out into the hallway to see what is going on. Soldier B grabs the teenager, drags him into the lounge and they

55

both end up on the sofa. Soldier B connects with one, two, then three blows. Angela jumps on his back, ripping his shirt. She hears a snap but continues to hang on to him like some sort of tiny rodeo rider.

Soldier B lets go of Nick for a split second.

'Nick, run! Go and call the police!' screams Angela.

The youngster manages to slide out from underneath the big soldier and bolts for the front door. Soldier B goes to run after him but trips and falls, giving Nick precious time to make it outside.

Angela looks down at her left hand. Her ring finger is bent sideways at the second joint. That was the snap she heard. She is confused because she can't feel any pain.

She looks up and sees Soldier B running at her. Angela scampers into the kitchen. But there is no escape from the kitchen – it's a dead end. She turns and Soldier B's hand slams into her throat, lifting her backwards. It is an uneven contest. He is more than twice her weight and many times stronger.

'Stop,' she gasps. 'What are you doing to yourself?'

Even in her panic she is wondering why she is saying this. Why isn't she saying, 'Stop, why are you trying to kill me?' Instead, she is worried about him.

The grip tightens. She can't talk anymore, and she is struggling to breathe. She grabs at his face, sticking her fingers – broken and otherwise – into his eyes. His iron grip relaxes a fraction, and Angela wriggles from his grasp and runs.

She is in the street now, sprinting past other army houses in only her underpants and a singlet top.

'*Nick!*' she screams. '*Nick!*'

Angela sees a vehicle approaching and she begins waving her hands in its headlights. It is one of the security guards who patrols the marriage patch.

'I need to find my son,' she tells the guard.

Angela gets him to drop her at the home of another base family. She knows Nick is close with their daughter. He isn't there so she gets the daughter to ring his phone. Nick answers and tells her that he is sheltering in their neighbour's house.

'I know you don't know us, and I'm sorry you're involved in this, but until the cops get here, we can't go home,' Angela tells the neighbours when she arrives. She is standing on their doorstep in nothing but her knickers and a singlet, with a badly broken finger.

Reluctantly, they let her in. Nick has already called the police and told them his mum has been attacked by Soldier B at Campbell Barracks.

'They would have known by Campbell Barracks that he was SAS,' says Angela.

In other words, Soldier B is potentially armed and dangerous. Where the hell are the police, wonders Angela. It is the early hours of the morning and she is hugging Nick on the couch in these strangers' lounge room. The woman is nice and gets Angela an icepack for her broken finger. The husband won't come near them.

'He used to give us strange looks all the time. Whether he heard about what [Soldier B] was like and didn't want to be familiar with him, I don't know.'

Maybe he is scared of him too.

After a couple of hours the police turn up. Angela can't believe how long it has taken them to come. She tells them what happened, they tell her they want her statement and that they are going to arrest Soldier B.

Angela knows this could end his career. This scares her.

'I just need you to get him out of there, so I can go home and go to sleep. I just want him gone,' she tells them.

But the cops want her to give them a statement. She is afraid and doesn't want to. But they keep asking her. She relents.

The police ask Angela if there are any weapons in the house. She is dumbfounded.

'Of course there is. There are knives and blades. He's in the SAS. Of course there are weapons in the house. There's a safe with guns,' she says.

Suddenly more police cars turn up. It has finally dawned on them who is inside the house, and how potentially dangerous he is. This man is a trained killer, one of Australia's most elite soldiers. This could turn into an armed siege.

Angela has an idea about how to defuse a violent escalation. She calls Soldier B's best mate, Matt, who is another senior SAS operator. If anyone is going to go in there and convince him to come out, it is Matt. Unlike his other Special Forces colleagues, Soldier B respects Matt. He listens to Matt.

'Don't go running in there,' Matt tells the cops when he arrives. 'You don't know what to expect.'

The police are told they are dealing with a battle-hardened veteran, one who is pissed, angry and who has several high-powered guns at hand.

Matt goes next door and lets himself in and finds Soldier B in bed asleep. He has passed out. Matt rouses him.

'Mate, you're being taken away.'

Soldier B goes peacefully. He is handcuffed and taken to the police station and questioned overnight. The police issue an order preventing him from contacting Angela and Nick for 72 hours. The next morning he is released into the care of the SAS. He will subsequently be charged with two counts of aggravated assault. I will later obtain the court documents outlining the charges, his scheduled court appearances, as well as Soldier B's bail undertaking, giving his address at the SAS barracks in the Perth suburb of Swanbourne.

'If a soldier was suspected of committing an offence like that it's classified as a notifiable incident and the commanding officer would be compelled to report it, irrespective of whether or not the incident was still under investigation,' says a serving senior ADF officer.

A former SAS member who was on the base when the incident took place also says the regimental brass would have been informed and taken it up the chain of command. Then they would respond like they always do.

'In these cases the SAS would visit the spousal partner and say, "We will deal with this because if the police are involved his career is over". The SAS had contacts with the police. They thought they were above the law.'

In other words, let us keep this in-house.

The brass knows exactly how much shit Soldier B is in. Aggravated assault in Western Australia carries a prison term of up to three years. A conviction will be career ending.

Soldier B is due to be deployed to Afghanistan in less than three months. He is a key member of 3 Squadron and one of its most experienced operators. He will be almost impossible to replace.

'You're not talking about a truck driver here,' says a senior officer. 'He's in a niche area where they have high competence demands and few people to choose from. I would expect that those in authority would have looked at it, balanced it, and said, "We've got to take him anyway, even if he's a bit of an arsehole."'

At home Angela is paid a visit by a regimental 'family resilience' officer. She has met the woman before at meetings of the SAS wives and partners.

'I was the big mouth at these meetings saying that they're coming home crazy, they're coming home punching the air. They're coming home talking to themselves in the mirror, having nightmares, drinking like fish. They're coming home not normal. What are you going to do about it?'

The SAS padre also stops by to check on her.

Angela wonders whether they are really worried about her, or whether they are more concerned about her speaking out about what goes on around the barracks.

'I feel they were worried that in court it would come out that in The Gratto, there is no drinking limit. There is a lot of bad shit that goes on up there.'

That bad shit includes punch ups between SAS colleagues. There are also strippers. Angela says some of the wives and girlfriends complain that they have a clear view from their homes of the strippers frolicking with their partners up on The Gratto's veranda. Luckily for Angela, her home doesn't have a view of the boozer.

But the Regiment's commanding officer surely can't be oblivious to the shenanigans at The Gratto. His house is just over the road.

One member of the Regiment breaks ranks and gives support to Angela as she deals with the police and the prospect she will be dragged into a messy court case involving her partner. This member has seen how the Regiment deals with in-house misconduct.

His support of Angela rankles others in the Regiment.

'I got a couple of phone calls telling me to back off,' he says. 'One said to me, "[Soldier B] is a great guy and this will stuff up his career. We will look after this."'

But in the end, the SAS doesn't have to worry about Angela. She knows that if she testifies against Soldier B his career is over. She doesn't want that.

After the no-contact order expires Angela and Soldier B can see each other. Matt drives him to the house and waits outside.

Inside they sit down, and he begins to cry. It is something Angela has never seen him do before and she feels pity for him. She knows he is deeply tormented, seemingly awash with demons he can't control.

Soldier B takes her hand with the broken finger and begins kissing it.

'I'm sorry I did this to you. I can't believe I hurt you.'

'Maybe this can be a turning point,' she says. 'We can look at my distorted finger and go, "That was the day our life changed for the better".'

60

The finger is permanently disabled, but they agree to start again. In tears, he apologises to Nick, who tells him he forgives him.

There is one problem. Soldier B still has to front court on two charges of aggravated assault.

At the first hearing Angela tells the magistrate she does not want to proceed with the charges.

'You're a battered woman,' says the magistrate. 'Are you going to sit there and stand up for him, are you? You need to speak out.'

But Angela is adamant. She stands by her man.

Later a senior police officer calls her. He tells her she could have been killed in the assault.

'Strangulation is classified as attempted murder,' he tells her.

'If he wanted to kill me, he could have,' she says.

'Oh no, he was very intoxicated. So I think you had one up on him. But a few more minutes and you would have been dead,' says the officer.

They want her to testify. She won't budge. She and Nick write letters to the court saying that a conviction will end a distinguished military career. Soldiering in the SAS is Soldier B's life.

At the next hearing Angela waits in the lobby while Soldier B walks in to front the court. The police liaison officer sitting next to her leans over.

'So you're not going to testify?'

'No, I told you that in the letter,' says Angela.

'He needs to be charged. This is your last chance,' the police liaison warns. 'If it happens again, we can't help you. You can't bring this back.'

'That's fine,' replies Angela.

The police liaison stands up.

'Fine. We will get these papers signed and you can go.'

The liaison officer walks over to the two police officers who took Angela's statement on the night of the assault and gives them the news. The case cannot proceed.

Inside the court, the charges against Soldier B are dismissed for 'want of prosecution'.

In this case, it means the key witnesses won't testify.

The police liaison officer watches Soldier B and Angela walk out of court hand in hand alongside Nick. The three of them find a coffee shop to celebrate the dismissal of the charges.

'You really do care about me,' he says to Angela and Nick. 'Thank you so much.'

Two days after the aggravated assault charges are thrown out Soldier B is awarded a Commendation for Gallantry at a ceremony at Government House in Perth.

The decoration is for 'acts of gallantry in action while a team commander' during a previous deployment in Afghanistan.

In a light purple dress she picked herself, Angela watches on as the plain orange ribbon adorned with gold-plated flames is pinned to Soldier B's broad chest.

His honour and place in the Regiment is reinforced.

Within weeks he will be back in the action in Afghanistan with 3 Squadron SAS. There, he will be at the centre of several violent incidents, including a suspicious killing. It will be remembered for its sheer sadistic brutality. It is a killing that will scar those of his colleagues who witness it, and it will haunt others who are ordered to cover it up.

4

GIVE HIM A TASTE

'Now you see how it is here. Somewhere in the
war there's supposed to be honour.
Where's the honour here?'
Afghan Mujahedeen leader 'Masoud', *Rambo III*

The patrol 2-I-C raises his index finger. One minute until the chopper hits the landing zone.

It's 7 May 2012 and Braden is opposite the 2-I-C. He is wedged in the Black Hawk seat between the SAS patrol scout and a Waka. Like the other Wakas, he is a Hazara from the country's north. The patrol scout reefs the chopper door open. Green fields and bands of trees whip by. They are flying low.

Braden, the Bear, has his monitoring device in a pouch over his chest, and a large antenna bent over his shoulder. He is wearing red wraparound sunglasses and his M4 assault rifle is barrel-down, upright between his legs.

He has been in Afghanistan for more than two months now. He has witnessed the death of Rahul and the killing of the detainee that followed, a shooting Braden believes was ordered as revenge. He remembers the bound prisoner being placed on his knees, Soldier A motioning with his gun, then the burst of fire from the Waka.

He remembers thinking, Oh fuck. That's an execution. Okay, we're executing people now.

They are about halfway through their deployment. Some in the squadron are becoming frustrated. They are playing by the rules, but they are being fucked over by the Afghan authorities.

63

'We would put [detainees] in the detention facility, and they would be back out three days later,' says an SAS patrol commander on the 3 Squadron rotation in 2012. 'So you go, "What the fuck are we doing?" It was just bullshit.'

Braden listens to the angry complaints from the patrols about the revolving door of the detention centre.

'We may as well just fucking shoot them,' he hears one of the operators say.

They are risking their lives to capture the targets, and then those targets are walking out of jail and picking up a weapon again.

'What the fuck are we doing here?' asks Braden.

Then there is telling friend from foe. It is clear the Taliban exploits this. Sometimes they stand and fight, other times they hide their weapons before the helicopters land and then pick up a hoe and play farmer.

Braden wonders what the strategic mission is. He knows that other great powers have come to Afghanistan only to sink into an inescapable quagmire.

'I knew that the Soviets had been there. I knew that the English were there at some stage,' he says. 'You're looking around, you're like, "How did these people beat the Soviets at the height of their power? They're goat herders, simple people".'

It was all so much clearer and cleaner in *Rambo III*, thinks Braden.

Their destination this fine spring day is the hamlet of Deh Jawz-e Hasanzai, north of Tarin Kowt. It has long been a festering sore for the SAS.

The Black Hawk skims over the sparse groves and lush fields, passing just a couple of dozen metres above compounds containing homes and stock pens. They are very low now, level with a line of trees.

They are just metres off the ground and are coming in fast. The soldiers zip past a woman wearing a light robe and green head covering bolting towards a room inside a compound. She, like the other women of Deh Jawz-e Hasanzai, want nothing to do with these violent infidel

64

men from the West. Everyone in the district can hear the red beards coming.

Will the Taliban stand and fight today? Or are they hiding their guns and picking up their hoes?

The Black Hawk sets down in a field of young wheat next to the compound. The wheat is beaten flat by the downdraft of the chopper's blades, and it bends and rolls like green waves. The 2-I-C, a couple of operators and the dog handler sprint from the left door. Braden and the others disembark from the other side.

The soldiers head towards the compound where the woman in the green head covering was seen running to hide. The wheat is thigh-high, a month or six weeks from harvest. The men fan out and skirt around the compound towards a tree line. Above them the choppers keep watch. It looks just like a scene from a Hollywood action movie.

Today, Braden has been put in Soldier A's patrol – India Five. It also includes an SAS operator and four or five Wakas. They creep towards the target compound a couple of hundred metres away.

Another patrol – India Three – reaches the tree line first and crosses a large irrigation channel. On the other side is a poppy field. The light pink and magenta flowers are in full bloom. The large green bulbs are almost ready for scoring, to weep the milky gum that produces the opium.

The Americans have spent USD $1.5 million a day, every day, since the war began in 2001, fighting the opium war in Afghanistan. But they are losing and losing badly. The size of the national crop has grown four-fold while the Americans have been waging their war. Ninety-five per cent of the world's illicit heroin is now being supplied by Afghanistan, with the bulk of it passing through Europe.

But Washington persists. It is part of the wider war. Opium makes the Taliban USD $200 million a year, revenue it uses to buy guns, mortars, rockets and ammunition which it uses to kill American, Afghan and Coalition soldiers.

The poppy field is interspersed with trees, perfect cover for insurgents. One of the operators raises his weapon and looks through the scope. A poppy flower is wedged between the barrel and the scope. Nothing. He drops his weapon and keeps walking through the poppies.

The idea is for the various patrols to converge on the target. They are like a net closing around its prey.

'Ground force commander is requesting that last airborne call sign be inserted,' radios an India Three operator to the Black Hawks above. The commander wants the final chopper to land and disgorge its soldiers.

'Squirter from compound has been interdicted,' says the operator into the radio.

A squirter is presumed to be an enemy trying to escape or take up a better tactical position.

On one mission in March, multiple SAS patrols had chased a squirter for almost an hour across fields and irrigation channels, past compounds and confused farmers and frightened children, and down to a river flowing fast with the spring snow melt. Ditching most of his clothes and a pistol on the bank, the squirter had jumped into the fast-flowing water and had been carried away from the pursuing patrols. He thought he had made good his escape. But he did not count on the Black Hawks tracking him from above. An SAS sniper on one of the choppers shot him as he floated down the river. They talked about that shot for weeks.

Whoever this person is, today he has been caught alive in the SAS net.

Ahead through the poppies, hidden in a thick clump of trees, is another compound. It is their target.

A group of Afghan men are squatting out the front. Some of them have heard the helicopters. They know it is a raid and have come back to the compound to wait for the red beards. Safer here than out in the fields. Others have been told by the SAS soldiers to assemble at the compound.

Some of the patrol take cover under a tree about 50 metres away. They are assessing the situation.

The setting belies the tension. The sky is a brilliant blue, the fields are emblazoned in a sea of iridescent poppies, and the groves of trees create a feeling of bucolic serenity.

An India Three operator raises his rifle and takes another look through the sight.

'Friendlies coming in,' he says. 'India One.'

India One patrol has been dropped in after India Three and India Five.

Five minutes pass before India One arrives to join them. The patrol commanders and senior operators confer among the poppies. One of the India Three operators sucks back through his nose and down his throat and spits loudly.

'Cover Three-Zero. Cover Three-Three,' he says into the radio. It is a message that alerts the other patrols that some of the operators are moving in towards the compound and need cover.

'We're going to clear this lot,' says the patrol commander.

Dogs inside the compound begin to bark as they approach. One sounds like a brute, its bark more like the guttural roar of some medieval monster.

The red dots of the soldiers' laser rifle sights dart across the wooden entrance doors to the compound.

'*Raouza! Raouza!*'

They are ordering anyone inside to come out. An operator slowly pushes one of the doors open.

Suddenly something lunges at the operator through the doorway. His rifle is trained at it, ready to fire. It misses the operator by centimetres. It is a large black and tan goat. He doesn't flinch as it flashes past him and out into the fields.

'Men, women and children,' the operator says to the patrol commander. He is explaining who he can see inside.

'Get 'em out and get 'em seated in the public area will you, mate,' orders the patrol commander.

They enter the compound, guns raised.

'*Chenah*! *Chenah*!'

They are now telling everyone in the compound to sit down. The women pull their head coverings over their faces and huddle together in the shade with the children. A couple of men squat in the sunshine.

The interior walls of the compound are a labyrinth of rooms. There are at least 10 of them. Some have a single window, others are pitch black inside. The soldiers break into pairs, guns raised, and search each room one by one.

From the bright sunshine outside it takes the soldiers' eyes a split second to adjust to the gloom. Their breathing is hard. Anyone could be inside, waiting in ambush with a weapon to take advantage of their momentary blindness as their sight transitions from the light to the darkness.

Inside one room an operator finds boxes of food, some rugs and an umbrella. He emerges back into the light.

'Anything in there?' asks the patrol commander.

'Nup.'

Inside another room cups of steaming tea sit next to pillows on the floor. The red dot of the operator's gun sight dances across the walls.

Inside another a red curtain hangs across the room. The operator, weapon levelled, peels it back. Nothing.

The rooms have been cleared.

Outside in the courtyard a soldier is going through a man's pockets. He picks something out. A packet of cigarettes. He drops it on the ground. He pulls out a lighter. Drops it on the ground.

After all the men have been searched, their hands are ziptied behind their backs. They will be detained and taken back to Tarin Kowt for processing.

A soldier pulls out a marker pen and scribbles onto some tape. He writes 'I34 NOE1002'. I34 is the call sign of the operator who has detained the Afghan. The rest refers to the compound the Afghan has been found in. The soldier sticks the tape onto the bound prisoner's back. He moves down the line and repeats the process.

Two turkeys wander into the courtyard gobbling furiously.

Boom. Boom.

Nearby there is gunfire. It must be one of the other patrols.

Boom.

Another shot.

The turkeys swagger across the courtyard. The men of India Three move into a cattle yard behind the compound wall to continue their search.

Soldier A's patrol – India Five – has zigzagged its way towards the target compound from the other direction. A tree line near a creek gives them plenty of cover. Despite the shade, it is hot. The fact that Braden is carrying more than 30 kilograms of gear doesn't help. He is a lather of sweat.

As they approach the compound Braden sees him. The man in black. At least he thinks it is black.

He is tall for an Afghan, thinks Braden. About six foot. Thin, a bit of facial hair. Young, maybe 25 to 35 years old.

The man in black hasn't seen the patrol. He has just walked from the compound. He must know the foreign soldiers are around somewhere because a Black Hawk is hovering nearby. The noise is deafening.

It is not until the man in black gets to within 30 metres of the tree line that he first glances in the direction of the patrol.

He has seen us, thinks Braden.

The man in black reaches into his clothing. The patrol have their weapons pointed at his head and chest, fingers on triggers. The Afghan pulls out a small black device and throws it towards the creek. He puts up his hands in a gesture of surrender.

He has seen us all right.

Soldier A walks towards the Afghan. Braden thinks he hears one of them speak. Is it Soldier A or the man in black? He cannot tell.

Soldier A is 15 metres from the man when he raises his weapon. Not to his shoulder or to his eyeline, but to just above his hip. He is like a gunslinger with a lever action rifle pacing towards a bad guy in a 1950s Western.

Soldier A fires two shots from the hip. They slap into the chest of the man in black and the Afghan crumbles and falls back.

Braden freezes, his mind struggling to process what he has just seen.

The man in black is on the ground and isn't moving. The last little bits of his life are draining away, thinks Braden.

Soldier A is still walking towards the man in black. As he reaches him, he puts a bullet into his head. He doesn't even stop walking as he does it.

'It was almost like target practice for him,' says Braden, who is only a few metres from Soldier A.

Braden looks at the body. The back of the man's head has been blown out.

'Can you clear him?'

Soldier A wants Braden to go through the Afghan's pockets, to do a Sensitive Site Exploitation, or SSE.

Great, thinks Braden. Not looking forward to this. I have to search this guy whose skull and brains are everywhere.

He bends down and starts going through his pockets. A handker-chief. Some tobacco. Bits and pieces you would expect in the pockets of an Afghan man in the middle of nowhere.

Braden walks over towards the creek and finds the phone the man threw before he put his hands in the air.

Braden passes on the phone's details to the Charlie, the patrol's radio operator. He radios them back to Tarin Kowt, where they are run through a database and the results sent back. Nothing. The device is not of interest. It isn't on the target list. It is not on any list.

Braden is back searching the body when another member of Soldier A's patrol comes over.

'What happened?'

'[Soldier A] shot him,' says Braden.

'What was he doing?'

'Standing there.'

'Anything else?' asks the operator.

'He saw us, he threw the phone and then he stopped.'

'Oh, was he moving to gain tactical advantage?'

Braden knows exactly where this is heading. He shrugs.

'Sure.'

The man in black was tactically manoeuvring. That is what the patrol report will say. It will also say that he was a combatant who was carrying an ICOM. Under the Rules of Engagement, an Afghan carrying a radio could be a spotter and is therefore a fair target. The report will say the dead Afghan was engaged legitimately by Soldier A. And that will be that.

'They just make it easy and say, "Oh, he's moving to gain tactical advantage",' says Braden. 'So he said that to me and I just kind of went, "Okay, whatever. That's what he's doing".'

Braden doesn't want to argue with the operator. He knows the score.

As Braden finishes clearing the body they are joined by another patrol. With them is a dog handler and his dog, Devil.

Devil starts chewing on the dead man's shattered head. He is ripping at it.

What the fuck? thinks Braden.

'Can you get this fucking dog away?' he says.

71

The dog handler stares at him. At his feet, Devil is eating bits of the dead man's brain.

'No, give him a taste,' says the dog handler.

Fuck this, I'm done. Braden stands up. As far as he is concerned, he has cleared the man in black. Let the dog have him.

5

KING HIT

'Sitting in Saigon was like sitting inside the folded petals of
a poisonous flower, the poison history, fucked in its root
no matter how far back you wanted to run your trace'
Michael Herr, *Dispatches*

It began as an argument between two mates over a goat. But it would
end up with Tom sacked from his patrol.

A few days before the argument Tom had been reprimanded by
his patrol commander for missing the start of a meeting in the Ready
Room. He was getting lunch, unaware it was even on.

'What the fuck are you doing eating?' the patrol commander had
said when Tom walked into the Ready Room with his food. He felt
like a fool when he saw everyone gathered there.

'There's a general here to speak to us,' said the patrol commander.
'Put the fucking food down.'

'You didn't tell me there was a general here to speak with us. If you
had I would have been here,' said Tom.

Tom is skating on thin ice talking to his patrol commander like
that. In the SAS, the PCs are demigods. Their word is law. They
may be outranked by the officers, but these sergeants are vastly
experienced war fighters and are the dominant influence within the
Regiment. They are the prime movers behind its warrior culture, and
on the battlefield they lead from the front. Everyone obeys the patrol
commanders, and even the junior officers defer to their judgement in
planning operations and executing missions on the ground. The PCs
are so formidable they can have SAS operators like Tom sent home.

'The sergeants were more powerful than anyone,' says Tom. 'If they wanted to, and I saw this, they could ruin your career. They could ruin [officers'] careers.'

Tom suspects he was deliberately not told about the meeting, that he is being set up. It is not the first time that he has been excluded from things. After the briefing with the general, Soldier C had walked over to him.

'Mate, I can't fucking wait till they send you back to Australia,' he had said.

Braden Chapman, the Bear, is also approached by Soldier C.

'If you ever see [Tom] do anything not quite right, let me know,' he says.

Braden knows they are trying to build some sort of case against Tom. So too does medic Dusty Miller.

'It was a viper pit, they'd eat their own,' says Dusty. 'Tom didn't fit the mould, so he got singled out and persecuted dreadfully. I had no issues being his friend because a good person is a good person as far as I'm concerned.'

But it is a silly spat with his great mate Dusty that will trigger Tom's downfall and his removal from his patrol. By this time, 3 Squadron has been in Afghanistan for a bit over a month and the medic is planning some live tissue training and needs a goat to simulate a casualty that he can work on. He needs something that bleeds and breathes.

It is a weekend and Dusty has had trouble finding a goat and the training isn't ready to go as planned. Dusty asks Tom for help.

'Mate, I'm happy to give you a hand,' says Tom. 'But because I'm in the patrol I can't really just leave and go and get goats with you and help set everything up. When it's ready let me know and I'll be more than happy to come and do it with you.'

This pisses Dusty off. He thinks Tom wants the day off. It is a silly misunderstanding but it will set off an argument.

'If I ask you to fucking help me, you're fucking going to help me. It's as simple as that. I'm not fucking telling you. I'm ordering you,' says Dusty to Tom. Pulling rank is not something Dusty likes to do, especially with mates.

Braden hears them arguing. That's weird, he thinks. Those two are usually close friends, as tight as they get.

'Tom basically spoke down to him,' says Braden. 'Dusty just tore shreds off Tom. And they got over that really quickly.'

But not before Soldier C walks past. He is not going to waste this opportunity.

'He went straight off to [the patrol commander] and reported Tom,' says Dusty. 'Like a fucking schoolboy.'

As far as Dusty is concerned it is a minor blue between two mates and it has been sorted out. But the patrol commander doesn't see it that way. He wants Tom out, and this is his opening. The patrol commander comes to see Dusty in his room.

'What happened between you and Tom today?'

'Nothing, mate,' says Dusty. 'Just a bit of a disagreement. I fucking sorted him out.'

But the patrol commander has already taken things up the chain of command. Tom's alleged insubordination is put on a 'record of conversation' with the squadron sergeant major.

'It's all bullshit,' Tom tells the SSM. 'It was a misunderstanding. Dusty and I are fine.'

'They knew we were good mates,' says Dusty. 'They just thought it was the perfect situation to try and break that up or cause a rift.'

The next day Tom is called in again and this time 3 Squadron's officer commanding is there. The spat over the goat has gone up the chain of command. Tom is told he is being removed from the patrol. He is also told that he has to move out of the room he shares with the operators, and that he will be bunking in with the support staff.

Tom is furious. He has been sacked over an argument about a fucking goat.

They also want to humiliate him – an operator – by making him room with the 'crap hat' support staff. But Tom is fine with that. He likes the support guys and mixes with them already. Dusty and Braden are his mates.

Told to toe the line or he will be sent home, Tom is put in charge of a patrol of Wakunish soldiers.

'I remember Tom being almost happy about it because he got to go and deal with the Wakas,' says Braden. 'He enjoyed the language. He didn't have to deal with that patrol anymore that he didn't like. But even I could see that he'd been basically sacked.'

Tom has been in charge of the Wakunish before, during Rotation 15 in 2011, a role he was commended for.

'Your outstanding leadership and mentoring of your Afghan Partner Force, throughout your deployment, substantially contributed to the development of their operational capability,' wrote the commander of Joint Task Force 633, Major General Angus Campbell. 'Your tireless dedication and acceptance of additional responsibilities, often requiring you to lead a team of Afghan partner forces, was instrumental in the successful conduct of numerous partnered operations.'

Tom is a mere trooper. Running a patrol of Wakas is usually done by a sergeant. Tom's apparent promotion after being sacked from his patrol puzzles him.

'Why are they appointing me to a position which is effectively a patrol commander, with greater responsibility, if they are questioning my ability to perform?' asks Tom.

He knows the answer to that, and so does Dusty. It has nothing to do with performance or ability.

'Tom's more of a thinker. He's very intelligent, but he's personable,' says Dusty. 'But to those guys he was a weirdo.'

Tom says they also question his sexuality, joke that he is a 'poof'. This is despite the fact he has a girlfriend back home.

One time in Tarin Kowt someone steals Tom's sneakers and training gear, douses them in petrol and lights it all up. They film it and pass the footage around for laughs.

'He was targeted by the arseholes because he was different,' says a fellow 3 Squadron operator. 'Tom was a good soldier. Tom could shoot, I mean shoot. Very capable operator. But different. Just didn't fit that, "I'm an SAS operator, let's get boozed, let's get tatts". He didn't fit that mould.'

'You know how they talk about the brotherhood? What a lot of crap,' says Tom. 'There was none of that.'

Tom may have been sacked from the patrol and relegated to the support staffers' room and to looking after some Wakas, but a couple of the operators are not finished with him.

A few weeks later he is in the accommodation block at Camp Russell. Some of the boys have been on the piss at The Fat Ladies Arms. It is the SAS boozer in the centre of the accommodation block, a place where the boys can blow off some steam after operations.

'It had the rules of the bar on the door,' says Dusty. 'The first rule of the Fat Ladies was don't mention Fat Ladies. So it was like "Fight Club". It was the wildest fucking thing.'

The Fat Ladies Arms is the scene of many rowdy and drunken nights. The bar's walls are decorated with scores of weapons captured by the SAS. There is an octagonal poker table emblazoned with the mascots of the three sabre squadrons – a redback for 1, a bushranger for 2, and the long-horned bull with demonic red eyes for the current inhabitants from 3 Squadron. At times, the soldiers play for serious stakes with their red, white and blue poker chips. There is the bar itself, complete with stainless steel fridges and a red illuminated 'The Fat Ladies Arms' sign above it. Next to the bar is a 3 Squadron poster.

At its centre is their unofficial motto – 'Drink, jump, fight, shoot and root'. Another sign declares: 'NO FAT CHICKS'.

There is supposed to be no boozing on deployments. So are the brass oblivious? Or are they turning a blind eye?

'Seriously, living in the Special Forces compound is a bit like living in a caravan park,' says one former SAS officer. 'You tell me. If an establishment like this, with parties like this, was happening in your caravan park, how could you not know? Makes you wonder how such huge parties could happen when the commander's office is only 50 metres away. They must have been wearing earmuffs and a blindfold.'

There are fancy dress parties at The Fat Ladies. During the 2012 rotation, 3 Squadron members dress up as Vikings and Roman centurions. Soldier B turns up one night as a gladiator, wearing nothing but a loin cloth and a leather shoulder guard and clutching a wooden sword. Others dress up as more contemporary figures such as Buzz Lightyear, Iron Man and Chewbacca. One SAS soldier dons blackface and a stick-on mohawk and comes as Mr T. One night, Iron Man passes out drunk so some of his mates grab a permanent marker and draw eyes on his eyelids and a penis on his cheek. He is so wasted he doesn't even move while they do it.

On another night, an inebriated SAS dog handler fires a pistol into the ceiling.

'[He was] saying to some female US helicopter pilot, "When was the last time you had a roof pop?",' says an SAS operator. 'She's like, "What are you talking about?" He goes, "Yeah, roof pop. We have them all the time. You had a roof pop?" He gets her pistol out of her shoulder holster, racks it and puts one in the roof.'

A female Special Forces support staff member there that night remembers the roof pop. How could you forget that? One other night after a torrid session at The Fat Ladies Arms, she cannot remember a thing.

'I wasn't pouring my own drinks. They were pouring them for me,' she says. 'I was very heavily intoxicated. I was so fucking hungover. I actually felt like I'd poisoned myself with alcohol. It was probably some sort of vodka. My lips were purple. It's the drunkest I've ever been.'

She later wakes up without any pants on in an operator's bed. She has no idea how she ended up there and what may have happened.

'They were making bourbon, vodka ... it took about a week or something to churn it out,' says Braden.

Another support staffer reckons the homebrew smells like nail polish remover. This rotgut doesn't just inebriate, it obliterates.

'There were stories about guys who shat themselves and walked it up the hallway,' says one Special Forces regular.

Dusty avoids The Fat Ladies Arms whenever he can. It is a cluster-fuck in there when the guys are getting on it.

'I'd go to bed and then suddenly there'd be a fucking bang on the door, "Where's the medic cunt? Get the medic out", and they'd make me drink with them. I was fucking knackered. So there'd be me drinking this homebrew shit, while they're all just fucking wasted. And I just want to go back to bed.'

Dusty does not escape the fallout from the big nights either.

'[One guy] he'd like turned purple,' says Dusty.

The SAS medic 'bags' him. He isn't the only SAS soldier who needs intravenous treatment for a killer hangover.

'So it'd be early morning, I'd be like cannulating people, putting bags of fluid up. Because they were all like fucking hungover so badly,' says Dusty. 'It was like something from the battlefield in the mornings. It was crazy. I'd just go around fixing fuckers up.'

Dusty isn't the only one who witnesses this morning-after carnage.

'I have seen SAS operators having to be IV'd before operations because they are so hungover,' says a former Australian Secret Intelligence Service agent who did several tours in Afghanistan.

Another time at the Fat Ladies a US pilot turns all paranoid after drinking the rocket fuel and he ends up with a black eye and a huge gash above his left eyebrow.

'And he's got to go and fly choppers and he's like, "Oh, I've been with the Aussies",' says Dusty. The medic stitches him up. It is not the only time he has to pull out the needle and surgical thread.

One night in the bar a patrol commander tests out his new combat knife by slicing open an engineer's arm.

'It was deep enough for it to be sutured. So I did it,' says Dusty. 'They were pissed, obviously.'

Just a couple of blokes blowing off steam, says one of the engineers.

'He slashed [his] arm ... he got stitches, so it couldn't have been a fucking tickle. Yeah, that was a mad night. It was a good night.'

The same patrol commander is particularly notorious for his drinking.

'He didn't inspire me as being a solid leader. He was just a functioning alcoholic,' says a 3 Squadron operator. 'Every time you went out with him he was either drunk or hungover.'

One night after a torrid drinking session, the patrol commander and an operator come looking for one of the Bears, a colleague of Braden Chapman's. Earlier, while out on a patrol, the Bear had fired at a target and the round had passed between two operators in front of him. They were livid about this loose shooting. Dusty and Braden are inside the support staff room when the door is kicked in. It is splintered off its hinges.

'Where's that Bear cunt at?' demands the patrol commander. He is carrying his knife.

For a second, Braden thinks they are asking about him.

'Which one are you referring to?' he says.

'The other cunt,' says the patrol commander.

But the other Bear is away working on a surveillance plane in Kandahar.

'Thank god he wasn't there,' says Dusty. 'I reckon he'd have been fucking beaten up.'

The patrol commander and the operator are not easily deflected.

'Which one's his bed?' says the patrol commander.

Braden points it out. The patrol commander begins stabbing and slicing up the absent Bear's mattress with the knife. He doesn't stop there.

'[The Bear] used to have pictures of his wife all over and [the patrol commander] stabbed the fuck out of every photo he could see,' says Braden.

'I mean [the patrol commander] was fucking unhinged,' says Dusty. 'He was completely unhinged.'

A week later the other Bear returns to find his bed trashed and his family photos hacked to pieces.

'Why didn't you fucking stop them?' he asks Braden.

'Are you fucking serious? Would you have stopped them if a group of drunken SAS guys came in, one with a knife, and starts going nuts and fucking up my bed? Would you have opened your mouth?' says Braden.

'Fair point,' concedes the Bear.

Some SAS veterans argue that a place like The Fat Ladies Arms is an essential pressure release for men being sent out day after day into enemy heartland on operations they might not return from.

'I think it's unrealistic to think you send a Western army to do the things they did or were required to do at that operational tempo without blowing off some steam and having a beer in a controlled environment. The Fat Ladies was that controlled environment,' says a 3 Squadron operator.

But rather than help operators blow off steam, one former SAS officer believes The Fat Ladies Arms contributed to anger, angst and violence among them.

'After combat, drinking like this is the most terrible way of dealing with post-battle trauma and issues. It's a disturbing indicator of the moral breakdown of an organisation,' he says.

It's not just boozing that goes on inside The Fat Ladies. There is a poker table which gets plenty of use. Sometimes they pull all-nighters and the stakes run into the thousands of dollars.

'We had lads in our fucking [accommodation] pull knives and shit like that because one lad owed another bloke 10 grand from poker,' says one Special Operations soldier. 'Fucking idiots. It's tax-free money. This lad who owed the other lad 10 grand is married. I was like, "Fucking hell, mate, you're gonna be divorced when you get back".'

This one night Tom has had a few drinks. But some of the others are wasted and things are getting heated.

'They'd had a big night on the turps,' says Tom.

That is about all he can remember of the night, and not because he was drunk. But others who were there do remember because it was so savage and senseless. What happens quickly spreads through 3 Squadron and the entire Regiment.

One of the operators, Trooper H, walks over and king hits Tom from behind. Unprepared for the punch, Tom collapses and his head slams on the floor.

He is out cold.

Dusty can't believe it.

'[Trooper H] is a good dude and a good mate,' he says. 'It was uncharacteristic of him. Tom was bullied. The worst case of bullying I've ever seen in my life.'

No one goes to Tom's aid. As he lies on the floor, they step around him.

'I think it may have affected their standing in the Regiment if they'd rushed over to assist me,' he says.

'It always seemed like people were distant with him,' says Braden Chapman. With Tom thrown out of his patrol, Braden is now one of his roommates. 'Other guys didn't want to be seen to be friendly with him knowing that people like [the patrol commander] didn't like him.'

Tom doesn't know how long he is on the ground before he picks himself up and stumbles to his bed. He will suffer a pain in the base of his skull for months to come. But he refuses to go to the doctor on base.

'I was concerned that if I go to the doctors they'll say, "What happened?" I didn't want to be put in a position of saying this happened and then it gets reported.'

Tom had earlier been told to toe the line by one of his superiors. The message is clear – do not violate the code of silence. He keeps quiet about the unprovoked assault.

Other operators come over to him later and help him fill in the blanks of what happened.

'Mate, are you okay?' asks one.

'Mate, how would you feel?' replies Tom.

'You hit your head really hard [on the ground] and they wanted to take you to the hospital,' says the operator.

'Oh yeah? Why didn't they?' says Tom.

'What happened was bullshit,' says another operator. But, like the others, he didn't help, and he doesn't report it. They toe the line too.

But word of the king hit is spreading through 3 Squadron like wildfire. Then it starts to circulate through the rest of the Regiment. An SAS sergeant based at Kandahar is concerned and talks to Tom about it.

'What's been done about it?' he asks.

'Nothing.'

The story makes its way back to Australia, to the base in Perth. Everyone knows about Trooper H knocking out Tom. All the sergeants and even some of the SAS officers have heard about it. But no questions are asked. What happens in Afghanistan stays in Afghanistan.

'There was no mediation process, there was no investigation, there was no one charged,' says Tom. 'Again, it relates back to the who's who in the zoo. If you drink with the right people and you're accepted as one of the cool kids, you can do no wrong.'

Tom feels very isolated, and very vulnerable. If a colleague, a man who also wears the coveted sandy beret, feels it is fine to king hit him, what else can he expect? If this soldier is then protected by the brotherhood, what more can they get away with?

He isn't the only fellow operator Tom is genuinely frightened of. There is also Soldier C and his former patrol commander. They have drummed him out of the patrol. They know that Tom knows what happened to the 'village idiot'.

Tom is at the point where he makes sure he is always the last one to put his M4 assault rifle away back in the Ready Room after they have returned from operations.

'I genuinely believed that if they'd have had the opportunity, if we'd raised certain things, that they had the capability – they'd already proven it – to put a bullet in the back of your head and just turn around and say it was the Taliban,' says Tom.

6

SARKHUME

'I remember us leaving that job and women were wailing.
There was smoke. It was like something from a Vietnam
movie. That's the best way to describe Sarkhume'
**Sergeant Dusty Miller, combat medic, 3 Squadron SAS,
Rotation 17 (February 2012)**

'The body needs to be cleared.'

Christina watches the Commandos in the footage standing over the Afghan's body. One of the Commandos bends down and begins going through the man's pockets. The Afghan could be badly wounded, though he appears dead to Christina. He is pretty messed up. There is blood all over his clothes, his head is back, his mouth is open, and his chest is still.

'The body needs to be cleared,' says the other Commando. He is impatient, he wants this done in double quick time. 'The body needs to be cleared.'

His voice is growing louder, more insistent.

The footage is taken from a camera mounted on the helmet of one of the Commandos. Suddenly the Commando searching the body is pushed out of the way. His comrade who wants the body cleared points his weapon at the dead man's head and fires two shots.

Christina shudders. It is early on in her deployment and she hasn't seen anything like this before.

Sapper Christina is on a six-month tour and has been in Afghanistan since October 2011. It is her first time in a war zone. Christina is the Handheld Imagery Data Base Manager for the Special Operations Task

Group in Afghanistan. She handles all the video and photos brought in by the SAS and the Commandos. She gets to see it all. Dead bodies, IEDs, weapons caches, prisoner mugshots, footage of operations.

'When the images came back I would know where the mission took place. Based on that I would use satellite imagery to then determine exactly where ... that photo was likely taken from,' says Christina. 'Each individual photo was individually metadata-ed. If it was an enemy killed in action, I'd find how he was engaged and where he was engaged, and I would put the information from the report against that specific image.'

It is time-consuming and detailed work, and an average day is 16 hours. But Christina loves her job. Despite being a lowly sapper, she gets to see everything that happens on every battlefield. She knows everything that is going on.

'On my deployment I lost count of the number of bodies I saw,' she says. 'I remember on one operation they came back with images of at least seven dead bodies.'

Christina is part of the Special Forces Fusion and Targeting Cell. The FATC is central in identifying insurgent leaders, bombmakers, and senior fighters to be targeted for killing or capture.

'So the Fusion and Targeting Cell had American analysts, as well as some other Australian intelligence personnel. They had database managers and would create packages,' she says.

'Packages' are intelligence briefs on Taliban targets. If you have a package created for you, it could mean you have a short lifespan.

'Usually it would have an objective name,' says Christina. Like the unfortunate Objective Yakuza Assassin. Other examples of objective names on the kill or capture list are Stiletto, Mohican Spear, Heget, Boxcutter and Yeti Aztec. Sometimes the packages also include the objective's tribe, age and father's name.

'It might contain [details of] the person they're trying to locate or a facility they're trying to locate,' says Christina. 'From there a mission briefing would be conducted which would have a whole heap of information, right down to the weather of the day.'

But some packages are sketchy, their detail vague.

'Some of them would say the objective had a beard. But most Muslim men had beards,' she says.

Christina is disturbed by the footage of the Commando shooting what she thinks is a dead Afghan. Mutilating or mistreating dead bodies is a war crime.

She decides to report it up the chain.

'Look, I've got this footage. I think it could contain something which may be a war crime,' she tells an intelligence officer posted with the Commandos.

He looks concerned and promises to investigate. Both Christina and the intelligence officer know that the SAS and Commandos are not supposed to be taking out personal video cameras. The last thing the military wants is a leak of unauthorised footage revealing what they like to call 'tactics, techniques, and procedures'.

'They were told not to wear helmet cams. Technically speaking, we shouldn't have that footage,' says Christina. 'I didn't see a lot of SAS with helmet cams, but I did see 2 Commando [soldiers] coming back from missions with Contours and GoPros [cameras] mounted on their equipment or their helmets.'

Christina asks regimental intelligence officers to give her any mounted camera footage, even though the soldiers aren't supposed to be wearing the devices.

'I kept asking for copies because we were often tasked to make [video] productions and we had little to no footage of operations,' she says. 'I thought the next best thing is getting a copy, at least then there is oversight and control.'

That is how she has the footage of the Commando shooting the apparently dead Afghan.

A few hours after she has reported the footage to the intelligence officer he comes in and pulls Christina aside.

'He said the footage did not contain a war crime and that I was to delete the footage and that I wasn't supposed to discuss it further,' she says.

Christina is conflicted. Does she obey the order and delete evidence of a possible war crime? Or does she keep the footage? She does both. Christina copies the footage onto a secure server she thinks only she has access to and then deletes it from the database.

But then the intelligence officer is back in her office. He has caught Christina out.

'He said that he'd found that on this server and I was to ensure that all copies were deleted of the footage,' she says.

She deletes the footage.

'I was trying to justify the reason that I was deleting it. But I knew that was wrong and I deleted it anyway.'

It is only early on in her deployment. This won't be the last time Sapper Christina is ordered to delete compromising images.

———

3 Squadron SAS is on another hunt.

They have been given the package. The target is Objective Young Apprentice, real name Mullah Hashim. He is a newly elevated Taliban commander who is renowned as a bombmaker.

This all part of an ongoing operation dubbed Tevara Sin, an intelligence driven mission targeting the leadership of the insurgency in Uruzgan. As part of Tevara Sin, the SAS can hit the ground at short notice, often between an hour and 90 minutes. Once the intelligence comes in, they scramble and go.

There are 28 SAS soldiers and 15 Wakunish on the raid. As well as Objective Young Apprentice, their other goal is to find weapons caches.

They are on their way in Black Hawk helicopters to the village named in the package.

Hazratullah is 14 years old. His homeland has been at war since he was three.

He doesn't know it, but the destination of today's Australian raid is his village. Sarkhume is about 20 kilometres west of the provincial capital, Tarin Kowt. It might only be a stone's throw from the capital, but Sarkhume is a place where Taliban and tribal warlords rule.

It is not the Australians' first visit to Sarkhume. The previous year, in June, a man was killed in a raid there. Villagers claimed he was a farmer working out in his fields.

Sarkhume snakes along a 1.5 kilometre stretch of river, and family compounds hug this waterway. The river is an artery. It is a district of cultivated fields and thick undergrowth. Perfect terrain for insurgents to ambush the Australians. On the outskirts of the village, the terrain rises and the foliage drops away to bare earth and dust.

Hazratullah is one of seven siblings. His father Haji Sardar is an almond farmer and keeps livestock to feed the family. He is also an important member of the village.

'He was a tribal elder and going to Jirgas [an assembly of tribal leaders] between people. Sometimes he was mediating. If two people had fought and clashed, he would make peace between them,' says Sarkhume villager Malik Dawood.

Haji Sardar also drives people to Tarin Kowt. But today he is not doing the Tarin Kowt run as he has just taught one of his other sons, Abdul Latif, how to drive.

'I might have learned how to drive a week or two prior to this. My father stayed behind, which led to the incident,' says Abdul Latif. 'I am responsible.'

Hazratullah is his father's favourite. He takes the teenager to the market and to the orchard. He wants him to go to school one day.

This spring morning Hazratullah is with his father when they hear the faint sound of a helicopter. They are in the family's guest room which soaks up the sunshine. It is also the place where the family gathers for late afternoon and evening prayers.

A few minutes later, at 9.37 am, the first Black Hawk touches down on the stony plain above Sarkhume. Soldier B is on this chopper. He is back in his element, heading out on a raid with his men, hunting their quarry. But he is lucky to even be in Afghanistan. If his partner Angela and her son Nick had pressed ahead with the aggravated assault charges, Soldier B would probably have been left out of this deployment. He might even have been thrown out of the Regiment. If he had been convicted, he could even be in jail.

Sixteen minutes after Soldier B's Black Hawk hits the ground, the second chopper sweeps in. Medic Dusty Miller is on this helicopter with the engineers, who go by the Echo call sign. It is just another day, another mission for Dusty.

'There was nothing special about it. It was like, "Yeah, we've got this information, we're going to go to this location." Again it was a kill/capture [mission] as per normal. I remember the objective's name, yeah.'

Hazratullah and his father are listening to the news on Haji Sardar's transistor radio when the first helicopter comes into view.

'He liked listening to the news. We were looking at the helicopters as they crossed the hill. They landed close to our home,' says Hazratullah. 'I stayed there, and my father headed to the garden. I was looking after the goats and the sheep which had been scattered by the helicopters.'

On the ground, the first SAS patrol begins clearing houses and compounds, looking for weapons and for Objective Young Apprentice.

'The foreigners came and kicked in the doors and they broke the padlocks and the cupboards and boxes. They tore the boxes open with bayonets,' says villager Shaista Khan.

Young Hazratullah watches as the Australians kick in the door of the mosque and barge into homes.

90

'They broke the glass in cupboards, mixed up all the household items, breaking into storage boxes,' he says. 'They were searching for guns. Whenever they found people they would blindfold and handcuff them, telling them to sit down there. No one would dare look at their faces. They had dogs with them.'

The Afghans are terrified of the Australian dogs. Like special forces in the United States, Britain and Israel, the SAS uses Belgian Malinois. A short-haired shepherd, the Belgian Malinois are celebrated by the Australians for their stamina, strength, intelligence and courage. On a mission the year before, an SAS dog called Kuga swam across a river and charged a Taliban fighter armed with an AK-47, exposing an enemy ambush position and possibly saving SAS lives. With the dog latched onto him, the insurgent shot Kuga five times. The dog was hit in the toe and twice in the ear. Another round struck his cheek and exited through his neck, while another entered his chest and went through his shoulder. Remarkably, after treatment in Afghanistan, then later in Germany and Australia, Kuga survived. But he died 11 months later.

While the Australians treat their combat dogs as equal and respected members of their team, Afghan civilians regard the Belgian Malinois as uncontrollable and savage. Today, in Sarkhume, that reputation will be reinforced.

Signals intelligence officer Braden Chapman is on the raid, but in a different patrol to Dusty. He is with 'Troop HQ' and is dropped with the troop commander and the radio operator on the far side of the village. To him, it is yet another day on the job in another dusty village whose name he doesn't know.

The raid proceeds without incident, until 10.15 am. That's when gunshots ring out. As Braden walks through the village, his radio crackles.

'Heard over the radio there'd been an EKIA and I remember hearing that somebody else was shot. That person wasn't dead.'

As they walk further through the village Braden sees a body on the ground.

'I could see a foot, the lower half of his legs. He was in longer grass or a bush ... we just walked on through.'

This was later discovered by Sarkhume villagers to be the body of Mirza Khan, killed trying to fight off an SAS dog. In his mid-20s, Mirza Khan worked in the wheat mill.

'He was a farmer with my father, helping my father in the mill. My father would bring wheat to the mill to get flour from it,' Mirza Khan's brother, Shaista Khan, will later tell an Afghan journalist I sent to Sarkhume to investigate the SAS raid.

Mirza Khan was going to have tea with two friends when he was seen by the Australians. His killing was witnessed by Hazratullah, who says the young man was set upon by Australian dogs.

'The dogs tore all his clothes. He was pushing their dogs away. They fired bullets and martyred him,' says Hazratullah. 'He was shot in his lower abdomen. He was shot in the leg. He was shot a lot in his chest.'

'I don't know how many bullets, but they had made holes all over his body,' says Hazratullah's brother Abdul Latif. 'He was riddled with bullets like a colander.'

Mirza Khan's mother is brought to see the body. At first Miraz Gula sees his eyes open, staring towards the sky, and thinks her son is alive. But then she comes closer and sees his horrific wounds.

'The clothing he was wearing was torn from top to bottom. It was torn to pieces. They had unleashed the dog on him,' says Miraz Gula. 'There was blood everywhere.'

So riddled with bullets is Mirza Khan's body that his family bury him in his clothes.

The Australian Defence Force will later claim that the young man 'was attempting to evade' the Australians. It will say he failed to stop when ordered to do so in Pashto. So he is shot dead. The SAS trooper who killed him does so 'as he felt for the safety of members' of his patrol.

My investigation will later prove all of this to be false. Mirza Khan was an unarmed civilian who was being mauled by an Australian dog when he was shot several times and killed.

After the shooting of Mirza Khan, the SAS and their Afghan Wakas continue to clear compounds along the river.

At 11.15 am Haji Sardar is out near his orchard when a shot rings out.

'They fired at [my father] in the garden,' Hazratullah later tells my fixer. 'My father was getting to the garden over a wall. They wounded him.'

When Hazratullah reaches his father, he notices that he is shot through the leg.

'He couldn't walk. Blood was dripping from his leg,' he says. 'They made him sit there.'

Dusty Miller gets a call to treat an Afghan man with a leg wound. The medic quickly assesses that the injury to Haji Sardar isn't life threatening.

'It was thigh. It was a through and through shot. It was fleshy and it wasn't arterial,' says Dusty. 'I'm good at my job. I treated it correctly. I fixed it. I put a compression bandage on it and then he was mine.'

The wounded Haji Sardar is Dusty's casualty, the medic's responsibility. The old Afghan is a good patient.

'He never really made a noise, just like most Afghans. They're just so stoic. I'd be hollering like a pig,' says the medic. 'A 5.56 [millimetre round] through the thigh. Oh my god, you can't imagine what that feels like.'

Dusty keeps the Afghan with him as he helps the other SAS soldiers blindfold prisoners, check their pockets and put whatever they find into bags. They have rounded up a lot of what the Australians call 'PUCs', or persons under confinement.

The Bear, Braden Chapman, is also there helping process the PUCs and had seen Dusty working on the wounded Afghan.

'I remember Dusty saying, "He's all good, patched him up, stopped the bleeding".'

Hazratullah is still worried for his father, because some of the Afghan men detained by the Australians are being beaten.

'Even if you had a simple look they would beat you with a gun on your head and roll you over. They would start kicking you. No one could look at each other or talk.'

Like they do on almost every operation, the Australians put bags and coverings over the heads and faces of the men they have detained.

Dusty wants Haji Sardar brought back to base for proper treatment.

'I'm thinking he's coming back with us because what he needed was a surgical wash out. He needed to be fixed,' says Dusty.

Dusty places the old man in the 'PUC train', the line of prisoners who will be put on a chopper and taken back to the Tarin Kowt base. There they will be processed and checked to see if they are on the target list. If not, they will be released.

'It was often my job to get this PUC train to the chopper so I'm normally on the arse end and I'm just pushing 'em along,' says Dusty. 'We had just gotten up. We'd left fucking two metres.'

Soldier B has grabbed Haji Sardar.

'I'm gonna take this guy, I've got this guy,' he tells Dusty.

'Why are you taking him? Where are you going?' asks Dusty. Soldier B does not answer.

Something isn't right. Haji Sardar is supposed to be getting on the helicopter to be taken back to Tarin Kowt for treatment. What does Soldier B want with the old man?

Braden hears Soldier B's response to Dusty's questions.

'[He] said, "I need to talk to this bloke" or something like that,' says Braden.

Watching on, Hazratullah sees an Australian with a 'painted face' handcuffing his injured father and taking him towards the village mosque.

'He was injured. They were carrying him. It was a big person who was carrying my father,' says Hazratullah.

Another patrol member says a Special Forces engineer attached to the SAS patrol was told to carry the wounded man by Soldier B.

Hazratullah wants to follow. He is concerned for his father, but the Australians warn him away.

'They took him inside the mosque,' Hazratullah says.

The mosque is a simple room up an alleyway.

From the compound, Hazratullah can hear shouts and cries coming from inside the mosque. He will later tell investigators from the Afghanistan Independent Human Rights Commission that he heard his father being beaten and tortured for between 30 minutes and an hour. Dusty believes it lasted only a few minutes.

'Whatever he did, it didn't take him long,' says the medic.

Hazratullah hears the cries stop and watches Soldier B emerge and then walk out of the compound. Soldier B catches up to Dusty who is herding the PUC train.

'Kilo, that bloke you had didn't make it,' he says.

'What?' says Dusty. His heart is racing. What the fuck is he talking about, he thinks. The guy had a flesh wound.

'He didn't make it,' repeats Soldier B with a shrug. He walks off.

Braden hears it too. 'He didn't make it.'

Braden looks at Dusty. The medic is shattered and visibly angry. Haji Sardar was his patient, his responsibility. But Dusty doesn't go after Soldier B. He knows what he is capable of, and he knows not to rock the boat.

What do you mean he fucking didn't make it, thinks Dusty. He begins racking his brain.

'Did I miss something? Did I miss an arterial bleed? No fucking way I did. The wound was through and through. I thoroughly checked it. The round hadn't hit the bone. I kept checking the wound as we were moving. He hadn't lost much blood. He had lost some, but I had it under control. He didn't even require a tourniquet. This guy was survivable. There was no way he could not have made it.'

Dusty knows that Haji Sardar has not died of his wounds. He knows he has been murdered inside that mosque. And he knows Soldier B has done it.

'He's a monster. He's a fucking animal. He really is an animal.'

It is not until the Australians leave that Hazratullah and the other villagers summon the courage to go inside the mosque.

Haji Sardar's eyes are closed. They try to rouse him, but they know he is dead. They examine his body. His torso is covered in bruises. There are boot marks on his chest and abdomen.

The women begin to wail. Hazratullah looks at the body. There is a neat dressing around his father's thigh. Someone has tried to treat him.

'Big fat boot marks were over his heart. You could see those boot marks all over his body, over his neck too,' says Hazratullah. 'He was dead. Before that he was fine. He was wounded, but not critically. He had been hit in the meaty part of his thigh, slightly wounded. They had martyred him.'

Dusty can tell immediately when the villagers realise what happened to Haji Sardar. He hears the women begin to wail.

'There was smoke. It was like something from a Vietnam movie. That's the best way to describe Sarkhume,' he says.

'I remember we heard wailing, women wailing and screaming,' says Braden. 'I remember someone going, "I guess they found the body".'

Soldier B has strangled him or bashed him, thinks Braden. There was no gunshot. He has done it with his bare hands. His bare hands.

On the chopper back to Tarin Kowt Dusty is furious. Sadistic as fuck. That's Soldier B all over, he thinks. This is bullshit. I didn't sign up to fix people up to have them killed. Fuck this, I've got to tell someone.

At Camp Russell Dusty pulls Tom aside behind their accommodation. 'Mate, you got five minutes for a chat?'

The medic trusts Tom above anyone else in the Regiment.

Tom can see that Dusty is shaken, that there is something gravely wrong. The SAS operator lights up a smoke and listens to his friend unload.

'Mate, I just had this patient taken off of me and he was fine. [Soldier B] took him off me and then came back and told me he didn't make it,' says Dusty.

'What do you mean?' asks Tom.

'He's dead.'

'You're kidding?'

'No,' says Dusty. 'He was my patient, and he was taken from me.'

Dusty keeps repeating those words. 'He was my patient.'

Tom knows that this will shatter his mate, that he will blame himself for Haji Sardar's death. That guilt will eat him up.

'I worked on this guy, he was my responsibility and now he's fucking dead,' Dusty tells Braden Chapman. Braden, too, can see the medic is devastated.

Dusty believes Soldier B is a psychopath who derives sadistic pleasure from killing.

'When he kills, it's like he has just gotten off,' says Dusty.

The medic remembers an earlier conversation on one of the first operations of the deployment. They are in a chopper about to hit the ground, and Soldier B is rolling his shoulders, warming up for the mission ahead.

'He goes, "I fucking love this shit. When I'm not here killing men, I'm in Canada killing bears." And I'm like, "Look out the window, Dusty". He fucking said that to me. And I knew then this guy's fucking mad.'

Back at Camp Russell the images taken from the Sarkhume raid are dropped into Sapper Christina's office. It is her job to log them and match information from the patrol report with the photographs.

She is working at her desk when there is a knock at her door. Christina is inside a secure room, so she gets up and goes over and opens the door. It is Soldier B. He comes in and closes the door behind him.

This isn't right, she thinks. Soldier B is a senior NCO. Christina has heard of Soldier B's reputation as a highly experienced SAS operator and an intimidating figure. Usually only the lowly ranked troopers, maybe the odd corporal, deal with Christina. What is going on? Why is he here?

Soldier B tells her he wants to go through the images taken at Sarkhume. Christina goes back to her desk, sits down and opens the file. Soldier B follows and stands behind her. Then he leans in and puts his hand on Christina's shoulder. She freezes. His grip is firm, but not tight. But Christina feels pinned down. She can hear him breathing in her ear. Soldier B is a big man, twice the size of Christina. Her heart is thumping.

Christina starts going through the photos from the mission to Sarkhume. There are about 20 of them.

'As we went through them he was looking at them all. And then he asked me to go through them again,' she says. 'He's like leaning over to look at the computer screen. He's pushing me down. He's leaning over the top of me.'

He tells her to stop on an image.

'Delete that one,' he says.

It is an image of a weapon that has been photographed in two locations.

'I know it was the same weapon because it had blue tape around the pistol grip,' she says.

Christina deletes it and they continue to scroll through the images. His hand remains vice-like on her shoulder. Her heart is still thumping.

'Delete that one too,' he says.

Christina looks at the photo. It shows a Special Forces engineer attached to the SAS patrol carrying an older Afghan man over his shoulder.

They are moving a dead body. That's why he wants me to delete it, she thinks.

The Afghan is slung over both of the engineer's shoulders, his head over the Australian's right shoulder, his legs over the left. The Afghan is being carried like a large slab of beef.

Christina doesn't know it, but the photo is of Haji Sardar. He is not dead. He is alive and is being taken to the mosque where his body will later be found. This picture is proof that Soldier B and the engineer moved the Afghan, and that they were the last people to see him alive. It is proof of an unlawful killing. Christina has no idea about any of that. She only feels that hand on her shoulder holding her down.

But there is something about the image of the engineer carrying the Afghan that gives Christina the creeps.

'He was smiling. The Australian soldier was smiling,' she says. 'The fact he was smiling in that image was really disturbing.' As well as the smile, Christina notices the engineer's rosy cheeks.

She deletes the photo. Only now does Soldier B's iron grip on her shoulder relax. He has gotten rid of the evidence that Haji Sardar was carried into the mosque. And it seems he has also deleted evidence that the same weapon was planted and photographed in two different spots.

Soldier B walks out. Christina feels like she is going to throw up.

'I didn't feel like I had the ability to say no. I couldn't tell him, "No, I'm not going to delete that". I didn't know what would happen to me if I did. So I just followed his direction,' she says.

A while later Dusty Miller comes into her office and asks her for the images from the Sarkhume raid.

'Don't worry, they've been deleted,' she tells the medic. She thinks that is what Dusty wants. That he has the same intentions as Soldier B, to cover up some bad things that happened on the job. It will be eight years before she finally understands what Dusty really wanted.

'I subsequently believe that he was trying to get evidence so that he could report the incident. Evidence which I deleted,' says Christina. 'He looked like he was going to burst into tears, and he walked out.'

Dusty doesn't remember going to see Christina. But he will never forget thinking what Soldier B would have done to him if he had reported the killing of Haji Sardar.

'He's that mad that he'd have probably fucking shot me.'

The next day some of the Sarkhume villagers turn up at the gates to the base with Haji Sardar's body.

'They were saying "Why did he get shot?" And they wanted money for it,' says one of the soldiers who was on the Sarkhume patrol. 'And they always want money. Why wouldn't they? You've got fucking nothing. And some guys turn up and fucking cap some bastard for no apparent reason.'

Six weeks after the raid the United Nations Assistance Mission in Afghanistan (UNAMA) passes on a petition from Sarkhume villagers alleging Haji Sardar and Mirza Khan were unlawfully killed. They also allege motorcycles were burnt, villagers beaten, a woman tortured, livestock shot, and property damaged.

A week later a representative of the Afghanistan Independent Human Rights Commission meets with members of the Australian-led Provincial Reconstruction Team and a legal officer from the Combined Team Uruzgan, of which Australia is a member. The AIHRC representative passes on complaints from Sarkhume villagers alleging that Haji Sardar and Mirza Khan were both civilians who were brutally murdered. The AIHRC launches its own investigation. After the safety of its investigators is guaranteed, the AIHRC visits Sarkhume.

The AIHRC finds that both victims were unarmed civilians and that the older man was beaten to death.

'It's a brutal way to kill someone. Sadistic as fuck,' says Dusty. 'I think I'd rather a bullet.'

The AIHRC investigation also finds that Mirza Khan was mauled by an Australian dog and then shot in cold blood without warning.

'How is it not cruel that they came and martyred my son? He had not committed any crime and he was not on any side,' says his mother Miraz Gula. 'My heart is completely broken.'

The AIHRC report says seven other people were wounded in the SAS raid, including a four-year-old boy named Zaibullah who 'was bashed with a knife on his back' by the Australians because he would not leave his father's side. A deaf man, Mohammad Wali, was badly beaten.

'He was a farmer. They detained him,' says Haji Sardar's son Abdul Latif. 'When he would look back and ask, "What did you say?", because he was deaf and couldn't hear properly, the Australians would beat him.'

Abdul Latif says the Australians hauled the deaf man into a storage area and tortured him.

'They would twist his balls and he would become unconscious. He passed out a few times. He has psychological problems now.'

The AIHRC also finds two motorcycles were destroyed by the Australians, and 11 village dogs and a cow shot.

'Our investigation shows, [and] our position remains the same, that civilians were harmed in this. The people who were killed were civilians,' says AIHRC chairwoman Shaharzad Akbar. 'The seven people who were injured were civilians. That's what our investigation indicates.'

Two months after the lethal raid a 'shura' or consultation is held between Sarkhume elders and the Australians, headed by Special Operations Task Group commanding officer and SAS veteran Jon Hawkins.

The shura is brokered by the Afghan warlord Matiullah Khan, who is a key Australian ally.

'If it wasn't for Matiullah Khan, the Australians wouldn't sit with us. He told [the Australians], "These guys are my friends",' says Shaista Khan.

Haji Sardar's older son Abdul Latif is at the shura.

'The leader of the Australians was a blond, huge man. He said that mortars are being directed at us from [the direction of Sarkhume],' says Abdul Latif. 'The Australians asked us for forgiveness. We told them that the person who passed on the reports [about the village and the insurgents being there], hand over that person to us.'

'They said, "We were mistaken. We were being misled and we were being given false information",' says Shaista Khan. 'We said we would forgive you but that person who passed on that information, we want that person handed over to us.'

The villagers refuse an Australian offer of cash compensation.

Four months after the Sarkhume killings the Australian Defence Force launches an investigation. It is called an Inquiry Officer Inquiry and is led by three investigators of officer rank. By the time they fly into Afghanistan to begin their work, 3 Squadron SAS has finished its deployment and left for home. The men of the Third Herd have been replaced by another task group of SAS and Commandos.

In Tarin Kowt, the investigators ask to travel to Sarkhume to see where the raid took place. But this is denied.

'The team was advised that, due to a continued high level of threat in the area from insurgents that no Australian Defence Force personnel were to be granted access to the site,' says the inquiry report.

Neither can they interview the Wakunish who were on the raid. They have been 'rotated away' from Tarin Kowt and are 'unable to be released from their duties to attend interviews'.

The inquiry officers are permitted to hold a shura with Sarkhume tribal elders in Tarin Kowt.

'They were polite. But the trouble was, they weren't there at the time the things happened [on the raid],' says one of the Australian Defence Force inquiry officers who was part of the Sarkhume investigation.

He has contacted me via my encrypted Proton email and agrees to speak to me on the condition of anonymity.

'They told a story which was pretty much identical to what we got from [the AIHRC investigator]. It wasn't completely consistent with what [was in] the complaint. And this is possibly why we didn't take them as seriously as we should have,' he says.

In other words, the Afghan version of events is largely dismissed. But the inquiry team are not the only ones who don't take the Sarkhume villagers as seriously as they should have.

The Special Operations commander in Uruzgan, Jon Hawkins, complains that the Australians 'copped some wild allegations' from 'hard tough farmers who were probably Taliban'. He also says the Australian investigators appear to have little understanding of the 'absolute chaos' of combat.

'People who have not been in combat have no idea,' Hawkins tells veteran journalist and author Chris Masters in Masters' book *No Front Line*. 'It is just absolute chaos yet [the Australian Defence Force Investigative Service] treat war as if it is a clinical event. It is not a clinical event. It is a complete and utter mess.'

After Tarin Kowt, the inquiry officers travel to Perth to catch up with 3 Squadron SAS members involved in the Sarkhume raid. But before they even begin interviews, a dangerous mindset appears to have set in.

'On the matrix given to us, and I suppose thinking with the presumption of innocence, we think, "Oh, Australian soldiers wouldn't do that, would they?",' says the Sarkhume inquiry officer who spoke to me.

Our SAS are the best of the best. They are trained to know when not to pull the trigger. How could they kill two men in cold blood? That is the mindset.

On the list of interviewees for the Sarkhume inquiry team is Dusty Miller. Ominously, he is told this by Soldier B who is also back home in Perth.

'You've got to come into the squadron,' Soldier B tells Dusty over the phone. 'There are some guys here from an investigation team.'

'Sure,' says Dusty. He doesn't know what it is about, and he doesn't ask. But Soldier B does have a question for the medic.

'We're good aren't we, Dusty? We're right?'

This is bad, he never calls me Dusty. I am always Kilo, my call sign. The medic knows what Soldier B is asking of him. He is asking him to keep his mouth shut, about whatever it is these investigators are delving into. Say nothing, don't tell them anything.

'Yes, mate. We're good,' says Dusty.

On the day of his interview Dusty walks into a conference room in 3 Squadron SAS headquarters in Perth. Before him are two of the inquiry officers, both lieutenant-colonels, who tell him they want to talk to him about what happened at Sarkhume.

'They showed me a lot of pictures of some dead people. You know, "Does this person look familiar? Blah, blah". And then they showed me some dressings and from memory they were definitely our dressings,' Dusty says.

One of the dressings is on the back of a child's head. The child is four-year-old Zaibullah and the photo they show Dusty is from the AIHRC report. The Sarkhume villagers claim the boy was struck by an Australian knife. Is the dressing one of ours, the investigators want to know.

Dusty bends the truth. No, it's not one of ours he tells them.

'I remember I was just playing the party line,' he says. 'Because I was in that position that telling the truth maybe was not probably best for me at the time.'

As for Haji Sardar, Dusty cannot remember either of the two investigators asking him a single question about the patient who was snatched from him and allegedly stomped and beaten to death.

'I don't think that came up. It doesn't stick out in my memory. It's in my mind that that incident was still very fresh, and it bothered me. And that's an understatement. But I don't honestly recall them asking me about that.'

Neither do they ask him anything about Soldier B.

'That's very strange, isn't it?' Dusty tells me years later. 'They were not looking that fucking hard. They were just stepping through hoops.'

And there is no photo of Haji Sardar's body to show to Dusty either. It has already been deleted by Christina months ago back in Afghanistan, on the orders of Soldier B.

Dusty remembers the interview going for about an hour. He has done what Soldier B has asked him to do. He has kept his mouth shut. On that front the inquiry officers have helped, because they have failed to ask him the most pertinent questions about what happened that day in Sarkhume. They have let Dusty Miller wriggle off the hook.

'Honestly, I was crapping my pants at the time,' says Dusty. 'I was non-committal to most of the questions ... I just played vague. So I sort of wasn't blatantly lying.'

Dusty knows what will happen if he volunteers the whole truth.

'You've got to understand that the context is I'm still in the job. I still want to be in the job ... I saw some pretty atrocious shit. I dealt with some terrible injuries. I dealt with death. I was pretty fucked up when I came back. I wasn't sleeping then either. Yeah, it was a pretty tough time.'

As well as Dusty, the inquiry team interviews a couple of the operators on the Sarkhume raid, including Soldier B.

'They're confident people. They're not sort of suddenly sweating and looking away and lighting up cigarettes like the bad guys do in B-grade cop movies,' says the inquiry officer who spoke to me.

'The more senior they were, the more confident they were. The more junior, like troopers, not so confident. But in retrospect, oh gosh, they all got their stories straight.'

The inquiry is an administrative examination and does not have the power to take evidence from a witness under oath. It has no powers to investigate criminal matters or allegations. It is toothless, and all about box-ticking.

Predictably, in its final report, the Inquiry Officer Inquiry finds that the Sarkhume raid was a legal operation. It asserts that both Haji Sardar and Mirza Khan were armed combatants and that both were justifiably killed.

But the investigation is a farce. A photograph in the report purporting to be of Haji Sardar is that of Mirza Khan, the much younger man who was also killed that day. They cannot even get the basics right. There is no photo of the second victim in the report.

'We may not have asked the right questions about, "Well, why don't you have the photograph [of the other victim]?" says the inquiry officer when he speaks to me eight years later.

The investigators find that Haji Sardar was mortally wounded after being seen with an AK-47 and after 'adopting a firing position'. The investigation finds no one was mauled by dogs and that there was no property damage. It finds that no child was beaten with a knife, nor does it find that the deaf man, Mohammad Wali, had his balls squeezed till he passed out.

The military does admit to the inquiry that they burned two motorcycles belonging to men the SAS thought were insurgents. It later pays compensation.

Allegation after allegation against the SAS soldiers on the raid is ruled by the inquiry officer report to be unfounded.

The inquiry team reports that 'no witness refused to answer a question, nor, as far as we can tell, answered one falsely'. The inquiry officers believe the SAS members, who have now had four months to get their stories straight. Despite all this, the investigators don't believe their evidence is lacking or their findings compromised.

Soldier B is exonerated by the inquiry. It finds the entire Sarkhume mission was lawful and justified. There are no adverse findings against anyone in 3 Squadron. They have gotten away with it.

'Most internal military inquiries are an absolute fucking joke. They're a farce . . . they're a box-ticking process to save their arse. That's all they are,' says 3 Squadron operator Tom.

Braden Chapman was on the Sarkhume raid. He saw Haji Sardar taken away and watched Soldier B return from the mosque and heard him utter those words to Dusty: 'He didn't make it.' But Braden is not interviewed by the inquiry. For years he will keep quiet about Sarkhume. That is what he is expected to do.

'When you're back at the unit people would make jokes about the size of the rug that they've swept everything under and that one day it'll all come out,' says Braden.

The inquiry officers have been intimidated by Special Forces mythology.

'The truth that underpins the reputation of the SAS is written from the patrol reports, by the patrols,' says one former senior Special Forces officer. 'Only good ever came out, not the truth.'

Truth is the first casualty of war, or so the old saying goes. No one really knows who said it first. The US Senator Hiram Johnson, the British Labour politician Philip Snowden, and even Aeschylus, the playwright who lived in ancient Greece almost 2500 years ago, have all been credited as the author of that proverb. There is another, lesser-known maxim: Journalism's first obligation is to the truth.

In August 2019 I am asked by Jo Puccini, my Investigations Editor at the ABC, to start digging into the allegations of Australian Special Forces war crimes in Afghanistan. She wants me to get as close to the truth as I can.

I am late to the party. Journalists from Fairfax and the ABC have already broken a series of astonishing stories that confirm that atrocities were committed. But I have some new leads. A colleague has obtained a cache of investigation reports written by the Afghanistan Independent Human Rights Commission. They are in Pashto and Dari, so my first task is getting them translated. A couple of weeks later the English translations arrive and I begin sifting through them. Sarkhume is by far the most promising lead.

With the help of a couple of brave Afghan journalists I track down the families of the dead men from Sarkhume for the first time. They contradict almost everything in the inquiry officer report.

I also lodge a Freedom of Information request with Defence for the inquiry officer notes and other documents for Sarkhume.

My FOI request is rejected because the release of these documents 'could cause damage to the security, defence or international relations of the Commonwealth', and because the material comprises information on 'the tactics, techniques and procedures' used by Defence during 'warlike' operations.

My request is also refused because it could 'jeopardise' an ongoing inquiry into allegations of Special Forces war crimes in Afghanistan by the Inspector-General of the Australian Defence Force. The IGADF investigation, which has been going for more than three years by this point, was sparked by rumours of atrocities and cover ups by the SAS and the Commandos.

It all smells like cover up and bullshit to me. And to Dusty Miller.

'It worries me that justice isn't going to be served,' he says.

For Christina, the mere mention of Sarkhume upsets her, even many years later. There is Soldier B's vice-like grip, holding her down in her chair. There is Soldier B in her ear, telling her to delete the two photos. Then there is the image of the smiling engineer carrying Haji Sardar.

'I fucking have nightmares about that shit,' says Christina. 'He was smiling like that. That's fucking sickening.'

Dusty Miller is also haunted by what happened at Sarkhume.

'All those things that I did went completely against what I believed in,' he says. 'Before that trip I would've said I would have never, ever done some of those things or fucking lied or covered for someone. So of course, that bothers me every single fucking day.'

But Dusty's distress, his psychological torment, will spur an old comrade into action. It will lead to more crimes being revealed, more cover ups exposed.

'Seeing Dusty broken kind of crushed me,' says Braden Chapman.

In October 2019, seven and a half years after he was part of the Sarkhume raid, Braden reads my online story about the families of Haji Sardar and Mirza Khan. He thinks of Dusty. He thinks it is time the real story, from within the SAS and the patrols, is told.

'So I was, "Fuck it, I want to support him". And then I came across your article and saw that Proton.'

This was my encrypted email address attached to my online story. Braden clicks on the email link and begins writing.

Maybe, for once, they won't get away with it.

7
KILLING FIELD

'It's one thing to say don't commit atrocities on the battlefield.
It's another thing to say don't get caught doing atrocities'
Disgraced former US Marine Corps
Lieutenant-Colonel Oliver North

Every journalist yearns for a Deep Throat. A source inside the room when momentous decisions are made. A witness to a terrible crime. An insider to an elaborate conspiracy. An exposer of insidious corruption.

Deep Throat was the name given to the secret informant who helped the *Washington Post* journalist Bob Woodward and his colleague Carl Bernstein expose the involvement of the Nixon Administration in the Watergate scandal. Woodward and Deep Throat, later revealed to be FBI associate director Mark Felt, would signal each other by moving a flowerpot or by making coded markings in a copy of *The New York Times*. Sometimes they would meet in an underground garage at 2 am. These liaisons and the information Deep Throat imparted would lead to the downfall of the President of the United States.

Often sources or whistleblowers will contact journalists by sending them an anonymous tip. As many of my colleagues will attest, most of these tip offs turn out to be false leads or total rubbish, a complete waste of time. Personal grievances, conspiracy theories, elaborate fabrications, petty political point-scoring, the incoherent ramblings of someone with too much time on their hands. If you call yourself an 'investigative journalist' you will see your fair share of all of that.

One time I received an email tip off that promised to be the scoop of the century: 'ASIO have suits that enable them to remain invisible to the human eye in normal lighting (you could not see them 20 cm from your face) and allow them (operatives) to pass through walls, this tech was first documented by the Palestinians, when Israel invaded in 2002.'

The email that landed in my inbox on the morning of 29 October 2019 would prove to be a much more credible and verifiable tip off. What it contained was dynamite, and it would lead to us broadcasting, for the first time, visual proof of an Australian war crime in Afghanistan. It would also lead to a federal police murder investigation.

The email came from someone calling themselves 'Usernameanon'.

'Just some info on SAS war crimes I witnessed. And other info you might find useful ...'

Usernameanon, it would turn out, had a gift for understatement. The anonymous correspondent said they had deployed to Afghanistan with the SAS in 2012. Usernameanon wrote of witnessing unprovoked violence by Soldier B.

'He loved hurting people and the only time I seen him happy was the day or 2 after he had killed someone.'

The email ran for almost two pages and contained incredible and shocking detail. Usernameanon chronicled a series of alleged unlawful killings by 3 Squadron SAS in Afghanistan in 2012.

He wrote how he was with Dusty Miller when Soldier B grabbed the wounded Afghan and took him away, only to emerge later and say, 'The guy didn't make it'. This was Sarkhume and the killing of Haji Sardar.

He detailed how Soldier A ordered an Afghan soldier to execute a captured man who was on his knees. He told how he witnessed Soldier A shoot an Afghan man who had his hands in the air, how he 'shot him twice in the chest and once in the head after he hit the ground'.

Except the author did not use 'Soldier A' or 'Soldier B'. He spelled out their names.

'I hope this helps Dusty and whoever is out there seeking justice for the people of Afghanistan who were the real victims of the disgusting war.'

That was the author's sign off. There wasn't a name. But I had his email address.

I wrote back asking for any more detail he could give me. Usernameanon responded by sending me some photos of Soldier A and Soldier B in the field. He had definitely served with these men.

We continued to correspond. He told me about other incidents. Soldier B striking a child. An Australian dog being sooled onto an Afghan civilian for no reason. How he had also been attached to US special forces at Bagram Air Base in 2013 and involved in tracking targets to be killed. How he had watched people on a screen being torn apart from the air.

Then the emails stopped.

As a journalist, keeping a source on the hook is a delicate and nerve-racking business. The idea is to tease out as much information as you can and, in this case, to eventually try to coax the source to go on the record. But if you badger or bombard them, they can become frustrated or uncomfortable and slip away into the untraceable labyrinth of the cyberworld.

Weeks went by. I was fretting that I had let my Deep Throat slip away.

But then an email popped into my inbox. It was from another address. It was Usernameanon, except he had changed his name.

'Forgot my password for the other account and had to create a new one. Sorry. Have you been trying to get in touch?'

A sense of relief flooded through me. It was now heading towards the Christmas holidays. It was time to step out of the cyber shadows. I asked him if he would be prepared to meet. He agreed.

A week later I sat waiting in a hotel lobby interstate, exactly as we had arranged via encrypted email. I still did not know his name, or what he looked like. The meeting time came and went. More minutes ticked by. I caught the eye of everyone who came into the lobby who I thought could possibly be a former SAS soldier. No, not him. Too old. Or him.

Then a solidly built guy in jeans with a beard and black hair curling out from under his baseball cap walked in. He saw me and came over.

'G'day.'

'I'm Mark,' I said. 'Thanks for coming to meet me.'

He didn't offer his name and I didn't ask. I knew he would tell me when he was ready. We went up to the room I had booked and sat and talked for several hours.

The guy in the baseball cap was quietly spoken, expressed himself in considered sentences, and often there would be long and slightly awkward silences as he pondered his answers to my rapid-fire questions. He wanted to be precise. If he didn't know something, he told me so. I could tell that he was burdened, almost crushed by what he had witnessed while with 3 Squadron in Afghanistan.

He provided more detail on the killings he had seen. I scribbled frenetically as he spoke. At the end of our chat he handed me an SD card.

'You can copy that if you want. It's a load of photos and videos from over there. All sorts of stuff.'

I couldn't believe it. I started copying the files. There were hundreds of photos and dozens of individual videos. I clicked on a few of the videos and he identified the SAS operators in the footage and explained what was happening on the patrols that we were watching. But there was no way we would have time to go through it all. He agreed that I could email him with questions about anything in the files.

I held out my hand and he shook it.

'I'm Braden by the way,' he said.

As I flew home – an encrypted hard drive with the images and video always within reach – I wondered if I would ever see Braden again.

———

'Directly to the front! Two guys moving right to left behind the wall!'

The camera, mounted on the SAS soldier's assault rifle, is like a scope. You can see what the operator is aiming at as the rifle recoils with gunfire, the spent shells spitting out the side of the weapon. This is war unvarnished and unedited. It is literally from the viewpoint of the SAS soldier. It is the heat of battle, you can almost smell the gunpowder. You can hear the tautness in the soldier's voice as he directs fire. It is kill or be killed.

I spend days and days going frame by frame through the videos. There are MTV-style highlights reels of battles and blasts set to heavy metal music which the SAS soldiers have edited together themselves. In one, an explosive charge shatters a door and sends lethal shards of timber cartwheeling towards the SAS soldiers who set it off.

'Fucking hell! Think I was a bit in the open there,' says one operator as he is enveloped in a cloud of dust and debris.

Another scene shows an SAS operator approaching a young Afghan man who has his hands up. The little red dot from the operator's gun sight dances over the man's torso and across his face. The Australian grabs him by the scruff of the neck and slams him face first into a mud wall.

The highlights package ends with a 'Third Herd' bull symbol and the names of all the 3 Squadron operators and support staff on the tour flash up on the screen. It reminds me of the end of a movie when they roll the actors' credits. All of these names will be very helpful for my investigations.

There is vision of the patrols shooting dogs.

'Shot the cunt right in the snout and he ran off,' says one operator as they creep through a compound.

'Kick the shit out of that cunt,' says another operator. He is not talking about a dog. He is talking about an Afghan man being hauled out of a room.

'Are they the two little butt monkeys?' asks one operator on another raid as he points to two Afghan youths. '[They're] all butt monkeys,' replies his mate.

There are walls of compounds being blown up, houses being burned, SAS soldiers posing with the Confederate flag, a patrol blowing up public buildings, some operators threatening to bash Afghan civilians, and soldiers cuffing and blindfolding prisoners.

'Chuck bags over their heads, mate,' remarks one.

There are missile strikes on compounds. In one, a hapless cow almost cops it. The beast bolts away.

'Very fucking Mogadishu,' says one SAS operator as they stroll out of a village from where knots of thick black smoke are rising. They have just poured petrol over the satellite communications equipment from the village's Public Communications Office and lit it up.

In another video an operator starts up an Afghan's motorcycle and rolls it off a cliff. They all laugh.

'And back to you for stunts,' says the soldier filming. It is like he is throwing back to a commentary box.

There is the battle of the mud bunker when Rahul, the Afghan Wakunish soldier, is killed. The camera swings past Rahul and if you slow the vision down you can see a few frames of his face. He has taken a bullet through the eye and his brains are seeping out of the back of his head. Dusty is cradling him.

Other times the soldiers are just sitting around. Patrolling can be dull, repetitive like *Groundhog Day*. But I know from my days reporting in war zones in the Middle East that it is when it is quiet that the soldiers talk. It is when the truth comes out. When secrets are revealed, or disquiet voiced. When they blow off steam.

'Should've just killed everyone in the village, then nobody could use it. Just go the scorched earth theory,' says one SAS operator as he and his comrades sit on the ground one day waiting for choppers to pick them up. It is the bluster of a young man trying to impress his more battle-weary comrades.

'Fucking bitches going off,' complains an operator in another video. They have just walked from a village they have cleared. One of the older women there had chastised the Australians for hauling her and the other women out of their homes and for scaring a cow that then ran away.

'Bitches,' says another soldier, mindlessly.

'That's why we need to bring back raping,' says the operator.

'Raping,' nods the soldier. You can tell he is thinking, 'Whatever'.

———

It is Friday evening, 6 pm. I am in the office. I am down to the last hour of footage. I have spent more than a week trawling through it, frame by frame. Patrol after patrol.

There is some powerful stuff in these videos. But nothing that shows war crimes. There is talk. In one, an operator talks about a kid being killed, about 'cunts' being shot. It suggests something very bad has happened. But the footage doesn't show anyone being shot or killed. Except for the mud bunker battle in which Rahul and the Taliban fighters were killed. Soldier A clearly had his blood up, but it does not appear he has breached the laws of war. The Taliban had fired first.

I click on a video labelled 'FILE0185'. It is 13 minutes and 12 seconds long.

It begins, like many others, with an SAS patrol in a Black Hawk chopper. They are on another mission.

I can see the two American pilots up front, and gunners hanging out each side of the Black Hawk.

The SAS patrol member wearing the helmet camera is someone I don't know. He is not one of the regulars who has filmed the vision I have watched in the other files. This guy is one of the dog handlers.

I know this because he looks down and sitting at his feet in the chopper is his combat dog.

They are flying over what the SAS soldiers call 'the green'. Out the window on the left in the distance I can see another Black Hawk zipping along.

Sitting next to the dog handler is the patrol commander. It is the patrol commander who is notorious for his drinking and for wielding his knife back on base. The door gunner on the right raises two fingers. Two minutes until they hit the ground. The dog handler holds up two fingers to acknowledge the warning.

The chopper is low now. They are close to the target. Up front, the pilot raises one finger. Everyone acknowledges. The patrol commander slips off his headset and slides open the Black Hawk door. They are skimming over the tops of trees. The door gunners now have two hands on their weapons, and they lean out of the side of the chopper. They are ready to shoot back if they take ground fire.

The chopper banks to the left, straightens and drops sharply, landing in a field full of green wheat. It is 3 minutes and 21 seconds into the video. I check the metadata. It dates the footage as late May. It makes sense. The wheat is just weeks from the summer harvest.

The SAS patrol is out of the chopper in a flash, fanning out and dashing through the wheat towards a tree line.

The dog handler is out in the lead, just behind the patrol scout who is wearing a bandana. The patrol scout is Soldier C, one of the operators who has helped get Tom kicked out of this patrol.

Earlier in the deployment, he and Tom had clashed up at the SAS shooting range after Soldier C fired at the feet of some young Afghan kids who were scavenging for bullet casings.

'Those rounds could have quite easily ricocheted and hit one of the children. And he's swearing at them, "Fuck off!" And I turned to him and said, "What the fuck are you doing?"' Tom tells me. 'He was allowed to run riot.'

Braden Chapman saw Soldier C strike Afghans while on operations: 'If they were not doing exactly what he wanted he might be a bit heavy-handed, just punch them or something like that.'

During the deployment he has his head shaved into a mohawk. I see a photo of him wearing a skull mask while getting ready to go out on an SAS training exercise back in Australia. Dusty sees him carrying a machete on operations in Afghanistan.

Others say he is a good soldier. He has won a Commendation for Gallantry on a previous tour.

'He's a nice guy. All killers are nice guys,' says another 3 Squadron operator.

Led by Soldier C, the SAS patrol skirts around a compound, running between its mud wall and an irrigation channel which is lined with trees. They can conceal themselves here. But so, too, could Taliban fighters. Overhead the choppers are circling, ready to provide covering fire.

As they approach the end of the mud wall Soldier C slows to a jog, as does everyone behind him. They are still in the tree line, but it has thinned out and doesn't provide as much cover. Suddenly Soldier C stops and crouches.

'Hey, man's over there!'

He is looking out to their right. Then he is off again. The dog handler heads right, across a narrow plank bridge running over an irrigation channel, and he emerges into fields of young wheat.

'Quake, heel.'

I now know the dog's name. That should help me find the handler's name. The handler lets him off the leash. A Black Hawk flies over the fields in the distance as Quake trots along in front. At one point the dog turns to cross the irrigation channel.

'Quake, come,' says the dog handler calling him back.

It is at this moment the dog handler sees the man the patrol scout spotted. The Afghan must be about 100 metres away. He is standing, frozen amongst the wheat. Quake takes off.

'*Laasoona porta ka!*' screams the dog handler as he stops and raises his weapon at the man.

It means 'hands up'. It is a warning in Pashto contained in the Australian military's 'Rules of Engagement' card. It tells soldiers that before opening fire they 'are required, if time permits, to give a warning in a loud clear voice'.

But the Afghan does not raise his hands. He can see Quake tearing towards him. The man drops down into the wheat.

'Quake, down!'

It is no use. The dog is not going to stop, it has a target, and it is trained to attack. Soldier C is up ahead walking towards the Afghan in the wheat as two Black Hawks move slowly overhead. The SAS is watching this unfold from the sky.

The dog handler has now caught up to Soldier C at the corner of the wheat field. Amongst the green wheat a young Afghan man is kneeling on the ground trying to fight off Quake. The dog has latched onto him and it isn't letting go.

The Afghan is terrified, and he whimpers as he attempts to get free of the dog.

'Quake, leave! Quake! Heel!'

As the dog handler calls off Quake, Soldier C casually walks around the Afghan. He doesn't even bother to point his rifle at the young man, who is now on his back with his legs drawn up towards his torso. It is only when he stops within a couple of metres of the prone man that Soldier C levels his weapon at him.

The young man is quiet, and he is contained. There is something red in his right hand. I stop the footage, rewind and look at it again frame by frame. They are red prayer beads. The man is dressed in a collarless white overshirt and loose-fitting white pants that look like they end just below the knee. He wears a brown traditional vest and old worn shoes. The Afghan is looking up into the barrel of Soldier C's assault rifle. The big Australian towers over him and the young man is petrified.

The dog handler swings his head to the right. Another SAS patrol member is walking along the path towards them. As he takes up position under a tree about 40 metres away, two gunshots are heard off in the distance.

'Down! Down!'

Quake is itching to tear into the young man again. I can hear the dog handler's heavy breathing in the footage. He is either puffed from all the running, or his adrenalin is pumping. Possibly both.

Soldier C has the man covered. The situation is under control. Soldier C is even looking around to assess if there are any other threats. But everything is calm. The Afghan is motionless on the ground amongst the wheat, clutching his red prayer beads. He is not moving a muscle.

Like in the other videos I expect to see the Afghan plasticuffed and blindfolded and detained. But something else happens.

'Do you want me to drop this cunt?'

Soldier C has turned to his left and is talking to the dog handler who is about 20 metres behind him. Soldier C is looking down the barrel of the dog handler's helmet camera. I can't see his eyes because he is wearing sunglasses.

It takes me a second to realise what he is asking. He is asking the dog handler if he wants him to kill the man on the ground. What do you say to that?

The Afghan is not moving. He remains as still as can be, his legs drawn up. He can't understand this strange language and does not know that his very life hangs on the answer to Soldier C's question.

'I don't know, mate. Hit ***** up.'

The dog handler does not want to make the call. He is telling Soldier C to ask the patrol commander.

Soldier C swivels around the other way, again taking his eyes off the Afghan. It is clear that he does not regard the young man as a threat whatsoever. If he did the young man would be already dead.

'*****, you want me to drop this cunt?'

He is talking to the SAS patrol commander who is squatting on his haunches under a tree about 40 metres away. There doesn't appear to be any response. Soldier C asks a third time.

'You want me to drop this cunt?'

I am transfixed. Surely, he is not going to shoot this guy.

The squatting figure under the tree looks like he raises his hand to his throat or chin. Is it a signal? Or maybe he is signalling to someone else out of shot for an answer. (Months later I will get the audio of the footage professionally isolated and amplified, and it sounds very much like the patrol commander's response to the question about whether Soldier C should drop the Afghan is 'yes'.)

Within a couple of seconds, the first shot has left the patrol scout's rifle.

The Afghan on the ground shudders, his legs spread apart.

The dog handler's head swings right to the figure under the tree, who is watching the killing. Then Quake is off towards the young man. Like the other combat dog who Braden Chapman saw chewing on the head of the dead Afghan, it seems Quake wants a taste.

'Quake, no!'

The patrol scout squeezes the trigger again. Then a third time. By now Quake is back in frame and has latched onto the Afghan.

'Quake, stop! Leave!'

The Afghan's body shakes. It is the dog pulling at him. As it does, blood from the top of the man's head sprays over the wheat in an arc. A second pump of blood paints the wheat, powered by the last couple of beats of the Afghan's heart.

'Quake, leave!'

Finally, the dog obeys and lets go of the dead man. Soldier C then slowly walks off through the wheat.

I go back and check the times. Thirty seconds has elapsed from the instant Soldier C first points his rifle at the Afghan to the moment he kills him. The last 30 seconds of this man's life. Half a minute spent in frozen terror. In that entire time the young man has not moved. He is under control and is not a threat.

'No! Heel!'

Quake has returned to the dog handler, who is admonishing the dog like you would a naughty child. He leans down and strokes the dog's neck.

I cannot believe what I have just seen. I look around to see if any of my colleagues in the office have witnessed the killing. There are only a couple of people about on this Friday evening.

I close the lid of my laptop. I need to ring my editor. We have footage of a possible war crime by the Australian Special Forces in Afghanistan.

———

We have a killing. But we don't have all of the ingredients of a killing. We don't have the name of the victim. We don't have a location, or a date or a time.

We do have a lead, and that is the metadata from the dog handler's helmet camera. It gives 26/05/2012 9.56 pm as the date and the time the footage began rolling.

But that can't be right, because this is a daytime operation. The date could be right, as 3 Squadron SAS was in Afghanistan then. May was when things were heating up. They were out almost every day. That is when the wheat was tall and green.

I know the identity of the patrol commander. I can easily find out who was in his patrol. As for the dog handler, there were only a few on that SAS deployment.

It is time for me to go and see some contacts, men who might know more about this.

One Saturday morning I am at home. I am playing the video of the killing, over and over. I must have watched it more than 100 times by now. There is something in it that I find familiar. But I can't put my finger on it. I keep focused on the victim, going through the footage frame by frame like some obsessive homicide detective.

Then it strikes. It is not the victim I recognise – it is the wheat. Green wheat, spread flat, some of it painted with blood.

I run into our spare room and start rummaging through a pile of manila folders and paper. It is in here somewhere, that report into Sarkhume. The thing is, the report didn't just look at Sarkhume. It also investigated two other killings.

I find the report and start flicking through it. Sarkhume is the first investigation and it takes up most of the report.

Then I see it. It is a photograph of a man in white lying among flattened green wheat, a red arc of blood surrounding his head like a ghastly halo. His blood is over the wheat. What looks like a dark vest is spread out next to him and he is wearing pants that do not cover his lower legs. There are blotches of fresh red blood on his chest and smaller spots on the leg of his pants. Items purportedly found in his pockets are spread out on his vest. What looks like a handkerchief and a tobacco tin. There is also a mobile phone and a two-way radio known as an ICOM.

The report says the ICOM was found with the body and the mobile discovered back along the route the man took. It says the mobile was found to be 'associated' with the main target of the operation, an insurgent commander and bombmaker code-named Objective Young Akira. His real name is Mawlawi Payendi.

I turn the page. There is a gruesome close up of the victim's head showing bullet entry wounds in his neck and face. It also shows the exit wounds. The top of the Afghan's head has been blown out, exposing pieces of brain. These photos were taken by the SAS soldiers on the patrol. The blood is still fresh and is pooling in the Afghan's mouth. It is not a pleasant sight, but I force myself to look at every square millimetre of the photo. Then I see them in the bottom left corner next to the Afghan's shoulder. Red prayer beads.

The report also identifies the shooter. It is Soldier C. Within days I confirm that Soldier C is still serving in the Special Forces.

The dead man's name is Dad Mohammad. The report says he was killed during an operation on 28 May 2012 near the village of Deh Jawz-e Hasanzai. This is two days later than the date on the metadata. But I know the date in the metadata is out because it puts the daylight operation at almost 10 o'clock at night.

The Defence report says that a few days after the killing tribal elders from the village met with Australian military representatives to complain that a disabled man, about 25 or 26 years old, had been shot, stabbed and killed. The elders said the victim, Dad Mohammad, had one leg which was shorter than the other. His younger brother, Jamshid, will later tell my fixer that Dad Mohammad's disability affected many aspects of his life, including his ability to walk.

'From the time of his childhood, when he was seven years old, he was crippled because of his leg. There was some mass in his soft muscles,' says Jamshid.

Surgery did later alleviate some of his problems with his leg.

The 28 May raid involved 36 SAS and 30 Afghan troops. The report says there was intelligence suggesting Objective Young Akira was going to be holding a shura with other insurgents in Deh Jawz-e Hasanzai. The mission was signed off by the Commanding Officer of the Special Operations Task Group, Lieutenant-Colonel Jon Hawkins.

At 4.02 pm the first Black Hawk helicopter hit the ground. This is the chopper in the helmet camera video which lands in the wheat field. According to the report, Dad Mohammad is killed just minutes later.

The report states that the SAS spotted multiple Afghans running away from the target area. It claims that one of them was Dad Mohammad. It says that the Australians in the choppers dropped smoke and flares in Dad Mohammad's path in an attempt to stop him fleeing. They suspect he is a 'spotter', or someone who reports on the movement of Australian forces to the Taliban.

Suddenly Dad Mohammad starts to move towards an irrigation channel in what the report says is an attempt to evade the SAS
cordon. It states he was called on to stop several times by soldiers on
the ground, but these calls are ignored. He is 'tactically manoeuvring'.
This is yet another ROE 'violation' that will seal Dad Mohammad's
fate, according to the report's authors. Crucially, the report also says
he is seen by Soldier C carrying an ICOM.

The report goes to pains to point out that Soldier C has acted
within the Rules of Engagement. It says that he hasn't just received
formal ROE training, but that he has also done a refresher course. It
is Soldier C's third tour of Afghanistan and he is confident he knows
his ROE.

He tells investigators he considered the Afghan a direct threat, one
that had to be engaged for self-defence. He tells them he shot the
Afghan from 15 to 20 metres away.

All of this is clearly bullshit. None of it squares with the video.
In the footage the Afghan is not 'tactically manoeuvring'. He is not
ignoring calls to stop. He does not appear to have an ICOM in his
hand, just a set of prayer beads. And he is not killed in 'self-defence'
from 15 to 20 metres away. He is quiet, compliant and contained. He
is terrified. He is shot from almost point-blank range.

Like Sarkhume, the report is littered with errors. In one instance
it calls the victim 'Dad Mahammoud'. It says that there is no chest
wound. But a Defence source will later tell me that Soldier C hit his
mark with each of his three shots. How could he miss at that range?
Dad Mohammad was shot in the chest.

As for Soldier C, he is not interviewed by the inquiry officers for
their investigation. Instead, he provides a written statement 10 months
after the killing. The inquiry officers believe everything he tells them.
Like Sarkhume, they do not travel to Deh Jawz-e Hasanzai.

In conclusion, they find that during their inquiries a 'consistent
and convincing pattern of evidence emerged from which it was clear

that each [witness] ... was telling the truth and had not had the intent to concoct an untrue account of what happened in the lead up to, and on the day of, the relevant operation.'

The report finds that Soldier C is well acquainted with the rules of engagement. Predictably, it rules that Dad Mohammad was lawfully killed.

So, given all the discrepancies, is the killing in the Defence report the same killing I have on video? If it is, there has been one hell of a cover up. It requires precise collusion among not just the patrol on the ground, but possibly the Black Hawk crews hovering overhead who may have seen it. It requires the patrol to plant an ICOM on the body for their report. It requires their superiors to ask no questions. And finally, it requires all of those called before the Defence inquiry officers to lie, and to lie by telling the same story.

We make the decision to dispatch our Afghan fixers to Deh Jawz-e Hasanzai. These are brave and highly experienced journalists who must leave the relative safety of Uruzgan's capital Tarin Kowt and travel to Taliban-controlled territory. They must be discreet. If they are not, they could get themselves and those they talk to in a world of trouble. They could be killed.

They come back with nothing. As we feared, they are detained and questioned by the Taliban, then sent packing. They want to wait a few weeks and try again. They go and come back with interviews with the relatives of a man killed in a foreign forces raid. Nothing matches – the name, the dates, the time of day. They have the wrong killing.

I have purposely withheld key details about the killing of Dad Mohammad from my fixers. All I gave them is a date and a name. I don't want anyone coached or any interviews contaminated.

We send them back. A couple of weeks pass, then they return with two interviews. One is with Abdul Malik, the father of Dad Mohammad.

Abdul Malik tells our fixers he was in Kandahar the day his son was killed. He got a phone call to tell him his son was dead so he immediately returned home.

'The women from my home told me [the story]. The raid was happening, and people were screaming, "The Americans are coming". Everyone was trying to hide. [My son] was also coming towards home when [the soldiers] faced him and finished him,' says Abdul Malik. 'He did not have a rifle, a Kalashnikov or a sickle on him ... they can arrest him. Why did they have to kill him?'

'He was married and had two daughters,' the victim's younger brother Jamshid will later tell my fixer. 'The youngest one was about a month old and the other was three years old at that time.'

When Abdul Malik returned to the village that day Dad Mohammad was ready for burial.

'He was in a shroud. Because of my grief I was sitting over there [away from him]. I asked, "Where is he?" They said, "He is there". I went to see. His face had wounds. I covered his face and told them to take him to the graveyard.'

Abdul Malik went to see the wheat field where his son died.

'The wheat was flattened all around,' he says.

The second interview is with farmer Abdul Khaliq. He was in a nearby field when the Australians swept in. He was returning from taking his sick daughter to the doctor.

'The helicopters landed next to me. The soldiers had their faces painted in green colours. They had dogs as well. There were Hazaras with them as well who said to me, "Come here, you son of a bitch".'

Abdul Khaliq says he was bitten on the head and fingers by an Australian dog. The soldiers then told him he was being detained, so he handed his daughter over to an elder. He was taken to another part of the village. As he and other prisoners were sitting, they heard something in the distance.

'We heard gunshots. We were facing the wall when the shots were fired.'

Abdul Khaliq and four other village men were put on a helicopter and taken away to Bagram Air Base. He spent the next 18 months in prison. The Australians accused him of using a child – his own daughter – as a human shield. He claims that the charge was made up.

'I learned about Dad Mohammad's killing [in prison] from a visitor. They told me, "Dad Mohammad is finished",' says Abdul Khaliq. 'Dad Mohammad was like me, he was a farmer. He didn't have a problem with anyone. He was quiet. No one in the district said or heard anything bad about him. Dad Mohammad wasn't hanging around with the Taliban. He was a good man. His time was up in this world. I was told that his face was swollen and covered in blood. He wasn't recognisable.'

The interviews are dynamite. They confirm everything in the video. I even confirm that Abdul Khaliq was one of the five prisoners taken back to Tarin Kowt that day. Everything matches: the wheat, the clothing, the prayer beads, the blood spatter, that the wounds were inflicted by someone standing above and to the left side of the victim. We are 98 per cent sure. But we need to be certain.

There is still the problem of the date. The Defence investigation found that Dad Mohammad died on 28 May. But the metadata on the helmet camera worn by the dog handler puts the date as 26 May. I know that is wrong from the time stamp – 9.56 pm.

A few days before we are due to go to air, I get a call. It is from an impeccable source inside Defence. I had told the source about what I have, and the problem with the dates. The source tells me the video and the report are the same incident.

We are 100 per cent. We can now get the story to air.

——

'This is a war crime.'

Chris Barrie isn't just any old soldier. He was the Chief of the Australian Defence Force between 1998 and 2002. He has watched the *Four Corners* program 'Killing Field' showing the killing of Dad Mohammad recorded on the helmet camera and is stunned by what he has seen.

'The man was not armed, the man was in a docile situation, and he was shot. If this was to happen on the streets in Australia, [it] would be a simple case of murder.'

The program also broadcasts Braden Chapman's eyewitness accounts of the killings involving Soldier A and Soldier B. Initially reluctant to commit to anything on the record, Braden had agreed to mull over my request for an on-camera interview. I didn't want some silhouetted, anonymous figure in my story. For it to have power and impact, it needed Braden to step out of the shadows, to defy the brotherhood of the SAS and its code of silence, and to show his face and to tell his story to the audience. But that carried a risk. He would be exposing crimes involving the most lethal soldiers in the Australian military.

'I believe that by going public you protect yourself,' I told him. 'You become a public figure, a whistleblower who has exposed the truth. That makes it harder for them to come after you.'

A journalist desperate for the story would say that. But I believed it. A couple of weeks later, after speaking with his wife, Braden got back to me. He would do the interview.

His descriptions of the killings he saw are mesmerising. His measured and coherent delivery give his interview credibility and a raw power.

The *Four Corners* story also shows footage of SAS patrols burning compounds, rolling motorcycles off cliffs and laughing and soldiers talking about 'shooting cunts'.

But it is the footage of Soldier C asking three times to drop the cowering Afghan in the wheat field and then squeezing the trigger that has truly shocked everyone. It has sent shockwaves through the corridors of power in Canberra. It has stunned the public too. The *Four Corners* story on the ABC website is viewed more than 1.2 million times in the first 24 hours. The vision of Soldier C in the wheat field towering over the frightened Dad Mohammad is on loop on all TV channels for days afterwards and the killing is being furiously debated on talkback radio.

The *Four Corners* program has damaged the hard-earned reputation and carefully crafted image of SAS operators as elite and noble warriors, men who use discriminate violence against a defined and menacing enemy. They are supposed to be Australia's most highly trained soldiers who distinguish between civilian and combatant.

The Prime Minister, Scott Morrison, describes the vision in the *Four Corners* program as 'shocking and alarming'.

The Defence Department says the program is 'serious and disturbing'. But there is no mention of whether Soldier C will be stood down. It will turn out that Defence doesn't even know who he is. Yet.

'Killing Field' has sent senior Defence leaders into a tailspin. Phones are ringing in Perth at the SAS base at Campbell Barracks and in Defence headquarters in Russell in Canberra.

Defence had dismissed the upcoming *Four Corners* story, thinking it would be a rehash of existing allegations or yet another report relying on the claims of anonymous figures hiding in silhouette.

'We're not really expecting anything,' said one senior Special Forces officer to a colleague a couple of days earlier. He has just seen the promo for the story. 'It's just going to trawl out the same old stuff.'

This is extraordinarily conceited. I had already sent Defence Media pages of questions about the incidents I would be covering in the program. Dates, locations, the name of the SAS squadron involved.

Ten minutes into 'Killing Field' the senior Special Forces officer gets a phone call. It is from a former high-ranking Defence officer.

'Are you watching this, mate?'

He is not. He is so confident the *Four Corners* program will turn up nothing new that he is watching a reality show on commercial TV.

'What the fuck are you doing? Turn the channel over to the ABC now,' says the former officer.

By the end of 'Killing Field' the senior Special Forces officer is stunned. He has gone from conceited dismissal of the program to 'Holy fuck!' in 45 minutes. His phone is also ringing off the hook.

Another who doesn't bother tuning in is SAS captain turned Federal Liberal Party MP Andrew Hastie.

'When the show came everyone's like, "You've got to watch *Four Corners* tonight. There's a *Four Corners* on". I was like, "This has been done to bits. I get it. [It'll be] a rehash of *60 Minutes* or something". And then my phone starts buzzing and it's like, "No, no. You've got to watch *Four Corners*",' says Hastie. 'I didn't realise that you guys had come across that cache of footage. I was shocked. Really shocked.'

He isn't the only Special Forces veteran left stunned.

'The shock of your story was they realised that despite everything that they've been doing [to fix Special Forces], and how positive it is, is that they still had, right in amongst their ranks, a disturbed individual called Soldier C, that they had no idea about,' says a former senior Special Forces officer. 'So it has the huge implied question. Fuck, if Soldier C was amongst us and we didn't know about it after all this, could others be there? And that it will make us look like idiots if we're claiming we've fixed Special Ops, but there's still people like Soldier C amongst the ranks.'

'I was furious. I was punched in the stomach angry,' says former Major General Fergus McLachlan. McLachlan has been retired for only a matter of months, having left the military as commander of Forces Command. It is the largest command in the Army, with 36,000 personnel. The 37-year veteran can't believe what he has seen on *Four Corners*.

'The culmination, of course, is the shooting. But to me, what was more troubling was the conversation,' says McLachlan. 'The missing piece that shocked me was there was no leader who took that individual (Soldier C) and moved him out of the fight.'

But that isn't the only thing that has bewildered Fergus McLachlan.

'Your program on *Four Corners* disclosed that a guy was still serving who other soldiers knew had done things that pretty clearly, in my view, are alleged criminal acts,' he says. 'How didn't we know about it? Why were these people still serving?'

Hours after the program goes to air, then Defence Minister, Linda Reynolds, releases a statement saying she is 'deeply disturbed by what has been aired' in the *Four Corners* report.

'I just bet up there in Russell [at Defence headquarters] and with Linda Reynolds, there would have been some really terse conversations going on about how the fuck could this have happened?' says the former senior Special Forces officer. 'Because your show had a very powerful impact, because there was a lot of fence sitters. And when they saw the whole program, it polarised a lot of people that up until then were being swayed softly one way or the other.'

The footage of the killing in the wheat field has changed the game. Some inside Defence are frantic. Who the fuck is Soldier C? Where is he? What is going on? More phone calls are made.

Among the men of 3 Squadron SAS, veterans of that deployment, there are also frantic conversations. Which cunt leaked that fucking footage? How did the frigging ABC get hold of it? One guy who is still serving is petrified. He wore a helmet camera through most of the deployment and his footage and voice are seen and heard throughout the story. He particularly fears Soldier B and worries how he will react to the program.

'It was like a real shock wave in that part of the defence organisation, a real shock wave,' says another Defence insider.

To Andrew Hastie, the killing of Dad Mohammad is 'morally repugnant'. 'Like any normal Australian, I had that visceral reaction. But also as a former Australian soldier myself who wore our flag on my left shoulder overseas on operations, I felt ashamed,' says the former SAS captain.

Hastie regards the vision of the killing of Dad Mohammad as the 'defining footage' of all the coverage of alleged war crimes in Afghanistan.

A senior officer within Defence compares the sight of Soldier C with his gun raised, towering over the cringing Afghan with another iconic and confronting war image. It is the black and white photograph of the Japanese soldier, sword held aloft, about to behead the blindfolded Australian prisoner kneeling on Aitape Beach in Papua New Guinea in 1943.

The Afghan embassy in Canberra is outraged by what the *Four Corners* program reveals. 'The Embassy calls for a complete, impartial and timely investigation of these allegations and trusts the Australian judicial system in this regard. If proven, the Embassy calls for the unconditional prosecution of the perpetrators.'

Stephen Rapp is a world-renowned expert on war crimes. He was the chief prosecutor in the Sierra Leone special court and the US ambassador-at-large for war crimes issues under former president Barack Obama. He believes there is a 'strong and indictable' case against Soldier C for murder as a war crime.

'Once a person is out of combat and unarmed and not able to do you damage or contact anyone that can do you damage, then they are a victim that you cannot shoot any more than you shoot you or me, if you were laying on the ground in your home country in front of our own homes.'

Braden Chapman is commended for appearing on *Four Corners*, for his courage in describing the killings he witnessed, and for breaking the code of silence inside the SAS.

'I think he did something that was very brave,' says former Defence chief Chris Barrie.

'He showed moral courage and he should be commended for what he did,' says Andrew Hastie. 'The Australian people should be thankful that we have people like him who are willing to stand for truth and justice.'

The day after the program Braden gets an email from the man heading up the Inspector-General of Defence inquiry into possible Special Forces war crimes in Afghanistan.

'You have done a very courageous thing, which I hope may be instrumental in shaping public opinion about these matters,' writes Paul Brereton. Brereton is uniquely qualified to run the inquiry. He is both a New South Wales Supreme Court judge and a Major General in the Army Reserve.

But inside Defence, some of the brass seem more concerned about who leaked the footage than they are about the atrocity it depicts. The same old story. But common sense prevails and a witch hunt for the leaker or leakers is discouraged. Senior Defence leaders realise that the damage has already been done.

But Defence is still sticking to its old playbook. Despite the outrage and shock of the program and of the footage of the killing, Soldier C remains an Australian Defence Force member. The Chief of Defence, Angus Campbell, who is a former SAS squadron commander, says he will not comment on the *Four Corners* story until after Brereton hands down his report. That is months away.

'In order to protect the integrity and independence of the inquiry, and the reputations of individuals who might otherwise be unfairly affected, the Chief of the Defence Force will not make further comment,' says an ADF statement.

But the pressure is building.

At 9.33 pm on 19 March 2020 – three days after the *Four Corners* broadcast – Defence releases a new statement.

'The Australian Army soldier referred to as "Soldier C" in the *Four Corners* program has today been identified and suspended from duty. The Australian Defence Force conducts its operations under strict rules of engagement and promotes a culture of ethical and lawful behaviour. These rules and cultural norms are enforced according [to] Defence's obligations under Australian and international law.'

Four minutes later the Defence Minister, Linda Reynolds, issues her own press release.

'Further to my public statement issued on Monday evening following the ABC *Four Corners* program, "Killing Field", I advise that I have today made a formal referral to the Commissioner of the Australian Federal Police regarding the incident involving the alleged serious criminal conduct of so-called Soldier C.'

Soldier C is now the subject of a war crimes investigation. Two AFP agents will soon begin crisscrossing the country interviewing former and serving SAS personnel. Their first stop will be Braden Chapman. The investigation is code-named 'Operation GNOTUK'.

The *Four Corners* story is also picked up by media around Australia and the world. The reaction runs for days:

'Film of Australian SAS soldier "killing defenceless Afghan" prompts investigation' *The Times*, UK

'Gruesome video shows special forces brutality as ex soldier alleges murder' *The Age*

'Australian forces accused of war crimes over shooting of Afghan man' China's *Xinhua*

'SAS killing morally repugnant, says Andrew Hastie' *The Australian*

'Horrifying moment an Australian SAS soldier shoots DEAD an unarmed Afghan man cowering in a wheat field in what's been labelled a "straight up execution"' *Daily Mail*, UK

'SAS soldier stood down after alleged killing of unarmed Afghan man' *The Daily Telegraph*

'Australian police probe soldier who shot unarmed Afghan' *France 24*

The *Four Corners* program also forces the SAS hierarchy to once again confront the spectre of what some of its soldiers did in Afghanistan.

The coveted sandy beret of the Special Air Service Regiment (SAS) with the badge depicting the sword Excalibur wreathed in flames and the motto 'Who Dares Wins'.

Butchering a goat during the SAS selection course in the Western Australian desert. In one test candidates are dropped in the middle of the bush to fend for themselves for days carrying 50 kilogram packs. Of the hundreds, only a few will make it through. But as one said, 'I was prepared to die on that course to get in'.

After battling through the bush for days on the Australian SAS selection course, the candidates get a food delivery - in this case offal mixed with blue food dye. On another course candidates got pigs' eyes on a bed of blue couscous. 'I looked at one and it was looking at me. I can still see it,' said one soldier who got through selection.

Playing nude Twister in The Gratto, the SAS boozer at the Regiment's base at Campbell Barracks in Perth. The Gratto was the scene of wild parties, drunken antics and nude chin ups. It was also a place where some soldiers drank from a prosthetic leg taken from a suspected Taliban fighter during an SAS raid in 2009.

Soldiers from Australia's 3 Squadron SAS in front of a US Black Hawk helicopter at Tarin Kowt, southern Afghanistan, in 2012.

Australian SAS medic Dusty Miller with 'The Drip Mile' trophy presented by SAS Regimental Medical Officer, Dr Dan Pronk.

The Drip Mile requires kitting up with a full combat load of 30 kilograms, running 400 metres and inserting a cannula into a live patient, then repeating the exercise successfully three more times to complete the mile.

The sign at the entrance to Camp Russell, the Australian SAS base at Tarin Kowt, Uruzgan Province in southern Afghanistan.

Soldier A sprays the remains of a mud igloo in a Kuchi Camp in Deh Rawood after it has been ripped apart by a thermobaric grenade. Inside was an insurgent bomb maker an Australian SAS team and their Afghan Wakunish counterparts were pursuing. The bomb maker and his cohorts opened fire and killed a Wakunish soldier, Rahul.

Australian SAS and their Afghan Wakunish counterparts form a guard of honour for the body of Rahul, a Wakunish soldier who was killed by an insurgent bomb maker. His body is taken to a helicopter to be flown back to his home region for burial.

Australian SAS Electronic Warfare Operator 'Bear' Braden Chapman and Combat Medic 'Kilo' Dusty Miller in the SAS Ready Room at Camp Russell, the SAS base in Tarin Kowt, Uruzgan Province, Afghanistan.

Braden Chapman out on patrol in southern Afghanistan. As an SAS Electronic Warfare Operator, known as a 'Bear', his combat kit includes an extra piece of equipment crucial to his role that gives him a 'line of bearing' to phones and ICOMs (two-way radios) used by the insurgents to communicate.

SAS soldier in an overwatch position in Afghanistan. The overwatch teams were armed with high-powered sniper rifles and the troop commander was often positioned in these elevated positions.

Soldier B, an SAS veteran and senior sergeant many of the men of 3 Squadron looked up to and even feared.

Australian SAS medic Dusty Miller and one of the Afghan Wakunish soldiers the SAS served alongside with a blindfolded detainee in the background. The Wakas were largely drawn from the minority Hazara population.

Transporting blindfolded prisoners inside a US Black Hawk helicopter back to Tarin Kowt. Australian SAS soldiers complained that the detainees would be handed over to Afghan authorities and then freed within days.

Australia's Special Operations Commander, Adam Findlay, hauls in all the SAS squadrons. He makes the extraordinary admission that war crimes by the Special Forces in Afghanistan may have been covered up. He blames the war crimes on 'one common cause'.

'It is poor leadership,' he tells the assembled SAS soldiers. 'In fact, it is poor moral leadership.'

Findlay warns them that it will take the Regiment a decade to recover from Brereton's report.

'Churchill had a great saying: "When you are walking through hell it is best that you keep walking". That's what we are going to do,' says Findlay. 'This is going to be a tough 10 years. And we have to rehabilitate the reputation and the capabilities and everything of this command ... we can't wallow in it.'

The Special Operations commander then praises those, like Braden Chapman, who had 'the moral courage' to speak out. He has a dark prediction for those who committed atrocities.

'You'll have to sleep once you leave the services. If your honour has been compromised, it will affect you for the rest of your life,' says Findlay.

The *Four Corners* program also shocks those who fought in Afghanistan as members of the SAS.

'Can you capture this guy alive?' says one former 3 Squadron operator and Afghanistan veteran, referring to Dad Mohammad. 'Yeah, you can. Well then do that, because if you don't then you go to the laws on conflict, then it's murder. This is basic stuff. This is Soldiering 101 and these guys failed to get it, which pisses a lot of people off because we're supposed to be the best. The government spends a lot of money to train us up. And these dickheads aren't thinking.'

3 Squadron operator and veteran of that deployment, Tom, was not on the raid that left Dad Mohammad lying in the field. But he says it is clear from the footage that Soldier C has implicated his comrades in the killing.

'As a soldier, professional soldier on the ground, you do not turn to another and ask for permission. If you need to pull the trigger that's your decision and your decision alone,' he says. 'Because you need to live with the consequences after that.'

But he also believes the blame extends beyond Soldier C. Those around him should have stopped him while they were still capable. That includes the dog handler who deflected that terrible question, and the patrol commander who answered it.

'Hand on heart, I would have said, "No, no, you're not dropping that cunt",' says Tom.

'If you don't say no, you're complicit,' says the former 3 Squadron operator. 'And if you don't say anything, well, you're still negligent for not standing up to it.'

'You think you'd tell him, "Fucking cuff him and we'll keep going, take him with us",' says Braden.

As for Soldier C, Braden says, 'You can see he really wants to do it.'

Medic Dusty Miller says everybody knew it was an unlawful killing. 'The guy was unarmed. Soldier C just wanted to get kills up.'

The former 3 Squadron operator says SAS soldiers are scientifically chosen not to kill like this. 'We're selecting people to do a job, do a very strategic job,' he says. 'Not to go there and "do" the village. We are not there to do that. So you're disappointed to go, "You just said fuck you to every bloke in the Regiment, because that's not what we do. You fucking idiot, you deserve to go to jail for what you just did". Does the guy need to die? No, he doesn't.'

From his anonymous beginnings as Usernameanon in my encrypted email inbox, Braden Chapman is now the public face of former SAS members who want the truth of what happened in Afghanistan told.

He feels like he has done something to help his comrades who are broken by the moral degradation and murderous horror of the war. People like Dusty Miller.

'I think it's good that there is proof, actual video footage, because you've got all these people, like guys who have killed themselves or people like Dusty suffering,' says Braden. 'All that suffering is not in vain. Now it's coming out.'

But there is something that nags me about the footage of the killing of Dad Mohammad in the wheat field. There is something about Soldier C's calmness, how casual he is about the shooting. It is almost clinical. He is a very efficient executioner.

'You want me to drop this cunt?' Three times he asks it. Three bullets tear into Dad Mohammad. Then Soldier C walks off through the wheat, like nothing happened.

To me, it feels like he has done this before. Of course, he had. Two months earlier in what had already become known as the 'village idiot' killing.

8

IN CASE OF WAR, BREAK GLASS

When you're wounded and left on Afghanistan's plains,
And the women come out to cut up what remains,
Jest roll on your rifle and blow out your brains
An' go to your Gawd like a soldier
Rudyard Kipling, 'The Young British Soldier'

The patrol stands in a semi-circle around the Afghan's body. They are silent. Soldier C has just emptied the man's skull. The two shots were perfect.

Dusty reckons the man's brain hit the ground before he did.

It is two months before Dad Mohammad's killing in the wheat field. They are standing in another field, looking at the body of another Afghan killed by Soldier C. They will later remember this young man as the 'village idiot'.

Tom had seen Soldier C raise his rifle.

Maybe he is just taking a sighting through his scope, he had thought. They do that all the time. But the Afghan was only about 20 metres away. Close. Why do you need your scope at this range?

There was something not right about the young man. The way he looked, the way he limped away. He was disabled. He was scared shitless. Everyone could see it.

Then pop, pop. His head exploded. Perfect shots.

As they look down at the man's shattered head the patrol commander tells his 2-I-C to dress the body in a battle bra chest rig containing rifle magazines. The man was unarmed, so they need to manufacture a reason for killing him.

This isn't just the story of a killing. It is the story of a cover up.

They take photos of the dead man wearing the battle bra and the magazines.

'Move on,' says the patrol commander. They move on. The Afghan with the emptied head is left in the field. They don't even know his name.

———

'Ziauddin had a mental illness,' says Kalimullah. 'So he wasn't able to work well. He worked with his brothers.'

Kalimullah is related to Ziauddin through marriage and is appointed by the family to speak to my Afghan fixers about what happened on 28 March 2012. They have tracked him down in Kandahar and sit with him while he tells them over cups of sweet tea what happened to Ziauddin eight years earlier.

Ziauddin wasn't mentally ill. What Kalimullah means is that the young man had a brain injury. 'The Taliban beat him two years [before he was killed],' says Kalimullah. 'Because of this beating, he developed mental problems.'

The Taliban bashed Ziauddin until he was unconscious. No one remembers what he received the beating for. 'Maybe someone reported him due to a dispute or an argument,' suggests Kalimullah.

The beating leaves Ziauddin with cognitive problems. He is unable to work as he used to.

Ziauddin's family grows figs, pomegranates, cumin and wheat on their land at Paryan Nawa in the Shah Wali Kot region of Kandahar Province. Shah Wali Kot lies to the south, just over the border from Uruzgan where the Australians are based. Ziauddin's village of Paryan Nawa runs along both sides of a river and the land here is fertile.

When the first Black Hawk helicopter lands around mid-morning, the people of Paryan Nawa are in the fields harvesting cumin. Ziauddin is hanging around watching them. Sometimes they give him simple tasks to do such as carrying things. But because of his disability he isn't much help to them.

Ziauddin is about 100 metres away from where the chopper lands.

'He couldn't understand the situation very well. Because of his mental weakness he couldn't figure it out,' says Kalimullah.

He certainly can't figure out what the helicopter is about. The men who are running from it scare him too. They have painted faces, dark glasses over their eyes and strange weapons. One has a cloth covering his face. They are running towards him. He immediately starts towards home.

Ziauddin's older brother Shahabuddin is nearby harvesting the cumin and hears the helicopter land. He worries about his brother and is concerned that if the foreigners spot him they won't understand that he has a disability. Ziauddin will panic if he sees them.

Ziauddin is walking fast now. The men with the painted faces are getting closer to him. He is approaching an irrigation ditch on the edge of a field. Then he is dead.

'He was shot around the back of his head,' says Kalimullah. 'The bullet had pierced through the skull and his brains were spread away from his skull. His body was pale from blood loss.'

The villagers who later gather around Ziauddin's body can't tell that he has been shot twice because his head is a deformed mess.

Ziauddin's mother weeps over the body of her son. Gathering herself up, she pulls out a handkerchief and begins collecting pieces of his brain in it.

Kalimullah and Shahabuddin both say the Australians later came into the village and rounded up some of the men.

Shahabuddin is white hot with rage about what they have done to his little brother. He wants vengeance. 'I wanted to swear at them, but because I was unarmed people stopped me,' he says. They tell him if he abuses the Australians, they might kill him too.

Through an interpreter Shahabuddin is asked about his brother. He tells the story of how Ziauddin was beaten unconscious by the Taliban, how it had affected his ability to understand things, and how they have killed an innocent man.

A village leader, Mullah Asadullah, also confronts the Australians. 'You killed a mentally ill person,' he tells their interpreter. 'Why?'

By mid-afternoon, the SAS has cleared the village and the patrols board their helicopters and leave.

Ziauddin's body is taken up to the big cemetery that sits on the high ground above the village and is buried. At the place near the ditch where he was shot they pile up some rocks as a shrine. It is a Pashtun custom.

Tom doesn't remember going into the village that day. He doesn't remember much about what happened after the killing. But the 'village idiot' and his exploding head play endlessly through his mind. How could you forget that?

Before the *Four Corners* program 'Killing Field' I had emailed Tom. I had been told how he had been bullied mercilessly by some of his patrol, despite being a good soldier. I was also told he had left the SAS. I asked if we could speak. He was wary. But he agreed to meet me, discreetly at a hotel interstate. As we sat opposite each other I asked Tom to give me a character assessment of three of his former comrades.

Soldier A was 'respected' but a 'bit loose'. Soldier B was a 'psychopath'. Soldier C was an 'egotistical sociopath'.

He admitted that he 'was never in the group' and that he had been bullied.

'If you were in the boys' club you could do anything.'

He then spoke about guilt. 'I carry it every day, I think about it every day. Innocent people were killed.'

We talked for a few hours, but he did not want to go on the record. I could tell that he was reluctant to trust me. I couldn't blame him after the bullying he had endured, both physical brutality and psychological torment. We agreed to stay in touch.

Then the *Four Corners* 'Killing Field' program went to air.

For Tom, the program was a revelation. It was a validation of his own experiences on that deployment, a confirmation of his own belief that some of his comrades had gone rogue.

He decided he wanted to speak to me and to tell me what he had witnessed. It was then that he told me some details about the 'village idiot' killing, as some in the SAS had dubbed it. We agreed to meet again.

Then, one night at home, before our planned meeting, I got a call on an encrypted app. It was Tom. He had had a couple of drinks and wanted me to speak to someone who was with him. It was Dusty Miller.

I had tried to reach Dusty months before when I was investigating the killings at Sarkhume. But the message had come back that he didn't want to talk. He wasn't up to it. Now, over the phone, Dusty told me he wanted the truth to get out there.

'We did the wrong thing,' he said.

Dusty and I sit for hours and talk in his apartment. It is modern, clean and spartan. It is as far away from Afghanistan as you can get. Over there it is grimy, medieval, brutal. Everything in Afghanistan is untidy and complicated. The politics, the tribal culture, the war itself.

We talk about the day Soldier C killed the 'village idiot'. At this point, I still don't know the victim's real name.

'This guy was not fucking right. He was obviously intellectually disabled,' says Dusty. 'And I can't even tell you why. But this guy was not right.'

I ask him why he thinks Soldier C pulled the trigger.

'It was just so unnecessary,' says Dusty. 'Why would you do that? If somebody's running away unarmed, why would you shoot them?'

He pauses, then he answers his own question. 'He just wanted kills up. It was bloodlust.'

After a while we are joined by Tom. He is easily the messiest thing in Dusty's apartment. Despite the freezing weather, Tom is in a pair of paint-stained shorts and a flannelette shirt. He has got three days' worth of growth on his chin and his hair has that 'just out of bed' look about it.

Dusty is on the couch next to me. His beard is trimmed, hair perfect. In his late forties, Dusty is still very fit. Every week he runs about 40 to 50 kilometres and rides anywhere up to 600 kilometres. He looks like he could jump straight up and do a triathlon.

'This guy just took a life and he didn't need to take a life,' says Tom. 'Why? I have no idea. This is one of the things that runs through my head every single day.'

Tom had stood up and walked out of the debrief the day of the killing, after the patrol commander had commended Soldier C for taking out a 'high value target'. They all knew that was bullshit. Tom's walkout was an act of defiance, a challenge to the patrol commander's authority and a demonstration that he would not be part of the cover up.

'To get up during a debrief of an ops mission, it's career ending,' he says. 'But they knew they could do nothing because if they were going to say something I'd just go, "You want to take this further?"'

But isn't that the question? Why didn't he take it further? Should he have reported the killing as unprovoked, unnecessary, and unlawful?

'I would have been sent home,' says Tom. 'I would have been fucked over. Even worse there would have been a bullet in the back of my head out on ops.'

Sitting in Dusty's living room, I ask Tom if he is serious. There is no way anyone in his patrol would kill him, surely?

'I was in fear of my life,' he says. 'They were talking about throwing members out of helicopters because they weren't toeing the line. If they can shoot an innocent man in the back of the head just for the sake of killing someone, [they can] throw you out of a helicopter.'

Dusty is nodding as his friend speaks.

'You've got to understand that there were certain people that I've got to say were unhinged,' Dusty says. 'It's the only word I can really use. They're fucking unhinged.'

I already know one 3 Squadron soldier Dusty fears. It is Soldier B.

'He's a scary person,' Dusty had told me. He had used the exact same word as Tom to describe the veteran sergeant. 'He's a psychopath.'

'In case of war, break glass,' says Dusty.

Dusty was in Sarkhume. He saw Soldier B haul away his patient, the wounded Haji Sardar. He heard him say, 'He didn't make it', when he later emerged from the mosque. Dusty says he knows Soldier B killed the old man and killed him without mercy.

But that was not the only time Dusty was forced to cover for Soldier B, or to treat others who were on the receiving end of his savagery.

—

Dusty is fit and he is fast, but he can't catch the kid.

Soldier B has spotted the boy just after they have jumped from the Black Hawk. The kid is holding something that they can't make out.

'Kilo, fucking get that kid!' orders Soldier B.

In the foot race that will follow, Dusty will be at a distinct disadvantage. He is loaded down with more than 30 kilograms of body armour, medical gear and other kit, and is lugging his assault rifle. The kid also has the hometown advantage.

Dusty sprints across a field after the kid. The kid scampers over a low mud wall and disappears. A few seconds later Dusty is over the wall. In front of him is a compound. The kid must have run in there. The compound is a compound within compounds, a bewildering warren of alleys and rooms. Dusty ducks his head down alleys, into rooms, and over walls. The kid has disappeared. Dusty has lost him.

It is about this time the medic hears the choppers in the distance. He hears them come in, land and leave again. They must be picking up the patrols. With their departure silence returns to the district. It is deathly quiet, thinks Dusty.

'Righty oh,' he says to himself.

He is alone and he starts to backtrack, to retrace his steps. Down the alley, into the compound, through that alley, out the entrance, over the wall, across the irrigation ditch, into the field.

There is no sign of Soldier B or the patrol. He gets on his radio.

'Mate, where are you? Because this kid's fucking gone.'

Soldier B gives him the number of a compound that he is at. Dusty looks at the map and finds the compound marked on it. He has got a bit of a walk ahead of him. He is pissed off with Soldier B for leaving him on his own, deep in Taliban territory.

I might have my head chopped off, he thinks.

After a while Dusty makes it to the next compound. There he finds Soldier B holding an Afghan man up against the wall. The man is in bad shape. Blood is running down his right leg and both arms. His nose is flattened.

That's the worst broken nose I've seen, thinks Dusty. And I've seen a few.

Soldier B has just given the man a pounding and a combat dog has torn into the Afghan's legs and arms. Dusty slips on some black sterile gloves and sits the man down in a room off the courtyard of the compound and pulls up the legs of his pants. The dog bites are deep.

Dusty knows the damage the dogs can do.

'The dogs were just land sharks. We call them land sharks for a reason. They'd just fucking munch people. And so I'd be constantly treating dog bites.'

He starts to clean the bite wounds.

'He's the target,' says one of the patrol. The bashed man Dusty is treating is their objective, the biometrics analysis has confirmed it. That doesn't mean Soldier B can beat the shit out of him, thinks Dusty. But he will keep that thought to himself.

Dusty bandages the man's leg and treats the bite marks on his arms. There isn't much he can do for his nose. It is as flat as can be, having been punched in by Soldier B.

'He went for my sidearm,' says Soldier B to Dusty.

The medic is not going to argue with him. But he knows that is bullshit.

'I truly believe this cunt would have fucking shot me if I didn't play the game,' Dusty says of Soldier B.

The Bear, Braden Chapman, is outside with the others helping to process some Afghan men that have been detained. He watches as the troop commander walks over to Soldier B. He asks what happened to the Afghan with the flattened nose.

'He reached for my weapon,' says Soldier B.

Later Braden overhears the troop commander talking to an operator.

'[Soldier B] would have killed him if he had reached for his weapon,' says the troop commander. He doesn't believe him either.

It is yet another lie created by Soldier B, another cover up that he has drawn Dusty Miller and the others into.

'I think it's fucked. But at the end of the day, I want to go home as well,' says the medic.

Tom is also disturbed by Soldier B's violence against Afghans and by the apparent sadistic delight he gets when he destroys their property.

One day, Tom is on an operation when several patrols converge on a compound. One of them is led by Soldier B. They enter the compound and Soldier B shoos some cattle out. The Afghans inside can only watch as they bolt free. They are too frightened to protest. But what Soldier B does next will stun Tom and make him question why they are even in Afghanistan, and whether they are doing more harm than good.

Parked just outside the compound is a car. To Tom, it looks like an old jalopy that is shared by the villagers for odd jobs, trips into town and appointments with doctors.

Soldier B walks over to the car, leans in and shifts the gearstick into the neutral position. He then orders Tom and others in the patrol to help him push it through the main entrance into the compound.

What is he doing, thinks Tom.

'You sure you want to do this?' asks another operator.

'Just fucking do it,' snaps Soldier B. He is a sergeant, one of the demigods whose word is law.

They roll the car through the gates. The Afghans inside watch on as their car is brought to a stop in the middle of the compound. They are just as confused as Tom.

This is insulting, thinks Tom. This is where these people live, where they cook, where they sleep, where they do their laundry. It would be like them pushing a car into my living room, he thinks.

But it is about to get much worse than that. Tom watches as petrol is poured over the car. Soldier B walks over to it and lights it up.

What the fuck, thinks Tom. Why is he doing this?

But he says nothing. Next to him, the Afghan interpreter that works with the SAS patrol is furious.

'Why are you doing this?' he asks Tom.

Tom shakes his head. He doesn't have an answer. He has no idea why they have done this, other than to satisfy some sadistic craving within Soldier B.

A deep shame wells up inside Tom. He is part of this operation, he helped push the car into the compound. This really is a Strandhögg raid. As well as plunder and pillage, Strandhögg was Viking for burn.

Is this what I joined the SAS to do, he asks himself.

Acrid black smoke rises into the sky. The car is ablaze. A tyre pops, then another.

We are turning the entire population against us, Tom despairs. He thought he was coming here to help the Afghan people. Instead, he is barbecuing their cars.

9

SHINA

'I feel like they knew that no one was watching.
And they knew that they could get away with
pretty much whatever they wanted to'
**Christina, Handheld Imagery Data Base Manager,
Special Operations Task Group**

'Zulu Two?'

Braden Chapman's radio crackles. Zulu Two is his call sign.

The signals intelligence operator is on overwatch. From his position on the hill, Braden can see the SAS patrol clearing 'the green' below. Civilian compounds are scattered among the thick band of trees that hug the river. Moments ago, there were half a dozen or so shots and reports of enemy killed in action over the radio.

Later Braden will learn the patrol has killed two Afghans.

'Zulu Two?'

One of the operators wants something from Braden.

'Go ahead,' says Braden.

'Can you go up one channel?' says the operator.

The operator wants to talk privately. Braden flicks the radio up a channel.

'Chappie, you there?'

Off the main frequency, the operator can revert to nicknames. No one is listening in to this chat.

'Do you have an ICOM?' The operator wants a radio.

'Yeah,' replies Braden.

'You reckon you'd be able to get one over to me?'

Braden has to think quickly.

'Nope. Don't have a spare, mate.'

Braden wants no part of this. He knows the patrol has killed someone and he knows why they want the ICOM. It is to plant on the body of an Afghan. Under the Rules of Engagement an Afghan carrying a radio is fair game. They are classified as spotters who use the ICOMs to report on SAS positions.

Hours later they are back at camp in Tarin Kowt and Braden pulls the operator aside. He is a guy Braden likes and has never seen do anything dodgy. Braden wants to set him straight. He wants to explain the real reason he didn't want to give him the ICOM.

'I told him there's a noticeable difference between Taliban ICOMs and our ICOMs,' he says. 'We couldn't really plant the ICOMs I carried on an Afghani because they were too clean. Afghanis' equipment is always dirty so you can't really plant clean equipment on [bodies].'

'Cool, no worries,' replies the operator after Braden explains the situation.

On a later operation Braden is asked by another operator for an ICOM. He again refuses. He wants no part of these cover ups. But he is forced to watch as others plant radios they have brought with them or obtained from elsewhere.

'They hadn't got them off me but they'd definitely got them off somebody else and walked over and sat it next to a body,' says Braden. 'They'd just take a quick photo. And then they'd just leave it there.'

These planted radios are called 'throwdowns'. And it is not only radios being used to cover up unlawful, suspect or mistaken killings.

One day on operations Braden sees a Special Forces engineer carrying a couple of AK-47 assault rifles in a bag on his back. Braden hasn't heard anything over the radio about weapons being discovered. Not only that – the engineers were on the second wave of choppers and have been only on the ground for a matter of minutes, not enough time to rustle up some guns.

'Did you just find those?' asks Braden.

The engineer laughs. 'No, I brought them with me.'

He doesn't need to explain to Braden why he has brought the guns on the raid.

'If the guys have shot someone because they thought they may have been armed or something and then they worked out they haven't been, you're going to cover your tracks,' says Braden. 'Other members of my troop back in Australia, they did used to joke about how the same serial number was in every single photo of a dead Afghani ... inferring somebody was planting these AK-47s. That was the joke.'

One patrol commander on the same 2012 rotation also saw throw-downs used. 'I don't use fucking throwdowns,' he told me. 'I didn't care for it, [but] it didn't bother me.'

One AK-47 will become particularly notorious. It has teal-coloured tape around the stock and will be planted multiple times.

Dusty Miller says the engineer Braden Chapman saw carrying the AK-47s was the key player in providing the throwdowns.

'So when we found stuff they'd all go to [the engineer] and I can't think of anyone else that [throwdowns] would have come from, which is a shame,' says Dusty. 'I think that's where they got of a lot of throwdowns from.'

The use of throwdowns by the SAS is also detected by other agencies. Afghanistan is the largest station for spies from the Australian Secret Intelligence Service. ASIS helps to identify Taliban commanders and networks, and to map the insurgency's hierarchy.

The SAS acts as bodyguards for ASIS operatives when they go to meet their Afghan sources. Sometimes the SAS operators go and pick up the sources and bring them to a safe house to meet ASIS agents. These Afghan collaborators are essential for identifying targets to go on the Joint Prioritised Effects List or JPEL, the official register of enemies marked for capture or assassination. John Nagl, a counter-insurgency adviser to top American general David Petraeus, famously described the JPEL as 'an almost industrial-scale counterterrorism killing machine'.

The two sides – ASIS and the SAS – work closely together, but it is not always a collegiate relationship.

'We made them look good,' says one SAS operator who worked intimately with ASIS agents. 'They realised we were a necessary evil and, whether or not they liked us, they needed us. And they hated it.'

The feeling is mutual. ASIS officers are concerned that some SAS patrols are too loose with the rules of engagement, and that a few operators are out of control.

Then there are the incidents on the booze. During a rowdy night in Kabul an SAS trooper pulls a weapon on a female ASIS officer. In Kandahar at the 4 Squadron SAS bar 'Archers', a drunk ASIS officer pulls a pistol as a joke and waves it around. The officer is disarmed by the SAS operator manning the bar.

'You've got SAS on one side who are scientifically selected to have courage, initiative, teamwork, integrity, all those good things that make an Australian soldier. Then on the other side, you've got ASIS, who are scientifically selected to be the snakes in the grass: deceitful, conniving, sell their grandmother in a heartbeat,' says the SAS operator who worked with ASIS teams. 'You inject alcohol into that, it's just going to create friction.'

But there are other sources of friction. There is disquiet among some ASIS agents who have noticed the same AK-47 crop up in photographs from operations in three different locations. The weapon has tape on it.

'This doesn't make sense,' says one ASIS officer to his superior.

His superior takes it up with a senior officer within the Special Operations Task Group.

'I'll keep an eye on it and have a word to FE-Alpha,' says the senior officer, referring to the SAS. This is in 2009, three years before Dusty, Braden and Tom deploy on Rotation 17.

154

Incident, coincidence, pattern, thinks the ASIS agent. Throw-downs are a pattern.

During the 2012 deployment, Tom also sees a pattern.

'Often people who had been killed had weapons placed on them and were photographed with these weapons. That happened on numerous occasions.'

One of these throwdown weapons is given its own name. It is the 'Magic Makarov'.

'A Russian pistol, a Makarov pistol, appeared in photographs all across Afghanistan,' says Tom.

The Magic Makarov has been cropping up in photos since 2010. Dusty says the pistol (or more likely, pistols) became something of a running joke.

'There was Christina, who was the image girl,' he says. 'I heard this second-hand, that she'd gone to a number of PCs, patrol command-ers, and said that she's got photographs from a number of different jobs that we've done over the past three months or whatever, with the same Russian pistol appearing in it: The Magic Makarov.'

Dusty is talking about Christina, the Special Forces multi-media specialist whose deployment overlaps with his.

'I recall very vaguely speaking to someone about a pistol,' she tells me. 'I recall speaking to someone about a Makarov that continued to appear in images.'

But Christina is not sure. Every month she processes thousands of images brought back from operations. She is at it 16 hours a day.

During my research I am given a dossier of photos showing dead Afghans pictured with a variety of weapons and ICOMs. In one, an Afghan with a long white beard lies on his back, his eyes open and his mouth agape in a look of abject surprise. The dead man appears too old to be a fighter. But lying next to his bloodied right hand is a very clean Makarov pistol.

For Christina, patterns are emerging in some of the photos, and inconsistencies are becoming more pronounced in others. Some of the photos don't seem quite right. Christina is starting to suspect that throwdowns are being used.

'Sometimes there were images of a person who might be in a battle bra with magazines but no weapon,' she says.

Why would someone put on a battle bra but not pick up their weapon? she wonders.

I think immediately of the 'village idiot' killing. How the victim, Ziauddin, had been dressed in a battle bra containing a couple of magazines.

'On occasion there was equipment such as battle bras that looked too clean,' says Christina. 'This certainly rings some alarm bells for me.'

Then she sees images in which a body is photographed with a single grenade.

This makes me think of Sarkhume. The body of Mirza Khan, who had been mauled by an Australian dog and then shot, had been photographed with a grenade. Grenades are small and easy to carry, like Makarov pistols.

'There was some concern that weapons that appeared the same were appearing in multiple missions,' says Christina. 'There was the potential that they were planting weapons on people who they had killed.'

Christina also reviews a lot of the footage from Unmanned Aerial Vehicles or UAVs. She notices that, as a rule, the UAV cameras are pointed away from missions on the ground. Rarely do they capture anything of the operation itself.

'I feel like they knew that no one was watching. And they knew that they could get away with pretty much whatever they wanted to.'

The Brereton Inquiry into rumours and allegations of war crimes by Special Forces in Afghanistan will later confirm that UAVs would typically be pushed 'off target' once the SAS was on the ground. The inquiry would find some legitimate reasons for this – so that some of those watching the live camera feed from the UAV would not be able to observe classified SAS tactics, techniques and procedures, and because the UAV would be better used elsewhere for monitoring escape routes for enemy fighters.

The inquiry reviewed many hours of UAV imagery hoping to gain an insight into events on the ground and to further its investigations. 'However, the result was that the [UAV imagery] did not provide visibility of what happened on target,' the Brereton Report states.

The failure of the UAVs to feed back action from the ground isn't the only thing Christina finds strange. She is suspicious about the way some of the dead Afghans are positioned.

'Certainly, the earlier images of the deceased individuals, you would find them on their back with a weapon laid across their chest,' she says. 'It looked as though the person had been engaged and was deceased and then later on that weapon was placed on their chest.'

Christina wonders why many of these Afghans who have been shot seem to fall in the exact same way. Why is their weapon always diagonally across their chest?

'I feel like those images were staged.'

ICOMs, grenades, battle bras, weirdly positioned bodies. Christina is becoming more doubtful about what she is seeing and processing.

But she has already reported a suspect video. That was the video of the Commando shooting what looked like a dead Afghan twice in the head. She thought it was a war crime to mistreat the body of an enemy. But Christina is told to delete the video and not to mention it again. Do not rock the boat.

'I wonder how many images that I processed, that potentially had some sort of manipulation or involvement from Australian soldiers in order to make it seem like it was a legitimate killing?' says Christina. 'How frequently did that occur? How many incidences are we looking at?'

———

Dusty Miller watches as the Chinook flies away. He looks around at Forward Operating Base Anaconda.

Why would you put a FOB in a bowl like this? he wonders. The Taliban can fire down right into here. Anaconda is 3 Squadron's staging point for today's operation, which is in the wilds of Khaz Uruzgan north-west of Tarin Kowt.

Built by the US Green Berets, FOB Anaconda is about as isolated as it gets. Dusty looks over to a wall where the insignia of the United States Army Special Forces is painted. It depicts two crossed arrows over a stiletto knife. Underneath are the words '*De Oppresso Liber*'. To liberate the oppressed.

The base sits on a key rat line used by the Taliban to resupply fighters in both Uruzgan and Kandahar. In 2007, the Taliban launched a rare full-frontal assault on Anaconda, an attack repelled by 80 American, Australian and Afghan soldiers. The Taliban were scattered and they left behind more than 20 dead.

The next year a joint American and Australian SAS patrol was ambushed in a narrow valley in Khaz Uruzgan while on their way back to Anaconda. Nine Australians were wounded and one American killed in the rolling gun battle with a highly organised Taliban force. During the ambush, SAS Trooper Mark Donaldson sprinted 80 metres under fire to save a wounded Afghan interpreter, earning Australia's first Victoria Cross in 40 years.

3 Squadron SAS has been here before, and now they are back. It is 16 May 2012.

Dusty and the patrols will return to FOB Anaconda later. First, they have a target to hunt. They set off for a nearby village called Shina.

Shina farmer Sakhi Dad is irrigating his wheat when he hears the helicopters. He looks up and sees two of them coming up one side of the valley. Others are flying along the other side. They have come over a mountain the Afghans call Lewanai.

158

The first chopper lands in the valley. The valley is grassed and has a creek running through it. Compounds are scattered along its banks. The other choppers set down and disgorge their patrols.

The Australians are on the ground and the choppers back in the air within seconds. The SAS patrols are exposed here in the landing zone. To the left of the SAS soldiers the valley rises up, a perfect vantage point for spotters and snipers. They walk towards compounds in the greenbelt as the Black Hawks circle overhead keeping watch.

Sakhi Dad is nearby when they land.

'It became dusty. I walked from the wheat field, I had hay on my back,' says Sakhi Dad.

He wants to go to his home in Shina and gather his children. He wants the family safe and together when the red beards begin their raid. But it is too late. An SAS patrol has spotted him.

'They came from the side of the hill and they said, "Stop",' he says. 'They had coloured their faces. I couldn't figure out who they were.'

But the farmer refuses to stop because he is now very close to home.

'One of them ran at me and I don't know if he hit me with a gun butt or kicked me. But he hit me.'

The blow knocks the hay from Sakhi Dad's back and sends his shawl flying. An SAS soldier ties his hands behind his back and the farmer is hauled along with the patrol. Other men are also rounded up and they are taken to a compound and faced against a wall.

'They didn't allow anyone to look around. I didn't look at them,' says Sakhi Dad. 'Whoever looked at them they swore at and beat them. I was too fearful to look at them.'

Dusty is with another patrol that has stopped in a burial ground. Colourful little flags tied to sticks and poles flutter around them in the breeze. A compound is nearby. Someone spots a man in the wheat field next to the cemetery.

To Dusty, he is clearly a farmer. The Afghan is working in the middle of the field and nearby is a young boy. It could be his son or grandson. The boy looks about eight years old.

Dusty and another operator watch as an SAS soldier and two Wakas walk towards the farmer. The man has stopped working, and the boy watches on as the soldiers approach. Dusty can't make out who the SAS operator is. He is too far away, about 100 metres from Dusty. But the medic can hear raised voices between the farmer and one of the Wakas. The Waka raises his weapon and points it at the farmer from almost point-blank range.

What the fuck is going on, thinks Dusty.

The child starts to move towards the man. The Waka fires and the farmer drops like a stone. The boy screams and starts to run. There is another shot.

Dusty turns to the operator next to him.

'What the fuck?'

The operator doesn't reply.

The boy has reached the man and has thrown himself on the body. The child wraps his arms around him and screams.

Dusty hangs his head. This is fucked up, so very fucked up. This guy wasn't armed, and the Waka has just popped him. He can still hear the kid screaming. Dusty will never forget that screaming, or the sight of the boy trying to raise the dead man, his futile attempts to pull him up.

They walk on, out of the burial ground and away from the wheat field, leaving the boy to scream.

Abdul Wali is at home getting an axe when his brother Jalil rushes in. Abdul Wali is in his thirties and the eldest of seven children. Jalil is seven years old and the youngest, born to his father's second wife.

Their father, Abdul Walid, is an old man but is still farming. Today he has gone out with Jalil to irrigate their wheat, but now the boy is back at the house and out of breath. Abdul Wali knows something bad has happened; he has heard the helicopters.

'Where is our father?' asks Abdul Wali. His black eyes stare into his little brother's face searching for an answer.

'They have shot him!' cries the boy. 'They pointed a gun at him and he bled. He fell down and then he started to get up, but they shot him again. He just lay there.'

'Stay here,' says Abdul Wali.

Abdul Wali doesn't care if the Australians shoot him – he wants to get to his father. The old man is a proud Afghan and served in the military in the days of Mohammed Daoud Khan, the first president of Afghanistan. He has endured tragedy, including the death of his first wife. But since his second marriage and the birth of little Jalil, old Abdul Walid is happy again and is a respected elder in Shina.

His son Abdul Wali is heading down to the creek when he spots the Australians and some Wakas on the other side.

These men are huge, thinks Abdul Wali. Their faces are painted in stripes of green and black and they wear gloves.

One of the foreigners waves his hand towards Abdul Wali, beckoning him to approach. The Afghan wades through the creek. He is searched and ordered to follow them. Along the path he passes Habib Aaka, a Shina elder.

'They have killed my father,' Abdul Wali tells him. As he speaks an Australian soldier cuffs him around the head and throws him into an irrigation ditch. Looking up, the Afghan sees the soldier level his weapon at him. But another soldier comes over and says something to the SAS operator. The operator lowers his gun and Abdul Wali pulls himself out of the ditch. He has had a close call.

Abdul Wali is taken to the compound where the other detainees are, including Sakhi Dad, and is ordered to sit and face the wall like the others. Suddenly there is more gunfire in the distance, followed by a tremendous explosion.

'They have destroyed Abdul Kabir's yard,' whispers one of the bound men near Sakhi Dad.

'Shut the fuck up!' says one of the SAS soldiers. The prisoners don't know what he is saying, but they know what he means.

Another villager is brought to where the prisoners are sitting. They can hear him whimpering in pain. Sakhi Dad, Abdul Wali and the others are too frightened to look around and see who it is.

More gunfire is heard. Some of it is in the distance, some much closer.

Dusty and his patrol are walking towards the compound when they hear the explosion. IED, thinks Dusty. He waits for his radio to crackle into life and for someone to ask him to treat someone's wounds. But it is silent.

The blast has been caused by a charge set by one of the engineers. It is to blow a hole in a nearby wall so the patrol can enter another compound.

Dusty has reached the compound where the prisoners are. He can see them squatting, hands bound behind them, facing the wall.

'Kilo, got a guy over here. You need to treat him.'

They take him over to an Afghan who has blood dripping down his arm. Those fucking dogs again. It is the whimpering man. He has at least two deep puncture wounds to his bicep. Teeth wounds. And a large tear along his forearm. Dusty starts to clean the wounds and suture up what he can.

Why do they sool these fucking dogs onto people? thinks Dusty. He has dealt with so many dog bites already on this deployment. Injuries caused by the Australian land sharks.

Dusty looks down and notices a spreading patch of blood around the crotch area of the Afghan's man dress. The medic pulls out his scissors and cuts away the cloth around the wound.

Fuck me. The Afghan's scrotum has been torn open by the dog and his testicles are exposed. The medic has seen his fair share of wounds, but this is horrific.

But to some of his comrades it is all good for a laugh.

'You playing with that jundi's nut sack, mate?' says one operator.

'Hey, Dusty, good luck fixing that prick's ball bag,' laughs another.

The black humoured banter doesn't bother the medic. This is just how the blokes cope with the terrible wounds they see.

But Dusty is worried. The injury is complicated and serious, the man is in terrible pain and he needs surgery. He jumps on the radio and asks Soldier B, the ranking soldier on the operation, to come over and take a look.

'This is serious,' Dusty tells Soldier B when he arrives. 'This guy has to come back with us.'

'No fucking way. He's not coming with us. Just fucking fix him,' he replies.

'This guy's fucking testicles are on his lap,' says Dusty. 'What do you want me to do here? We can't fucking leave him. He'll die if we don't take him back.'

'He's not coming. And we're exfiling shortly, so you've got to fix him. You'd better hurry up.'

Dusty knows he is not going to win an argument with Soldier B. He doesn't give a fuck whether this guy dies or not, thinks the medic. He gives the Afghan a big shot of morphine, because he is in excruciating pain and what he is about to do is going to hurt even more. He begins cleaning out the wound, washing it out as best he can. Helping him out is Scruffy, one of the operators.

'Oh, fuck. Fuck me,' says Scruffy. Scruffy was once a medic, but this injury is even making him squeamish. Dusty has got what remains of the Afghan's manhood in his hands.

'Are you serious, Scruffy?' says Dusty as he cleans the wound. 'You've been sent over to give me a hand and all you're doing is fucking squirming.'

After the clean out Dusty makes sure the man's testicles aren't torsioned or twisted, then he does what is called a delayed primary closure.

It isn't a full suturing of the wound. He has deliberately left the closures loose so any infection can seep out.

'Hurry up, Kilo. We're out of here.'

It is Soldier B again.

'Nearly done,' says Dusty.

He then jabs the Afghan with 2000 milligrams of Ceftriaxone, a broad-spectrum antibiotic he hopes will kill any infection.

Dusty calls over the interpreter. The wounded man is too out of it to remember what the medic is about to say. So he gets the interpreter to explain what needs to happen to one of the villagers.

'Tell this guy there is a FOB [Forward Operating Base] not far from here. There are some 18 Deltas [Special Forces Medics] there. If he takes this bloke there they can fix him and he needs antibiotics. If he doesn't he may die of infection.' Dusty knows that the wounded man stands little chance without getting antibiotics.

It is time to go. As Dusty walks away he knows he has done all he can. But that probably won't be enough.

That bloke is a dead man, thinks Dusty.

After what feels like hours, Sakhi Dad, Abdul Wali and the other detainees who are squatting against the wall hear the beating rotors of the helicopters fade and then disappear.

'They are bringing more soldiers,' whispers one of them. He thinks the choppers will return with more troops and is scared.

'No, they have left,' replies another.

The men now believe it is safe to cut off their ties and check on their families.

Lying nearby is Mohammad Naim. There is blood all over his ripped clothes and his arm is bandaged. He is groggy but conscious enough to tell them about his encounter with the Australian dog.

Before the raid began he had been having tea at his house with Mullah Mohibullah, the imam of Shina's mosque. The imam had hurried home when the raid started, while Mohammad Naim had decided to stay inside the family compound. It would be safer there. He was planting tomatoes when the Australians arrived at his door. One of them was holding a dog on a leash.

One of the big soldiers spoke to him, but the Afghan could not understand his language. There was no interpreter with them. All Mohammad Naim could do was reply in Pashto that he could not understand.

Suddenly the dog lunged at him. It tore at his arm. Mohammad Naim couldn't believe the power of its jaws as it latched onto him, sending jolts of pain up his arm. He tried to fight it off. The dog let go, but then it snapped at his groin. It had gripped on to his testicles and was shaking its head from side to side, and he could feel it tearing him. It was excruciating. Mohammad Naim fainted.

He woke up near the other detainees, and one of the Australians with a painted face came over and started tending to his wounds. The Australian was not as big as the others and he had a reddish beard under the streaks of camouflage. He was gentle and thorough, and he injected him with a needle and cleaned Mohammad Naim's arm. But when the Australian noticed his groin and all the blood, he looked concerned. The Australian cut away his pants and shook his head. He spoke to another soldier, a big man with massive shoulders and a stern expression. Mohammad Naim did not know what they were saying, but it sounded to him like they were arguing.

Now, after the Australians have gone, he feels no pain. It is the morphine. But it will soon wear off. He is told by one of the villagers that the Australian who treated him wants him to go to the base of some other foreigners and get more treatment. But Mohammad Naim doesn't want anything to do with any foreigners.

To the other detainees, freed of their binds and no longer forced to stare at the wall, the damage from the SAS raid is immediately obvious. One of those who has been untied is wheat farmer Sakhi Dad who was knocked flying by the Australians while trying to get home from his field.

'They blew up three houses, two motorcycles of the villagers. They even shot dogs in the village,' he says. 'Around seven, eight, or ten dogs were shot. Of course, the dogs were barking, so they would shoot them. If they saw a donkey, they shot it.'

They are not the only things that have been shot.

'Your brother-in-law has been martyred,' one of the villagers tells Sakhi Dad.

He finds Jan Mohammad's body lying among a grove of silver-berry trees near an irrigation channel. The dead man was about 20 years old and engaged to be married.

'He wasn't able to work because his brain didn't work properly. His brother was mentally ill and so was he,' says Sakhi Dad. 'He was not able to do farming or work with the crops. He would do some irriga-tion and look after the cow or a lamb. That's all he did.'

Jan Mohammad was grazing a black cow from the village when the Australians came in their helicopters.

'When the cow heard the planes, it ran and he ran after it,' says Sakhi Dad. 'Soldiers came his way ... and saw him running. I don't know what they thought, that maybe he is a Talib and running away or a civilian that is running away. They shot him straight away in the head.'

The bullet takes the top of Jan Mohammad's head off. It sounds very similar to the way Ziauddin, the so-called 'village idiot', was killed.

Sakhi Dad and half a dozen villagers carry Jan Mohammad's body to the mosque to prepare it for burial.

Abdul Wali heads straight to the wheat field where his father was working when the Australians arrived. He discovers that his little brother Jalil was not the only witness to Abdul Walid's death. An elder, Mr Aminullah, also saw the killing and tells Abdul Wali what happened.

'[The Australians] called on my father and my father went towards them along with ... Mr Aminullah,' says Abdul Wali. 'They were together at the time when they went towards them ... and they shot [my father].'

Abdul Wali says his father was hit in the abdomen and neck. Mr Aminullah was not harmed.

The old man lies where he was shot, covered in a shawl. Little Jalil tells his older brother that one of the Afghan soldiers with the Australians put the shawl on him and turned him towards Qibla, the direction Muslims face when performing their prayers.

Abdul Wali picks up the old man's body. His hands quickly become slick with his father's blood as he carries him to the mosque.

In the village the old man's body is placed next to that of a third victim. It is Mullah Mohibullah, Shina's imam, who was having tea with Mohammad Naim when the raid began. His body is found among some trees.

'I looked at his face and saw that he was missing the top of his head. So I covered him,' says Abdul Wali.

Abdul Wali thinks it is a stab wound. But it is a catastrophic bullet wound that has blown out the top of the imam's head.

The people of Shina claim the SAS patrol has murdered three innocent civilians.

'These two [Jan Mohammad and Abdul Wahid] were not Taliban at all. One was an elderly person from the village and the other was mentally ill. The third was the imam of our mosque,' says Sakhi Dad. 'They killed innocent people.'

More than 200 people come from across the district to attend the funerals. The bodies are buried in the cemetery with the fluttering flags where Dusty Miller and his patrol paused on their way into Shina.

Years later the SAS raid still traumatises the people of Shina.

'We were scared,' says Sakhi Dad. 'If we heard [the sound of helicopters] we would hide in a cave out of fear. We thought they will beat, shoot and kill us again.'

A grieving Abdul Wali leaves Shina, swapping his farm for a plot of land in the mountains where he feels safer. He has returned to his home village to speak to my fixer about what happened on 16 May 2012. It is a reluctant visit.

'I hate this place, I don't like it here,' he says. 'I don't like this place, where my father walked and sat ... he was on his own land since childhood. He never stole or did badly to anyone. He was an elderly person. This is impossible to forgive, and I won't forgive it.'

Abdul Wali says he wants to avenge his father's death, no matter how long it takes. 'Among us Pashtun we say, "The older it gets, the stronger and fresher it becomes". It does not fade away.'

The story of Shina doesn't finish with the killings of Abdul Walid, Jan Mohammad and Mullah Mohibullah. Eight years after the raid I will discover that the same weapon – an old AK-47 with a rust mark near the trigger guard – was planted on two of the bodies. Dusty Miller has seen this Kalashnikov taken out on raids before.

'It had been used multiple fucking times,' he says. 'It did the rounds.'

Abdul Wali and Sakhi Dad are telling the truth. Their dead family members were unarmed civilians.

Shina is a study in the art of the throwdown. It is a study in how to get away with murder. Shina makes it clear that many in 3 Squadron SAS knew about these cover ups. They witnessed throwdowns being placed on the bodies of Afghan civilians and they kept quiet.

A former 3 Squadron SAS operator says those who planted weapons perpetuated a cycle of deviant behaviour, one that corrupted everyone around them by making them complicit in killings and cover ups.

'They're masters of manipulation. They're masters of fooling people. They're these chameleons who shape and influence. You put those people in an environment where violence is encouraged, and they just transition into psychopaths,' he says.

'They certainly were rogue. They did what they wanted when they wanted. They got away with murder,' says Christina.

The Special Forces multi-media specialist now knows that she catalogued images of innocent people whose bodies were photographed with throwdowns. It makes her feel sick.

'I feel like for a very long time I've been holding on to this enormous secret. It's been really eating away at me.'

She is not the only keeper of secrets.

———

'Mate, it's ridiculous,' says the operator.

'It is ridiculous,' says the patrol commander. 'If I thought it would make any difference, I'd say something to him.'

They are standing against the mud wall of a compound, next to a dry irrigation channel.

The metadata on the video says it was filmed on 17 May 2012. The day after the raid on Shina. It is one of the SAS helmet camera videos given to me by Braden Chapman. And what these men are about to discuss is astonishing. It is a litany of complaints about the behaviour of Soldier B. I know this because they use his name.

'His eyes rolled back like a shark,' says the patrol commander. 'He's a fucking idiot.'

Soldier B was on the operation at Shina. Are they talking about something that happened during the raid there?

'He was totally compliant,' says the patrol commander. He is talking about an Afghan.

'Mate, I was more worried about –'

'Getting shot,' chimes in the operator.

'Getting shot while he was swinging his weapon around,' says the patrol commander.

'I was on the other side from where the PUC was. Thought I was going to get shot,' says another operator standing nearby.

A PUC is a person under confinement, a detainee, a prisoner. A PUC has been shot by Soldier B. Was it one of the three men killed in the Shina raid?

Soldier B's SAS comrades are in shock. The veteran operator has been loose with his weapon, he is out of control. They think he could have killed any one of them while swinging his gun around.

'It's fucking bullshit. I'm not happy with it,' says the patrol commander. But he won't say or do anything about it because Soldier B is more senior, a vastly more experienced SAS operator.

On this deployment, Soldier B is in charge of handling prisoners in the field and getting them back to base.

It appears this one prisoner didn't make it back.

The operator spits. 'It's just do what I want, bash who I want, shoot at whoever,' he says.

'Yeah,' nods the patrol commander.

'Kill a kid, oh well, just keep shooting cunts.'

'Exactly.'

'Bash more cunts.'

'Shoot a kid,' adds the patrol commander. 'Shoot some fucking grandparents.'

I can't believe what I am hearing. They are talking amongst themselves about possible war crimes. They are talking about a comrade who has gone rogue.

'Execute someone in front of fuckin' –'

'Support staff,' says the patrol commander.

'Not even just support staff but other fuckin' –'

'Agencies.'

'Terps [interpreters] and that.'

'Went into the office yesterday, and one of the engineers went, "Yeah it happened – he just took him around the corner and fucking shot him",' says the patrol commander.

'You can't do it in front of anyone but a fuckin' operator,' says the operator.

'You can't do it in front of anyone. You don't do it front of anyone ... it's so wrong on so many levels,' says the patrol commander.

Dark clouds are forming on the horizon.

'When [Soldier B] was smacking out of nowhere, I thought he was going to shoot me by accident. Shoot through him,' he says.

Shoot through who, I wonder. The prisoner?

'It's just like, [he] was fucking like an animal.'

The operator snorts up through his nose and down his throat. He spits loudly towards the irrigation channel.

'We're definitely not trying to win the war anymore.'

The men fall silent. Thick, black, acrid-looking smoke billows from behind a mud wall. The patrol is burning something.

Hours later several SAS patrols are waiting on a grassy plain for the helicopters to pick them up. It has been a long day. The wind buffets them. One operator turns to another.

'Too much. Today is too much.'

10

THE WELL

'But who in war will not have his laugh amid the skulls'
Winston Churchill

The target is a senior insurgent leader codenamed Objective Oberon. Real name Nek Mohammad. He is an HVT: a High Value Target. Nek Mohammad is Taliban royalty, and always travels with heavily armed bodyguards. He has slipped the SAS's net before, but they have intelligence suggesting he is at a particular compound. They do not want to lose him again.

Tom pulls his kit together in the Ready Room:

M4 assault rifle and 10 magazines
9mm pistol and 3 magazines
Survival knife
Two grenades
Body armour
Webbing
Medical kit
Target map
Target list
2 litres of water
Plasticuffs
Radio and spare battery

Tom jumps on the scales to weigh himself. They all need to do this so the flight crews can calculate the total weight they will have on the Black Hawks. 125 kilograms. That means Tom is carrying 35 kilograms of gear.

It is June 2012, three-quarters of the way through 3 Squadron's deployment. By now, Tom and the other operators have dozens of missions under their belt and can be ready to roll in a matter of minutes.

Along with Tom, Soldier A will be in one of the lead choppers with his men. As a patrol commander and 'partner force handler' overseeing the Afghan Wakunish soldiers, he has also had a busy tour. Some of the guys still talk about how he took out the Taliban inside the mud igloo early in the deployment, after the Waka Rahul had been killed. They respect Soldier A's balls, and his willingness to put himself in the firing line and finish the job.

Medic Dusty Miller is on this job, but he will again be in the second wave with the Echo call sign, the engineers. They will mop up behind Tom and Soldier A's patrols which are tasked with the initial clearing of the compound.

At the entrance to the target compound Tom and Soldier A are met by the headman. Sometimes Afghans will invite the Australians in and offer them tea. Not today. The headman is physically blocking their way, he is berating them. He won't let the SAS patrol in. He doesn't care how heavily armed they are.

'*Aram sa, aram sa,*' Tom tells him. Calm down, calm down.

But the headman is not budging. He is yelling at them.

This is strange, thinks Tom.

'There is something going on here. This isn't right,' Tom says to Soldier A.

He tells Tom to restrain the headman. Tom pulls the plasticuffs out of his pack and zips the man's hands together behind his back and sits him down by the entrance. The headman is enraged, and his yelling is getting louder. They leave him hollering by the door and enter the compound.

Inside Tom sees a group of women sitting in a huddle at the other end of the compound. He clears the rooms around its edges and finds nothing. Other than the women there is a tethered cow, a goat and some chickens. No Nek Mohammad, no weapons, just a huddle of women who don't take their eye off the Australians as they move about the compound.

'All clear,' Tom tells Soldier A. The patrol leaves the compound and moves off down the ravine towards a grove of almond and fruit trees.

A while later Dusty Miller and the engineers are sent into the compound to do a check. They are mopping up after the chicken stranglers, as some of the engineers call the SAS operators behind their backs. They don't dare say it to their faces. Sometimes the SAS patrols miss things. Sometimes they are under time pressure and can't clear everything properly. It is a quick sweep and move on. It is up to the engineers to do a more forensic search.

The women are still sitting in a huddle. One of the engineers lets his dog off the leash to have a sniff about. Another engineer spots a well with a metal lid over it near the women. An older woman is sitting on the lid.

The engineer leans his assault rifle against the compound wall and walks over to the woman on the lid.

'Fuck off,' he says, waving his arms in a shooing motion.

The younger women nearby know what he wants even though they don't understand his strange language. They move away, hurrying into the rooms that make up the perimeter of the compound. But the old woman on the lid won't budge.

'Fucking move, move, move!' says the engineer. He is standing over the old woman. A Wakunish soldier has joined him in front of the well and is training his weapon at the lid.

Finally, the woman gets up and joins the others who have retreated to the rooms. The engineer walks around to the other side of the well, stops and kicks off the lid.

Suddenly a hand holding an AK-47 assault rifle thrusts out of the well and there is a burst of fire in the direction of the Waka. The Waka flies backwards. He has been hit square in the stomach at almost point-blank range by the burst. He lands on his back in the dirt and is still.

Holy fuck, thinks Dusty. There is some bastard inside the well.

Dusty and the engineers dash for cover behind a wall and begin firing at the hand. This is one of these times that Dusty is a soldier first, a medic second. But his instinct is to get to the Waka. Is he alive or is he dead? Surely, he can't have survived a round from point-blank range. But if he's wounded, I can help him, thinks Dusty. But I need to get to him fast.

'Kill these fuckers!'

It is the engineer who kicked the lid off the well. He has retrieved his M4 and is firing at the hand as he runs for cover. Another engineer is on his knees in front of Dusty letting off bursts at the well. The medic, too, is firing. Dirt and pieces of mud wall – flicked up and dislodged by the AK rounds – are showering Dusty and the engineer.

The hand keeps popping up and shooting blindly.

His magazine empty, and the fire from the well stopped for a second, Dusty sees his chance. He starts crawling towards the Waka.

In front of him the hand holding the AK-47 pops out again. The hand is twisting and turning, sending bullets in an arc across the compound. Dusty is on his stomach in the dirt, like a goanna, slither-ing towards the Waka. He thinks it is only a matter of seconds before he is hit. Dusty gets to the Afghan and grabs him by his body armour and starts pulling.

This bastard is heavier than he looks, thinks Dusty.

Bullets flying, adrenalin pumping, Dusty drags him behind a wall. It is an impressive feat. The Waka is much bigger than the Australian, but the lean medic is renowned for his pound-for-pound strength.

Sheltering from the gunfire behind the wall, Dusty perches over the Waka. The stocky Afghan is looking up at him, blinking.

Fuck, at least he's not dead.

Dusty begins a primary survey of his torso – crotch to ankle, armpit to wrist. I can't see any blood, Dusty thinks. The Waka is wincing and reaching down to his stomach. Dusty rips off the Afghan's body armour and lifts up his shirt. There is a massive red bruise near his navel. Then Dusty realises. The AK-47 round has hit the bottom part of the plate of the Waka's body armour, but only just. A couple of centimetres lower and it would have pierced his lower abdomen. The big Waka will be fine.

Down in the ravine, Tom and Soldier A's patrol hear the first burst.

'Is that an M4?' asks someone.

'Mate, that's an AK,' says Tom. 'It's coming from that fucking compound.'

The patrol sprints back up towards the ravine. They can hear more bursts of AK-47 fire as they reach the entrance to the compound. Tom looks inside and sees a hand sticking out of the well. It is holding the AK-47 and spraying it everywhere. There is someone inside the well.

Tom can see Dusty hunched over a Waka behind a small mud wall. The Afghan must have been hit, he thinks.

Tom takes aim and starts firing at the hand. It is precise suppressing fire – one shot per second. Soldier A runs over and tells Tom to keep it up. He then sprints towards the well as bullets fly past him. Soldier A reaches it and drops in a grenade. Everyone is in awe of his courage.

'[Soldier A] controlled that entire contact, that close quarter battle,' says Tom. 'He was amazing that day.'

Having tossed his grenade down the well, Soldier A pulls back, firing as he retreats. He takes cover. There is an explosion, but then the hand and the AK pop out and begin firing once again.

What the fuck?

Tom dashes in and drops down another grenade and retreats. But the hand keeps coming out.

The soldiers reckon there must be some sort of tunnel network connected to the well shaft, offering the hand a refuge from the grenades which must be falling all the way to the bottom of the well. They wonder if it is the same hand, or if there is more than one fighter hiding down there.

The engineer behind the wall throws a grenade. It misses the well, rolling past it and stopping next to a terrified cow tied up behind it. It explodes and tears the poor animal to pieces.

Soldier A decides to drop a thermobaric grenade down the well. He hopes that just like the battle at the mud igloo, a thermo will finish things once and for all. A 'thermo' uses oxygen from the surrounding air to generate a high-temperature explosion and a massive blast wave that can rupture the internal organs of people even on the fringe of the blast.

'That was his choice of weapon,' says Tom.

Soldier A asks for more suppressing fire as he prepares to once again make the dash.

'Mate, fucking get back! It's not worth it! Get the fuck back!' screams his 2-I-C. He thinks Soldier A is pushing his luck by making another charge.

But Soldier A takes no notice. Rather than take the direct route to the well, he skirts around the perimeter of the compound, getting as close as he dares to the well before tossing the thermo down the hole.

The blast sends dust, dirt and something else out of the well. That something else turns out to be bits of flesh and bone. The engineer who killed the cow sees what looks like a knee land on the ground nearby. Tom sees the knee too, and a hand and what he thinks is a heel.

Tom hears moaning from inside the well.

This is gruesome, he thinks. When are these guys going to die?

Tom and Soldier A approach the well and they pour more gunfire into it. Then they decide to regroup. They believe there are at least three men inside the well, and that one is still alive, possibly in a tunnel running off the well.

They have one last weapon left in their arsenal. An airstrike. A US Apache gunship helicopter is called in and the SAS patrols pull out of the compound and up a hill next to it. It is the perfect vantage point for the spectacular show they are about to see.

They can hear the beating of the Apache's blades getting louder. Below them, tied up on the outside of the damaged compound, is another cow. No one has thought to untie it before the Hellfire missile hits. Too late now.

Dirt and dust shoot up silently from inside the compound and the wall is torn apart. A split second later the sound of the blast reaches Tom and Dusty and the other SAS soldiers up the hill. The thunderous wave of noise rolls down the valley. The cow panics but can't break its tether. But other than the deafening blast it is unharmed.

'Not a bad shot,' says someone.

Dust billows from the compound and is picked up by the wind and swept down the valley. The Apache peels away. The Australians go back inside to see what is left of the well.

Braden Chapman, the Bear, is also there.

'I remember they looked down there after the Hellfire hit it and it looked like there was a big tunnel system down there,' says Braden.

The battle of the well has shown the SAS at its best. Acts of valour and selflessness, displays of true grit and teamwork. The firefight has also demonstrated that their enemy is prepared to fight to the death.

'Even though they're our so-called enemy, I take my hat off to them with regards to their tenacity to never give up and to continue fighting right to the very end,' says Tom. 'It was quite remarkable, respectable.'

The SAS has fulfilled the mission and killed their target. Biometric testing will later reveal that Nek Mohammad, aka Objective Oberon, was down the well. The two other fighters were his bodyguards.

'They must have seen us landing,' says one of the engineers. The Taliban commander and his bodyguards were well hidden by the time the first SAS patrol entered the compound.

Under bursts of fire, Soldier A and Tom risked their lives to get grenades down the well.

'Tom should have got a pat on the back for that,' says Dusty. 'He's no coward.'

Neither is the combat medic. He crawled under fire to pull a wounded Afghan comrade to safety. Like Tom, Dusty doesn't get a pat on the back either. But he does make a friend for life.

After the air strike, Dusty takes another look at the Waka's stomach. The bruise above his navel is the size of a grapefruit and is slowly deepening from scarlet to purple.

'You're a lucky man,' says Dusty.

'Thanks to Allah,' says the Waka.

'No, mate, thank ADI, because that's what saved you,' says Dusty, referring to the company that manufactured the body armour. 'Point-blank range. You don't normally walk that off.'

Even though he has probably saved a life, Dusty feels a rising anger and a moral confusion. He has just gone through a near-death experience.

Inside the compound he crouches down and picks something off the ground. Medically trained, Dusty recognises it as part of a human tibia, a piece of shinbone. A large piece of torn calf muscle is still attached to it.

'Hey, Dusty, stick it in a bag and put it in your pouch,' says one of the operators with a grin.

It is a joke, but the medic's blood is up. Dusty pulls out a knife, cuts the flesh and muscle off the bone and puts the piece of tibia in a plastic bag and puts it in his pouch. He wants to give it to the intelligence officers back at base. These are the guys who sit in the safety of their offices assigning the Taliban targets and expecting the SAS patrols to capture or kill them. The geeks, as Dusty calls them. They have done this before with bloodstained ICOMs taken off the bodies of dead insurgents. The patrols have brought them back and dropped them on the decks of the geeks.

'It was their macabre way of saying, "This is the fruits of your labours, guys. Congratulations",' says Dusty.

After they land back in Tarin Kowt, one of the patrol commanders turns to Dusty.

'You got that bag?'

Dusty digs it out of his pouch and gives it to him.

'I know for a fact he placed it on their desk,' says Dusty.

None of the geeks dared say anything about this gruesome gift.

'It's barbaric and it's just not normal,' Dusty tells me years later. 'But at the time, it was completely normal to me. It was a joke and it's not a joke. That's a fucking human being, regardless of who they were.'

It is another thing to add to the list of incidents that haunt Dusty Miller.

'Everyone had become desensitised,' says Tom.

Dusty later comes to understand that by taking the tibia he has contravened the laws of war.

'You just got caught up in this bullshit, this moral shift comes into play,' he says. 'I'm not proud of it.'

War, by its very definition, is death, destruction and injury. That is the physical consequence. But there is another consequence of the trauma inflicted by war, one that ethicists call moral injury.

'What I think of as moral injury is where that experience is so overwhelming that we just can't get beyond or can't function because of that sense of guilt or shame,' says Deane Baker, a military ethicist who specialises in moral injury. 'That makes you sort of dysfunctional as a human being.'

Moral injury is not a diagnosed condition. As a concept it is still being researched and understood.

'It's still very much being thrashed out,' says Baker. 'It's an interesting one because it's being approached from different disciplinary angles. A lot of the work has been done by psychologists, but philosophers also think of this as something that they have something to say about.'

Afghanistan is the perfect war for moral injury. It is a 21st century conflict, awash with ambiguity, fought by a shape-shifting enemy, and defined, ultimately, by a sense of pointlessness. It is a war without battle lines, a conflict without an end.

'I think what moral injury is, it is a situation or situations that confront us to such a degree that [our moral values] get damaged in some kind of way,' says Deane Baker.

Like with Dusty and the tibia.

Moral injury can infuse people with a sense of betrayal. It can cause them to lose trust. It can make them aggressive. Put simply, moral injury is a wound to the soul.

Moral injury is Dusty Miller watching as Haji Sardar, his wounded patient, is carried away. It is Dusty feeling powerless to intervene. It is Tom watching the 'village idiot's' head explode, and then being forced to be part of the cover up. Moral injury is Braden Chapman being warned by Soldier B that he will need to get used to him putting a gun to people's heads and pulling the trigger. It is Braden replying that he is 'good to go'. It is Christina being ordered to delete photographs, even though she knows it is wrong. It is Soldier B's hand on her shoulder, pushing her down in her chair.

'Moral injury is damage to a person's moral framework, to their basic conception of what's right and wrong,' says Captain Roger Herbert.

Herbert is a former member of the United States Navy's elite SEAL team who led missions during the 1989 invasion of Panama. The six week military conquest was launched to overthrow the Panamanian general turned dictator Manuel Noriega who was wanted by the

US for drug trafficking and racketeering. Herbert is now a professor of Ethics at the United States Naval Academy where recruits are educated and commissioned into the Navy and Marine Corps.

'If a soldier perpetrates an act that transgresses a deeply held moral value – is forced to kill a child soldier, for example – then the act of taking that child's life is the trauma that results in moral injury,' he says. 'But it's not necessary for the soldier to perpetrate the act. Witnessing such an act can also be morally traumatic or even fighting well and honourably in a war that seems unjust.'

The Taliban's repeated violations of international law made a difficult war even harder to fight. It presented Coalition troops with a complex series of moral dilemmas and questions that often had to be solved and answered in a split second. The most fundamental of which is, who is a combatant and who is not.

'Insurgents deliberately seek to degrade the capacity of counter-insurgents to distinguish between combatants and non-combatants,' says Herbert. 'But while it's illegal and immoral, blurring the line between soldier and civilian is an effective guerrilla strategy. If counter-insurgents can't reliably make this distinction, then over the course of a protracted campaign they, inevitably, will make mistakes and harm non-combatants. When this happens, insurgents are ready to leverage the wrongful killing or destruction for propaganda value.'

As the war in Afghanistan ground on, doubts about its strategic aims and its success or failure grew louder. These doubts were most pronounced among those on the ground doing the killing.

'There's been that question of, "Why are we really here? Are we really helping? Is this really about the defence of our nation?"' says Deane Baker. 'And when you start to see people's lives shattered because of a war that you're involved in, and you're not entirely convinced, or you don't have a good account of why this is important and worthwhile, I think that's a real potential source of moral injury.'

Most Australian Special Forces soldiers did multiple tours to Afghanistan. Their exposure to moral trauma was amplified by deployment after deployment, and by the counterinsurgency campaign they were prosecuting.

'We've never really had a war quite like Afghanistan where we've sent people back and back and back,' says Deane Baker. 'Essentially, we've asked a very small number of people to engage in probably more combat than any Australian ever. Perhaps somebody needed to stop and think, "Hey, what impact is this having on them? Have we overstretched them? Have we really asked too much of them?"'

11

THE CASE OF
ALEXANDER BLACKMAN

'For in that sleep of death, what dreams may come,
When we have shuffled off this mortal coil'
Hamlet, **William Shakespeare**

'Why couldn't you just be fucking dead?'

The British Royal Marines are standing over the wounded Taliban fighter. To them, he is beyond help. The Afghan, who is lying face down, has a sucking chest wound. He whimpers.

'Stop fucking whingeing,' says one of the Marines.

The fighter is part of a group of Taliban that has just attacked a remote British command post named 'Talaanda'. An Apache helicopter gunship has fired 139 rounds at the insurgent. A few have hit him. The Afghan is a bloodied mess.

The Marine patrol that has gone to find the man cannot believe he is still alive.

The patrol commander, Sergeant Alexander Blackman, suggests they move the insurgent out of sight of the helicopter that is hovering over the field. They pick him up and drop him several times before dragging him to the side of the field.

'Anybody want to do first aid on this idiot?' asks one.

'No,' they say in unison.

'I'll put one in his head if you want,' says another.

'No, not in his head, 'cause that'll be fucking obvious,' says Blackman.

The patrol commander looms over the wounded Taliban fighter. The man just won't die. They roll him over onto his back. His face and body are covered with dry grass and his eyes are open. He is breathing.

Blackman asks where the helicopter is, and he is told that it has gone. The patrol commander crouches down. He has a nine-millimetre pistol in his hand. He places the barrel of the pistol against the wounded man's chest and squeezes the trigger.

The insurgent's upper body and arms begin to writhe, his head shakes. His breaths become shorter and more laboured.

'There you are, shuffle off this mortal coil, you cunt,' says Blackman. 'It's nothing you wouldn't do to us.'

'I know,' says a Marine standing nearby.

'Obviously this doesn't go anywhere fellas. I just broke the Geneva Convention,' says Blackman to his comrades.

'Yeah, roger, mate.'

Blackman hops on the radio.

'Fully dead now,' he says.

The camera is switched off.

The patrol is in a field in Helmand Province. It is 15 September 2011, and this killing has been caught on the helmet camera of one of Blackman's fellow Marines.

The footage is later discovered by the Military Police during an unrelated investigation. They find six clips that reveal in unstinting detail what happened to the Taliban insurgent.

In November 2013 Alexander Blackman is convicted of murder and sentenced to life with a minimum term of 10 years. He is dishonourably discharged from the Royal Marines.

Less than four years later his conviction will be quashed, and Blackman will be a free man. How did he get away with murder?

At the time of the killing in 2011, Sergeant Alexander Blackman is on his fifth combat tour. The Royal Marine Commando has been to Iraq three times, including for the 2003 invasion. His first tour of Afghanistan was back in 2007.

He is a battle-hardened 13-year veteran of the Marines. His service is regarded as 'exemplary' and for this deployment he has been appointed as troop sergeant. The senior non-commissioned officer, the troop sergeant is typically the most experienced soldier in the troop. Blackman is put in charge of Marines deployed to Command Post Omar, an isolated base in Helmand Province.

Lying to the west of Kandahar and Uruzgan, Helmand is the main area of operations for British forces in Afghanistan. The British haven't seen fighting like this since the Korean War in the early 1950s.

Helmand is a snake pit of Taliban. It is their centre of opium production, meaning it is vital to funding their insurgency. Here, the Taliban don't just kill. They are known to brutalise, behead and string up the limbs of their victims.

More than 450 British service personnel will die in the Afghanistan war, the vast majority in Helmand. One of them is Blackman's troop commander, killed three months before the wounded Taliban fighter is finished off by Blackman in the field.

When Alexander Blackman is convicted of murder at his trial in 2013 there is a public outcry. His supporters include the journalist turned spy turned novelist Frederick Forsyth, the author of internationally bestselling thrillers like *The Day of the Jackal* and *The Dogs of War*.

Forsyth and Blackman's other supporters do not claim the former Royal Marine is innocent of killing the badly wounded Taliban insurgent. Of course he killed the man. Forsyth writes that Blackman 'snapped for a few seconds'. He says men like the Royal Marine Commando deserve allegiance, not to be hung out to dry by the brass.

'If you ask your men to go into hell, you ask them to give you their unswerving loyalty. When they come back out, those that do, you give them your unswerving loyalty in return.'

In 2016, based on new information from Alexander Blackman's family and a new defence lawyer, the Criminal Cases Review Commission is asked to consider the strength of Blackman's conviction. It concludes it should be reviewed as potentially unsafe. It accepts evidence that at the time of the killing Blackman was suffering from an 'adjustment disorder'.

'It's a bonafide psychiatric diagnosis,' says Professor Neil Greenberg.

Greenberg is a forensic psychiatrist. He also served in the British Armed Forces for 23 years and just like Alexander Blackman he has earned the coveted Green Beret of the Royal Marine Commandos. He has also deployed as a psychiatrist and researcher to Iraq and Afghanistan.

He says adjustment disorder is an exaggerated reaction to one or more significant life events, one that can move from being a reaction to a mental health disorder that manifests itself in depression, anxiety, and an inability to cope.

'It can lead you to becoming impulsive when you're not normally. It can lead you to being aggressive when you're not normally,' says Greenberg. 'You think more negatively, or you think more angrily. So you might feel emotionally tearful or you might feel very sad. You might not go out very much, you might drink more alcohol, you might take more risks.'

Greenberg says a person with an adjustment disorder can plan and act with apparent rationality. That could explain why Blackman wants to drag the wounded Taliban fighter out of sight of the helicopter, and why he doesn't want to shoot the Afghan in the head. He wants to shoot him in the chest where the man is already badly wounded. It will hide the crime.

In 2017 the Supreme Court reviews Blackman's conviction. Neil Greenberg has met with Blackman and reviewed the Marine Commando's notes and military record. He gives evidence about Blackman's mental state at the time of the killing. The court describes Greenberg as a very impressive witness.

'Clearly he's done something which is terribly wrong. There's no two ways about it,' says Greenberg. 'The question ... for the court is, what was his intention at the time he shot the injured insurgent? Was he intending to kill him? Or did he think that he was dead, and he was desecrating a body?'

The court quashes Blackman's sentence. It decides to swap Blackman's murder conviction with one of 'manslaughter by reason of diminished responsibility' and he is re-sentenced to a 'determinate' period of seven years. Under this determinate sentence he is eligible for release halfway through the term. A month later Alexander Blackman walks free from prison.

The court also orders that the 'dishonourable' aspect of Blackman's discharge from the Royal Marines be substituted with 'honourable'.

So how did the court come to such a dramatic decision?

It accepts the evidence of three psychiatrists, including Neil Greenberg, who say that at the time of the killing Blackman was suffering from an 'adjustment disorder of moderate severity' that was capable of substantially impairing his ability to exercise self-control.

The Supreme Court finds that his decision to squeeze the trigger was 'probably impulsive' and he was impaired in his 'ability to form a rational judgement about the need to adhere to the standards and the moral compass as set by [Her Majesty's] Armed Forces'.

In other words, Alexander Blackman is so stressed and damaged by war and by what he has experienced his judgement is diminished to the point that he is broken. He may be a highly trained and experienced Commando, but he has gone past his breaking point.

'There isn't any such thing as a Rambo-type, Arnold Schwarzenegger soldier who can face all sorts of stressors and appear to be invulnerable,' Greenberg tells the court. 'That sort of person only exists in the cinema.'

Writing with his usual flourish in the British press, Blackman supporter Frederick Forsyth spells out what the Royal Marine and his J Company comrades had to endure in Afghanistan.

'J Company was undermanned, posted to a hellhole mud-brick compound with no roof or shelter in what has been described as "the most dangerous square mile on earth" … they saw severed limbs of dead mates hung from the trees to taunt them, found the flayed-alive body of a soldier taken alive by the Taliban, carried their colleagues with severed legs to the "CASEVAC" [air evacuation] helicopters, some alive, some dead.'

Blackman was beset with his own personal struggles. The court is told that his father died just before he flew out for his second tour of Afghanistan. When his troop commander is killed in March 2011, it leaves Blackman in charge of the isolated command post. CP Omar is undermanned. Blackman is deprived of sleep. He is almost killed in a grenade attack a month before the killing. There is an IED explosion on average every 16 hours.

'As a Marine, you get on with it because that's your job,' says Greenberg. 'Then, of course, people started dying, which happens on operations. And slowly he changed from being a kind of tolerant, firm leader to someone who was more irritable. To someone who started to believe that he was particularly being targeted.'

The court concludes that the patrol commander had developed a hatred for the Taliban, one fuelled by the desire for vengeance.

Blackman's unit has to patrol between five and ten hours a day over rough ground in heat of 50-plus degrees Celsius carrying at least 45 kilograms of gear. Blackman refuses to let some of his corporals go out on patrol.

'He took it on himself because he didn't have any children and they did,' says Greenberg.

The Royal Marine Sergeant starts to act strangely. A comrade describes him as 'a husk of his former self'. Blackman's wife says that during leave to scatter his father's ashes in the UK, Blackman is always looking at the ground. She asks him why. He explains that he has to always be on alert for IEDs, just like in Afghanistan.

To his supporters, Alexander Blackman is both an exponent of violence and a victim of it. War defines him, then it breaks him.

Professor Neil Greenberg says that '20 to 25 per cent of combat troops deployed to Iraq and Afghanistan at some point suffered from a mental health difficulty'. He says that in 2012 and 2013 about a third of those diagnosed with a mental health difficulty were suffering from adjustment disorders.

Even highly trained Special Forces troops have their breaking point.

'There is nobody who is impervious to suffering with mental health difficulties,' he says. '[Special forces soldiers] love their kids and they go out and enjoy windsurfing or whatever they do. They are normal people who have a certain amount of determination and resilience and zeal and also physically are able to cope with the very arduous challenges of selection to join the Special Forces. They are not robots or automatons.'

So does that mean that Australian Special Forces soldiers could have been suffering from adjustment disorders too? Could this be a reason for some of the unlawful killings and unjustified violence? Could we see Australian Special Forces soldiers charged with war crimes invoking adjustment disorders as part of their defence?

The Brereton Report will conclude in 2020 that 'it can be anticipated that, in the light of the frequency of deployments, and conditions not dissimilar to those relied on in *Blackman*, mental health defences including adjustment disorder will be invoked'.

'Any legal defence that doesn't take the adjustment disorder avenue is giving up a free pass,' says one former Special Forces officer. 'In light of the huge questions around our own chain of command, culture, higher accountability and fumbled strategy, it will be a turkey shoot for the various defence teams to bring in senior ADF commanders and paint a picture that their client was immersed in a sustained *Apocalypse Now* environment which contributed to significant adjustment disorder pressures.'

Neil Greenberg has watched the *Four Corners* program 'Killing Field'. He has heard Soldier C ask three times, 'Do you want me to drop this cunt?' He has seen Soldier C put three bullets into the cowering figure of Dad Mohammad in the wheat field.

Greenberg can't and won't comment on the mental health of any of the SAS soldiers in that patrol. How can he? He hasn't met them. He doesn't know them. But there is one aspect of this killing he will go on record about.

'Soldiers work together in teams,' he says. 'What's the rest of the team doing? What's his sergeant doing? What conversations have gone on? Like, "Hey, mate, what's up? Why are you behaving like this?" Where is the leadership? Soldiers don't operate by themselves.'

But as a former Commando, Neil Greenberg also understands the stresses of the battlefield, the split-second decisions that soldiers must make, and the life-altering and legal consequences of those decisions.

'The consequences of making the wrong decision could be the loss of life for you or your colleagues and the consequence of making the wrong decision another way could be that you've committed a war crime.'

It can be a fine line.

12

STIRRERS

'Recruits tended to be unusual to the point of eccentricity,
people who did not slot easily into the ranks of the regular army,
misfits and reprobates with an instinct for covert war and little
time for convention, part soldiers and part spies, rogue warriors'
Ben Macintyre, *SAS: Rogue Heroes*

The operator is on his haunches, struggling to get his balance. One false move and he will give the game away. Next to him the two strippers are demonstrating much better poise and dexterity on the Twister mat. They are bent over, heads down, rears in the air, hands flat on the blue and yellow dots. All three of them are stark naked. Surrounding the twisting trio are SAS operators, regimental support staff and their guests, stubbies and cans in hand, cheering them on.

The music is blaring, and the booze is flowing. One SAS support staffer wearing Australian flag boardshorts is lying flat on his stomach on the carpet of The Gratto. He wants a better view of what the strippers have on show. Above him, stuck to the wall of the bar, is a road sign to Baghdad, liberated by the SAS during the 2003 Iraq War.

'It was like a footy club on steroids,' says SAS medic Dusty Miller.

It is a very fitting comparison. One senior officer likens the SAS to that other Perth institution, the West Coast Eagles AFL team of 2006–2007, regarded by many as the league's champion outfit when it comes to illicit drug use.

'The culture is high performance, high party, drugs. It's no coincidence that the Eagles and the SAS hung together in Perth and were all mates.'

In 2015, Brownlow medallist and former Eagles star Ben Cousins breaks into Campbell Barracks, some say to obtain drugs. The SAS barracks is an old hangout of Cousins', though since his much-publicised drug-fuelled fall from grace, the operators have been giving him a wide berth.

The befuddled Cousins is apprehended after a comical 'low-speed' pursuit through the barracks' streets.

Back on the Twister mat the blonde stripper is now gripping a leg each of the SAS operator and the brunette stripper, both of whom are leaning backwards supported by their arms and other leg. It is a precarious position. Everything is on display, and the SAS operator has a fair few rum and cokes onboard and is starting to wobble. The blonde stripper totters and grabs the other leg of the operator, who topples backwards off the mat and knocks over his can of rum and coke onto the carpet. Game over. Everyone in the circle around them is laughing and cheering. The strippers sit on the floor and give each other high fives. Who dares wins. Their naked opponent laughs, grabs his can and strides off to join his mates. Stirrers 2012 is in full swing.

Run by the ranks, the annual Stirrers Parade celebrates the birth of the SAS. It is part piss-up, part piss-take and has been a fixture of the regimental social calendar for decades. All the SAS squadrons come together at Stirrers in a rare gathering of the Regiment.

'That time of year is upon us again and as always Stirrers will no doubt remind everyone of the good, the bad and the ugly throughout the year,' reads one email invitation to the members of the Regiment.

Christina is among the crowd. She is back from her tour of Afghanistan, a deployment that has troubled her. Christina is still haunted by that hand on her shoulder holding her down, by Soldier B telling her to go through the photos from the Sarkhume raid and to delete that one, and that one. Photos that could implicate him in the killing of Haji Sardar. But with a tap of Christina's finger on the mouse they are gone.

Christina takes another swig of her drink. Stirrers is an opportunity to blow out some cobwebs and forget all the shit. But even
Stirrers is part of the Regiment's warped culture, and for Christina this
year's event will come back to gnaw at her.

Like everything involving the alpha males of the SAS, Stirrers is
competitive and often combative. Rugby games are contested. Costumes
are donned. Skits are performed. Members are mocked. Even training
mishaps are the subject of black humoured sketches. One year they even
sent up an accident which left an SAS soldier a paraplegic. The guy was
sitting in the audience.

'The skit was the norm to make light of mates and anything that
happened,' says a former operator. 'In the mid-80s a trooper was
arrested and put into Fremantle Prison. He committed suicide by
suffocation, wrapping Glad Wrap around his head. This was played
out on the parade. His close mates didn't see the funny side.'

One of the funnier Stirrers skits was when one of the SAS operators, Alex, mocked up a news bulletin. Dixie Marshall, the popular
presenter of Perth's Channel Nine News, was even part of the gag and
the network let Alex film the whole thing in their studio. In Perth, the
SAS are gods.

'Good morning, and welcome everybody to this special news
bulletin,' begins Marshall, clearly enjoying the joke. 'Since the overdose
of a Commando soldier in Afghanistan this year, popular opinion is
emerging within the Australian Defence Force confirming that the
Commandos really are a bunch of dickheads.'

Trying to remain poker faced, she continues her introduction
down the barrel of the studio camera.

'Many soldiers' opinions of the Commandos vary from being very,
kind of, knobbish to fully-fledged cocksuckers of the ocean-going
variety,' Marshall reports.

Her co-anchor is Alex, the SAS operator who has also written the
skit for the Stirrers Parade.

The sketch has the men of the Regiment watching in the SAS hangar pealing with laughter. The 'news report' includes vox pops of people on the street, including several homeless men, who are asked their opinion of the Commandos. Or as newsreader Dixie Marshall calls them, 'these pack of tools from Sydney'.

Dickheads, rubbish, disgusting, are the nicer responses from people who are clearly in on the joke.

Pack of wankers, answers one young boy.

It is very much a light-hearted dig at the SAS's Special Forces rivals. The Commandos are an easy and obvious target for regimental ribbing. But sometimes the humour at Stirrers turns dark and inwards. Sometimes the annual event is used to settle scores, and to dispatch internal enemies. And it is done very publicly, Caesar-like.

The year after Alex's news bulletin skit, revenge is delivered swiftly and without mercy. The crosshairs come to rest on a junior SAS officer, a diligent young major who failed to adhere to the code of the so-called 'NCO Mafia'. This cadre of non-commissioned officers regards most of the junior officers, like the young major, as blow-ins who spend a few years in the SAS before posting out to chase promotions elsewhere.

'[He] was by far one of the best officers the Regiment had ever had,' says 3 Squadron operator Tom of the young major. 'He was highly intelligent, highly capable.'

The NCO Mafia is run by the sergeants, the senior non-commissioned officers. Some believe this mafia has managed to hijack the proud culture of the SAS, that they have become the Regiment's centre of power. Battle-hardened, revered and decorated, the sergeants have much more experience and respect from the men than do the junior officers who are supposed to run the show.

'The sergeants are there forever. The captains, the officers, are there for three years,' says one SAS operator. 'Sergeants have massive street cred, massive experience, whereas the officers just go, "I'm here to lead and manage. I'm here to make sure that the training is organised, and the ammunition is allocated, and the ranges are booked"... the guys on the trigger – the sergeants – they're leading the guys on the ground. They've got all the warfighting experience.'

The major in the crosshairs of the sergeants knows how powerful the NCO Mafia is. One day in the officers' mess he sits down at lunch with four 'greenhorns', young officers from infantry and cavalry units trying to make selection in the SAS. One of them is future Liberal MP, Andrew Hastie.

'Guys, you're expendable. Just remember that,' he tells them.

His words will prove prophetic. The major will soon see just how expendable junior officers like him are. This year, the war fighters in the NCO Mafia have him firmly in their sights. They will not miss their mark.

In the hundreds-strong Stirrers audience are some serious brass, including generals and a former head of Special Operations Command. The squadrons are doing their best to out-skit each other. Everyone is having a laugh, even if some of the 'humour' is as dark as the Afghan night and just as lethal.

The sergeants take to the stage and call up the major. They had all served in Afghanistan together that year, and the sergeants were not impressed. The major is regarded by most in the Regiment as smart, competent, but a little picky. He is prepared to sacrifice populism for professionalism. But to the sergeants he is a pompous upstart, a troublemaker. To them, his greatest sin has been to try to hold them to account during their Afghanistan deployment.

'He was calling out these patrols,' says a former senior Special Forces officer. 'He was pushing back on the sergeants. He was complaining to his SOTG [Special Operations Task Group] commander and back to Australia and all of that.'

The major reports the heavy drinking at The Fat Ladies Arms too.

The sergeants are outraged, and they fight back. They complain about the major behind his back to the chain of command.

'In the theatre this involved coming up with false accusations about [the major's] performance,' says the former officer. 'That's undermining an operational commander in war. In an American sense, that's go to jail for years sort of stuff.'

Stirrers is an opportunity for the sergeants to finish him off once and for all, to 'decapitate him', according to the former officer.

Up on stage in front of hundreds, the sergeants hand the major the 'Cock of the Year' award. An annual award handed out at Stirrers, it is a prize designed to mock, to denigrate, and in this case, downright humiliate. It works. As the crowd, including the senior brass, applaud and laugh, the major slinks off stage.

'You've got sergeants who basically completely destroy a standing [junior officer],' says the former senior Special Forces officer. 'To look out over a sea of faces and see the entire unit, including the bulk of the chain of command of Special Operations are there and laughing hilariously at your expense. Where is your standing as a leader out of that?'

The major's reputation and self-esteem are in tatters. The sergeants are jubilant, and their power is reinforced. It has been driven home in the most public of ways. Other junior officers in the crowd have got the message too. Take on the NCO Mafia and you can expect the same humiliation. The brass will not back you against the sergeants – they will join the laughter.

'It killed him. It broke his trust,' says Andrew Hastie, an SAS captain at the time who was mentored by the major. 'Then [to have] the officers who you expect to back you up, not support you. I mean they say politics is bruising. But I always say warrior politics is the fiercest politics of all. He had the most humiliating thing done to him of all.'

The decapitation of the major was not spontaneous, and it was not unauthorised. It was thoroughly planned and executed with the approval of those above him.

'[They] basically wanted him out,' says the former officer. 'And basically, [the sergeants] knew they had top cover to do what they did.'

The year after being awarded Cock of the Year the major resigns from the SAS. He hasn't just been decapitated, his head has been stuck on a pike, for all to see. The NCO Mafia are untouchable. They remain the true power of the Regiment.

'That was an extremely vicious ... way for NCOs to twist the knife that they put in someone's back. It was appalling,' says Tom. 'You're losing these brilliant soldiers, these brilliant minds with years of experience, all because of some sergeant who's got an axe to grind to get back at someone who's pissed them off.'

'I think the symbolism of the Cock of the Year is that [the NCOs] weren't even accountable to their chain of command,' says Andrew Hastie. 'Good order, discipline and all the rest of it, is what makes military units work. You've effectively got the Diggers being openly insubordinate to one of the senior commanders and the chain [of command] tacitly supporting that.'

'You've got all these junior officers seeing these senior officers present when these completely inappropriate events are occurring,' says the former senior Special Forces officer. 'You want people to say, what was wrong with the culture? Why didn't people speak out? This is illustrative of the enormous power of the sergeants. They didn't take it. They were given it. So you're talking about a chain of command that basically let the sergeants get too much power.'

But the savagery and spite of Stirrers will become even too much for the brass. In July 2016, the Commander of Special Operations, Jeff Sengelman, sends a minute to the Chief of the Army.

'This activity's conduct has previously been marred by poor judgement and inconsistent oversight that compromised the chain of command, placed the reputation of the unit and the Command at risk, and weakened unit cohesion,' Sengelman writes. 'Most critically, it damaged the reputation and dishonoured the service of quality people, often leaders, within the unit.'

The skits are 'becoming less about light-hearted fun and more about grinding axes and settling perceived scores'.

New rules are brought in. Each Stirrer's Parade will be run by an appointed Stirrer who will be held accountable for everything that happens at the annual event. Skits are to be vetted and no 'character assassination' allowed. All video submissions will be fully reviewed before they are shown, and no one will be allowed to take photos during Stirrers. All drinking must stop 10 hours prior to the next training day. No member will be forced to drink alcohol against their wishes and no drinking games will be permitted.

'Nudity is prohibited,' states the directive.

It sounds more like a list of rules for a high school football team having an end of year trip to the Gold Coast rather than a directive to Australia's most highly trained and elite soldiers.

Through Freedom of Information I obtain almost 20 pages of documents from Defence about Stirrers. It is clear the chain of command knew that it had a serious problem with the parade for years.

'Becoming poisonous and divisive,' states one 2016 background document headed 'Stirrers Parade'. 'Destruction of long-standing tradition … not humorous … CO currently reviewing the risks – esprit-de-corps/moral/personal humiliation.'

At the top of the list of concerns is the Cock of the Year award.

'Now a morally bankrupt and gutless attack with no intent except to humiliate through a mob mentality for self-protection … Cock of the Year is the lazy and cowardly option in its current form.'

'Who here would be happy to be pulled up in front of the [Regiment] as Cock of the Year and humiliated?' the document poses.

The Cock of the Year award has come to symbolise everything that is broken or wrong with the Regiment. Senior leaders who laugh along and do nothing, junior officers who are humiliated and intimidated into silence, and sergeants who set the rules and brutally punish those who break them. This toxic atmosphere did not just prevail in Afghanistan, it seeped into the SAS barracks in Perth and it was effectively endorsed by the brass in Canberra. This deviance was normalised.

'This is about the leaders and the culture,' says the former Special Forces officer. 'This is about why the people that tried to be whistle-blowers would ... get destroyed or turned on.'

The whistleblowers, like Braden Chapman on *Four Corners*, are now being held up by the ADF and Special Operations Command as the personification of the Regiment. They are applauded for their moral courage. But for years, those who dared to speak out like the junior officer were ostracised or attacked. The leadership didn't applaud them – it tore them down.

'You're just talking out of school, you're talking out of turn. You're a grass,' says SAS medic Dusty Miller of the attitude towards those who dared to speak out. 'I think that the culture had become that fucking toxic.'

———

The cheering is getting louder as the leg is passed around. Stirrers 2012 has moved beyond nude Twister and now Das Boot is getting a run. Christina watches as everyone takes a long swig from it and passes it on. Soon it will be her turn.

Das Boot isn't a boat. It is a prosthetic leg taken off a dead Afghan, supposedly a Taliban fighter. He was killed during an SAS raid in 2009 and his prosthesis souvenired as a trophy by the men of the patrol. Ten years after his death, Nine Newspapers reported that Victoria Cross recipient Ben Roberts-Smith was under investigation by the Australian Federal Police over the alleged execution of the Afghan with the prosthetic leg. The media outlet said that SAS members who witnessed what happened were prepared to testify that Roberts-Smith, then an SAS corporal, had unlawfully killed the man. Roberts-Smith is suing Nine Newspapers over a series of reports that he claims portray him as a war criminal. He denies all wrongdoing and says that any killings in Afghanistan were lawful.

The incident, known as the Whiskey 108 killing after the name of the compound where the Afghan died, will become the focus of an investigation by the Inspector-General of the Australian Defence Force, with allegations the man with the prosthetic leg was *hors de combat*, or out of the fight, when he was killed.

I had seen a photo of 2 Squadron SAS, known as the 'Bushrangers', with Das Boot in Afghanistan. It is a group picture. Ben Roberts-Smith is there, holding his assault rifle and towering above the rest of his squadron. Standing out the front of the men, like their leader, is an operator wearing a Ned Kelly wraparound steel helmet and breast plate. In each hand he holds a rifle, 'stick 'em up' style.

It is a spectacularly choreographed shot. Above them all fly a Black Hawk and two Apache helicopters firing decoy flares. To the left of 'Ned Kelly' at the front of the squadron is an operator down on one knee. In his left hand is a black board with 'Das Boot' painted in white lettering. This is the stand the SAS has had made that the leg usually sits in. The prosthesis itself is in the kneeling operator's right hand. He is gripping the leg by the shin, his head thrown back, his lips to its rim. He is pretending to drink from it.

The leg is taken back to Campbell Barracks in Perth and used in drinking games by SAS operators and support staff up at The Gratto. Though some think hygiene is more of an issue than where the actual leg itself came from.

'Seeing guys hand it around and drink beer, whiskey and stuff out of it, it's like, "No, I'm not going to drink that because it looks fucking disgusting",' says one SAS operator. 'If it blows your hair back, whatever.'

Medic Dusty Miller drinks from Das Boot because that is what everyone else does.

'It's not the finest prosthetic limbs that are made over there,' he says. 'It was that fucking pack mentality. We all got carried away with it.'

As the leg approaches, Christina is feeling no pressure at all. She is 'shit faced, a piss wreck, almost blackout drunk'. She is getting into the spirit of Stirrers, she has become absorbed in the culture, she wants to belong. Christina can no longer distinguish between what is right and what is wrong.

Christina is helped up onto The Gratto's bar. The leg is passed to her. Gripping it, she tips the prosthesis back and drinks. She can't even tell what she's pouring down her throat. Could be beer, or whiskey or rum. Or all of the above. Whatever it is, it tastes like shit. Those crowded around her in The Gratto cheer as she downs it all, to the last drop.

Christina passes the leg over to the next person. It is about the last thing she remembers before she passes out and is carried over to the old accommodation at the barracks.

She wakes the next day to a killer hangover. Through the haze Christina grabs her phone and calls her girlfriend Emma. She will be worried about her.

Emma answers and asks how her night at The Gratto went. Christina was texting her as the night wore on, her messages becoming more and more garbled. Christina tells Emma about all the mad shit that went down, and how she drank from the prosthetic leg. She draws a sense of pride from skolling from the leg. It is a sign Christina has been accepted by the group.

'Wow. I can't believe you drank out of that thing. That's really sad and disturbing,' says Emma. 'Why do they use it as a drinking vessel? That's sick. That is someone's leg and they're using it as a trophy. What about the poor man it belonged to?'

Emma's words jolt Christina. After she hangs up, she starts to think about what her girlfriend said. How Emma is disgusted by what she did. Emma has become the conscience that I have lost, thinks Christina. I've become indoctrinated. Why did I do that?

Christina now feels like she has devalued that Afghan's life by drinking out of his prosthetic leg. Even if he was Taliban. That doesn't matter. She knows being pissed is no excuse. She wishes she could go back and have the courage to tell them to stick their fucking leg up their arse.

Christina is haunted by what she and the Special Forces did in Afghanistan. Now she is home, and she is appalled by what she is part of.

'I still somehow found myself completely absorbed and taken by the culture to the point where I'd drink out of a deceased person's leg. I wish I could take it back. But I can't.'

13

THE DEATH OF DIDDAMS

'Every day and every night that our soldiers continue to fight
in Afghanistan, every day that we have troops overseas in
harm's way, you hope the family will not be receiving some
fateful news – but they do. That is the thankless reality of war'
Prime Minister Julia Gillard, 14 August 2012

3 Squadron SAS is just a few days away from heading home. It has
been a busy rotation. Some say it has been the most successful of any
of the 17 Special Forces deployments so far. More drugs seized by
the Commandos, more enemy fighters killed or captured by the SAS,
and more weapons and explosives seized or destroyed than on any
other rotation.

Members of 2 Squadron SAS have arrived at Tarin Kowt to do a
handover. The Bushrangers are replacing the Third Herd.

The deployment for the Third Herd has not been without its
casualties. Rahul, the big Waka, was killed in the first few weeks,
mowed down by the Taliban hiding in the mud igloo.

Then in late June, Quake was killed during an operation in a valley
north-west of Tarin Kowt. Just as he had done to the unarmed Dad
Mohammad in the wheat field, the SAS combat dog had charged at
two Taliban fighters lying in ambush behind some rocks. Quake had
latched onto one, but the other had then shot him through the chest.

A week later, on 2 July 2012, 3 Squadron is off on what many of
them reckon will be the last job of the deployment. They are heading
to Qala-e-Naw in the restive Chora Valley. Their mission is to take on
some insurgents who have been harassing US Navy SEALs based there.

It is what they call a hot landing. Bullets are zinging into the US Black Hawks as the Australians come in to land near the green belt. The SAS patrols know that when they hit the ground they will have to move fast. There is little cover where they are landing, while the Taliban are well established in thick trees and are already finding their mark.

'When the chopper came down to land on the riverbed there were guys with guns across the other side of the riverbed hidden from us,' says Braden. 'I could hear bullets tinging off the chopper. I was at the door and I remember looking at the other guy on the door and he raised his eyebrows. We were both kind of thinking, "Well this is a good start".'

The Bear, Braden Chapman, sprints as fast as he can from the chopper. What a time to die. On the last fucking job of the deployment.

Across the river from Braden and his patrol the Taliban fighters are spraying everything they have got at the Australians. They are well hidden in the dense foliage.

'It was almost like rainforest,' says Braden. 'It was really thick.'

Behind the insurgents the ground rises sharply, giving the enemy a formidable firing position. Braden hears another Black Hawk come in.

'[That] patrol got dropped halfway up the hill [behind the Taliban] with another patrol,' he says.

Braden's patrol is exposed, and the fire being poured at them is heavy. But they have to hold tight. They are a cordon – their job is to squeeze the enemy and cut off any avenue of escape while the other patrols close in for the kill.

In his book, *The Crossroad*, 3 Squadron SAS operator Mark Donaldson says they spotted the enemy the moment they jumped from the choppers. Donaldson sees one carrying a PKM machine gun, and he opens fire. He misses, but the insurgent is shot by Soldier A's team of Wakas.

Heavy fire is coming from the building that is the target of the SAS raid. The soldiers are firing at enemy fighters as they 'squirt' from it in a bid to escape.

'Dudes were shooting them as they ran across the creek,' says Braden. 'Some of them looked 15, 16 years old. I saw two, maybe three guys sprint across and I didn't see any of them with guns.'

One guy makes it across despite drawing fire from at least two SAS operators. Others are hit and killed. Maybe they are unarmed because they have left their weapons behind in a desperate bid to escape.

Nearby, Soldier A ambushes one Taliban fighter coming out of a tunnel. He kills two more at close range in thick bush. One is armed with a rocket propelled grenade launcher.

Not far from Donaldson's position there is another battle raging. It involves the patrol commanded by Sergeant Blaine Diddams. A veteran of seven Afghanistan deployments over 11 years, 'Didds' is regarded by many in the Third Herd as a fine soldier and a bit of a larrikin. When he isn't out on operations, he is often seen around the poker table at The Fat Ladies Arms back at camp.

Diddams' team is locked in a fierce battle with two fighters armed with AK assault rifles and PKMs.

Donaldson hears Diddams come over the radio.

'Frag out!' he shouts.

It means grenades are exploding. Then there are more bursts of intense fire and another radio message from Diddams.

'Devil's down.'

Devil is one of the combat dogs. Mark Donaldson was his handler on an earlier tour.

'Devil's down. Dog's down,' reports Diddams.

Donaldson doesn't know it yet, but Devil is dead. He has been shot after running at the insurgents engaged by Diddams' team. The dog has latched onto one of the arms of the Taliban fighters and in the struggle the fighter has shot Devil through the back of the neck.

But then worse news is relayed over the radio.

'Didds is hit, he's down.'

There is immediate concern among the men of 3 Squadron. Is he alive? How badly wounded is he?

Through his earpiece, Braden Chapman listens in as one of the other patrol commanders radios through to the troop commander.

'Go one up,' the patrol commander says.

He wants to transmit a message off the main frequency they are using.

'No signs of life,' says the patrol commander on the other channel. 'No signs of life.'

He is talking about Blaine Diddams.

Tom is back in the control room at Tarin Kowt watching live footage of the raid being beamed out by an unmanned aerial vehicle above the field of battle. He can see the SAS soldiers running and firing.

'Then we got, "Friendly shot, friendly shot",' says Tom.

The control room asks who has been shot.

'Three-one,' is the response. That is Diddams' call sign. But then the news gets worse.

'No pulse. No pulse.'

Dusty Miller is also back at base. The medic has been bumped from this raid. They tell him it is because it is a nursery mission, a handover with 2 Squadron. They need Dusty's spot. He is furious.

'They said, "The medic's not going, we're putting a 2 Squadron bum on the seat". I said, "This is crazy. You call it a nursery job. But really, it's just as fucking dangerous as any other job. Why are you bumping the medic?"'

They tell him they have PAFAs on the raid. Patrol Advanced First Aiders. These soldiers are trained in advanced first aid and are like civilian paramedics. They are nowhere near as good as a fully trained medic, thinks Dusty.

Dusty had seen Diddams just a few hours earlier while they were brushing their teeth after breakfast. The two men are not close. They had got off to a rocky start before they had even landed in Afghanistan. The beret-qualified veteran and the medic support staffer had sat next to each other on the way over on the plane. Diddams had ignored Dusty.

'I was this crap hat,' says Dusty, referring to his non-operator status. 'Originally he didn't like me. It was obvious he didn't like me. But as the trip went on, things improved ... I think he saw that my commitment was like 110 per cent.'

In Afghanistan, the medic had helped the patrol commander out with a dental problem and the frost between them had thawed. That morning at the sink before the operation the two had had their most convivial chat of the deployment. With just a few days until they shipped out, talk inevitably turned to home.

'You good, Dusty?'

'Yeah, good, mate. Be good to get home. It's been full on.'

'Yeah, it's been a big trip.'

Those were the final words the two had spoken, about going home in a few days' time. Now Dusty is bursting to get on a chopper and get to the wounded SAS operator. He doesn't know it yet, but it is Blaine Diddams. The scene of the raid at Qala-e-Naw is about 10 minutes' flight away. But they send the new doctor instead.

There is nothing anyone can do, even if they were there. Blaine Diddams has been hit by a round that has passed through his clavicle and hit his aorta. He was behind a small rock wall and had risen to fire at the Taliban fighters when he was struck above his chest plate. But one of the PAFAs is working on him, despite there being no signs of life.

As the battle rages on, Donaldson hears over the radio that they have got Diddams out. They have loaded him onto an aeromedical evacuation chopper, and he is just minutes away from the Role 2 medical facility at Camp Russell. As the evacuation chopper takes off, the door gunners in the Black Hawks above sweep in with a terrifying burst of fire.

'Those door gunners really opened up,' says Braden. 'They killed a couple of guys.'

The gunners want the evac chopper to get in the air and back to the Role 2 medical facility back at base safely and as quickly as possible.

At the Role 2 just minutes later, Dusty watches as they bring Diddams in and continue to work on him.

'I just see all the tatts on his legs and arms. I knew straight away it was Didds. I expected it to be one of the fucking newer guys for some reason,' says Dusty. 'I didn't expect it to be someone like Didds.'

After a while the medical team stops. There is nothing more they can do. Blaine Diddams is dead. He is Australia's 33rd fatality of this long war.

'They called it after a period of time and it was fucking gut wrenching,' says Dusty. 'I can't say I was close mates with Didds. He was a complex character. No fucking way did I want to see any of our boys not come home. That was my job. It bothers me every day pretty much that we didn't all come home.'

The soldiers on the fateful raid have landed back at base and returned to Camp Russell. They have killed 12 enemy fighters but lost one of their own. Everyone is shattered. Diddams was supposed to be going home with them in just a few days.

They strip their gear and weapons in the Ready Room.

'Some people were crying. They were shaken up,' says Tom.

One of them is the PAFA who worked on the patrol commander while under fire.

'[He] walked over and he was crying. He just started hugging people,' says Braden.

Later, Diddams' comrades gather to say their farewells.

'I remember we all lined up,' says Braden Chapman. 'There was like a big cooling refrigerated shipping container and I remember his body was in there and everyone went through and had to pay their respects.'

'We all went through and said goodbye to him,' says Tom.

The men gather for a drink. They have done more than a hundred missions on this deployment and they cannot believe that their last time outside the wire would bring such tragedy.

'It was the end of our tour so they couldn't do anything about it,' says Braden. 'I remember guys saying that that's the worst thing. They can't even go back to that area and fuck up the Taliban because we're done.'

A few days later 3 Squadron SAS leaves Afghanistan, along with the body of Blaine Diddams.

'We landed at this air base [back in Australia],' says Tom. 'His wife was there. And that was just fucked up. It was just not a nice experience.'

As well as his wife Toni-Ann, Blaine Diddams has left behind a son and a daughter.

'This was a soldier's death – a death with honour, facing the enemy with his mates by his side,' the Prime Minister, Julia Gillard, will tell the parliament. 'Blaine Diddams' service and sacrifice will not be forgotten.'

The following year Diddams is awarded a posthumous Medal for Gallantry, the first of the Afghanistan war.

'To support his patrol and ensure mission success, he knowingly exposed himself to draw fire and lead assaults on insurgent position,' the citation read. 'His leadership and selfless acts of gallantry, which ultimately cost his life, were of the highest order and in keeping with the finest traditions of Australian special operations forces, the Australian Army and the Australian Defence Force.'

Despite their complex and often uneasy relationship, Dusty is devastated by the patrol commander's death. He feels he should have been on the raid that day, even though he knows in his heart of hearts that he could not have saved Blaine Diddams.

'That haunts me and haunts me to this fucking very day,' he says. 'I got home, and I mourned. He wasn't a good mate of mine, but to this fucking day I still mourn.'

14

THE TRACTOR JOB

'It was terrible. They were slaughtering villagers
like so many sheep'
**Sergeant Lawrence LaCroix, squad leader 1st Platoon,
Charlie Company, United States 1st Battalion, 20th Infantry
after the My Lai massacre, Vietnam, 16 March 1968**

Captain Louise walks out of the SAS Ready Room into the winter darkness enveloping Camp Russell. It's 15 December 2012 but she doesn't feel the bite of the frigid Afghan air. She only feels horror, a sickening horror brought on by the operator's confession.

He has just implicated himself and his patrol in a frenzy of slaughter committed only hours before. What he has told Louise amounts to an admission of a war crime, to a massacre of innocent civilians. Farmers. A child. Why did he tell her this? Was the operator trying to unburden himself?

Louise knows exactly why he has confided in her. She has known the SAS operator since they were both 14 years old and hanging out together in far north Queensland. By the time she was 16 they were in a relationship, and she was living with him and his mum and sisters. By the time they were 20, Louise and the operator, Soldier C, were married.

'He was very charismatic,' she says. 'He can be very protective. And can be very loyal.'

He can also be violent. Their 'on-and-off again' marriage is punctuated by violence. One time they were waiting to catch a bus down to Brisbane when Louise remarked on some pies in a shop.

'And I said, "Oh, look at those little pies". He thought I sounded stupid. So he kicked me. And I remember just seeing this look of absolute shock on this woman's face as she was standing by. I think that was the first real incident.'

There was the time when Soldier C was drunk, and he dragged her across the concrete outside a nightclub scratching up her legs. Then he spat on her. And the time he held Louise up against a wall by her throat. Louise remembers that happened after he had failed something during an SAS course.

'It is often when he's feeling like he's failed or something that he wants is in jeopardy,' she says of the explosions of violence. 'I should have just walked away.'

Louise thinks she knows part of the reason why Soldier C acts like this. It comes from a feeling of rejection, of having a father who was gone before he was born. A father he never knew. A figurehead he craved.

'When he must have been 23 – we weren't together at that point – he'd found his biological father, who didn't want anything to do with him,' Louise says. 'I think that was hard for him. I honestly think that almost everything he does is for approval.'

As a young man, Soldier C's dream is to join the SAS. To belong to the Regiment, to be an operator.

'He always feels this need to impress people that he thinks are stronger or higher than him, to try and fit in,' says Louise. 'I think that it really is just him trying to find where he fits in.'

Soldier C realises his dream of becoming an SAS operator, of fitting in. To do this he has to conform to the Regiment's culture. To Louise, aspects of that culture are sick.

'They were the big dogs, he wanted to be part of that. To me, it reminds me a lot of a book I read a while ago about outlaw motorcycle gang culture, and some aspects of it seem very, very similar to me,' she says. 'They consider themselves in some regard a bit of a brotherhood, and there's that loyalty there towards one another. But then there's also a fair amount of backstabbing and infighting.'

A registered nurse, Louise also wants to be in the military. In 2006, she joins the ADF as a nursing officer. A couple of years later she applies to go to Duntroon to become an intelligence officer. She finishes her intelligence training in 2010.

By 2011, Louise and Soldier C are off-again, for good this time. The relationship is over.

The same year he deploys with the SAS to Afghanistan. He goes a second time, on Rotation 17, in early 2012. This is the rotation in which Soldier C kills the 'village idiot' and Dad Mohammad in the wheat field. Not that Louise knows anything about that.

Now in December 2012, he is back for a third deployment. Louise is there too, on her first tour, as a captain and an 'S21' for the Special Operations Task Group.

'The S21 deals with current intelligence ... my role in that aspect was to put together daily briefs ... I was really excited to go,' she says. 'It was all that any of us wanted to do. And I really felt like we were doing the right thing.'

At Camp Russell, Louise works in the Fusion and Targeting Cell, or FATC. It has a staff of about 15 to 20 intelligence specialists supporting both the SAS and the Commandos. As the senior analyst for northern Kandahar, one of Louise's jobs is to find Taliban targets for them to capture or kill.

'There was a lot of [Taliban] leadership hanging around there,' she says of her patch. 'In the first half of the rotation we were putting together target packs of significant targets.'

Louise knew before she deployed that her ex-husband would be there and that they would be crossing paths at Camp Russell. At first, she tries to steer clear of him. But it is a small place.

'I mean you gravitate to anything that's familiar when you're in that environment. So yeah, he started to talk about what was happening out on patrol.'

Louise knows Soldier C sometimes likes to talk big. But some of what he tells her when they catch up bothers her. Is he exaggerating?

But on 15 December 2012 he tells her the story of a slaughter, a story she cannot forget or ignore. It is a story that will haunt her for years, distress her to this very day. It is a secret that only those in Soldier C's patrol know.

The job took place just hours before, in Shah Wali Kot. Northern Kandahar. Louise's patch.

Two SAS patrols – Zulu 1 and Zulu 2 – hit the ground near the village of Sara Aw. By the time they leave, more than a dozen Afghans are dead. A few are Taliban fighters, the rest are civilians. But the patrols will list them all as insurgents, legitimate targets who have been lawfully killed. It will become known among the men who went out that day as 'the tractor job'.

A few hours after Zulu 1 and Zulu 2 return from the operation Louise is hanging out in the SAS Ready Room when Soldier C begins talking.

'It was just that something big had happened on that job that day,' she says. 'I don't think he sounded like he was particularly horrified by it.'

But Louise can see that the men from one of the patrols that went out that day are shaken. These men are from Zulu 1, Soldier C's patrol. She can sense something is wrong. Soldier C and Louise are alone in the Ready Room now. He begins to recount what happened at Sara Aw around the tractor.

'He told me from his perspective what happened, which was that the patrol commander had accidentally shot one of these group of farmers. And then they made the decision that they couldn't leave anyone behind to tell [what happened],' says Louise. 'So they decided to kill all of them. And he described the fact that there was a very young person, about 13 or 14, there. He described shooting someone as they hid within the tractor wheel, cowering. I can't remember if that was the 14-year-old … I believe he said he shot more than one, but I can't remember the exact details. Honestly, it just sounded like a bit of a spree.'

Louise is stunned. She is sickened. She doesn't know what to say. This story has just tumbled from the mouth of a man she was married to, someone she has known since she was a girl in north Queensland, someone she had loved. She walks out of the Ready Room into the winter air.

The next day she goes into her office. She wants to look at the reporting and the photos from the job at Sara Aw.

'The imagery that I saw, it's all pretty close up. Head shots,' she says. 'There was imagery of someone who looked very young [who was] dead. He looked about 13 or 14. So a young adolescent.'

Not one of the photos of the dead near or around the tractor contains a weapon. But the reporting claims all of them are insurgents. It will say that Zulu 1 found a pistol, some magazines, a grenade and a battle bra. It reeks of a throwdown.

Louise can't remember how many died near the tractor. I will be told that it was about six Afghans. All civilians.

She goes to see her Officer in Charge, a woman she trusts, a colleague known for her ethical leadership.

'I think something's happened on that patrol yesterday,' Louise tells her. 'I do think we need to look at it further.'

The OIC passes it up the line, to the lead intelligence officer for the Special Operations Task Group. Louise also mentions her concerns about the tractor job to the information officer, telling him about the photo of the dead teenage boy. The information officer has used that image in a leaflet they plan to drop on an area known to be sympathetic to the Taliban. The leaflet has a blunt message:

217

IF YOU TAKE PART IN HOSTILITIES, WE WILL COME FOR YOU. After Louise tells him of her concerns about the photo he removes it from the leaflet.

Other than that, nothing happens. Nothing is said, no one comes to see Louise about it. She is conflicted. Does she kick up a fuss and demand they investigate? Or has she done all she can, and does she let it drop? She respects the commanding officer of her rotation. But she decides against taking it all the way up the chain.

'The CO was a good man, a leader of character. He would've at least investigated it. One of my regrets was not taking it further,' she says. 'But I was so afraid to say anything because you're in such a vulnerable position as a female over there. I was worried that I was putting myself in danger if I did say something, and that I wouldn't be believed.'

Louise worries that not only will she be sent home if she takes it up the chain, but that her physical safety will be at risk.

'Absolutely. One hundred per cent. That was the biggest thing for me. I was terrified.'

Louise also wonders about the villagers at Sara Aw, about the family members grieving for their dead loved ones, the wives and the children.

'What would have happened to them afterwards? I mean the reality is that they would have been given away. Given away to other male members. They would have had their whole livelihoods taken from them ... you just lose everything.'

Months before I had met Louise I had been told about the slaughter at Sara Aw, about the frenzy around the tractor. I had dispatched one of my fixers to the village in northern Kandahar to investigate what was believed to be the worst one-day death toll of alleged unlawful killings by Australian Special Forces in Afghanistan. The following is based on their testimony and that of multiple Australian sources.

———

Mohammad Nasim is in his field when he hears the Black Hawks. It is almost midday and the other farmers of Sara Aw are also in their fields. Some, like Mohammad Nasim, are irrigating. Others, like his brother Abdul Salim and Mohammad Zaher Shah, are loading onions into sacks and stacking them on the village tractor. Mohammad Zaher Shah is only 13, but he is expected to help in the fields too. Once loaded, the onions will be taken to a nearby town to sell.

The helicopters are moving towards Sara Aw. Mohammad Nasim can see them now in the distance. Three of them. They belong to the foreigners, the ones who shoot anyone they see. There is a fourth Black Hawk but it has peeled away from the other three to land the SAS mission commander and his team in an elevated overwatch position.

It is 15 December 2012 and the SAS has scrambled to get to Sara Aw after receiving intelligence about Taliban hiding near the village. Two patrols – Zulu 1 and Zulu 2 – as well as Afghan Wakunish soldiers are in the three choppers heading for this isolated speck in Shah Wali Kot in northern Kandahar.

Mohammad Nasim watches as the three Black Hawks fan up dust as they hit the ground close to Sara Aw about a kilometre or two to the west of him. They have landed near a cluster of buildings outside the village that the locals call 'the nomad houses'. They are guest houses for people visiting or passing through. Their current occupants are not pleased to see the Australians and their Afghan allies.

'There were three Taliban in the nomad houses,' Mohammad Nasim says. 'They resisted.'

Another Sara Aw farmer, Abdul Qadus, has also heard that Taliban are sheltering in the nomad houses. Like the other villagers, he is too frightened to ask them to leave.

'We did not know where they had come from or where they were going. During the raid, they resisted,' he says.

As the Black Hawks touch down the Taliban fighters sheltering in the nomad houses open fire. Bullets whizz past the SAS operators from Zulu 2 and their Wakunish comrades as they return fire and look for cover.

The chopper with the other SAS patrol onboard – Zulu 1 – has shot back into the air. Reports of squirters nearby have come in and Zulu 1 is going to chase them down.

Around the nomad houses the firefight is fierce, but the men of Zulu 2 are among the best trained soldiers in the Australian military and one by one the Taliban fighters fall to their accurate fire.

But not all of it is precise. A child is also hit, possibly by a ricochet. He will later be treated and airlifted to Kandahar. He will survive.

When the shooting stops the SAS will report four Enemy Killed in Action around the nomad houses. Two more, deemed to be squirters, are shot nearby. But are they combatants or civilians? The villagers from Sara Aw say they were unarmed farmers.

'Those two were near the Taliban at the time of the killing, I witnessed them,' says Abdul Qadus. 'They shot them and killed them. There was nothing [weapons] with them.'

As Zulu 2 battles the Taliban fighters at the nomad houses, Zulu 1 is hunting the 'squirters' reported nearby. From their Black Hawk, they spot them in a field below. The Afghans are scattering like ants in all directions.

But they are not squirters, they are farmers. Among them are Mohammad Nasim, his brother Abdul Salim and 13-year-old Mohammad Zaher Shah, who has stopped loading onions onto the tractor and is bolting for cover like everyone else.

'Everyone was terrified,' says Mohammad Nasim.

In another field, Mohammad Zaher Shah's older brother Hazrat Shah has watched the helicopters approach and has jumped on his motorbike and headed home.

'You are home!' says his mother when he walks in. She too has heard the helicopters sweep over.

'Yes, but my brother is still out there. I hope he will be okay,' he says.

'They are all farmers, they will be fine,' she replies. 'They will not shoot farmers.'

Back in the field, the men of Zulu 1 are in the helicopter watching the figures below scatter. The patrol commander, Sergeant T, orders the American door gunner to lay fire around the dispersing Afghans. He wants them to stop running and to remain in the fields. This violates the Australian Rules of Engagement that prohibits the firing of warning shots, but the American doesn't mind that. He opens up with his gun as the Black Hawk sweeps around in a circle, slamming a ring of fire into the earth below. The Afghans below stop running and most retreat back towards the tractor seeking cover.

The Black Hawk lands in the field. Leading Zulu 1 off the chopper is Sergeant T, who immediately opens fire towards the farmers sheltering around the tractor. Taking the cue of their patrol commander, Soldier C and another trooper also start shooting at the Afghans cowering around the tractor. One of them is young Mohammad Zaher Shah. Mohammad Nasim's brother Abdul Salim is also shot.

'When the shooting started they were shooting people indiscriminately,' says Mohammad Nasim. 'Some of the people irrigating were shot, some were shot in the onions. Some people got to the tractor and they were shot in the tractor. They were intentionally killing these people.'

'The people were scared,' says farmer Abdul Qadus. 'Some of them were running from one side to the other to try to make themselves safe. But some were shot and killed.'

Another Sara Aw villager, Rahmatullah, is also trying to hide from the rampaging Australians. He watches as some of the farmers try to shelter from the SAS bullets.

'[They] shot them at the tractor. They were shooting people intentionally. They were mass shooting,' he says. 'One [of those killed] was Mohammad Azim, my brother.'

Five civilians are killed by the SAS soldiers around the tractor, among them the young Mohammad Zaher Shah. The teenager is shot near the onions he was loading to take to sell in the city.

Abdul Qadus will also be hit during the SAS raid. But he is lucky. His wound is not serious and he will be taken to the provincial hospital in Kandahar. Before he is flown away, he confronts the Australians.

'I asked them, "Why are you killing these civilians? They are civilians. These are our maternal and fraternal cousins. Why are you shooting these people?"'

He gets no answers to his questions.

Two other Zulu 1 patrol members are not involved in the killing around the tractor. When the Black Hawk had landed, they had chased after a 'squirter'. After a long pursuit, one of the soldiers had shot the man dead when he reportedly refused to stop. Soon after the other soldier had apprehended another Afghan he had come across on the way back. He has now brought him back to the field where the tractor sits. As they enter the field the detained man spots the carnage, the bodies of his fellow villagers lying on the ground. He is understandably terrified. He is right to be scared.

The patrol will later claim that the man reached for one of the soldier's weapons. That the Afghan went for his gun. What is not in dispute is that the farmer is shot dead by Sergeant T. He is the 13th person to die during the raid on Sara Aw.

Photos are taken of the dead and, separately, an odd assortment of weapons. A useless grenade. Some magazines. A pistol. A battle bra.

Then Sergeant T pulls the pin from a thermite grenade and lobs it at the tractor. These grenades are a 'sabotage' weapon that can be used to destroy equipment and machinery. Their flames are so fierce they can burn underwater. The tractor goes up.

The SAS patrols will later report 13 enemy killed on the Sara Aw raid. Villagers Abdul Qadus, Mohammad Nasim and Rahmatullah all say 14 people died that day. Three Taliban fighters and 11 civilians.

The villagers compile a list of names of the civilians for my fixer.

Faiz Mohammad (Mohammad Zaher Shah)
Omar Jan
Abdul Salim
Mohammad Azim
Sakhi Jan
Wali Jan
Gulab Khan
Gran
Abdullah
Toor Jan
Nazar Mohammad

Australian sources will tell me that up to 11 of the so-called 'Enemy Killed in Action' from the Sara Aw raid could have been farmers. Civilians targeted in an orgy of shooting.

Back at his home, Mohammad Zaher Shah's brother Hazrat Shah is worried. It is now well over an hour since the helicopters landed and he fled on his motorbike.

'I will go and ask about my brothers,' he tells his mother.

'I want to go with you,' she says. 'Maybe the raid is not finished and they will stop you.'

They hop on the motorbike and ride to the field near Sara Aw where the men and boys were loading the onions. But at the field, all they find is a motorcycle and the tractor. Both have been burned. Then they spot other things on the ground.

'There were bits of brains and other things, shoes,' says Hazrat Shah. But there are no bodies.

Hazrat Shah and his mother hop back on their motorbike and head to Sara Aw's mosque. As they pull up a villager approaches them.

'Your brother has been martyred,' he says.

Hazrat Shah's mother collapses off the back of the motorbike. He rushes to help her. Holding his mother, he enters the mosque where all the bodies have been brought.

'All of them were martyred,' says Hazrat Shah. 'All of them had been shot in the head. My little brother, just 13 years old, was among them.'

Almost nine years after his brother's death, Hazrat Shah will show my fixer a photo of the teenager. It shows a serious boy with intense brown eyes and the wispiest hint of down on his top lip. Perched above his thick head of hair is a traditional taqiyah cap, its sequins glittering in the light.

Mohammad Zaher Shah is the boy that Captain Louise will later see among the photos that the patrol will bring back. The boy of about 13 or 14 in the imagery that she will look at after being told by Soldier C about the mass killing. His head will be shattered.

Speaking to my fixer, Abdul Qadus describes what he saw that day the Australians swooped in from the sky in their Black Hawk helicopters.

'They were practising their hunting,' he says. 'They were vicious and cruel people.'

The so-called 'tractor job' will later become the single biggest alleged atrocity investigated by the Brereton Inquiry into Australian Special Forces war crimes.

———

For Captain Louise, Soldier C's admission about the frenzied killings at Sara Aw has made her begin to question everything. About what they are doing in Afghanistan. About what is really happening on the patrols. About herself.

'The secrets that I started keeping, the secrets relating to the tractor job in particular, was horrific. It's really horrific,' she says. 'And I really became complicit in that.'

During her rotation Louise hears jokes about throwdowns. About AK-47s, ICOMs and battle bras being planted on bodies. There are jokes about Afghans being killed after 'moving to a position of tactical advantage'. She knows this term is being used to explain away the unlawful killing of innocent people.

Then there are the Afghans they are keeping in detention at Tarin Kowt, people she believes shouldn't be there. Louise knows this because she believes she is responsible for at least one instance of it.

'We had someone who could have been an Objective. Maybe wasn't. Probably wasn't,' she says. 'It was actually my decision to send him back to the high-level prison and keeping him in prison and actually name him as the target which it turned out he wasn't. We didn't find out until after I got home that he wasn't. I didn't do the right thing.'

Then there are the Objectives themselves, the insurgents they collect intelligence on, the high value targets they put on the JPEL (Joint Prioritised Effects List) to be killed or captured.

'Certainly, toward the end [of my rotation], I started to think that we were starting to make Objectives out of people who were, I'd say, pretty low level, which was something that always sat really badly with me,' says Louise. 'I really had to ask myself sometimes, "Are we going after anyone of significance? Or are we turning farmers into Objectives?" In the end, I felt like we were working to keep the operators happy by giving them work to do.'

Even some of the target packages Louise puts together she believes fail to meet the threshold 'to become Objectives'.

'It's not hard to turn someone into an Objective,' she says.

In early 2013 Louise's deployment to Afghanistan comes to an end and she goes home to Brisbane to the 1st Intelligence Battalion.

'Toward the end of my rotation I really kept to myself a lot by that point,' she says. 'I just didn't like what we were part of anymore.'

225

Louise feels complicit, like an unwilling co-conspirator to a crime. She is the only one outside the patrols that were at Sara Aw that day who knows about the massacre at the tractor.

'I fully decided – despite the fact that I had really, really been challenged by it – that I was going to keep what I knew to myself because I was so worried about what might happen to me and my family if I said something,' she says.

Louise will keep her mouth shut about the tractor job for almost eight years. But then in March 2020 she tunes into *Four Corners* and watches helmet camera footage of a man she instantly recognises, a man looming over a cowering Afghan in a wheat field. She watches, horrified, as her former husband pumps three bullets into the unarmed Afghan.

'It was shattering. For me, it was like, "I'm actually keeping a much bigger secret",' says Louise. 'Once I saw [the *Four Corners* program] I realised I couldn't keep it to myself, because I couldn't let any of those incidents … be seen as a stand-alone incident, because I knew that it wasn't. And I just think those people deserve so much more. And they deserve to have justice for what happened to them.'

15

THE GOAT FUCKER

'Those who can make you believe absurdities,
can make you commit atrocities'
Voltaire

The booze is flowing in The Fat Ladies Arms on 6 January 2013.
They are raising a glass to a fallen warrior. One of their own. Earlier
in the day out on operations the SAS lost a much-loved member,
a loyal combat specialist who died while saving his partner's life. He has
sacrificed all for an SAS comrade.

The wake for Fax is in full swing.

The combat dog had been in Afghanistan for more than six months
and was on his second straight deployment. Fax had been kept in the
country after his handler from 2 Squadron SAS returned home at
the end of their tour. It was thought he should stay on during the winter
rotation to give him some more experience. Fighting in Afghanistan
usually winds down over the winter. But the SAS is keeping busy
chasing targets despite the cold and the snow, and Fax's death is a
reminder that the enemy remains stubbornly lethal.

The SAS had gone looking for an insurgent bombmaker hiding
out in Langar, a Taliban badlands, west of their base at Camp Russell.
According to the 'Australian War Dogs Combat Profiles' on the
aussiewardogs.com website, the patrol came under fire as soon as it
landed near a dry riverbed. An insurgent on higher ground had the
SAS covered, including Fax and his handler Lance Corporal 'JA'
who were particularly exposed as they were both out ahead of their
patrol. Fax charged at the insurgent and latched onto him but was

shot twice during the melee. The website says the insurgent was then 'neutralised' and Fax's wounds treated at the scene. A medevac heli-copter was called to take the dog back to the hospital on base for urgent treatment. But Fax was declared dead on arrival.

'There can be no doubt that Fax's actions on 6 January 2013 directly saved the life of both [Lance Corporal] JA and members of his patrol,' states the account of Fax's death on the *aussiewardogs.com* website. 'It was an excellent example of the courage and determination required of a [Combat Assault Dog] in the SASR.'

Fax has joined Devil and Quake in the pantheon of fallen SAS canines. Their loyalty, courage and service won't be forgotten. Back at the SAS barracks in Perth, a memorial will later be built for them and it will be adorned with a poem by a former soldier.

Some of the men of the Regiment will honour their loyal mates in a different way, with a rather unique ritual. It will involve special memorial dog bowls, dedicated to each dead canine, kept at The Gratto. On special occasions these stainless steel bowls will be brought out, filled with beer or spirits, and the guys will pass them around and drink from them. One visitor to The Gratto will be invited to swig expensive Limeburners single malt whisky from one of the dog bowls. While Fax is honoured by his SAS mates with a bowl of remem-brance, the Defence Force brass will bestow more formal honours by awarding him the Canine Operational Service Medal for his service in Afghanistan.

But tonight, on the base at Tarin Kowt, just hours after Fax's death, the SAS soldiers he served alongside are drowning their sorrows for their fallen mate in The Fat Ladies Arms. It is going to be a long night.

———

Some of those on the Black Hawk nurse throbbing heads. It has only been a matter of hours since they farewelled Fax and a few of the operators have had too much booze and too little sleep. The SAS patrol is made up of a mixed group, with some drawn from 3 Squadron.

They have a target location – a village called Nawjoy in the Char Chineh district of Uruzgan. Nawjoy is cradled on the southern side of a sharp bend in the Helmand River. Rising in the fabled Hindu Kush mountains, it is Afghanistan's longest river.

They have a target, a 'person of interest' said to be in that village. He is a man called Mawlawi Sher Mohammad. But there is a catch. Mawlawi Sher Mohammad is not on the JPEL, the official list of targets that can be killed or captured. He is a person of interest, meaning he can only be engaged by the SAS in self-defence.

On the ground in Nawjoy, Abdul Azim can make out the faint beat of the helicopters in the distance. It is around 9 am and the sound of the Black Hawks strikes fear into Abdul Azim. Most people in Nawjoy are now heading home. They don't want to be out in the open when the foreigners land.

'Everyone was running because of their cruelty,' says Abdul Azim. 'I was frightened so I hid in the well.'

He will spend the whole day hiding in the well in his yard, only emerging after the Australians have left.

Farmer Ghafoor Jan is collecting corn when the helicopters land on the outskirts of Nawjoy. He watches as the SAS jump out and immediately begin cordoning off the village.

'All the village was besieged – no one could get in or out,' he says. 'There was no single Taliban in our village when the foreigners came.'

But the SAS's apparent objective – Mawlawi Sher Mohammad – is in the village. Ghafoor Jan knows exactly where he is, because he is Mawlawi Sher Mohammad's brother-in-law. Mawlawi Sher Mohammad is an important member of the Nawjoy community.

'He was the imam in our mosque,' says Ghafoor Jan.

'He was a religious scholar. He was teaching the kids in the mosque. All the children of the village were his students,' says Abdul Azim. 'When he would finish teaching the children, he would do farm work on his land.'

Both men deny that Mawlawi Sher Mohammad had any ties to the insurgency.

'He had no links with the Taliban. He was not the Taliban's man,' says Ghafoor Jan.

From their homes, the people of Nawjoy watch as the Australians enter the village with their combat dogs. They are big men, and their faces are disguised with camouflage paint.

'The women told me the story about the kind of people they were. They had blackened faces, grey guns, and red beards,' says Abdul Azim, who was hiding down the well. 'There were interpreters with them. The interpreters, they were asking for Mr Mawlawi.'

Mawlawi Sher Mohammad has finished his lessons with the children and is now standing with a group of women from Nawjoy. Abdul Azim says he was told by the women that an SAS interpreter walked over and asked the imam his name.

'He replied, "My name is Mawlawi Sher Mohammad, and I am the imam of this village",' says Abdul Azim. 'The women told us that he said, "I have no connection with the Taliban. I am teaching the village children".'

The SAS believe they have found their man.

'They took hold of Mr Mawlawi by his hand and they forcefully pulled him away from [the women],' says Ghafoor Jan.

'The Australians were talking to him through an interpreter. The women said, "We pleaded a lot with them. Do not do this. For God's sake, don't take him away from us",' says Abdul Azim. 'The women said, "[The soldiers] told us, we will have a few words with him".'

Mawlawi Sher Mohammad is taken to a stable next to his home. Villagers say they heard at least two shots from inside.

It is hours before the Australians leave. When they climb into their Black Hawk helicopters, they take with them 14 men from Nawjoy. The villagers say they left behind burned motorcycles and a car. After the SAS is gone, Abdul Azim climbs out of his hiding spot in the well in his yard, while Ghafoor Jan heads to the stable to find his brother-in-law.

'He was lying on his back,' says Ghafoor Jan. 'His head was in the stable and his feet were in the doorway. He'd been shot with two bullets, in the chest.'

'His corpse was in a very disrespected situation. He had been dragged into the stable. This is a place for animals,' says Abdul Azim, who also saw the body. 'His head was in the stable and his feet were sticking outside.'

The Australians have got their man, or so they think. In fact, they have killed – or have they murdered? – the wrong man.

The Afghan they have left lying in the hay in the stable is not their 'person of interest'. He is not Taliban.

The dead man, Mawlawi Sher Mohammad, was in his early thirties and was married and had three daughters. He was a civilian. His misfortune was that he shared the same name as the SAS's person of interest. For that, he was killed in cold blood.

———

Major Jeremy Ross has basically been told to fuck off by the SAS.

'I was very clearly told by the Officer Commanding of [the SAS] that I was not welcome, I wouldn't need access to their area.'

Jeremy Ross is the S2 for the Special Operations Task Group on Rotation 12 in 2010. As the S2 or senior intelligence officer, he is in charge of more than 30 staff: human intelligence specialists, analysts, technical officers.

'[As] part of the S2 team, you had the intelligence fusion centre,' he says. 'Their job was to find targets. We could also dynamically target.

So if we had a target and it was ticked off – it was on the JPEL (Joint Prioritised Effects List) – you had legal tick off, command tick off.'

That means the target can be captured or killed.

But the SAS don't want a bar of Major Jeremy Ross, even though he is leading the intelligence team helping to pull together their targets and objectives. The SAS has their own SCIF, or Secured Compartmentalised Intelligence Facility, and while some of Ross's staff work inside it, the S2 has to ask permission to enter.

'I have to knock on the door, and they'd sort of come and say, "What do you want?" I'd say, "Can I speak to the [Officer Commanding]?" To me, that's just bullshit.'

Jeremy Ross isn't just a senior intelligence officer. He is also a beret-qualified Commando. Maybe that is another reason for the SAS rancour. But as the S2, he regards himself as being above the 'pissing competition' between the two often-bitter rivals.

'Whether it's sitting apart from each other in the messes, squabbling at the Officer Commanding levels as to what Intel is provided ... it was petty and toxic,' he says of the rancour between the SAS and Commandos. 'In the gym, where it was a common gym, there was just no talking between the two force elements.'

The secrecy and hostility of the SAS is nothing new to Jeremy Ross. On an earlier rotation to Afghanistan while working for the Defence Intelligence Organisation, Ross had been refused access to SAS patrol reports.

'It was made clear that ... these were all highly classified pieces of information and that we'd probably have to vet them fully, then they wouldn't be worth anything,' Ross says. 'I had the highest [security] clearances in the land ... the Americans were happy to give us really anything we wanted. But not the Australian SAS patrols.'

The message is unequivocal. The SAS don't want to share their patrol reports, and if they did they would be so heavily redacted or expurgated they would be indecipherable.

To Ross, the SAS is very much a bottom-up organisation, a regiment in which the tail wags the dog. Unlike in the Commandos, the junior officers in the SAS are largely sidelined while the senior NCOs wield a corrosive combination of power, fear and control.

'The charisma of some of these guys can't be understated. They're truly charismatic guys, some of them,' says Ross. 'Their street smarts are beyond belief. Professionally, they've done a lot of killing. So they've got kudos. They're certainly lethal, influential guys and they run that unit really, really hard.'

As for their superiors – the junior officers of the SAS – they are 'roadkill'.

'These guys are specifically picked either to be malleable, entirely malleable young officers, or completely hard charging thugs like the boys,' says Ross. 'But they identify very quickly if you've got a modicum of a moral compass, or you're not going to be able to drink the Kool Aid. Then you're too hard.'

As the S2, what is worrying Jeremy Ross most of all is the influence of the NCOs, particularly the SAS patrol commanders, when it comes to who they are targeting out on operations. He is becoming suspicious that they are identifying and killing targets based on intelligence from unknown or unreliable sources. Ross knows that some of this intelligence is not coming from his unit.

'They're getting intel from other sources and prosecuting and going and conducting operations. I was very uncomfortable with that. And I was just going, "Where are you getting that information from?"' says Ross. 'At the end of the day, a lot of our training is to write intelligence reports to understand that people can bullshit you, can feed you a load of shit, to actually go and prosecute a target to run their own sources through you.'

In other words, Afghan sources could be using the Australians to settle disputes and blood feuds, or to take out tribal enemies or business rivals. One of those who could be exploiting the Special Forces to prosecute his own tribal vendettas is their main Afghan ally in Uruzgan, the warlord Matiullah Khan.

With Khan, the Australians are in a bind. He is a powerful man, made very wealthy, some say, through extortion and corruption. A close ally of President Hamid Karzai, he is a chieftain whose private militia has been given official status. Ignore him, or worse, rebuff him, and it could cost Australian lives. What Matiullah Khan runs is essentially a protection racket. The Special Operations Task Groups have no choice but to do a deal with the devil.

'SOTG learned really quickly that for survival and protection, Matiullah Khan could provide it,' says Jeremy Ross. 'Being aligned to Matiullah Khan meant that you were kept significantly safer. But then you legitimise him.'

Ross, then with the Defence Intelligence Organisation, is asked in 2006 to assess Matiullah Khan, and specifically, whether it is prudent for the Australian Defence Minister to meet the militia leader during a visit to Uruzgan.

'I knew that [Khan] was a very tenuous character. But I did recommend that [the Minister meet Khan]. Now there was big push back from the Dutch,' says Ross. 'The Dutch said, "You know, you're legitimising a murderer". My take on it was, better the devil you know.'

Dutch investigative journalist Bette Dam believes the devil played the Australians like a fiddle.

'By elevating strongmen with vested interests, their intelligence was compromised from the start,' Dam, who was based in Uruzgan, wrote in *The Australian* newspaper. 'The [Australians] allowed themselves to be used by local allies, who competed with each other for Western military resources to empower themselves as tribal leaders. Some then used those resources to target their rivals.'

The wiliest of these strongmen in Uruzgan was Matiullah Khan. Bette Dam says anyone who was not with the Afghan militia leader was immediately regarded as an enemy, and those enemies were all labelled as Taliban. In one notorious incident, Khan tied a man to the back of his car and had the poor victim dragged around until he died.

In Tarin Kowt, Jeremy Ross hears from the Australian Special Forces what happens to other perceived enemies out on joint operations with Khan's men.

'What he did on the ground was horrific. Some of the patrol commanders in the early days would come back and say, "Oh, my God, what they did was disgraceful",' he says. 'Killing people … non-combatants or people who had obviously surrendered.'

Another Australian intelligence officer believes Matiullah Khan, known to the foreigners as 'MK', genuinely wants to protect Uruzgan.

'Of course, he used people to his advantage as well,' the intelligence officer says. 'So there was a checkpoint that had some young boys that [the Afghan army soldiers] were sexually assaulting. So MK sent his guys in and had them all slaughtered. He had those guys killed … he's obviously a warlord but I don't think his heart was in the wrong place.'

Despite their unease, many of the Australians like the gregarious MK. The bond is particularly strong with the SAS, who Jeremy Ross believes are unwittingly or knowingly doing Khan's bidding by going after targets who are his rivals.

'I have no doubt that his biases would have meant that he was protecting his own patch. That's why he became so, so close to many of the patrol commanders in SAS. They were on a first-name basis with Matiullah Khan,' says Jeremy Ross. 'It was such a strong relationship between the SAS and Matiullah Khan. Occasionally they were pressed upon to distance themselves, but they couldn't.'

The warlord is very generous to his friends, and as revealed by the ABC in early 2021, he regularly presented Rado watches worth more than $1000 to Australian Special Forces soldiers in Uruzgan. Jeremy Ross says some of the SAS patrol commanders were recipients of MK's largesse.

'They would routinely talk about watches being given to them from Matiullah Khan. He had so much money,' Ross says. 'He was a very clever man, Matiullah Khan.'

Clever maybe, but the corrupt warlord would meet his end about 18 months after his Australian allies departed Uruzgan, killed in a Taliban suicide bombing.

To Jeremy Ross, the warlord was a master manipulator, the devil they needed to know in Uruzgan. But the S2's biggest headache are men who wear the same uniform – the SAS patrol commanders. They are becoming too cocky. They are taking over the targeting, they are becoming the self-appointed experts. The intelligence staff are being cut out of the loop. For Ross, the senior intelligence officer of this Special Operations Task Group rotation, this is a dangerous development, and he worries the SAS is not doing its due diligence.

'Do the due diligence of providing correct intelligence so they can go out and actually kill someone. If they're going to kill someone, like finish a person's life, that is actually needed.'

But an experienced SAS patrol commander, who spoke to me on the condition that I did not disclose his identity, said the target information provided by the intelligence staff was 'a bit how's your father', hinting the SAS was forced to rely on its wits and intel.

'They didn't really have their shit in the one sock. But that's all we had to go off,' he told me. 'The whole thing was incompetence from the top down.'

Jeremy Ross believes the intelligence his team collected and provided was verified and solid. He suspects the SAS were either getting backdoor intelligence from the Americans or were running their own human sources. He wonders whether the targets they were killing out on operations were legitimate or whether they were prisoners and innocent civilians being used to get the kill count up.

'They were just junkyard dogs,' he says of the SAS. 'There's very little oversight of what they do outside the wire.'

But to the SAS operators risking their necks, Jeremy Ross is yet another Intel geek desk jockey who has no idea what it is like outside the wire. To doubt the operators, men who put their lives on the line almost daily, and to question what happens out on the ground, is regarded by the SAS patrols as unforgiveable disloyalty.

But the S2 isn't the only one who is sceptical about where the SAS is sourcing some of its target information from. Some of the Australian Secret Intelligence Service agents in Afghanistan believe the SAS is going well outside its remit and is handling its own human sources.

There is also pressure put on ASIS officers by the SAS to add names to the JPEL, the kill/capture list. Arguments are sparked when ASIS agents question where the SAS is getting its intelligence from.

'It's classified,' an SAS patrol commander says to one incredulous ASIS officer who dares to ask.

'It was all bullshit,' says one former ASIS agent of the attempts by the SAS to add names to the JPEL.

The manipulation of the JPEL would later be highlighted by Dr Samantha Crompvoets, a sociologist commissioned by the then Special Operations Commander, Jeff Sengelman, to undertake a review of the Command. After dozens of interviews with special forces insiders, Crompvoets was left with the impression that there had been a large number of unlawful killings that had been 'reverse engineered'. The implication was that names of Afghans were put on the JPEL after they had been killed out on operations, in order to legitimise the killing.

———

The report submitted by the SAS patrol after the Nawjoy raid reads like many others. It states that the objective – in this case, Mawlawi Sher Mohammad – was a combatant. It claims that he was armed – in this case with an AK-47 assault rifle, and that he was killed in self-defence after taking up an ambush position inside the stable. The patrol report concludes that he was engaged and lawfully killed. There is no violation of the Rules of Engagement or the Law of Armed Conflict.

But the Afghanistan Independent Human Rights Commission will later complain that the Australians have murdered Nawjoy's imam. It will allege Mawlawi Sher Mohammad was a civilian and was unarmed. If this is the case, then the SAS patrol's post-operational report is a sham, concocted to cover up a cold-blooded murder. It means the AK-47 was planted on his body and photographed by the patrol. The Australians will respond to the AIHRC by re-asserting that Mawlawi Sher Mohammad was a Taliban insurgent. But Mawlawi Sher Mohammad's name was never on the official JPEL kill/capture list to begin with. He was merely 'a person of interest'.

The death of Mawlawi Sher Mohammad will later be investi-gated by the Inspector-General of the Australian Defence Force as part of its inquiry into rumours and allegations of Special Forces war crimes. In the frame is an SAS patrol member who is alleged to have killed the Afghan while he was unarmed, under control and not engaged in hostilities. He will also be accused of planting the AK-47 on the victim's body. But he isn't the only one facing the prospect of war crimes charges. The patrol member's superior on the Nawjoy mission is accused of failing to exercise control over his subordinate and of failing to do everything in his power to stop the killing. He is also alleged to have been complicit in the subsequent misreporting of events.

That is what the Inspector-General's report will conclude. But almost everyone who was on the actual operation at Nawjoy that day struggles to remember what happened. No one recalls the killing of Mawlawi Sher Mohammad. Did they have too much to drink at Fax's wake? Were their heads a little too fuzzy that morning? Or is this a case of selective amnesia?

But the SAS patrol members do remember one thing from the Nawjoy operation. It is a recollection of what one of the SAS snipers in an overwatch position saw through his rifle scope. It will become one of the funniest yarns of the Afghanistan campaign. Through his scope, the sniper sees a lonely shepherd up on a ridge fucking a goat. Everyone remembers that. They will laugh about it for years to come. The sniper even snapped off a photo of the amorous Afghan. But no one remembers Mawlawi Sher Mohammad being killed and left amongst the hay in the stable. What is so unusual about a dead Afghan?

16

CIRCLE OF FRIENDS

'Let me remind you that you must never think of yourselves
as an elite. To do so would be bad for you and bad for your
relations with the army and it would undermine those
splendid qualities, to which you are wedded, of humility in
success, and of a constant sense of humour. No, you are not
an elite force. You are something more distinguished'
David Stirling, founder of the British SAS

It is 2 am and the candidates are sitting on milk crates in the building
they call 'The Embassy'. It is part of the vast Bindoon Training Area,
about an hour's drive north of Perth. Bindoon is where the SAS
conducts much of its selection, drills and training. As well as The
Embassy there is a mock-up suburban village where soldiers can do
live-fire shooting exercises involving moving targets.

'They've got robots that cruise around the streets,' says a former
SAS operator. 'Imagine a Dalek on a Segway, and you can dress them
up in clothes and hats. And there's 15 to 20 of them. And you can
shoot from anywhere.'

Tonight, those sitting bleary-eyed on the milk crates under the
floodlights are not on the selection course to be SAS operators. They
want to be the Regiment's next generation of officers. One of them is
cavalry officer Andrew Hastie.

This is the officer selection module, which is largely made up of
back-to-back tutorials and gut-busting bursts of PT at godawful hours
of the day and night. But tonight, inside The Embassy, Hastie and his
fellow candidates are doing a session called 'circle of friends'.

'You're sat on a milk crate with high beams in your face,' says Hastie. 'Then a horseshoe of officers and NCOs are asking you very personal questions about yourself.'

There are debates, and ethical dilemmas are put to the candidates.

Not yet 30 years old, Andrew Hastie wants to join the SAS because it is the toughest job in the military.

'I've always been somewhat of an individual, a bit of a loner, and the prospect of soldiering in small teams, the prospect of soldiering in very tough environments ... has always appealed to me,' he says. 'The SAS offered both a challenge, physical and intellectual. But I didn't anticipate the moral challenge that it would pose.'

Hastie is about to be confronted by one of those moral challenges. The next session in the officer selection module is called a TEWT – tactical exercise without troops.

'At Duntroon we used to call them a PENIS – pointless exercise not involving soldiers,' says Hastie.

For this TEWT the officer candidates are broken up into groups. They are given the floor plan of a casino. This is a scenario-based exercise in which they must display ingenuity, stealth and rat cunning. It also involves role play.

'We were told that we were there as part of an AFL team. And you had the hots for the captain's wife. You're the vice-captain. And you had to work out how to have a secret liaison with her in the casino building whilst the team was celebrating end of year functions,' says Hastie.

The mission appears to be straightforward. You have 30 minutes to come up with a plan to fuck the captain's wife. But for Andrew Hastie it is anything but simple. A committed churchgoer whose deep Christian faith is shared by his wife, Hastie is stunned and conflicted by the task they have been given.

In the 2010 documentary *SAS: The Search for Warriors*, the Commanding Officer of the SAS describes the selection course as an exercise in breaking an individual down to reveal their true character.

The SAS is about to get a taste of Andrew Hastie's character. It isn't just about his faith and his moral compass. To him, this exercise also violates principles drummed into him during officer training at the Royal Military College at Duntroon and at the Australian Defence Force Academy (ADFA).

'You do a lot of ethical leadership training and then ... you're being asked to basically betray, in a scenario, your wife and your mate,' he says. 'It was designed to shatter your moral framework that ADFA and Duntroon gives you ... I sat there, and I thought to myself, "This goes against everything I believe. And I'm not going to do it". So I just prepared to fail there and then. I just refused to do it.'

The next morning the officer candidates are called up to brief the trainers on the plans they have formulated to pull off their illicit hook up inside the casino. Hastie, like the others, is exhausted. They have had little sleep, they have done back-to-back PT. They have been sat on milk crates at 2 am and peppered with personal questions in the 'circle of friends'. They have been broken up into groups for the TEWT and asked to come up with a plan to secretly fuck the fictitious wife of their pretend AFL team captain.

Hastie knows that what he is about to do will cost him selection in the SAS. His turn comes to tell them how he has planned the clandestine sexual liaison. He stands.

'I'm not briefing it,' he says. In other words, he has no plan. He won't be part of it. Hastie gives no reason and sits back down.

Andrew Hastie is later surprised to learn that he hasn't failed selection. But the CO of the Regiment wants a word.

'I acknowledge that you refused to do one of the exercises, and I accept that,' says the CO. 'But you've got to be prepared to explain why.'

The junior officer acknowledges that as a legitimate point. Maybe he should have explained why the task was in conflict with his Christian beliefs, his moral values, and his training as a military leader.

'But nonetheless, my thought about it was, "Why were we doing a tutorial like that?" Something deliberately deceitful, that done in a military context would seriously undermine unit cohesion and morale,' Hastie says.

He might have passed officer selection, but he still has a whole slab of training courses to get through before he earns the sandy beret of the SAS.

This is going to be a hard couple of years. This is the culture I'm up against, Hastie thinks.

—

His nerves are so bad he struggles to eat breakfast most mornings. He believes they are trying to get rid of him, to fail him on CQB. The Close Quarter Battle course is a 12-week shooting package and Andrew Hastie needs to pass. But the NCOs running it are making his life hell. Not even the senior officers dare mess with this cabal of hardarse sergeants.

'They weren't instructors – they were just bullies. So you'd be learning how to strip an MP5 [machine pistol], a USP pistol, your M4 [carbine], do all these complex drill movements and people are just abusing you.'

But Hastie believes their real problem with him has nothing to do with his performance on the CQB course. He thinks he is being targeted because of his beliefs, because he is different. Because he isn't a booze-guzzling trigger puller who loves getting wasted up at The Gratto with the rest of the boys while they ogle strippers' breasts.

During another course, candidates must do a swim test in a heated pool in the Perth suburb of Claremont. Not Hastie.

'I had to do my swim test in the middle of winter in the barracks pool. You're basically hyperventilating when you get in the pool,' he says. 'I felt like the system at that point was working pretty hard to get rid of me. And I had to choose whether to dig in or quit. And I decided to dig in.'

But digging in isn't enough to get Andrew Hastie through the CQB course. He knows his CQB isn't great, but the SAS is desperate for officers. Why aren't the instructors working more closely with him to make him a better shooter, to make sure he passes?

Hastie puts in the extra hours trying to improve his CQB, but it isn't good enough for the NCOs running the course. They have their reasons for not liking this God-bothering young officer. And one day when the hat is passed around to help fund some fun up at The Gratto they strike.

'They basically just rubbed me out [of the CQB course] when I refused to tip in money for strippers,' he says. 'I was just thrown to the wolves.'

Andrew Hastie refuses to darken the door of The Gratto. To him, it represents the amoral underbelly of SAS culture.

'I thought it was disloyal to wives who spent a lot of time away from them. And then, inevitably, they'd return home on a Friday afternoon, evening, completely drunk. If I was in that situation, I wouldn't be in a good position to be a good dad or husband.'

Having failed CQB, Hastie will have to do the course again. It will mean he will have to wait at least another six months before getting his sandy beret.

The young officer has come into the Regiment reading biographies of British SAS founder David Stirling and legendary SAS soldier and saboteur Paddy Mayne who operated behind German and Italian lines in North Africa and Europe in World War Two. He assumes that the Australian SAS honours that free-spirited and free-wheeling tradition, where diversity of thought is cherished and encouraged, and where rugged individualism is celebrated and central to the Regiment's unique fabric.

'That was what I expected, people who were exceptional soldiers but who were able to think outside the box and were prepared to circumvent the chain of command like David Stirling did in the Western Desert during World War Two in order to fulfil the mission,' Hastie says. 'And then I get there, and it feels more like a bikie gang. There is no freedom at all. You're treated like garbage if you don't conform.'

Mess with the 'gang' and there are serious consequences. To Hastie, that was rammed home when the junior officer was awarded the Cock of the Year award at Stirrers. The young officer had taken Hastie under his wing and had later warned Hastie and the other officer selection candidates that they were expendable. 'Just remember that,' he had said.

Andrew Hastie passes the CQB course on his second try and is given his beret. He is now a captain in the SAS and knows it will only be a matter of time before he is sent over to Afghanistan. He is worried about a culture he sees as extremely unhealthy and weird, and he fears that in Afghanistan that deviance could compromise their standards and even undermine their mission.

'Once you transplant that culture onto the battlefield and you have a few bad leaders, unethical leaders, forcing Diggers to do bad things, what are they going to do?'

The young captain already knows that bad things are happening in Afghanistan. He has heard from people within the Regiment that operators are taking matters into their own hands.

In 2012, he asks an SAS operator recently returned from a deployment to brief his troop about his experiences. The veteran operator talks to Hastie and his men for more than half an hour.

'And the one point he kept hammering home was, "Do not be too quick to take someone's life. People are doing stupid things. And people have fired without cause. Or done worse. Don't do it",' he says.

The talk makes Hastie uneasy. He decides to have a chat to his troop sergeant. With his first full deployment to Afghanistan with his squadron looming, the SAS captain is grateful to have the troop sergeant by his side. He is a decent and experienced soldier prepared to take the hard decisions, to put his morality ahead of popularity when it comes to the operators under his command. The troop sergeant is not a member of the NCO Mafia.

'We've got to be on the same page here,' Hastie says to him, referring to their impending deployment.

'I'm not going to Afghanistan to put dirt farmers on their knees and shoot them in the head,' replies the troop sergeant.

———

It is last light and the crews on the helicopters are warning that fuel is getting low. Captain Andrew Hastie has skidded his way down the slope near the village of Olum Ghar to join his soldiers. He has been dropped above the firefight. Hastie knows that if they don't leave soon they will have to stay the night.

It is 28 April 2013, and Hastie and his team from 1 Squadron SAS have been in Afghanistan for two months. It is Hastie's first full deployment to the country and his role as troop commander puts him in charge of the patrols on the ground. It means he must manage all the sergeants, corporals and troopers, and make sure they are sticking to the mission.

Linking up with his men, Hastie sees the bodies of three Taliban fighters on the ground. But then he does a double take. He cannot quite believe what he is seeing. The right hand from each of the dead insurgents is missing. An SAS corporal has cut them off with a scalpel and put them in bags to take back to base.

'My brain wasn't processing what I saw. Because it was one of the black swan moments, right?' says Hastie.

He is told by the patrol that this is a biometric technique the SAS has been told to follow when they are under time pressure. Taking fingerprints, hair samples, DNA swabs and processing weapons and phones can take time and be dangerous, especially if a patrol is exposed or under fire. Then there are problems with some of the biometric tests. A lot of the Afghan fighters are also farmers and manual labourers, and their fingerprints are often worn away. The SAS are told that laboratory testing is the gold standard. So the SAS corporal has severed the hands with a scalpel to take them back for identification. There is another reason why they want to be sure about the identities of the three men they have shot.

The SAS has scrambled to Olum Ghar to capture or kill Objective Rapier, whose real name is Abdul Hai. To the SAS he is like mist. He is their most elusive quarry, their most dangerous enemy. They will do almost anything to get Rapier.

He runs the key IED network in Uruzgan, and that makes him a lethal force. He operates across Helmand and Kandahar provinces too. He is said to be behind Australian deaths. One of them is Signaller Sean McCarthy, killed in 2008 by a roadside bomb comprised of two anti-tank mines. Intelligence suggests Rapier never sleeps in the same bed twice, rarely uses phones. When he does, he throws them away afterwards. He is known to slip over into Pakistan.

But some doubt that Rapier even exists. A senior ASIS agent believes Special Operations intelligence staff have assembled him from a series of ambiguous or incomplete reports. He reckons Rapier is a mishmash, a sewn together Frankenstein of insurgent leaders rather than a single individual. The agent reads the intelligence reports on the elusive Rapier. In some he is over six feet tall and 100 kilograms, in others he is a slip of a man weighing less than 60 kilograms. The ASIS agent dubs him Keyser Söze, after the chief antagonist in the Hollywood thriller *The Usual Suspects*. A figure of legendary ruthlessness, Söze strikes fear into the hearts of those who cross him. But is he real or is he a phantom? Maybe he is both. As one of the characters in the film remarks about Söze, in a line borrowed from the French poet Charles Baudelaire: 'The greatest trick the Devil ever pulled was convincing the world he didn't exist.'

The SAS is convinced Rapier exists. To them he is 'the white whale', their extant and abiding obsession that is seemingly always one step ahead.

The SAS has been hunting Rapier since 2007. Back then they thought they had him in their net. But as they closed in, one of their long-range patrol vehicles hit a mine, tearing the front end off it, sending the engine block flying and injuring its four occupants. By the time the SAS regrouped, Rapier was gone.

The Commandos went after him in June 2009. But they didn't come close. Later that year, Rapier was said to have escaped again, slipping through a Dutch cordon disguised as a woman.

It is almost four years before another decent chance arrives to catch or kill him. If he even exists. And that time has come.

On 28 April 2013 the Australians think they have their man. Intelligence suggests Rapier is at a compound near Olum Ghar in Zabul Province, due east of the Australian base at Tarin Kowt.

A force of 120 SAS and Commandos launch in Black Hawk and Chinook helicopters. The mission is described in detail by veteran journalist and author Chris Masters in his book, *No Front Line*. It recounts how four alleged Afghan insurgents were killed in the raid, and how a 'shit storm' will soon erupt.

Two of the dead Afghans have been shot in the face. That makes it harder for the SAS operators to determine if one of them is Rapier. But the engineers with the SAS patrols are armed with technology that is mobile, instantaneous, and supposedly foolproof. It is technology that is designed to identify targets, no matter how badly maimed or disfigured they are. It is an American-developed Secure Electronic Enrolment Kit or SEEK machine.

'We always carried a SEEK,' says a Special Forces engineer who deployed to Afghanistan and who went on dozens of operations with the SAS. 'The SEEK had the fingerprinting technology, iris scanning ... the SEEK had all the information uploaded. So if you took a fingerprint and it matched, well, then you'd get a match on the SEEK.'

So why not use the SEEK on the dead Afghans?

The SAS corporal has used the scalpel to sever the hands of three of the men because the Special Operations engineer with the SEEK is somewhere else and light is fading. The corporal thinks it is quicker and will be easier to take the hands back to base for thorough biometric testing and analysis.

'I always understood [the cutting off of hands] grew out of operational necessity,' says Andrew Hastie. 'We kept talking about, "Yeah, we don't have enough time to get decent fingerprints and all the rest of it".'

About a week earlier a sergeant from the Australian Defence Force Investigative Service (ADFIS) had led a training workshop at the Special Operations engineers' lab back at Camp Russell. The focus of the training was biometrics and sensitive site exploitation or SSE, the process of collecting and cross-referencing material such as phones, retina scans and fingerprints out in the field.

Andrew Hastie isn't at the meeting, but is briefed about what was said afterwards.

'This [ADFIS] guy was telling the guys, "Fingerprints are difficult. If you can get a finger, great. If you can get a whole hand, excellent",' says Hastie. 'But he was comparing his experience in Iraq, collecting body parts from suicide bombers with practice out in the targeting environment or a targeting mission, which is what we were doing. So I just never assumed that that would happen at all.'

In other words, it is easy to collect body parts from a suicide bombing in Iraq. But in Afghanistan, they must be harvested.

Australian Special Operations soldier, Corporal L, was at the workshop. He is on his second deployment to Afghanistan and he remembers the ADFIS sergeant talking about retina scans, DNA and fingerprints. He recalls that towards the end of the briefing one of the Australians asked a question.

'It was a joke. It was like, "What about cutting fingers and hands off?" That was the question asked, with a smile and a laugh,' says Corporal L.

The question may have been a joke, but the response was not.

'And they said, "Yeah, you know, in a dire scenario you could do that",' says Corporal L.

One SAS trooper will later claim that the experts described the removal of hands as the 'gold plate solution'.

Another said someone asked, 'So you're sweet with us bringing back a hand?' The reply reportedly went, 'Yes … you've got to do what you've got to do on the battlefield'.

The ADFIS sergeant leaves the meeting thinking the SAS members now regard the severing of hands as legitimate. 'That's all they were focused on,' he would say later.

Corporal L says it was obvious to the soldiers in the meeting that the mood and tone of the discussion about severing hands was light-hearted. 'It wasn't a serious conversation. I think everyone was sort of having a laugh with the fact that that was being done,' he says.

In other words, the Australians were not asking permission to cut off hands or digits. Corporal L says they were already doing it. 'So that was sort of just confirming that it was done, because I think it was a bit of a joke it was being done. I must say, it wasn't being done to hundreds of people. It's probably just a handful. It wasn't so wide-spread. It was probably just a couple of shooters, maybe one or two engineers [who were doing it].'

But Corporal L isn't comfortable with the practice and tells his team not to do it.

'I was in my little group of five people, which is four SAS and me,' he says. 'I remember I told the Cats [SAS operators] I was with, not to do it. I was like, "There's no need to ever do this. Because you just take a fingerprint. So there's no need".'

Despite later reports about the SAS cutting off the hands of dead Taliban, supposedly so their biometrics could be taken later, Corporal L says it was the engineers in the Special Operations Engineer Regiment who initiated this gruesome ritual.

'I think it started with a thumb and forefinger and then escalated to the hands. Thumb and forefinger are the ones you need because that's the stuff you grab [with],' says Corporal L. 'If I'm a bomb builder, the thumb and forefingers are the things that I am mainly grabbing the pieces of tape with or pieces of equipment with. They are the main ones you need if you're going to get a fingerprint match. The other ones are almost redundant.'

Corporal L first sees this in an evidence bag. It has a couple of fingers in it.

'It was sort of shown in jest, like, "Ha ha, look at this, we've got some fingers". But I was never impressed. I was mortified really, because how do they know these people weren't alive when they were doing it,' he says. 'People were doing it not necessarily because they needed to – it was because they were enjoying it. It was fun. Like "one-up me". Start with the fingers and then move to the hands.'

Corporal L says the practice was macabre, and different tools were used for different body parts.

'Secateurs for the fingers. I saw the secateurs. I think they were run of the mill garden ones. And then for the hands, I know people used to carry machetes, and especially little battle axes ... they could have been using tools that they got out on site. There was shit lying around everywhere.'

The SAS corporal hunting for Rapier used a more precise instrument – a scalpel. But in the end, the severing of the hands will all be for nothing. The Australians don't know it yet but Rapier has once again slipped the net. Maybe, like Keyser Söze, he was never there.

In the helicopter heading back to Camp Russell, Troop Commander Andrew Hastie is growing increasingly troubled by what he has seen. Three dead insurgents all missing their right hands.

'You just know when something's like, "Okay, this is weird". I went straight back ... I walked back from the apron with one of the patrol commanders. I was talking to him about this issue,' he says.

'I then get up to outside the headquarters and I get the engineers and I have a chat with them and say, "What's the go with this? Where'd this come from? What's this practice you're talking about?"'

Hastie then takes it to the captain running the engineer detachment and then further up the chain to the OC (Officer Commanding) of his squadron, Luke Sanders.

'[It's] emblematic or symbolic of what war does to people over time, and the way it degrades people's moral sensitivities and compromises your restraint and your ethical decision making,' says Hastie of the severing of the hands.

'The warrant officers, the sergeants, all the [Explosive Ordnance Disposal] techs knew this was happening,' says Corporal L. 'After every mission, you'd get together and you'd just chat to your mates about exactly what happened, including if you did or did not cut people's hands off. So it wasn't a secret. Everyone knew that this was going on, including the commanders. It was done for fun. It wasn't done for a tactical need. There was not a single mission with the SAS where I thought there was a tactical need to actually do that.'

A veteran of more than 100 missions, Corporal L confronts his sergeant about it, telling him there is no need to cut off hands and digits.

'Why are you doing that when we have more than enough time to take fingerprints and evidence the normal way without having to fucking cut people's hands off?' he complains.

After Hastie takes the issue up the chain, everyone is told the practice of severing hands will cease immediately.

But word of this grisly practice will quickly leak out of Camp Russell and the Australian Special Operations Task Group.

'I think it ended up in *The New York Times* and the front pages of our newspapers and [Prime Minister] Julia Gillard made comment on it,' says Hastie. 'The issue is, "Guys, you're making media headlines here. Can you just tone it down?"'

———

'What are you Australians doing? Don't you understand? Gus, if this was any other nation's unit, I would send it home.'

General Joseph Dunford, commander of the International Security Assistance Force (ISAF) and commander of all United States forces in Afghanistan, has threaded his way through the crowd. The parade at ISAF's Kabul headquarters has broken up and the four-star general has Fergus McLachlan in his sights.

McLachlan knows why the top US general in Afghanistan is chewing him out. It is about the severed hands.

'I'm working for you. I'm not in their national chain of command,' McLachlan tells Dunford.

That is true. Fergus McLachlan is a Major General in the Australian Army but he has been seconded to ISAF Joint Command in Kabul as its chief of plans. He is working for Joseph Dunford, not the Australian Defence Force. He has nothing to do with Australia's Special Forces operating in Uruzgan in the country's south. But as an Australian he is a natural target for Dunford's wrath.

McLachlan's key task for ISAF is to prepare and execute the drawdown of American and allied forces in Afghanistan from 80,000 personnel to fewer than 15,000. This is the official policy of the Obama Administration as it tries to extricate the US military from the mire of America's longest war, and to hand over security to Afghan authorities in 2014. General Joseph Dunford has been handpicked by President Barack Obama to lead the process.

But an Australian SAS corporal armed with a scalpel on an operation near a remote village no one has ever heard of in the country's south is threatening to cause Dunford yet more grief with the Afghan president. Hamid Karzai is approaching the end of his second, and last, five-year term. Once an American favourite, the wily Karzai is starting to turn on his old enablers.

'He's difficult and prickly, and every time the Four Star [General Dunford] goes down there, Karzai's looking for ways to belt ISAF,' says Fergus McLachlan. 'His political mandate has become so that he has to be seen to be standing up to the foreigners.'

The severed hands incident is a perfect free kick for Karzai.

Fergus McLachlan has been at ISAF Joint Command for a couple of months. He has met his new boss Joseph Dunford before, in Darwin, when the US general had been the assistant commandant of the Marines.

'He is the most impressive military leader I've worked with,' says McLachlan. 'The best leaders have the ability to move from high strategic – you know, literally talking to the president – down to kicking tyres with privates and corporals.'

But today, after the parade, Dunford is kicking Fergus McLachlan.

'We knew each other really well,' says the Australian general. 'And he gave it to me.'

McLachlan tells Dunford he will pass on his message. It is clear. The Australian SAS needs to understand the strategic mission and objectives in Afghanistan and to stop undermining them. Put bluntly, the SAS needs to stop fucking up.

'We were supposed to be transitioning out. We were supposed to let the Afghans fight ... and yet Australia was still this kill or capture or decapitate [force],' says McLachlan. '[The SAS had] become the shoot 'em up boys.'

Fergus McLachlan tells General Dunford that he does not believe the severing of the hands by the SAS is a war crime. But he knows the PR damage it has done the Americans, the Australians, and the whole ISAF mission.

'What that was, was evidence of a level of brutalisation. But also a lack of strategic awareness,' says McLachlan of the severing of the hands. 'How did they become so brutalised that this guy thought that was okay?'

The problem for McLachlan is that this is not the first time the Australian Special Forces have embarrassed Dunford and ISAF, and given Karzai an opportunity to belt the US Four Star.

Two months before the severed hands affair, in February 2013, a civilian casualty (CIVCAS) incident flashed up during the ISAF morning battle update briefing.

'Discussion of the implications of the Uruzgan CIVCAS. Two Kuchi shepherd boys killed, as young as six and eight,' Fergus McLachlan wrote in his diary. 'Multiple reports to the palace. President of Afghanistan told today.'

Once again, SAS troop commander Andrew Hastie will be at the centre of this drama. Again, the incident that sparks Hamid Karzai's ire will not be Hastie's fault. But what happens will trouble the young captain for the rest of his life.

On 28 February, Hastie and his men are on a reconnaissance mission in the Shahid-e-Hasas district of Uruzgan, a place long regarded by the SAS as a hornet's nest of Taliban. The US Green Berets have recently pulled out and left the Afghan National Police to fend for themselves in a remote patrol base in one of the district's dusty valleys. Not surprisingly, the morale of the Afghan police is through the floor. Hastie arrives at this lonely outpost with a few gifts for the Afghans: some batteries and cartons of Red Bull. Then he sits down with the police commander for a cup of tea and a chat. The mood is tense. The commander tells Hastie that the Taliban are preparing to attack the outpost. As the two men talk, the SAS captain's electronic warfare operator comes over.

'We're getting a lot of chatter. It's Taliban chatter about getting a rocket and waiting for the Black Hawks to return,' the Bear tells Hastie.

The Bear says he will triangulate the ICOM chatter and try to get a direct bearing to it. He soon pinpoints the location. It is a man with some sheep and donkeys not far from the outpost. He has an ICOM, and he is spotting for the Taliban, telling them where the Australians are and what they are doing. The shepherd is waiting for the Black Hawks to come back to pick up the SAS patrol and when they do he will radio that information to the Taliban. This is when they could strike.

Hastie confers with his senior sergeant and his Joint Terminal Attack Controller. The JTAC's job is to direct combat aircraft and fire onto targets.

The SAS captain must make a judgement based on all the information he is getting. Is there a threat? Yes. Do we have a bearing to the spotter? Yes. Hastie runs through his checks and consults his Bear again. There is still chatter. Hastie has no choice. The safest and most effective way of killing the spotter is with an Apache helicopter gunship and its 30-millimetre canon. Hastie orders the JTAC to coordinate the strike, and as the ground commander, his coded initials – Alpha Hotel – are passed onto the Apache crew. This is his call, his responsibility.

Two Apaches approach the target. Hastie and his men are watching the spotter and his animals when they hear the helicopters open up. But the spotter is unharmed. Hastie's stomach drops. The Apaches are firing at the wrong spot. They are aiming at something hundreds of metres away from the spotter. What have they hit? The Apaches are ordered to stop firing, as Hastie grabs his medic and a couple of other SAS soldiers and they start running to the place the choppers were targeting. By this time, the spotter has legged it and the chatter has stopped.

The SAS soldiers reach the spot where the Apache canon fire has hit. The scene is heartbreaking. There, on the ground, are the broken bodies of two little Afghan boys. Toor Jan and his brother Odood had been gathering firewood when they were torn apart from the air. Like the spotter, they too were with their livestock.

The SAS medic bends down and picks up one of the boys. He looks over to Hastie.

'There's nothing we can do,' he says.

The mistake has been made by the Apache crews. They have assumed the spotter had moved, and that the two boys were the target.

If they had stuck to the grid reference given to them by Hastie's JTAC, Toor Jan and Odood would still be alive.

Andrew Hastie is devastated, and immediately reports the civilian casualties.

'I thought to myself, this is how it ends, a green-on-blue in the middle of nowhere, after two little kids have died innocently. It's the worst feeling I've had,' says Hastie. 'Totally crushed. Absolutely heartbroken. There was no joy in the job from that point onwards … this is a miserable, miserable place to be.'

Back at base, Hastie sits down with his Commanding Officer and talks him through the tragedy. It is a tough moment, one made harder by the fury coming from the Afghan president's office.

'I am confident Karzai knew within 20 minutes of it happening,' says Hastie. 'It was a terrible incident that had strategic consequences.'

An investigation is launched, and it is decided to give the family of the dead boys a 'tactical compensation payment' of $5000. A delegation is arranged to fly out and see the family and hand over the money. But Andrew Hastie is not invited to come.

'For whatever reason headquarters decides we will keep those involved in the incident out of the reconciliation process. I sort of accepted that, although it felt really strange. It didn't really sit right with me.'

As the delegation is preparing to leave to see the family, Hastie is down at the helicopter pad chatting with one of the Afghan interpreters. Talk swings to the trip to pay the family.

'Are you coming? Where's your gun? Where's your body armour? Where's your helmet?' asks the interpreter.

'No, no. I am being kept out of it,' says Hastie.

'No, you must come. This is about Afghan honour. You're it. You're the guy,' says the interpreter.

Hastie knows he should go. He sprints over to his OC (Officer Commanding), Luke Sanders.

'I need to be on this flight,' he tells him.

'Yep. Grab your weapon and your body armour and helmet,' says Sanders. Sanders has kept Hastie together since the CIVCAS incident, and he has absorbed a lot of the heat directed at his junior officer from up the chain. To Hastie, Sanders has been a godsend and an example of true SAS leadership.

The delegation flies out, meeting the family at an Afghan police station. The family is represented by an uncle and a brother of the dead boys. When the meeting begins Hastie is not part of those sitting with the family; instead he is part of the security detail for the Australians. But after the payment is made and the meeting is winding up, the captain makes his move, walking to the centre of the room.

'I'm the guy who gave the order. I just want to say I'm sorry,' Hastie tells the uncle and the brother.

The uncle looks at the Australian.

'I forgive you,' he says.

The brother says nothing.

'You could see there was a lot of hatred and anger from the brother,' says Hastie. 'But I thought for his grieving process it was important he could at least see someone, the person who took legal and moral responsibility for it.'

The investigation into the deaths of Toor Jan and Odood would later clear Andrew Hastie of any fault. But that does not assuage his sadness and sense of grief for their family.

'I think and pray for that family every February 28 and in between,' says Hastie. 'They're still carrying the cost of losing two sons who would now be 16 and 14. The lesson to me was there's nothing really glorious about war and it comes at a human cost. It's not a boy's own adventure.'

Up in Kabul, the strategic consequences of this tragic mistake are being made abundantly clear to Major General Fergus McLachlan. The chief of plans at ISAF Joint Command is told by a very senior

ISAF colleague that the incident is regarded as extremely serious by the Afghan leadership.

'And if these [incidents] continue it could result in a premature end to the mission. That was, Karzai could kick us out,' says McLachlan.

But there is another incident. The Australians open fire on two men on a motorcycle who do not stop at a checkpoint. One of the men is an Afghan policeman.

On top of that, the Australian Special Forces are flunking one of Dunford's key metrics – letting Afghan forces take the lead on operations. The number of Afghan soldiers on missions is supposed to be double that of Coalition forces. That is Dunford's combat ratio rule. But the Australian Special Forces simply ignore it.

'It was clear that we were already seen as a unit that was out of step with the strategic environment. We were supposed to be backing off,' says McLachlan. 'We were supposed to be transitioning out. We were supposed to let the Afghans fight.'

But the SAS is doing the opposite. Fergus McLachlan believes they have been seduced by the kill/capture creed of legendary US Special Operations commander Stanley McChrystal and his notion of Special Forces soldiers as 'snake eaters'. The Australian general says the men of the SAS have swallowed the American Kool Aid. They are even starting to look like the American operators.

'When you get on and off a plane coming in and out of Afghanistan, you'd see these guys. Early on, they were wiry, lean, tough looking. And by 2013 they look like second rowers for the Wallabies [rugby union team]. They've got arms like my thighs, they've got Maori war tattoos, they've got bespoke equipment. They've become something completely different.'

The Australians are treading on thin ice with General Joseph Dunford. Not only is he juggling President Obama's troop drawdown, but there are furtive attempts to initiate peace talks with the Taliban. There are also the ongoing and complex problems with Pakistan's often duplicitous Inter-Services Intelligence agency that controls movement across the porous border with Afghanistan. And of course, Dunford has the cantankerous Karzai constantly on his case. The severing of the hands by the SAS is almost the last straw for the US general.

Canberra gets the message. The Special Operations Commander, Gus Gilmore, is dispatched to Afghanistan to mend fences. Fergus McLachlan summons the chief of Australia's Special Operations Task Force – the lieutenant-colonel running the SAS and the Commandos – up from Tarin Kowt to Kabul to explain to him their strategic failures. It is time to have it out.

'We are in transition; we're trying to run a successful election. We've got all these other pressures that you should be aware of. Do you know about these things? If so, why are you not passing it on to your people?' General McLachlan asks the Special Operations CO. 'Why are your guys still making these decisions?'

They are on their last chance. If not for the hard-earned kudos and status the SAS has already garnered over more than a decade of operations in Afghanistan, and if not for General Dunford's abiding respect for the Australian Special Forces, the men of the Regiment would probably already be back in Perth. McLachlan believes one more monumental fuck up and it could all be over for the Australian Special Operations Task Force. For the Americans, the stakes are too high.

Major General Fergus McLachlan believes that, at their best, the SAS is the equal to any and every special operations unit in the world. Their agility and their teamwork are without peer. But by 2013, he says something had gone seriously wrong with the Regiment.

'The drinking, the bullshit beards and the rolled-up sleeves and whatever equipment they wanted,' he says. 'I genuinely feel something had broken in the command and control chain ... we knew it was the worst governed unit in the Army.'

The Australians are appearing regularly on General Joseph Dunford's battle updates. For all the wrong reasons.

17

THE GOOD SOLDIER

'Every soldier thinks something of the moral aspects of
what he is doing. But all war is immoral and if you let
that bother you, you're not a good soldier'
US Air Force General Curtis Le May

I decide to ring Soldier A. What is there to lose? I need to hear his side
of the story.

I have heard from many SAS veterans that he is a fine soldier,
a natural leader, a man of rare courage.

'Very well respected, very highly regarded as an operator and there
was never any doubt as to his capabilities,' says an SAS operator
who was trained by Soldier A.

You can see those capabilities during the battle at the mud igloo
at the Kuchi camp in Deh Rawood. While other operators want to
pull back and get an attack helicopter to put a Hellfire missile into the
igloo, Soldier A waves them all away.

'I got him, mate. Go!' he says to another operator wanting to
retreat.

He then slots a new magazine into his assault rifle and empties it
into the remains of the igloo and the Taliban inside. He is going to
finish it, and he does.

In the SAS, there are tribes within tribes. The Regiment splits its
operators into three disciplines – land, air and water. Soldier A is a
'watery'.

'The wateries do a harder course,' says a former water operator.
'It's like another selection. It's like the Navy SEALs but for 12 weeks.

You're being a diver. So you're an SAS soldier and a Navy SEAL. With that comes a level of ego and arrogance because you've got to be fitter because of the marine environment, and you've got to be more trained and more skilled as well.'

In Afghanistan, the water operators are renowned for their toughness and their ruthlessness. Some of them will become notorious for being at the heart of the darkness, for demanding others follow unlawful orders, and for showing no mercy to prisoners or civilians.

But the former water operator says Soldier A was different.

'He had the skills but not the swagger of the other wateries,' he says. 'He was one of the better ones.'

He is clearly a complex character, and something of a paradox. A lethal exponent of the art of exquisite unpleasantness, a Special Forces veteran of more than a dozen deployments to war zones and, it appears, a man not afraid to show his emotions when it comes to children being harmed.

One operator tells me how he ran into Soldier A back at the mess at Tarin Kowt after an operation. Soldier A looked shattered.

'You all right, mate?' asked the operator.

'Some things you can't unsee,' said Soldier A.

He told the operator how the SAS dog handler on that day's raid had pulled the quick release on his dog, and how it ripped into an Afghan child.

'The dog was ragdolling the child in its jaws. They were able to get the dog [off] but the kid was pretty badly hurt,' the operator told me later. 'Anyone who's affected by seeing children get hurt, it's probably a good indicator of where their moral compass points.'

But is this man, as Braden Chapman has told *Four Corners*, also a cold-blooded killer? A man prepared to shoot an Afghan who has his hands up? A man who ordered a Waka to execute a bound, kneeling prisoner?

Soldier C out on operations, a blindfolded detainee squatting behind him. Soldier C would later be shown in a video broadcast by *Four Corners* shooting an unarmed Afghan cowering in a wheat field.

An SAS soldier dressed as a Viking at a party in The Fat Ladies Arms at the Australian SAS base at Tarin Kowt. On the wall is a 3 Squadron poster with the motto: 'Drink, jump, fight, shoot and root'.

An SAS soldier in blackface and dressed as Mr. T inside The Fat Ladies Arms. The bar would become notorious for heavy drinking, with some hungover SAS soldiers needing to be 'bagged' with an IV drip the morning after big sessions so they could go out on operations.

Playing poker in The Fat Ladies Arms on a table emblazoned with the redback, bushranger and bull symbols of 1, 2 and 3 Squadrons SAS. One Special Operations soldier remembers the stakes at the table sometimes running into thousands of dollars.

Sarkhume villager Hazratullah, who watched as his wounded father Haji Sardar, who was being treated by combat medic Dusty Miller, was taken away by an Australian SAS soldier into the village mosque. The Afghan elder was allegedly beaten to death by the Australian, known as Soldier B.

Abdul Latif, the elder son of Haji Sardar, who was allegedly beaten to death by an Australian SAS soldier. After the death of his father, Abdul Latif attended a shura, or meeting, in which he claimed the Australians asked for forgiveness.

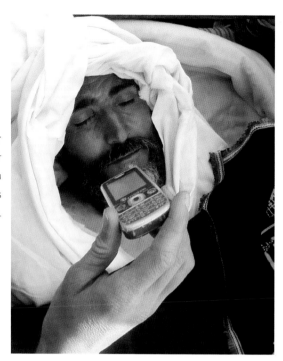

Sarkhume villager Haji Sardar in his burial shroud. 'Big fat boot marks were over his heart. You could see boot marks all over his body,' said his son, Hazratullah.

An Afghan compound burning during an SAS operation. Soldiers would sometimes burn compounds of suspected Taliban as well as telecommunications equipment at Public Communication Offices in villages and towns. 'Very f..... Mogadishu,' remarked one SAS operator after his patrol had just poured petrol over the satellite communications equipment from a PCO and lit it up.

Still shots from the *Four Corners* program, 'Killing Field' which showed Soldier C killing a frightened and prone Dad Mohammad. The footage caused shockwaves around the world and resulted in an Australian Federal Police war crimes investigation. It also sparked a new line of investigation by the Brereton Inquiry, the independent Australian Defence Force inquiry into war crimes in Afghanistan.

Abdul Malik, the father of Dad Mohammad, the young Afghan who was shot dead by an SAS soldier as broadcast in the ABC *Four Corners* program, 'Killing Field'. 'He did not have a rifle, a Kalashnikov or a sickle on him. They can arrest him. Why did they have to kill him?' he says of the Australian SAS.

Australian SAS combat dog Quake and his handler. Quake was seen in the *Four Corners* program 'Killing Field' latching on to Afghan, Dad Mohammad, who is later shot dead by an Australian SAS operator. Quake was later killed on another raid.

Soldier A peering down the remains of the well in which insurgent leader Objective Oberon was hiding with his bodyguards in June 2012. When the lid was lifted, a hand holding an AK-47 had popped out and began firing, hitting an Afghan Wakunish soldier in the chest plate of his body armour. After throwing grenades down the well, the SAS called in an air strike and hit the well with a Hellfire missile. The Wakunish soldier survived.

The Wakunish soldier involved in the battle of the well against insurgent leader Objective Oberon in June 2012 shows the bruise after he took a bullet to his body armour. During the battle he was dragged to safety by medic Dusty Miller. 'Point-blank range. You don't normally walk that off,' said Dusty.

Australian SAS medic Dusty Miller treating an Afghan punched in the face by SAS Soldier B and mauled by an SAS dog. It was the worst broken nose the medic had seen. Soldier B claimed the Afghan had gone for his sidearm.

Dusty Miller treating an Afghan whose scrotum was torn by an SAS combat dog. Despite the medic fearing the man would die of infection, his superior officer refused to let Dusty take him back to base for proper surgery. All Dusty could do was advise the man to seek antibiotics. I later tracked the Afghan down alive. He had taken Dusty's advice.

US Black Hawk helicopter pilot and door gunner in Afghanistan. In 2012, the Australian SAS used the American aircrews to get them to their targets out on operations.

Left: Rahmatullah, who claims his brother was shot by an Australian SAS patrol near a tractor in a field at Sara Aw village. At least 13 people died in the raid. The villagers say 11 were civilians. 'They were shooting people intentionally. They were mass shooting,' he said.

Right: Mohammad Zaher Shah who was killed during an Australian SAS operation near a tractor in a field at Sara Aw village. Just 13 years old, he was among at least 13 people who died in the raid. 'All of them had been shot in the head,' says the dead boy's older brother, Hazrat Shah. The villagers say 11 of those killed that day were civilians.

Like US, British and Israeli special forces, the Australian SAS uses Belgian Malinois as combat dogs. A short haired shepherd, they are celebrated for their stamina, strength, intelligence and courage. At least three – Quake, Devil and Fax – would die on operations in Afghanistan.

SAS soldiers in The Gratto at the SAS base at Campbell Barracks in Perth drinking alcohol from dog bowls in honour of their fallen combat canines. One visitor will be invited to swig expensive Limeburners single malt whisky from one of the dog bowls.

Dusty Miller treating an Afghan man bitten by an SAS dog. 'The dogs were just land sharks. We call them land sharks for a reason. They'd just f...... munch people. And so I'd be constantly treating dog bites,' said the combat medic.

Major Jeremy Ross, intelligence officer for the Special Operations Task Group on Rotation 12 in Afghanistan. Ross says the SAS were 'junkyard dogs' who operated with little oversight outside the wire.

SAS troop commander Andrew Hastie returning from an operation in Olum Ghar, Afghanistan, in April 2013 after he discovered an SAS corporal had cut the right hands off three dead insurgents. A troubled Hastie reported it up the chain of command. '[It's] emblematic or symbolic of what war does to people over time, and the way it degrades people's moral sensitivities and compromises your restraint and your ethical decision making.'

SAS troop commander Andre Hastie with Afghan tribal elders during his 2013 deployment to Afghanistan. In February 2013 Hastie apologised to the family of two Afghan boys killed in an air strike against a suspected insurgent spotter. The US Apache crew did not use the grid reference supplied by Hastie's team and they fired at the wrong target, killing the boys.

Australian Major General Fergus McLachlan, right, with his boss, General Joseph Dunford, commander of US Forces in Afghanistan and the International Security Assistance Force. McLachlan was charged with executing the drawdown of American and allied forces. Dunford expressed concerns about the behaviour of some of the Australian SAS undermining their efforts and was angered by the reports of soldiers severing the hands of dead Afghans.

3 Squadron Australian SAS operator Tom at an ANZAC Day ceremony at
Camp Russell in Afghanistan in 2012. Tom left the SAS in September 2016 but
he still struggles to put his experiences and the incidents he witnessed behind him.
'The wrongs need to be righted . . . and the people in Afghanistan who were killed
who shouldn't have been killed deserve a voice.'

When I showed Tom this photo eight years later, he refused to believe it was him.
The chiselled Digger is no longer. The erect, clean-cut SAS operator in the photo
never left Afghanistan.

I had tried to reach him. But the Australian Defence Force had made it clear that he was a serving SAS operator and that I could not speak to him. Because of that we made the decision not to name him, or Soldier B or Soldier C, in the *Four Corners* story. We would not be judge, jury and executioner.

The ADF also refused to answer any of my questions about Braden's detailed eyewitness allegations against Soldier A, claiming it was inappropriate while the Inspector-General of Defence inquiry into war crimes was still ongoing.

After 'Killing Field' went to air I got Soldier A's number. I had been told he had now left the Regiment. Now was the time to dial it. I listen to it ring. I expect no answer. I am ready to leave a voicemail message.

'Hello, it's ****.'

It is him. I have rehearsed my line. I want to keep it short, just a quick introduction. I am not going to make any excuses for the *Four Corners* story. I don't feel there is any need to, and if I do try to explain why I did what I did, I suspect he would see that as weak. I just want to give him an opening and see if he will speak to me.

'Hi, it's Mark Willacy here. I did the *Four Corners* story. I was hoping we could have a chat.'

Nothing. Silence. I am waiting for the phone to go dead. Maybe it has already? But then I can hear him breathing on the other end of the line.

'I don't think I should talk to you. What have I got to gain from talking to you? They tell you I had pancreatic cancer?'

'Yes, I had heard that.'

I had been told by several of Soldier A's SAS comrades that he had cancer, that it was in his pancreas and spreading. I was told by a couple that he only had a short time to live. I decide not to ask about the cancer just yet. He will see that as fake sympathy, a cunning attempt by a scumbag journalist to appear human.

'I was pissed off with you, mate,' he says. 'Because no one ever tried to speak to me and get my side of it. And this went to air, right?'

He is just like his comrades have told me he would be. No bullshit, taking the lead, on the offensive. He fires questions at me like he unloads a magazine from his M4 assault rifle into a Taliban bunker. Straight and rapid.

I explain that I wanted to talk to him for the *Four Corners* story. That I had gone to Defence at the time, but that we had been warned that serving SAS soldiers could be charged for talking to us. At that stage I didn't have his direct number. Now I did, and I wanted to hear his side of things. And I remind him that I didn't identify him in the *Four Corners* story, even though I knew his name.

'Because of that *Four Corners*, I'm right up there with the top five now,' says Soldier A.

He is talking about the Special Forces soldiers who are being investigated by the Inspector-General of Defence. I assume the top five refers to those alleged to have committed war crimes.

'Is that what they've told you?' I ask.

'I must be, right?' he answers. 'I have no doubt the federal cops are listening to this fucking phone call. It doesn't matter. I've done nothing wrong. All I've done is tried to be a good soldier and make sure everybody under my command came home safe and sound, that's including that bloody Braden, who is just a kid.'

I decide to get straight to the point and to Braden's allegations. I have to in case he decides to hang up. Did he order the Waka to kill the prisoner? Did he shoot the man with his hands up?

'I'm not going to go through it with you now,' he says. 'I'll wait till whatever falls out of all this shit.'

He explains that he doesn't want to give me his version of events because he has spoken to the Inspector-General about it. He says he is not allowed to talk about it. I tell him I am allowed to ask him anything I want.

'I just don't want you to put it out there because it'll fuck me even more. As it is, I'm already under the pump. I don't know anything about anything.'

But then, unprompted, he starts talking about the battle at the mud igloo, the firefight in which the Waka Rahul was killed.

'There were four guys in there, all gunned up with hand grenades and everything. They shot the fella next to me,' he says referring to Rahul. 'If you've ever been shot at as many times as I have, it's not a fucking game.'

Soldier A explains that, yes, he was the handler for the Wakunish soldiers. But he stresses that he was not their commander. Is he trying to deflect responsibility for the killing of the prisoner, when Braden says he motioned to the Waka to shoot the bound man just days after the battle of the mud igloo?

'So I'd take [the Wakas] back, I'd train them and then we'd go out and do jobs. All right. So when it comes to me ordering them to do stuff, they just do their own thing anyway,' he says.

So he didn't order the Wakunish to shoot the prisoner? That's what I want to know. Braden says it was to avenge the killing of Rahul.

'What a load of fucking shit,' he says. '[I don't go out and say], "I'm gonna get some revenge for the Wakunish guy who got killed last week." I don't give a fuck about that, because that's the game.'

That's the game, and in Soldier A's eyes Braden has broken the rules of the game.

'He was saying stuff in that article, and he said it to you, that basically made me out to look like an arse clown, when I've always been a professional soldier. I've always done the right thing,' he says. 'And you're making split [second] decisions which he'd never comprehend because he's always standing there with dinner plate eyes going, "What the hell is going on?" Running around with guys who have done multiple, multiple trips and been shot at multiple, multiple times. I'm so fucking angry.'

He calls Braden a kid, a sack of shit, and tells me the Bear has lost his marbles.

'I took him under my wing. I bet he didn't fucking tell you that either, did he?'

I tell him that Braden did tell me that, and more.

'He said, "I actually had him up on a pedestal",' I reply. 'He said, "I thought he was the best sergeant we had". So he did say that.'

'So what's his agenda then? To try and ruin my fucking life?'

We talk for 45 minutes. I tell him that I am writing a book and would like to come and see him, to sit with him and hear his story, his version of events.

'If you don't talk to me, I'm going to have to write it without you. Simple as that,' I say. I know he is a man who doesn't mind plain speaking.

'I'm happy to talk, if you're going to write a book,' he says. 'That's what you do, you write books, you blokes. But you need to get the facts right. If I can't defend myself, it's just fucking wrong.'

A few days later I message Soldier A and tell him I am flying to see him. We agree to meet out the front of the place I will be staying at 10 am the following Monday. He responds with a thumbs up emoji.

But a couple of days before our meeting I get a message from him. He tells me he is not comfortable meeting a journalist.

'Plus, my loyalty lies with my brothers and the unit and to forfeit that trust makes me no different to all these other cowards,' he writes. 'I'm sure you understand.'

I ring him and tell him it is important we meet, for the very reasons he put forward on the phone when we first spoke. He wants me to get my facts straight. I can't do that without talking to him, I explain. If he wants to defend himself, he needs to see me. He relents. The meeting is back on.

On Monday at 10 am I am on a bench outside the place I am staying. At 10.05 am I send him a message to confirm that I am on the bench. At 10.10 am I ring Soldier A. No answer. I get the feeling he is not going to show. But I am reassured by the fact that he is the type of bloke who would have the guts to tell me if he wasn't going to come. He is a straight shooter, in every way, I remind myself. I sit tight and wait.

Then a guy on a Harley Davidson rumbles by and parks. I know immediately from the man's physique it is Soldier A. He is not a big man and he has told me over the phone he has lost a lot of weight since the cancer diagnosis and treatment.

The man is wearing a black, open-faced helmet, and a bandana printed with skulls covers his mouth and nose. Black sunglasses conceal the rest of his face. But I know it is him. I wander over.

He slips off the helmet, bandana and glasses. I am struck by his eyes. Large and blue and piercing. I remember what I was told by that Special Forces veteran about Soldier A. 'Fucking mad, psycho eyes.' But they are not mad or psycho. They just emanate an intensity, a candour, that bores right into you. They follow you like the red dot of a laser gun sight.

'How are you?' I say and hold out my hand.

He slips off his glove and offers his hand.

'I'm good. Sorry, I'm late. I couldn't find the place.'

We decide to talk at a coffee shop up the road. On the way we make small talk, until a man passing us lets go of the leash of his rather large dog. The dog darts across our path.

'Control your dog, mate,' says Soldier A. His tone is even, but firm.

The man looks at him and is about to say something but stops. He has seen the eyes, their blue intensity. Maybe, there is a flash of menace in them too. We walk to the cafe and he orders a lactose-free coffee, explaining that his stomach is quite delicate because of cancer surgery.

We sit and I notice one of his eyes is bloodshot. He senses what I am looking at.

'I'm training for a fight,' he says. 'I want to raise some money for pancreatic cancer research.'

He then tells me one of his sparring partners got him a good one right in the eye. Despite all he has been through with the cancer, Soldier A is still up for a fight.

'I copped a few today,' he says. 'It's ruthless.'

Soldier A is one of the Taliban's feared red beards, though his ginger whiskers are now also flecked with grey. His hair is cropped short, accentuating his widow's peak. He tells me how he was diagnosed with pancreatic cancer in 2018 after suffering from jaundice.

'It's a miracle I've gotten this far because it was inoperable,' he says. They said, "Plan your funeral".'

But after chemotherapy the cancer started to shrink. He tells me about the nine-hour operation to remove the remainder of the cancer. How they took half his pancreas, some of his stomach and duodenum, all his gallbladder, and then sewed what remained of his stomach to his large intestine. Hence the lactose-free coffee.

'When I eat, you can't maintain any nutrients, so you got to take tablets to keep going. That's why I'm only 69 kilos,' he says. 'I'm just buggered, mate. But I might kick on for another five or ten if I'm lucky.'

We talk about his life, how he is a fellow Queenslander. How he broke horses on big stations in the far north. 'On the cattle station you're always getting smashed,' he says. 'You jumped on a young horse before the sun even come up and you usually bite dust then.'

He tells me how he almost had a career in horse racing. 'I'd had an amateur jockey licence as well because I was only 50-something kilos when I was 18. I did three races, Camooweal and a couple of other places,' he says.

I ask if he ever won a race.

'Got a third,' he replies.

But instead of a life of horses and the vast expanses of north Queensland, another career beckoned. At 19 he joined the navy and became a clearance diver. In 1991 Soldier A went off to the first Gulf War on HMAS *Sydney*.

He returned to the Middle East in 2004, working in Iraq on a military security detail, the same time I was in Baghdad working as a foreign correspondent for the ABC. We talk about how we have both been to Basra and Kirkuk, and about how the same hotel we stayed at in the capital was later ripped apart by a suicide bomber.

He says he was the first clearance diver to transfer to the SAS. He tells me about the tragedies that followed.

In 2006 Soldier A was on HMAS *Kanimbla* with an SAS detachment off Fiji. He was supposed to go up with his sniper team on a Black Hawk for a training exercise, but because he had a cold he decided to dive instead.

'Which was a lucky call in the end,' he says.

Soldier A was in his dive gear and had just hopped into the boat when the Black Hawk came into land on the *Kanimbla*.

'It came round and hit in the tail section. The rotor section landed behind my boat. And I said to the guy diving, "Get around there because I reckon it's gone over the side."'

They made their way around the ship but on the other side there was no trace of the Black Hawk, its crew or the SAS team onboard. It had sunk.

'There's nothing left there at all, like nothing happened. Then blokes started bobbing up and I jumped in with my fins and swam over to a couple and we were dragging them back to the boat and we were swimming around dragging blokes out of the water, trying to count guys and we had three blokes with broken backs I think.'

There was no sign of the chopper pilot, Captain Mark Bingley. But after what seems like an impossibly long time, a head bobs up to the surface.

'I swam over to him and it was the pilot, Bingers. I was trying to give him CPR, but I couldn't get on top because of the waves.'

Bingley is dead. So too is SAS Trooper Joshua Porter.

'The young fella went to the bottom with the helicopter,' he tells me. I can see the incident still pains him.

Porter's body was later recovered. Everyone else on the Black Hawk made it out.

The following year Soldier A and a mate were driving through torrential rain at Somersby north of Sydney when they came across a family trapped in a car in the middle of a raging creek. Soldier A could see the mother and father and at least two children inside the car. With the help of some others, Soldier A tied a strap to his waist and waded out into the floodwaters. The father had managed to open the door of the car, but while trying to get out he had been pinned.

'He was stuck [around] his waist, facing out, in the top of the door. Like he'd tried to get out at some stage and the pressure of the water stuck him against the door. So he was stuck.'

'Get my kids, get my kids,' yelled the man.

'I'll get your kids when I get you, mate,' replied Soldier A.

He began throwing the other end of the strap to the father, missing with his first attempt. On the second throw the man grabbed onto it. But the floodwaters had grown more powerful, and as the man tried to pull himself free with the strap the car was picked up and it began to roll. As it did, Soldier A caught sight of one of the kids in the back of the flooded vehicle.

'The boy was nine I think. I saw him. He was dead though. When the car rolled I sort of got a look in the car and saw him.'

The father, pinned by the door, went under with the car. Scrambling out of the water Soldier A and the other would-be rescuers ran along the bank, tracking the bobbing car until they could no longer follow. The bodies of Adam Holt, his partner Roslyn Bragg and their daughters Madison and Jasmine, aged two and three, and their nephew Travis, aged nine, were later recovered. Their car had plunged into the creek when a culvert under the Old Pacific Highway collapsed during the violent rainstorm. A Coroner's inquest would later find that the local council repeatedly ignored warnings about the road and the rusting culvert beneath it. Even a layperson could have foreseen the collapse, the Coroner found. Neglect and incompetence had cost five lives.

As he tells me about his desperate bid to save the family Soldier A looks away, those piercing blue eyes betraying an anguish that he still lives with.

'I went to the inquest and all. I met the family,' he says. 'They asked us to give evidence at the inquest.'

I ask him if he told them how he tied the strap to his waist and waded out into the floodwaters to try to save the family.

'I told them the whole thing.'

Then there was Afghanistan, just months later.

Soldier A was with SAS patrol commander Matthew Locke when he was shot and killed in October 2007 during an engagement with the Taliban.

'I was right next to him when it happened,' he says. 'I crawled out to get him, and I could tell straight away he was dead. We were still taking fire, so we dragged him back into cover and then the boys worked on him. But you could tell straight away, you know, when he's staring up into space.'

After these close calls and the deaths of the family and his comrades, Soldier A says he went off the rails for a while.

'It was just a shit year with three things and everyone sort of died at my feet. I was like, "What the fuck's going on?"' he says. 'But it is what it is.'

After all of that, it was back to Afghanistan for another deployment. He lightens the mood by telling me a funny story, about the time his patrol went into a village. There is a shura, a meeting, going on among the Afghan elders and the SAS patrol finds nothing suspicious and moves on. It is after they have left that the Afghans from the shura get on the radio and challenge them to fight.

'They said, "Send the helicopters away and then fight us like real men",' Soldier A says.

The choppers are called off and Soldier A orders the interpreter to get on the radio. Tell them we're ready to fight, he says. But the Afghans are then seen running away. Soldier A orders the interpreter to get on the radio again. Tell them they're a bunch of pussies, he says. The interpreter looks at him, wondering if he is serious. Do it, he says. He laughs as he recounts the story, and his blue eyes smile.

It is time to talk about the 2012 deployment. His eyes sharpen and the laughter falls away. Soldier A tells me he had more kills than anyone on that deployment. That is because his area of responsibility was 'the bowl'. It is the area around the provincial capital Tarin Kowt, a patchwork of villages, compounds, valleys and peaks that are notorious Taliban strongholds. It is the kills I have come to talk about.

I want to know about the day Braden Chapman says Soldier A killed the Afghan with his hands up. The day Braden says Soldier A ordered him to go through the dead man's pockets, the day the combat dog chewed on the Afghan's head. The day the dog handler said, 'Let him have a taste'.

'He's talking about him searching the body. We would never get him to search the body. You don't expose blokes to that. Because to me, it's nothing,' he had told me over the phone.

He had dodged my questions then. Now I want him to answer them. Did he shoot the guy?

The Afghan didn't have his hands up, he says. He explains that the man had a blanket around him and Soldier A could not tell if he was armed or not. So he shot him.

When they searched the body did they find any weapons? I ask.

No, he wasn't armed, he replies. But I acted within the Rules of Engagement, he says. Braden is full of shit, he adds. He claims the Bear wasn't fit for the 2012 deployment and that one time he had passed out during training back in Perth.

Soldier A then reflects on his career, and how he was – in his words – a good soldier.

'A lot of this stuff is unremarkable to me after ... 20-something years in Perth [at the SAS] and 14 deployments I did, operational deployments.'

He lists them. Iraq. East Timor. Somalia. Afghanistan multiple times.

'War is a dirty thing, as you know, mate,' he says. 'We did more combat than anyone in Vietnam did ... I'm just saying that my unit and the 2 Commando guys, we got shot at a lot.'

But did they shoot people they were not allowed to shoot? Did they cross lines? Did they break the Rules of Engagement?

'I would never call myself a warrior, but that's obviously what we are. That's what we do. That's what we love to do. That's what we've been trained to do.'

Soldier A is poised, he is bold, he wants to set this nosy, naïve, ill-informed journalist straight.

'What I've been training to do for the last 25 years, every fucking day, I've been training to kill dudes. That's all I've ever fucking done. You're a journalist, so you've been trained to be a journalist and talk to people like you're talking to me now,' he says. 'But for me, and my cohorts, that's all you've ever been doing the last 20 years is training every day how to kill people better. And that's a fucking fact.'

I ask him about his 3 Squadron comrade, Soldier B, about his reputation for unwarranted violence, and the allegations that he enjoys killing.

'He is probably my best friend,' he says. 'He's the real deal, mate. Where you've got a job like we do, you need blokes like [Soldier B] ... it's not all fucking rainbows and unicorns and little flying bunnies running around ... he's a great soldier.'

And Soldier C? What about him?

'He's fantastic, mate. He was in my team the year before.'

Like a good soldier, he anticipates my next attack, my next attempt to flank him. He knows I am going to ask about Soldier C and the killing in the wheat field from my *Four Corners* story, footage that set off a media and political firestorm.

'We don't go around shooting blokes willy nilly,' says Soldier A. 'We just go in there and just do the job, because it takes bad men to do bad work in the end.'

Fuck this. I am going to push him on this, on why Soldier C killed Dad Mohammad in the field, why he shot a man who was terrified, unarmed and still on the ground.

'Seriously, if you've got to ask three times [to kill him], you take your eyes off the guy three times, you're spinning around,' I say. 'This guy is on the ground with his knees drawn up, holding his bloody prayer beads.'

'Yeah. I'm not going to comment on that, mate.'

He has dodged the question. No full-frontal assault this time, just a quick retreat. Maybe there are some battles Soldier A prefers to avoid. But then he stuns me.

'In actual fact, I wish I'd got fucking blown away on that trip in 2012. At least I'd have me name up on the wall. I wouldn't be slowly rotting away here.'

He is talking about the memorial at Campbell Barracks in Perth known as 'The Rock', which is etched with the names of the 48 SAS soldiers killed on deployment or in training. Some of those killed, like Blaine Diddams, were Soldier A's mates. He is also talking about the cancer, the slow rot inside him that could finish what the Taliban could not.

After the cancer diagnosis Soldier A and his wife separated.

'Marriage breakdown on top of it all and then you come out on *Four Corners* and kick me right in the guts.'

Then there are his three children who he helps care for, including twins with special needs.

'They were born [at] 25 weeks, that's why they're special needs,' he says. 'This is why you're doing your thing and you go away, and you come back, and you sacrifice everything.'

We talk again about the 2012 deployment, the close calls.

'I nearly got blown away three times on that trip.'

About the fog of war on the battlefields of Afghanistan and the shape-shifting enemy.

'How do you differentiate between a combatant and a non-combatant, right, in that split second?'

About the mission in Uruzgan.

'I was only going there to make sure me mates came home safe. I don't give a fuck about any big picture bullshit. None of us did.'

About how pointless it all was.

'We'd get guys, we knew they were bad guys. We would put them in the detention facility, and they would be out three days later.'

About the senior officers and generals who gave out the orders, set the missions, and ran the war.

'At the end of the trip, all the medals and honours and awards come out and none of the Diggers got anything. But all these fucking officers did.'

About what the Inspector-General's inquiry will find.

'They're just going to take the "A" out of SAS and we're going to be SS. We're all going to be arseholes. We're all going to be labelled as fucking murderous pricks.'

And finally, about him.

'I'm like a cat with nine lives to be honest,' he says.

I wonder how many of those lives he has used up. Soldier A has outfought many enemies, he has survived tours to Iraq and Somalia, he has seen off the Taliban on multiple deployments, and he has fought cancer to a standstill through chemotherapy and surgery, a cancer that usually kills 90 per cent of those who get it within five years of diagnosis. But is he truly the good soldier he says he is?

'Every bloke I've shot over the years there's a thousand I didn't shoot. That's just how it is, mate,' he says. 'When we were overseas I wasn't the nicest bloke. I wasn't there to build bridges and schools and shake hands with locals. I don't give two fucks about that.'

Soldier A declines my offer of another coffee. We have been sitting and talking now for two hours. Sometimes he is quiet and reflective. Other times, like when he talks about the family who were washed away in their car and who drowned before his very eyes, he is clearly emotional. One time, when describing the battle of the well and how he was nearly killed by the hand holding the AK-47, he leaps to his feet and acts out how he got behind the attacker and dropped down some grenades.

'That footage, is there more to come out?' he asks. He is talking about the more than 10 hours of footage I got from Braden, the helmet camera vision that I used in my *Four Corners* report.

'Yes,' I tell him. I am planning to run a story showing three of his comrades standing around talking about Soldier B killing a prisoner. It will be running in two days' time, but I don't tell him that.

'Does it involve me?' he says.

'No, it doesn't.'

'I should hope not. I don't think there would be, because I'm pretty down the line with it,' he says.

Soldier A believes there is no footage of him doing anything wrong, because he doesn't cross the line with his soldiering.

As we walk back to his Harley Davidson, he tells me how he is joining a veterans' motorcycle club. He has no time for outlaw gangs, they are scumbags.

Back at his bike he puts on the skull bandana and his helmet. He slips his sunglasses over those intense blue eyes. He is invisible once again. He holds out a gloved hand and I shake it. He promises to stay in touch.

A couple of months later I am awarded the Gold Walkley for 'Killing Field'. I am bombarded with phone calls and messages of congratulations. A few days later another message flashes up. I open it. It is from Soldier A.

'Congratulations on ur (sic) award.'

I'm stunned. Is he serious? Or is he taking the piss? He is known for having a quirky sense of humour. I have won Australia's highest honour in journalism for a story in which he stands accused by a comrade of committing one war crime and ordering another. As I am pondering these questions another message from him appears on my phone.

'Not being sarcastic either BTW.'

18

WHERE OTHERS FEAR
TO TREAD

'A war begun for no wise purpose, carried on with a
strange mixture of rashness and timidity, brought to a
close after suffering and disaster, without much glory
attached either to the government which directed, or
the great body of troops which waged it. Not one benefit,
political or military, was acquired with this war'
**British Army Chaplain George R. Gleig on the
First Anglo–Afghan War of 1839–1842**

The instructor looks down at the groggy candidate.

'Give me your rifle.'

The candidate has barely had an hour's sleep. He has just returned
from a long pack march in the Stirling Range, 330 kilometres south-
east of Perth. It is rugged country, with bluffs rising over a thousand
metres and a unique topography that creates its own weather conditions. After bashing his way through thick bushland for days with
bugger all food to eat the candidate has collapsed into a deep sleep,
only to be woken a short time later for a snap rifle inspection. It is part
of the mind games the instructors like to play.

It is 1987 and candidate Jeff Sengelman is determined to pass
selection for the SAS. A jungle warfare instructor at the Army's
Canungra Barracks in Queensland, 25-year-old Sengelman is on a
career trajectory to becoming a senior officer. But he wants something
more exciting, he dreams of a life of boys' own adventure. The SAS is
the perfect place for that.

Ever since he was head of cadets at Ipswich State School in south-east Queensland, Sengelman has wanted to be in the army. The grandson of a garbage collector who lost most of his fingers on one hand while serving in Bougainville in World War Two, he was the youngest graduate from the Army's Officer Cadet School. Now the boy from Ipswich wants to join the army's most elite unit.

The SAS selection course is legendary for its sheer physical and mental torture, its mind-bending sleep and food deprivation, and its crushing attrition rate. Only 10 to 30 per cent of those who start get through. During three weeks of hell there are solo navigation exercises over days covering more than 70 kilometres. There are 2 am parades in full kit with weapons. There are scenarios involving secret patrols in 'foreign lands'. Then there is Exercise Happy Wanderer. Candidates are dropped into isolated bush with a 50-kilogram pack to carry. They have four to five days to move undetected through more than 100 kilometres of rugged terrain. They are hunted by an 'enemy force' armed with dogs.

'You've got no clothes,' says one SAS operator. 'So you've had to make your clothes out of hessian, a big roll of hessian. You start sewing up clothes. You're looking like cavemen running through the bush with sticks and improvised stuff.'

'We're doing our escape and evasion process, travelling by night across the West Australian bushland,' says another operator. 'Doing ten, fifteen kilometres a night following the stars.'

Sometimes when they are dropped in the scrub the candidates are given a goat. They know exactly what to do with it.

'We had to gut the goat and cut the goat up into meat and divvy it up between 17 or 18 blokes and then dry the meat,' says an operator.

For the candidates, one goat among more than a dozen men lugging heavy packs through endless scrubland only goes so far. Hunger soon sets in and the scramble for food means eating whatever bush tucker they can scavenge. Even if it means recycling.

'Quandong,' says one SAS trooper. 'They're like nuts, berries, that emus eat. Emus will shit out the nut. You look for the emu poo and go through it and crack the nut and eat the nut ... It was just three weeks of just starving and being chased.'

That is a gourmet meal compared to what one trooper remembers from his selection. Having battled through the bush for days, the candidates get a food delivery.

'The truck turns up and two trays come out with a bit of foil over the top, and you're so fucking hungry. You are so running on fumes. And it is this moment of, "Right, this is the last feed you're going to get for the next four days. Consider that".'

The instructors peel back the foil. The men stare down at their meal, and it stares right back at them.

'It was a bed of pigs' eyes with their eyelids and eyelashes,' says the trooper. 'On a bed of couscous that was blue.'

Starving, and with the prospect of little or no food for another four days, these SAS candidates have little choice.

'If you don't ingest this, and put this into your body, there's no way you'll get through the next four days,' says the trooper. 'I was gorilla fisting these things. I remember them exploding in my mouth and thinking to myself, "I need to get as much fuel for my body" ... and the thing about pigs' eyes, they're like human eyes, that's the worst bit. I looked at one and it was looking at me. I can still see it.'

Those who can't swallow pigs' eyes and who fail the many other gruesome physical and psychological challenges of selection are RTU'd: Returned to Unit. Others who can't stand the sheer hell of selection can fill out a Withdrawal at Own Request form. But if you do that you will never be allowed to try for selection again.

'I actually ate [the form] I was that hungry,' jokes one operator. 'You need something in your stomach.'

Jeff Sengelman is determined to make it through. If he doesn't, it is back to Canungra and a career as yet another staff officer.

'He was quiet, reserved,' says Bruce Armstrong, also a candidate on the 1987 SAS selection course. 'But you could absolutely sense that he had a very strong but quiet determination to get through the course.'

'He would not mind me saying this, but Jeff was by no means the fittest in the group,' says Greg de Somer, who was often paired with Sengelman on the selection course. '[But] he's very dogged and determined, and that's what they're looking for.'

But Sengelman has an Achilles heel. It is no secret to his friend de Somer or to anyone else on the course for that matter. That includes the instructors, many of whom are grizzled veterans of the Vietnam War. These old timers, with their stony-faced scowls and machine gun bark, have one key task.

'They just apply pressure,' says de Somer. 'I went on the course knowing you're not going to get praise ... if you did a five-kilometre run and came first and got a really good time, they'd give you a hard time for not trying hard enough ... they'd say, "The guy you beat by a minute actually did better because he gave his all. You didn't. You were cruising, you're a bludger".'

'Physically, but importantly, mentally, they test your absolute limits to see where you sit,' says Armstrong. 'It's the constant lack of sleep, of telling you you've failed at everything you do ... they're always looking for some way to physically punish us and to make sure that you're right at the point of physical exhaustion ... a lot of guys took themselves off the course. So it's hard.'

One of the instructors is about to target Sengelman's potentially course-ending vulnerability, one that has earned him the nickname Rusty. Bruce Armstrong is further down the line, watching with trepidation as the instructor barks at his spent comrade.

'Give me your rifle.'

The exhausted Sengelman snaps to. The instructor is looking at him, waiting for the candidate to hand over his semi-automatic SLR.

Sengelman knows the rifle is chock full of dust, dirt and grime. He didn't clean it once while he was out on the Stirling Range. Instead of pulling it apart and cleaning it when he got back from the march, he chose to hit the sack. Sheer fatigue trumped maintaining weapon cleanliness and operability.

'Jeff's nickname was Rusty because he always had rust on his weapon,' says de Somer. '[The instructors] knew if they want to pick on someone for a weapon, you'd go to Jeff first up. And chances are you'd get a bite … and sure enough he got done.'

The candidate hands over the SLR.

'[The instructor] looked down the barrel of his weapon and said, "There's rust in there",' says Armstrong. 'And I don't think there was anyone who was in that line who wasn't thinking I've probably got rust in my weapon as well. But I think the truth is that they were trying to find a mental chink in Jeff's armour.'

Having already found rust down the barrel of Sengelman's SLR, the instructor presses the takedown latch on the side of the weapon and tries to break the rifle open to check it further. But the latch won't depress, and the rifle won't open. All that grime and rust has seized it shut.

The instructor throws the rifle back at Sengelman.

'You open it up.'

Sengelman knows that if the instructor can't open the SLR, then he certainly can't. Desperate, the candidate begins slamming the butt of the rifle into the ground in a desperate effort to break it open. Next to him in the line, another candidate begins to laugh. Then the instructor starts to chuckle. But within seconds his laughter fades to silence, and the instructor's face turns to thunder.

'You're off the course,' he tells Sengelman. 'Go pack your bag.'

Sengelman can't believe it. He is not even halfway through the selection course and he has blown it. The exhausted ex-candidate shuffles back to his bunk and collapses.

285

'I got told plenty of times that I'd failed on certain events I'd passed, but they tell you you'd failed anyway, just to mentally see where you were,' says Bruce Armstrong. 'We all got the same in one way, shape or form, that, "You're failing ... it's all over for you".'

In the morning Sengelman hatches a plan to test whether the instructors are playing psychological games with him. He will stay put. He will refuse to leave the course. What has he got to lose?

'[The instructors] applied pressure to see how he reacts,' says fellow selection candidate Greg de Somer. 'And clearly he didn't react to it, and just dug his heels in and stayed on.'

'What the fuck are you still doing here?' screams the instructor when he spots the failed candidate. 'Get your gear. Go!'

But like the latch on his rusted rifle, Sengelman won't budge.

Sengelman's stubbornness, his refusal to quit in the face of defeat, his downright chutzpah, bemuses the instructors.

'Okay, dickhead. If you want to hang around we are going to torch the shit out of you.'

He can stay. But if he wants to continue, the instructors will keep their promise to do everything to make his life hell. They will break this cocky bastard.

It is decided the unflushable candidate will get his own personal instructor whose job it is to smash Sengelman till he submits.

But the candidate persists. The special attention seems to drive him on.

One day towards the end of the course the candidates are ordered to run up a hill with a colleague over their shoulders. Sengelman is given his dead weight.

'No. I want this guy,' he says pointing to one of the instructors. He is a big man, much larger than Sengelman's designated partner.

Sengelman slings the big guy over his shoulder and sets off up the hill. The instructors shake their heads. The stubborn prick just keeps going. He won't be stopped. He reaches the top of the hill with the big bloke still onboard.

But on the very last day Sengelman is stopped in his tracks. A virus, coupled with three weeks of relentless adversity and privation, has stripped a lot of weight from him. He collapses and wakes up in hospital.

Coming to, his first thought is, Have I failed selection?

But from his hospital bed Jeff Sengelman is told he has passed. He is one of just a handful of officers who has got through the mental and physical torment of selection. His friends Greg de Somer and Bruce Armstrong are others.

'I lost 10 kilos,' says de Somer. 'Statistically, of 35 officers [who started] only five get through roughly. So it's competitive.'

The candidate they call Rusty has cleared the first hurdle to joining the Special Air Service Regiment.

Sometimes it pays to be a stubborn bastard.

———

It is Jeff Sengelman's first day with his feet under the desk as Special Operations Commander Australia or SOCAUST. Nearly three decades after refusing to be kicked off SAS selection he is back. But as SOCAUST, Major-General Sengelman isn't just in charge of his old Regiment. As well as the SAS, he is the head of the Commandos, the Special Operations Engineer Regiment, the Special Operations Logistics Squadron, and all Special Forces training. He also runs the Special Forces' domestic counterterrorism deployments.

'I formed a private view that they couldn't have picked anyone better to do it,' says Bruce Armstrong. Sengelman's old SAS selection comrade would become a captain in the Regiment before finishing his military career as a colonel and then running a large corporation. 'I think that was the hardest job there was in the Defence Force at that time, to take on that command and leadership role of SOCAUST.'

Sengelman's people are expected to be the best of the best, the most versatile and adaptable members of the military. One year they may be sent away on operations to places like Afghanistan, the next they may be engaged in the counterterrorism unit, and the year after that they may be seconded to clandestine activities with ASIS.

Based in a windowless sub-basement at Special Operations Command in Canberra, Sengelman is a rare thing for a SOCAUST. He is one of the few insiders who left Special Operations and went off to do other things in the military. He has been the Deputy Chief of Army. He has commanded 28,000 personnel, ten times the number of people he will lead in Special Operations. He has been the director of strategic operations for the legendary US General and counterinsurgency specialist David Petraeus in Iraq. He has been the head of Modernisation and Strategic Planning for the entire Australian Defence Force, a role that puts him in charge of preparing the military for future challenges and threats. It is a job Sengelman tackles with gusto.

'I was a kid that liked to dream about the future and what could be,' he tells the Blenheim Partners leadership podcast series *No Limitations*.

From his office in the windowless sub-basement, the former school cadet from Ipswich is now a two-star general in charge of all of Australia's Special Forces. But Sengelman quickly starts to realise his future as SOCAUST could involve cleaning up an almighty mess. He has been away from Special Operations for five years and a lot has changed. For a start, the forever war in Afghanistan for the SAS and Commandos has been over now for 12 months. The last rotation – the 20th – departed the country and returned home in December 2013. The Australian SAS had first arrived in Afghanistan in October 2001. The Special Forces would eventually deploy to the country in three phases: 2001–2002, 2005–2006 and 2007–2013.

Despite the constant rotations and frenetic tempo of deployments, Afghanistan gave the SAS, in particular, a purpose and a focus.

It has defined them and won them plaudits in the media and from Australia's political leadership. But now the war is over there is a danger. It is a vacuum, a silence, that the SAS doesn't know how to fill. For Sengelman, this is a dangerous thing. He needs to re-orient and re-focus the Regiment, and that could take a year or two.

Greg de Somer believes Sengelman is the perfect candidate to repair and re-shape Special Operations.

'He came at a very pivotal time,' says de Somer, who also rose through the Regiment to become an Officer Commanding of an SAS Sabre Squadron. 'He identified things very early on ... I'm quite proud of him.'

'Jeff is a thinking officer and leader in a relatively rare way. I don't think there are too many like him,' says his other close friend Fergus McLachlan. 'He's a terrific guy, but he's tough.'

By this time Major General McLachlan has completed his 12-month tour of Afghanistan as the Chief of Plans for the Commander of the International Security Assistance Force, US General Joseph Dunford. For his service there, McLachlan will be awarded the United States Legion of Merit. He has now returned to Big Army back in Australia. McLachlan notices that a dangerous 'us' and 'them' mentality has developed between the Army and Special Operation Command. He believes his mate Sengelman is just the man to put a dose of salts through the chicken stranglers and trigger pullers of the Special Forces.

'I took some initial perverse satisfaction out of the fact that [Special Operations Command] was getting some scrutiny,' says McLachlan. 'We didn't know where it was going to lead. But I'd been in Afghan-istan, I knew there was alcohol. We knew these things in Big Army.'

In late 2014, just before Jeff Sengelman takes over as SOCAUST, Western Australian police get a tip off. Searching the home of an SAS member in Perth, they find a large cache of ammunition and weapons parts. They have been stolen from the SAS firearm magazine at Campbell Barracks, exposing a massive hole in how the Regiment regulates and accounts for its explosive ordnance and controlled stores. Some fear the ammunition and weapons parts are being sold to bikie gangs.

But this is not just a worrying theft of supposedly secure SAS equipment and stores. It is an example of the significant governance and discipline problems at the Regiment. The SAS is purportedly the most audited unit in the army. So why isn't something as deadly serious as missing ordnance being picked up?

Jeff Sengelman has a visit to the SAS in Perth scheduled in his diary, his first as SOCAUST. But in light of the revelations about the theft of ammunition from the SAS magazine, that trip across the continent will have to be brought forward. Sengelman is ordered by the Chief of the Defence Force, Mark Binskin, to get on a plane and get over there to find out what the hell is going on. So much for the welcome mat being rolled out in Perth for the new SOCAUST. Instead, Sengelman is heading west to kick some SAS arses.

'As a commander, I knew that these were indicators that something was wrong,' he will later tell the *No Limitations* podcast. 'What's going on? Back in those early days, these weren't stories about war crimes.'

Stolen weapons parts and ordnance are not the only problems confronting the SOCAUST. The command he leads has become inbred and stale. The headquarters Sengelman has inherited is riven with gossip and leaks. His old regiment, the SAS, supposedly the most elite in the entire Defence Force, is tired and some say in an apparent state of dysfunction. Many of its officers opt for mateship over leadership and turn a blind eye to bad behaviour by their subordinates. No one is held accountable, and this further undermines discipline and the chain of command. If anything, management of the Regiment has become bottom up. The battle-hardened NCOs, veterans of multiple Afghanistan tours, are running the show. They have become the tail wagging the SAS dog. There is also a smug elitism rising from the ranks, and a deep sense of entitlement rooted in their Afghanistan

290

heroics. There is an arrogance of exceptionalism and self-glorification around the place that would be unacceptable anywhere else in the Defence Force. The culture and values of the Regiment are seemingly adrift, and many fear that deviance has been normalised.

Even within the SAS itself, rival tribes have emerged. One group wants the Regiment to stay faithful to its original purpose, that of reconnaissance and surveillance. They believe the true spirit of the SAS is personified by the legendary phantoms of the jungle, the Viet Cong's feared Ma Rung. But another faction has embraced the American concept of the Special Forces as ultimate warriors carrying out secretive kill/capture missions. It is these adherents to Stanley McChrystal's snake-eater doctrine who have triumphed as the dominant tribe.

Over the more than decade-long course of the Afghanistan conflict, Australian and American Special Forces conducted many combined operations, and on occasion had to fight their way out of Taliban ambushes together. Their bond has been forged by blood and bullets.

But Sengelman believes this bond has become unhealthily close. Australian Special Forces soldiers are spending more time embedded, attached or visiting their American and British counterparts than they are spending with their fellow Australian units. It is time for a re-balancing. Sengelman directs Special Forces elements to join ADF exercises each year and to work more with Australian conventional forces. Special Forces NCOs are encouraged to cross over into Big Army for a while if they want promotion.

But have Sengelman's efforts to re-balance come a few years too late? Elements of the SAS leadership have already embraced with gusto that US kill/capture approach to operations. In the final couple of years of the Afghanistan conflict – 2012 and 2013 – the thrill of the hunt and discredited Vietnam-era kill counts have underpinned SAS operations. The increasing number of Afghan deaths – insurgent and civilian alike – reflect that. The war is now over. The dead in

Afghanistan are long buried. And kill/capture is seen by many as a grotesque failure.

'That kill or capture [concept] was past its used by date,' says former Army general Fergus McLachlan. 'I think we just killed the older, more moderate [Afghan insurgents]. And we just made angrier, more violent ones.'

Six months after his appointment as SOCAUST, Jeff Sengelman emails the Chief of Army, David Morrison, formally advising his boss of the scale of the problems at Special Operations (including the SAS) and how he plans to address them. Governance and culture are among his priorities. Sengelman is directed to proceed with his plan.

Within weeks he has removed control of Campbell Barracks in Perth from the Commanding Officer of the SAS and appointed another lieutenant-colonel to run the base. It is too much for the SAS CO to run the base and the busiest and most specialised combat unit in the Australian military. The Regiment is put on an operational pause. The only thing that remains a priority for the SAS is responsibility for domestic counterterrorism. Everything else is on hiatus until the SAS gets back to a healthy footing.

Soon after comes a bombshell. The Australian Secret Intelligence Service, whose agents had served alongside SAS members in Afghanistan, tells Defence leadership about nearly 100 serious incidents its personnel witnessed in Afghanistan. These are incidents, including alleged unlawful killings, that involve Australian Special Forces, predominantly the SAS. One ASIS agent has complained to his superiors that in one case the SAS killed everyone inside a target vehicle including his source. The source was their inside man and was supposed to be spared. The ASIS agent is furious, accusing the SAS of indiscriminate killing. It can take ASIS agents months, sometimes longer, to identify and cultivate informers. The list of incidents outlined by the spy agency is concerning, but Defence cannot talk directly with ASIS personnel about what they allegedly witnessed. That is off limits.

The ASIS complaints and the persistent whispers about atrocities in Afghanistan cannot be ignored any longer. But who can Jeff Sengelman trust in his old Regiment?

'I reached the point as a leader when I knew that if I couldn't elicit from my own soldiers the truth, and if I didn't have a relationship with them that believed enough in me to at least tell me their stories about what they thought was going on, then actually the very foundations of my position as SOCAUST, my unwritten contract as a leader, would be held in some doubt. I knew I had to try something different,' he said.

He calls a meeting of SAS sergeants and higher ranks.

'I brought in the bulk of the members of the Regiment in a single room and I asked them to tell me their stories. But I asked them in a way that encouraged them to believe in me. So I expressed my concern about what was going on and why. I invited them to each write me a letter to tell me honestly what was going on in their own words.'

Sengelman tells them he will respect the privacy of the letters they submit. He promises to resign his commission if he ever breaches their trust by showing anyone else the correspondence. The letter writing exercise is Sengelman's version of a truth and reconciliation commission. If you confess, you get a fresh start. But he warns that if they raise criminal behaviour, he will have to report it.

At the meeting he tells them that the SAS is at a tipping point. This is their last chance to come clean. If they fail to do that, it is out of Sengelman's hands.

'Okay, sir, we get it,' he is told.

In all, Sengelman will get 209 letters from the men of the Regiment. Many of them are emotional and raw, and they express sadness and regret about what they have done. Most are about consuming alcohol in Afghanistan. Some talk about drugs. These are not war crimes. But the binge drinking and the use of drugs on deployment is a symptom of wider problems in Afghanistan and at home – domestic violence, poor decision making, normalised deviance and loose leadership.

'I did for a fleeting moment think that we were the metaphoric equivalent of the Titanic just about to hit the iceberg. So I grabbed the wheel and I pulled hard right,' says Sengelman. 'We missed the iceberg, but we lost a lot of bark in the turning. But we turned and we were still afloat at the end of it.'

The SOCAUST writes back to all 209 correspondents.

He poses practical and philosophical questions to them. What is their purpose as SAS operators and members? How do they define who they are and their culture? Are they the exceptional warrior at the pinnacle of warcraft who can find and finish the enemy? Or are they a soldier of the highest moral outlook who practises ethical behaviour and displays integrity of character? Sengelman believes the men of the SAS should aspire to be both but must always prioritise the latter.

But there is a core of resistance building against Sengelman within the Regiment. Some old hands think the new boss is stirring up shit that would be best left alone.

'He wasn't in Afghanistan. He doesn't understand what's going on,' says one.

'Sengelman is using this to promote himself,' complains another.

This sentiment isn't just confined to those calloused Afghanistan veterans within the NCO ranks. A senior colleague tells Sengelman to 'ease up a bit'. Others, some of them old friends, go quiet on him. It is a lonely time.

'I did apologise to Jeff later because as he peeled back the onion and it had got rotten, we were slow to understand how much load he was carrying,' says his friend and fellow general Fergus McLachlan. 'It is a very isolated time for Jeff. I think his mates have mobilised since, but we at the time didn't know how deep it was going ... it was pretty much Jeff on his own.'

'I think we all had an idea that it was going to be tough,' says Sengelman's comrade from selection and former SAS captain Bruce Armstrong. 'We knew that, but I don't think any of us had any idea how hard that command was going to be. And I think talking to him after, I probably should have reached out. It was an incredibly hard time for him.'

But Sengelman's letter writing exercise seems to have pricked some consciences. The SOCAUST is now being told stories that hint at atrocities committed by Australia's most elite soldiers. He is told that people were killed in Afghanistan who should not have been killed. That radios and weapons were dropped on bodies. There is not a lot of detail about the when, where or who. But these stories are disturbing, and they keep coming.

'It was people from within Special Operations who told the stories, not outsiders. People inside. Our own people came forward and shared those stories,' Sengelman says.

'Australian soldiers have the best bullshit detectors of any Australians I know ... and I suspect Special Forces soldiers are even better,' says Fergus McLachlan. 'So they had to perceive that he was fair dinkum and going to follow it through or they wouldn't have disclosed anything, because they were vulnerable.'

The evidence that atrocities were committed in Afghanistan is growing. In his headquarters in the sub-basement, the SOCAUST meets with about a dozen visiting SAS captains.

'I am hearing stories of incidents and war crimes. I don't want any details but as the SOCAUST I want to know how broadly this goes,' Sengelman tells them. 'How many of you have heard stories of war crimes? Put your hands up. This won't go any further than this room.'

All but one raises his hand.

As part of his review of Special Operations Command, Sengelman calls in someone he trusts, an outsider. Samantha Crompvoets is a sociologist in her late thirties who has done studies for organisations ranging from police and emergency services to the Australian Football League. Her Canberra-based firm specialises in organisational change and culture. Crompvoets has also done reviews for the Defence Department and worked with Jeff Sengelman before.

'I was kind of a known quantity,' she says. 'The stuff they'd got me to do previously was a bit sensitive.'

Sengelman commissions Samantha Crompvoets to study how Special Operations Command (SOCOMD) 'integrates, operates and co-ordinates with other ADF and whole-of-government capabilities in support of Australia's national security'. This isn't about war crimes, more about how the Special Forces fit with other agencies, and what those agencies think of the people and units under Sengelman's command.

'What he engaged me to do was look at how the national security community perceived Special Operations Command, what was their capability in terms of domestic counterterrorism,' says Crompvoets. 'That was my terms of reference. Go and talk to a whole lot of very senior people across a whole lot of agencies and government and see what they think.'

The interview list she is given contains names from the Australian Federal Police, the spy agencies ASIO and ASIS, the Department of Foreign Affairs, and the Department of Prime Minister and Cabinet.

'It was pretty high-level people,' says Crompvoets.

Predictably, the assessments of the Special Forces and their capabilities are glowing.

'People just said, "Yeah, they're amazing",' says Crompvoets. 'But what became really clear is ... they didn't actually know what they did. Some of these really senior people didn't even know the difference between SAS and Commandos.'

No one has anything bad to say, though Crompvoets is told of 'rumours' of odd behaviour by the SAS.

'They're all a bit "off the reservation" was the phrase people often used,' she says. 'There were these questions, questions about exactly what they did in the shadows … there might be some things that are quite unpalatable to government or the public.'

Samantha Crompvoets is confused. These interviews are shedding very little light on what the Special Forces do and how they fit with other agencies. Then there are these vague rumours about them going off the reservation.

'I was like, "Why do I not understand what the fuck is going on?" I just don't get what they're all alluding to,' says Crompvoets.

She wants to understand more, but she won't be able to fill in the blanks by talking to the brass and those in the upper echelons of the security agencies.

'So I went back to Jeff and the [Chief of Army Angus Campbell] and said it would be great to talk to some other people internally so that I can better understand how SOCOMD works,' Crompvoets says.

She is given a new list of names. She is told she can add anyone to the list that she thinks will help her research. Crompvoets starts working through her new lot of interviewees.

'What really came up then was that history of the Commandos versus SAS,' she says. 'Absolutely toxic. SAS not wanting to touch the bags of Commandos if they had to move a whole lot of stuff … they would be constantly bitching about each other. Not just that, withholding information from each other so they couldn't do their job. It was really sort of petty, but actually quite risky behaviour, really undermining capability.'

The men from the rival regiments are only too happy to bad mouth each other to Crompvoets. Their internecine hatred is both petty and disturbing at the same time. But it soon leads her down a darker path.

'When I started to have these conversations a couple of little things started slipping out, about things that weren't quite right,' Crompvoets says. 'Initially, people just started referring to Abu Ghraib or My Lai.'

The My Lai massacre during the Vietnam War and the Abu Ghraib torture and prisoner abuse scandal in Iraq were human rights violations that to this day tarnish the reputation of the US military. What are her interviewees trying to tell Samantha Crompvoets?

Word is now spreading through Special Operations about Crompvoets and her research project. Her phone is beginning to ring day and night.

'I remember one person phoning me and just saying, "I just want to talk to you about some stuff that I know happened in Afghanistan",' she says. 'He was talking about farmers being executed, and also talking about the planting of weapons on people … I just thought, "Fuck, I need to ask more questions".'

But some don't like Samantha Crompvoets asking questions. She feels some of the officers in Special Operations Command are trying to railroad her.

'It was like, "Okay, civvy chick, you've done your bit now. You don't really get it. Off you go, that's enough",' she says. 'I knew I was pissing them off.'

She asks Jeff Sengelman what she should do.

'I remember Sengelman saying to me, "You don't talk to anyone in SOCOMD anymore, any of the people working in SOCOMD Headquarters. None of them can be trusted."'

Just weeks after Samantha Crompvoets begins her research, one of the more destructive elements of SAS culture will be celebrated in front of hundreds of people. At a ball at the Hotel Realm in Canberra for the veterans' charity Soldier On in August 2015, a decorated and respected SAS operator makes a speech. In it he jokes about getting on the piss with a comedian who had come over to Afghanistan to entertain the troops. To the vast majority in the audience, which includes a former prime minister and some top military brass, it is a harmless gag delivered by a man of undeniable moral fibre and physical courage. Everyone thinks it is pretty funny. But to a few in the crowd it speaks to the normalisation of alcohol misuse and abuse, a chronic failure of discipline within the ranks, and a visible lack of leadership in theatre.

If one of their role model warriors, a man of unimpeachable integrity, is making jokes about being on the grog in Afghanistan, what other behaviours were acceptable over there?

Samantha Crompvoets has also heard the stories of the boozing in Afghanistan from the soldiers she has been speaking to for her research. But it is the other stories that really disturb her. Crompvoets has by now been told about competition killing, the cover ups of atrocities, 'psychos' in the Regiment with a bloodlust, and how patrol commanders were responsible for 'the worst of it'. There is a disturbing, yet unverified, story about the SAS slitting the throats of two 14-year-old Afghan boys who they decide might be Taliban sympathisers.

'I spoke to a lot of people who were really broken by it, who were really devastated that that was their organisation, who were frustrated that nothing had happened. Really frustrated,' she says. 'The most disturbing thing was people saying, "Yeah, that was what happened all the time. It wasn't this one thing that happened once. And I've been really traumatised by it. This was just the way it was. This is what people did. These were routine, regular occurrences, patterns of behaviour".'

It is time for Crompvoets to seek some advice about the terrible stories she is hearing about Australian Special Forces in Afghanistan. What she has been told is like nothing she has ever come across before. This is all well outside the scope of her original brief, and Crompvoets wants to know what to do with this troubling information. She goes to see Jeff Sengelman and Angus Campbell. Campbell gives her some simple advice.

'Bad news doesn't get better with time. Write it all down.'

Sengelman advises her to provide two separate reports and to disclose everything.

'So it had to be separate,' says Crompvoets. 'It was much more freeing to me to be able to write them separately.'

In early 2016, Crompvoets submits her reports to Sengelman and Campbell. The first report aligns with the original contract of

providing a snapshot of how Special Operations Command integrates, operates and co-ordinates with other military and government
agencies. In it there are no specific allegations of war crimes. But
there are allusions to domestic violence, behaviour involving drugs
and alcohol, and 'unsanctioned and illegal application of violence on
operations'. Crompvoets also writes of the disregard for human life in
Afghanistan and the perception of a complete lack of accountability
at times.

It is in her second, seven-page report titled 'Insights and reflection' that more specific concerns are raised about unlawful killings
and cover ups.

'It was sanctioned psychopathic behaviour,' Crompvoets reports
one participant as telling her.

'You'd just stand there while things were going on thinking, this
is fucked. But what can you do?' another is quoted as saying. 'If they
don't trust you, that's it – you basically get pushed out and it's pretty
much the end of your career.'

The sociologist admits in her second report that the details of the
events she has been told about are scant. But what isn't ambiguous
is the sense of frustration and anger felt by those soldiers who know
about what happened in Afghanistan.

'As stories trickle out, and they inevitably will, the legacy of [Special
Operations Forces] will perhaps no longer be the "fine capability" held
in such high regard politically and internationally,' she writes in her
second report. 'Rather it will be a story about accountability, trust and
blood lust that will stain the organisation for a long time to come.'

Crompvoets knows this second report will cause a stir in Canberra.

'I knew it would go to the Minister,' she says. 'I knew that it would
be escalated. I clearly felt sort of vulnerable.'

She worries she will be dismissed as a civilian 'know-nothing' who
has never been to war. But Crompvoets is convinced that what she has
been told, and what she has included in the seven-page report, is true.

It has to be, because many of those from within the Special Forces that she has spoken to have taken great risks.

'One person in particular was scared for his life. He said, "If anyone knew I was saying this …" He just felt like he'd be killed or something.'

Jeff Sengelman has heard pretty much the same things that Crompvoets has detailed in her 'insights and reflection' report. Her accounts of what she has been told are yet more confirmation that SAS operator discipline has broken down and that deviance is entrenched and even institutionalised. It also bolsters Sengelman's belief that it will only be a matter of time before these rumours and allegations become public.

But Sengelman has much more than Crompvoets' reports in his bottom drawer. He has the 209 letters sent in by SAS members, and other stories of disturbing behaviour he has been told about. This has become too big.

On 9 March 2016, Major-General Jeff Sengelman in his capacity as SOCAUST writes to his boss, the Chief of Army Angus Campbell, and advises him of a range of deeply disturbing stories that have come to his attention. These stories imply that serious or criminal behaviour may have been committed in Afghanistan. Sengelman writes that 'some of these matters are widely known and circulated within the Command'. He believes there is sufficient substance to the stories, which appear to stretch over a decade, to warrant a detailed inquiry. But most revealing in his correspondence to Angus Campbell is Sengelman's belief that some of these unsettling stories were known to those up the chain of command.

'My cursory understanding of these matters suggest that a range of leaders with Special Operations backgrounds have been aware of these stories but failed to formally report them through agreed mechanisms.'

The SOCAUST asks Angus Campbell for his guidance on how to proceed.

In response, Campbell requests that the Inspector-General of the Australian Defence Force (IGADF) conducts 'scoping and assessment as to whether these rumours can be substantiated'. These persistent rumours involve deviance from professional standards, the existence of a culture of silence, activities outside or contrary to the Rules of Engagement, and systemic failures by the Special Forces chain of command.

The IGADF is a statutory office holder appointed by the Minister of Defence and, crucially, is outside the Australian Defence Force chain of command. In other words, the IGADF is independent and does not answer to the ADF. One of its main tasks is to ensure that the failures of military justice are exposed.

On 12 May 2016, the IGADF appoints Major-General The Honourable Paul Brereton AM, RFD, to determine whether there are substantive accounts or credible information relating to 'criminal, unlawful or inappropriate conduct' by Special Operations Task Group deployments in Afghanistan between 2007 and 2016. In simple terms, it is Brereton's job to find out if the rumours are true.

As a judge of the New South Wales Court of Appeal and a two-star general in the Army Reserve, Brereton is an inspired choice. He is a military man and a jurist of impeccable standing.

'He's so measured, so considered, and clearly super intelligent,' says Samantha Crompvoets, who has dealt with Brereton during some of her previous research. 'I found his manner so genuine.'

At Brereton's swearing in as a Supreme Court judge in 2005, then New South Wales Attorney General, Bob Debus, praised him for his technical argument, amenable disposition and exemplary service.

'Demonstrating your belief that everyone deserves a fair hearing, you have also stepped forth where others may have feared to tread,' said Debus. 'You have proved yourself willing to assist all those who come before our courts without fear or favour.'

The attorney general also noted Brereton's willingness to act pro bono for army veterans.

302

In his own speech, Brereton paid tribute to a man in whose footsteps he was following.

'Although he died when I was young, my father has been a great and lasting influence.'

Some would see an element of destiny in Paul Brereton's appointment to lead the Afghanistan war crimes inquiry. His father Russell Brereton was also a military officer, a barrister, and later a judge of the NSW Supreme Court. In 1945, Captain Brereton was appointed a War Crimes Officer for the Australian military. His task was to identify, track down and interrogate alleged Japanese war criminals.

'His job primarily was to investigate war crimes in Borneo,' says Paul Brereton. 'And then that culminated with the trials. He prosecuted the first of the trials.'

Those trials were on Labuan Island and Russell Brereton's first case involved a Japanese soldier accused of the massacre of more than 40 Allied prisoners of war.

With the Allies closing in on Labuan in June 1945, Sergeant Major Tsuruo Sugino was told to march a group of POWs inland and 'to dispose of them'. Those orders were followed with brutal effect.

With World War Two over, the captured Sugino was put on trial on Labuan in an army tent on the beach that would serve as a makeshift war crimes court. He was accused of failing to stop the killing of more than 30 POWs in one slaughter. On a second charge, it was alleged that Sugino had ordered that 15 POWs be shot.

While Captain Brereton's assignment was to prosecute Sugino, he was also determined to ensure the Japanese soldier got a fair trial.

'He was committed to ensuring that the defendants were able to mount a proper defence and that they had the resources necessary to do so,' says Paul Brereton. 'His initial revulsion, if you like, for what had happened, was ultimately balanced with a commitment to what we would call the rule of law and to seeing that justice was done, and that the accused be able to properly defend themselves and have a fair trial.'

Under the canvas of the tent on the beach, in the sweltering heat of Labuan, Russell Brereton opened the prosecution's case on 3 December 1945. He did so by detailing the atrocities committed against the Allied POWs by Sugino and his men.

'All were shot and bayonetted to put them out of their misery,' Captain Brereton told those gathered in the jury-rigged courtroom. 'I submit the act was a deliberate, calculated, cold blooded murder.'

The verdict would not be long in coming.

'Sergeant Major Tsuruo Sugino was today sentenced to death for having massacred 46 Allied prisoners,' reported Brisbane's *Courier Mail* three days later. 'He was found guilty after 15 minutes' consideration ... he is the first Japanese to be sentenced for crimes against humanity.'

Sugino was hanged the following year.

For Captain Russell Brereton, the Sugino trial would be the end of a long war that included stints in North Africa and New Guinea. The day before he left on his long journey home, Brereton was given some traditional Japanese calligraphy by Lieutenant General Masao Baba, the Supreme Commander of the 37th Japanese Army in North Borneo. The thick black brush strokes on rice paper translate to:

True heart is the core of everything

'Baba, who was ultimately hung on the basis of command responsibility for the death marches, had that presented to [my father] when he finished up in Labuan at the end of 1945,' says Paul Brereton.

The calligraphy would hang in Russell Brereton's chambers for decades. Today it hangs in his son's chambers.

'It's largely [in] remembrance of my father,' says Paul Brereton of the calligraphy and its message. 'I would like to think we were driven by similar influences in that way.'

Like his father, Paul Brereton would rise to the bench of the New South Wales Supreme Court. He would also be called upon to investigate alleged war crimes.

'In terms of the [Afghanistan] inquiry, I didn't particularly feel that that was part of the paternal legacy. But the judicial career, on the other hand, I certainly have felt I am treading in his footsteps there,' says Paul Brereton.

Like the Japanese atrocities of World War Two, the alleged war crimes committed in Afghanistan are senseless and shocking. There is no comparison in their scale. But what makes Paul Brereton's inquiry unique is who he will be investigating. While his father dealt with the systemic brutalities of Australia's Japanese enemy, Paul Brereton would have to get to the bottom of atrocities perpetrated against civilians, prisoners and non-combatants by Australian soldiers themselves.

Paul Brereton was stepping forth where most others would fear to tread.

For Australia's Special Operations Commander, Jeff Sengelman, the Brereton Inquiry is the start of another painful, but necessary chapter.

'I feel like a parent who's had to take their loved son or daughter down to the police station because you realise they've done something really wrong,' Sengelman says. 'Doing the right thing can sometimes feel really tough, mate.'

'I knew the pressure that was being put on Sengelman, massive pressure externally from people who have since left, telling him, "Okay, that's enough. You have delved far enough",' says Samantha Crompvoets.

'There is no process without Jeff Sengelman,' says Fergus McLachlan. 'There's no IGADF without Jeff … I look at Jeff and wonder whether I would have had the courage to keep digging to the extent that he did. I'd like to think I would, but I don't know.'

Jeff Sengelman – the grandson of a World War Two veteran, the school cadet from Ipswich, the SAS candidate who refused to quit – is now the commander of men in Paul Brereton's crosshairs, elite soldiers who will be accused of betraying military, moral and legal codes, Special Forces operators who will be investigated for the most heinous of war crimes, including the murder of prisoners and civilians. It is largely through Sengelman's dogged pursuit of the truth that they are in this position. Sengelman knows that truth is the only path to redemption for the SAS.

19

LORD OF THE FLIES

'When a country looks at its fighting forces, it is looking
in a mirror. What a society gets from its armed services
is exactly what it asks for, no more or less'
General Sir John Hackett, British Army

Samantha Crompvoets is ushered into the pokey room at Defence
headquarters in Canberra and shown to a seat. The sociologist and
a select few are being given a preview of the long-awaited war crimes
inquiry report written by the assistant Inspector-General of the
Australian Defence Force, Paul Brereton, and his team.

With Crompvoets is the director of the Australian War Memorial,
Matt Anderson, who has also been allowed to read a redacted version
of Brereton's voluminous report. Only the two of them are permitted in the tiny space because of restrictions in place for the Covid-19
pandemic. The others who are being given a preview are in neighbouring rooms. Supervising Crompvoets and Anderson is an army major.
She tells them that they are not allowed to take their copy of the
report, nor are they authorised to mark it or write notes in it. When
they are finished reading, Angus Campbell, who has been promoted
to Chief of the Defence Force since commissioning the report, will
come in and answer their questions. Then they will have to hand the
report back.

Samantha Crompvoets peels back the cover of the report. More
than five years have passed since Jeff Sengelman commissioned her
to look into perceptions of Australia's Special Operations Command,
research that would result in Crompvoets hearing stories of shocking

crimes and atrocities involving the SAS. Four and a half years have elapsed since Paul Brereton was appointed to head the inquiry into rumours of Australian Special Forces war crimes in Afghanistan. Very few thought it would take so long for the inquiry to be wrapped up and the report to be written. But then, no one knew what Brereton and his team would eventually uncover. It is now eight months since the Four Corners broadcast 'Killing Field', showing Soldier C killing the unarmed and terrified Dad Mohammad, footage that has caused shockwaves around the world.

Crompvoets begins reading. One of the first things she notices in the document are the many slabs of redacted text. But despite the blacked-out sections, the shock and power of the Brereton Report is immediately clear to Crompvoets. She has come into this room not expecting to be surprised by what it reveals, not after all the horror stories she has been told. But the report's contents are stunning. It is the scale, the vastness of the alleged atrocities. It is the cold-blooded killings. And the conspiracies and the cover ups. Crompvoets knew the release of the Brereton Report would be big news. But not this big. Like all but a few, she has not foreseen the historical significance of the report.

Oh fuck. This is really huge, she thinks. Crompvoets can feel the emotion welling up inside her. Brereton's report is dredging up all the terrible stories she has buried from years before. It is overwhelming her, and soon the tears come. Crompvoets has never cried about this stuff, not even during her research when she spoke with the broken and angry men who had witnessed atrocities in Afghanistan. But now she is sobbing in this little room in front of two other people. This report is beyond anything she expected. The army major supervising her comes over and hugs her.

'I'm so sorry,' says Crompvoets. She excuses herself and goes to the bathroom and cries some more.

People have told her that she will feel vindicated by the Brereton Report. That all those who had questioned her research, who had lumped all that shit on her and her work, would have to eat their words. Having read what Brereton has written, Samantha Crompvoets does feel something like vindication. But the prevailing emotion she feels is devastation. The allegations in this report will forever stain the Australian military. Crompvoets composes herself and returns to the pokey little room.

A while later Angus Campbell comes in to answer any questions that she and the War Memorial director have. In a few days the Chief of the Australian Defence Force will have to explain to the nation the shocking truth that lies within Paul Brereton's report. He will have to reveal some of the shameful secrets that have devastated Samantha Crompvoets.

—

'Rules were broken, stories concocted, lies told, prisoners killed. Once that rule was broken, so too was further restraint.'

Angus Campbell is staring down the barrel of the TV camera. His words, unvarnished and shocking, are being broadcast live to the Australian people from a theatrette at Defence headquarters in Canberra. I am sitting a few metres away from Campbell with a select group of journalists, listening as he responds to the war crimes report written by Paul Brereton and his team.

It is 19 November 2020. Four and a half years after he was tasked with investigating vague 'rumours' of war crimes, Brereton has delivered his report. What we are getting is the public version, much abridged and heavily redacted. Lieutenant-General Angus Campbell has read the full, unadorned version, all eight volumes and 3251 pages of it. It has rattled him. Addressing the press conference, Campbell's face is grave, and his words are clear, precise and paced. The Chief of the Defence Force has been rehearsing this speech for weeks, in full dress uniform and surrounded by his staff. Campbell knows the Brereton Report will set off a shitstorm.

On the walls of the theatrette around us are glossy photos of ADF personnel in action. A soldier in a helicopter with his unit. Troops helping an Indigenous community. These are the images the ADF want the public to see. A force for good. Personnel who uphold the values of honour, respect and community service.

The Brereton Report contains none of that. It is a document of sadness and shame. Of killings and cover ups. It recounts episodes and incidents that have never before been associated with the Australian military. The things it alleges are the acts of a ragtag army whose values seem more closely aligned with the Taliban enemy.

'Those alleged to have been unlawfully killed were all people under control, in lay terms, prisoners, farmers and other civilians. This shameful record includes alleged instances in which new patrol members were coerced to shoot a prisoner to achieve a soldier's first kill, in an appalling initiation practice known as "blooding".'

As a former SAS squadron commander, Angus Campbell was part of the 'who dares wins' ethos of the Regiment. Now, as the head of the entire military, he is trying to explain how that degenerated into 'who dares kills'.

'None of the alleged unlawful killings were described as being in the "heat of battle". None were alleged to have occurred in circumstances in which the intent of the perpetrator was unclear, confused or mistaken,' Campbell tells us.

No one can trot out the 'fog of war' to justify these crimes.

Prior to Angus Campbell's appearance, the journalists in the room have been given 90 minutes to read Brereton's redacted report. Despite the black slabs covering the names of the alleged perpetrators and much of the gruesome detail, the report is worse than I thought it would be. I scan its pages.

'There is **credible information** of 23 incidents in which one or more non-combatants ... were unlawfully killed.'

'A total of 39 individuals killed.'

'A total of 25 current or former Australian Defence Force personnel who were perpetrators.'

'The Inquiry has recommended that the Chief of the Defence Force refer 36 matters to the Australian Federal Police for criminal investigation. Those matters relate to 23 incidents and involve a total of 19 individuals.'

'Reports, rumours and allegations of war crimes in Afghanistan will continue to emerge.'

'I was prepared for something that was pretty terrible. But I was still shocked by the accusations,' says former Army Major General and Afghanistan veteran Fergus McLachlan. 'Brereton has told us war crimes were committed and that's now, in my opinion, a fact. I am convinced Australian soldiers were involved in war crimes ... and so it was incredibly upsetting.'

During the course of the inquiry, Brereton and his team have found and reviewed more than 20,000 documents and 25,000 images. They have interviewed 423 witnesses, with some cross-examinations lasting up to three days.

The inquiry has faced great challenges, including active resistance and deceptive conduct from some current and former Special Forces soldiers. They were up against a closely bonded culture 'in which loyalty to one's mates, immediate superiors and the unit are regarded as paramount, in which secrecy is at a premium, and in which those who "leak" are anathema'. There were those in the Regiment who thought Brereton's chance of penetrating the wall of silence was zero.

'He hasn't got shit,' boasted one SAS soldier at a barbecue in Perth the year after Brereton's inquiry began.

Like his comrades, that soldier has been trained not to break. The inquiry team have had to stare down witnesses who have employed resistance-to-interrogation techniques. These are operators who have been blindfolded, handcuffed, stripped naked, repeatedly interrogated and left in a sitting position for days as part of their training. Some of them have no hesitation about lying straight to Brereton's face.

But others have been of immense help to the inquiry. People who saw killings, were drawn into the cover ups, or who were made complicit through the threat of violence. Former Special Forces personnel like Braden Chapman, Dusty Miller, Tom and Christina. These are the people who faced threats, bullying and retribution for speaking out. But their testimony was vital. Without these witnesses the inquiry would have turned up very little.

In an email to Christina, Justice Brereton thanked her personally for her 'courage and assistance'.

'Some of what you have told me has been very important and helpful indeed. I know it cannot have been easy for you to do this, but I hope that having done so brings you some comfort and helps you to move forward with your life.'

But for months Christina resisted the urge to contact the Brereton Inquiry. To her, it seemed like yet another internal Defence investigation that would ensure that the reputation of the Special Forces was prioritised over justice. But the shame of her silence and that incessant gnawing of her guilt prevailed over her misgivings and fears.

'I hold to some degree responsibility for unlawful killings. I participated in cover ups by deleting evidence,' she says. 'Speaking to the IGADF is possibly the hardest thing I have ever done.'

'[The IGADF] were meticulous, they were thorough. They were relentless,' says Tom, who spent five and a half hours with Justice Brereton and his team. 'At the same time, they conducted themselves with an enormous amount of compassion and empathy.'

But Tom wasn't always a fan of the Brereton Inquiry. Before he was summoned to appear as a witness, we had met in a hotel room for a confidential chat.

'They can go and get fucked. I'm not being dragged into another military inquiry,' Tom had told me.

The former 3 Squadron SAS operator and veteran of three Afghanistan deployments believed it was yet another stitch up, designed to pin guilt on good soldiers who didn't fit in with the toxic culture of the brotherhood. Men the brotherhood wanted to force out.

'The previous military inquiries that I've been involved with were an absolute joke,' he had said.

From across the room I had listened to Tom rail against what he thought was just another bullshit inquiry.

'I think this inquiry is doing the right thing,' I replied. I had spoken to several other former SAS members who had already fronted up to the inquiry and had spoken in detail with the man leading it. 'I think Brereton really wants to get to the bottom of these war crimes.'

'I'm going to get charged with perjury if I don't go,' replied Tom.

With no other choice, Tom went. He told them about what he saw – the 'village idiot' killing, about throwdowns, about how some of his patrol bullied and even beat him.

'After attending the meeting with Justice Brereton and his team it became very, very clear to me that this was not a normal military inquiry that I'd been previously exposed to,' he says. 'They were absolute in their search for justice. Absolute ... they just wanted the truth. And they found it.'

Tom was now a true believer in Brereton and his mission.

Others were called in front of the inquiry not just as witnesses, but as possible perpetrators. Soldier A and Soldier C spent hours being grilled. But Soldier B was not interviewed. Some of his comrades tell me he went to ground and could not be located.

'He's gone bush,' one says.

I, too, failed to find him, despite engaging a registered and highly experienced private investigator at a cost of several thousand dollars. The investigator followed up a number of leads but Soldier B had disappeared. A researcher did manage to speak to two of his sisters. One promised to pass on my contact details, while the second hung up when the researcher asked for an email address for Soldier B or his lawyer to send questions to. For an SAS operator who prided himself on his fearlessness and was notorious for brutally confronting often powerless Afghan civilians, in the end Soldier B revealed himself to be extremely evasive and craven in the face of so many serious questions about his conduct.

The Brereton Report exposed everything we had discovered in our investigations for the ABC, and much more. How SAS reporting was manipulated and embellished. How Afghans who complained, like those from Sarkhume and those from Dad Mohammad's village, were dismissed as opportunists motivated solely by compensation. How inquiry officers, like those who investigated Dad Mohammad's killing, failed to exercise the requisite levels of suspicion and lacked basic forensic skills. How commanders blindly trusted their subordinates to do the right thing, and to follow the Rules of Engagement. How an aura was attached to the SAS operators who went outside the wire, and how this aura protected them from scrutiny. How a culture of cover up and secrecy allowed the killings to continue. As for the patrol commanders, they were 'demigods' who could make or break careers. These NCOs were the SAS's dominant clique who embraced the 'warrior hero' culture.

'It was at the patrol commander level that the criminal behaviour was conceived, committed, continued, and concealed, and overwhelmingly at that level that responsibility resides,' Brereton's report stated.

'I think when you look at those individuals who were patrol commanders, no, it doesn't surprise me,' says Trooper Jim, a former 3 Squadron SAS operator with several Afghanistan tours under his belt. 'The patrol commanders are in a really influential position. They're 20 years in the Regiment ... you're there because you've done the time, you've got the operations and the experience.'

Trooper Jim says the patrol commanders are just what the report says they are – demigods. They are men not to be questioned, let alone challenged. Trooper Jim gives me several names of soldiers, good operators, who were pushed out because the PCs simply disliked them.

'Just bastardising individuals over time to try to get them out of the unit,' he says. 'They were bullied out just because they had patrol commanders who hated them ... it was, "Nup, he sucks. I'm going to destroy him and get him out".'

Months before the Brereton Report's release, Trooper Jim had told me that all the unlawful killings in Afghanistan had been driven by half a dozen former comrades, or 'cancers', that had metastasised under weak leadership. After the report dropped, he was shocked.

'I can expect a patrol with one or two toxic individuals going rogue, but for it to be as widespread with 19 individuals, how do we get there? How did this happen?'

I am sitting across from Jim, having coffee. He pauses, before answering his own question.

'I know why. In those early days as far back as 2006, we let it happen. We reported these things. People spoke up. There was no consequences to what people were doing.'

Not only were some of the soldiers who were doing the wrong thing not punished, they were decorated. What message did that send to the younger, less experienced and more impressionable operators?

The report describes how Afghans who complained were regarded as money-seeking liars, and how – when inquiries were launched into alleged unlawful killings – the officers sent over to investigate lacked independence, curiosity and the right experience. It states how operators would simply lie to inquiry officers and their version of events would be blithely accepted.

'When a dumb arse inquiry officer comes over from Australia, he was putty in the hands of the operators,' says one former Special Operations officer. 'Every Afghan was assumed to be lying. The white guys were always believed.'

I remember the words of the inquiry officer who was part of the team that investigated the deadly raid on Sarkhume, how he and his colleagues never even considered for a minute that the two dead Afghans could have been unlawfully killed.

'On the matrix given to us, and I suppose thinking with the presumption of innocence, we think, "Oh, Australian soldiers wouldn't do that, would they?"' he had told me. He had described the SAS operators he had interviewed as 'professional' and 'confident' witnesses.

'They all seemed straight up and down,' he said.

He had also told me that maybe the inquiry officers didn't take the Afghans who complained about unlawful killings by the Australians 'as seriously as we should have'.

This leads me to the chief criticism of Brereton's report by some within the media and many ordinary Diggers. Accountability. While the inquiry found that the patrol commanders were the masterminds and drivers of the 'criminal behaviour', the brass was largely absolved of any direct responsibility.

'The Inquiry has found no evidence that there was knowledge of, or reckless indifference to, the commission of war crimes, on the part of commanders at troop/platoon, squadron/company or Task Group Headquarters level, let alone at higher levels such as Commander Joint Task Force 633, Joint Operations Command, or Australian Defence Headquarters,' the report concluded.

'I think it'd be impossible to assume that higher ups didn't know what was going on. It's as simple as that,' says former 3 Squadron SAS medic Dusty Miller. 'I really find it very hard to believe that the squadron commander level, that they didn't know what was going on, considering that they had a debrief with the PCs after every mission.'

'If, at the end of the day, [the leadership says] that they had no idea that this was going on, they shouldn't be there in the first place,' says Tom. 'Because they've lost one of the most important things, which is command and control.'

In 2019, while I was investigating the killings at Sarkhume, I rang the head of the Special Operations Task Group during

Rotation 17, Lieutenant-Colonel Jon 'Irish' Hawkins. I had read that the veteran SAS officer – who was in charge of all Special Forces operations during that rotation – had gone to Sarkhume after the villagers had complained about the killing of Haji Sardar and Mirza Khan. Hawkins had been quoted by journalist Chris Masters as saying that there were 'some wild allegations' from some 'tough, hard farmers who were probably Taliban'.

Over the phone the now-retired Hawkins told me he could not speak to me while the IGADF inquiry was underway. I should call him after it was completed, he said.

With the Brereton Report released, I texted him about having that chat. The next day Hawkins replied.

'Thanks for the text. Yes, the redacted Report has been released but I'm already assisting the AFP in related investigations into allegations stemming from the Report. I think you'd agree any comments by me may jeopardise these proceedings. I feel it's best that we don't talk and to let the AFP do their job as that is the only way justice will be properly served.'

I wrote back explaining I was writing a book hinged around the 2012 Rotation he was in charge of, and that my reports had helped the AFP investigations. I still wanted to talk to him.

'I hope this book will help people understand things,' I wrote.

There was no response.

As the commander of Forces Command, Fergus McLachlan was in charge of 36,000 personnel. He knows most of the Special Forces leadership, officers he believes would have acted if they had known that war crimes were being committed.

'But I am critical. Leadership involves curiosity, determination, sitting in quiet corners, listening, governance checks, visits,' says the former Major General. 'I think it's pretty clear that the high-performance Special Operations environment – when it was running well – made people overconfident about what leaders needed to do across the board.'

Former SAS captain Andrew Hastie believes some of the senior leadership did have a sense that war crimes were happening in Afghanistan, and that much of it was driven by the American concept of kill/capture the SAS had enthusiastically embraced.

'I mentioned it in 2013. I just said, "I've got big concerns with the way this whole targeting system is incentivising people taking matters into their own hands",' Hastie says. 'I made it very clear.'

And the response?

'It was kind of uncomfortable, "Okay, thanks. Thanks. You're an industrious terrier. I didn't need this dead rat on the carpet in front of me".'

As for what leadership expected of the trigger pullers, Hastie recounts a briefing given by a senior SAS officer inside the Counter Terrorism theatrette at Campbell Barracks in early 2010. It was a gathering of all the 353s – the operators.

'His exact words were – I can remember it as clear as day, "What I need you to do is be able to shoot cunts in the face, and then dine with the Ambassador the following night". And I went, "Okay, interesting".'

When it came to leadership, Paul Brereton's report did sheet home some blame to the brass on one issue. The problem was, whatever that issue or incident was, it was totally redacted. Titled Chapter 2.50, the only signpost that it was extremely grave and possibly sickening came in a stark sentence in an unredacted section beneath the slab of black.

'What is described in this Chapter is possibly the most disgraceful episode in Australia's military history, and the commanders at troop, squadron and task group level bear moral responsibility for what happened under their command, regardless of personal fault.'

The mysterious Chapter 2.50 quickly became a source of gossip, conjecture and media speculation.

Asked about it, the Chief of the Defence Force, Angus Campbell, said it needed to be legally redacted.

'Justice Brereton does describe something that is utterly disgraceful,' said General Campbell. 'It is shameful.'

The 'most disgraceful episode in Australia's military history' was not a particular incident or a specific killing. It was a pattern of grotesque behaviour; it was a psychopathic test of a trooper's blind loyalty to the patrol and to its commanders. It was blooding. This was the initiation rite of superiors telling junior soldiers to shoot a prisoner or a civilian, in order for the soldier to rack up his first kill. It was a welcome to the visceral business of death. It is worth noting that blooding occurred exclusively in 2 Squadron SAS, the 'Bushrangers', with many allegations centring on Rotation 18 in 2012.

'This would happen after the target compound had been secured, and local nationals had been secured as "persons under control",' Brereton wrote in his report. 'Typically, the patrol commander would take a person under control and the junior member, who would then be directed to kill the person under control.'

'Prisoners are sacrosanct, because the reality is you might one day be a prisoner,' says Fergus McLachlan. 'You're taught that from day dot of your service.'

Others believe blooding was more than just an initiation. Once the killing ritual was performed, the rookie soldier was locked into the group and bound by its secrets. A hold was now placed over him, one almost impossible for him to break. To break it would mean confessing to being a murderer.

Blooding didn't end with the killing. Afterwards, a cover story would be concocted to deflect any scrutiny, and the incident would be subject to an unwritten rule that the SAS enforced better than anyone – the code of silence.

Blooding is the ultimate form of manipulation. I remembered speaking to former Special Forces psychologist Louise Pitcher who deployed to Afghanistan twice, including in 2012. Pitcher had told me how at selection they looked for some psychopathic features when screening candidates, particularly high sensation-seeking attributes and risk-taking tendencies, as well as low levels of warmth. But the downside to this was that on occasion a true psychopath slipped through the screening.

'Psychopaths are manipulative by nature. They're very hard to detect,' she said.

Reading the report's section about blooding, I recalled one of the stories we had included in the *Four Corners* 'Killing Field' program. It recounted a raid on the village of Sola by the SAS in late August 2012. The men of 2 Squadron swept into Sola that night hunting for a rogue Afghan soldier called Hekmatullah who had turned his weapon on Australian soldiers and killed three of them. He had then fled.

The villagers told us that when the SAS arrived the men of Sola were in the mosque for evening prayers, which were being led by the Imam, Haji Raz Mohammad. With the imam in the mosque were his sons, including Rafiullah, who was a boy of eight at the time.

'When my father finished his prayer, they kicked him in the head while he was trying to stand up. His turban fell down, and they stood him up,' Rafiullah told my fixer. 'They tore his turban up into pieces and tied up the hands of the other people in the mosque. They beat me up and they said, "Why are you standing here, what did he give you?" I said, "He didn't give me anything". They beat me up very badly, and told me "Go home – why are you standing here?"'

The SAS patrol then dragged Haji Raz Mohammad, his adult son Abdul Jalil, and the other men out onto the street.

'[The Australians] were standing behind us. We were not allowed to talk. There was an interpreter with them. He was talking to us. Guns were pointed at our mouths,' said villager Noorullah.

The men were blindfolded. Later, the Australians would claim that the imam's son, Abdul Jalil, was shot dead after grabbing at a corporal's gun. This was regarded as plausible by investigators, and no further investigation was recommended.

But it is the death of Abdul Jalil's father, the Imam Haji Raz Mohammad, that has all the hallmarks of a blooding. Information I received from within the Regiment said that the imam was taken away, and a trooper was ordered by a superior to shoot the Afghan in the head. A radio was then planted on his body. This is also the account that the Brereton Inquiry investigated.

This killing is described in Chapter 2.36 of the report, with names and key details redacted.

'REDACTED *took a local national REDACTED who was unarmed and under control and therefore hors de combat, and not posing any threat, to a remote part of a compound, and forced him to the ground, and that REDACTED, upon the direction and/or with the encouragement of REDACTED then shot him in the head, killing him.*'

An ICOM was then allegedly planted on the body to conceal that Haji Raz Mohammad was not a combatant 'and to deflect or deceive any future inquiry into the circumstances of his death'.

Dark tales about blooding had seeped through the Regiment well before that rotation in 2012. Trooper Jim had heard about it being simulated at a pre-deployment 'Mission Readiness Exercise' back in Australia.

'You go with [weapons firing] blanks or paint and you do an activity, and the activities are replicated to the things you are going to be doing in Afghanistan,' he told me. 'It's all scenario-based stuff and you'll go in and execute the mission.'

Trooper Jim says during these simulated missions 'prisoners' would be taken.

'And I'd heard there were occasions where they said, "Okay, execute the bloke". One of the Diggers went, "What?" [The trainer said], "Yep. Double tap with blanks". And then [the trainer] had apparently said, "Okay, that's how it's going to be. Are you cool with that?"

The simulation of blooding was confirmed to me by another source, who said it involved the 'killing' of a PUC, or person under confinement, during exercises at the SAS training area inland from Lancelin, north of Perth. The source told me the name of the SAS trainer who urged the soldiers to 'kill' the 'prisoner'. It was the same operator identified by Trooper Jim. That operator would do multiple tours of Afghanistan.

I ask SAS captain turned Liberal MP, Andrew Hastie, about the practice of blooding, and if it gave him chills. He tells me that a few weeks after the release of the Brereton Report, he met with some Vietnam Veterans at Dawesville in his Perth electorate. He says he tried to explain it to them.

'I broke down because I just couldn't get the words out,' says Hastie. 'Lives have been forever ruined because of it. Afghan lives have been taken and destroyed. Families have been hurt. But moreover, Australian soldiers who joined for the right reasons, who wanted to do the right thing, were led astray by toxic and effectively evil leadership. And they deserved better.'

The Brereton Inquiry also concludes that it is the SAS patrol commanders who typically incited or directed their underlings to kill prisoners or Afghans under their control. The report says it is they who should be referred for criminal investigation. This should be 'in priority to their subordinates who may have pulled the trigger'.

Many of these men still bear the burden of psychological trauma and moral injury caused by squeezing that trigger. But the Brereton Report also found that when it came to that life-or-death moment, none of them ever stood up to their superiors and refused to be part of this blooding ritual.

'There is no evidence of any subordinate who was told or encouraged to commit an unlawful killing objecting, resisting or even questioning it,' the report states. 'This bespeaks a deference to superiors so extreme that it overrides legality and morality. It may also reflect a *Lord of the Flies* syndrome.'

A key component of blooding in Afghanistan was the throwdown. The Brereton Report said these throwdowns were often 'easily conceal-able such as pistols, small hand held radios ("ICOMs"), weapons magazines and grenades – to be placed with the bodies of "enemies killed in action"... in order to portray that the person killed had been carrying the weapon or other military equipment when engaged and was a legitimate target'.

Tom, Braden Chapman and Dusty Miller had all seen throw-downs planted on the bodies of unarmed Afghan civilians, people they claim were murdered in cold blood. Christina processed more than 25,000 photos and 250 videos, including images of bodies and weapons, during her time in Afghanistan. How many of those guns, grenades, battle bras and magazines that she saw lying next to or on dead Afghans had been planted?

The Brereton Report reveals that at least one junior officer believed men in his patrols were carrying throwdowns to fabricate evidence and to frame Afghans, and to justify their detention. The inquiry found he did nothing to stop the practice.

Sitting in the theatrette reading the report another line jumps out at me.

'Privately-owned helmet cameras were enthusiastically used in Afghanistan by some Special Operations Task Group members, which albeit unintentionally resulted in the exposure of at least one apparent war crime.'

It is a reference to the *Four Corners* 'Killing Field' program and the shooting of Dad Mohammad by Soldier C, all captured on the helmet camera of the patrol dog handler.

Inside the Brereton Report is a section labelled 'Consolidated Findings and Recommendations'. It is a chronological list of inci-dents investigated by the inquiry. I will spend hours matching the incidents with a timeline of more than a dozen killings that I have compiled and investigated over many months. It is difficult. Names, dates, locations, and other key or incriminating details in the report have been redacted. Large slabs of black are everywhere. But there is enough text left to put the pieces of the puzzle back together.

I find the shooting of Dad Mohammad that I had reported in 'Killing Field'. It talks about an Afghan male 'who was not participating in hostilities, being unarmed, wounded, and under control, and who was posing no threat.' It talks about a patrol member who 'aided, abetted and/or was knowingly concerned in the unlawful killing ... in that he assisted REDACTED to obtain the approval of REDACTED to kill' the Afghan man.

The patrol member knew the soldier was about to kill the man, and he 'failed to exercise control properly over his subordinate'. Was this the dog handler? He did outrank Soldier C. It was the dog handler, who, when asked by Soldier C if he wants him to 'drop' Dad Mohammad, replies: 'I don't know, mate. Hit ***** up.'

He has failed to exercise control over Soldier C. He should have said no.

The Brereton Inquiry found that several months after the killing in 2012, Soldier C 'lied to the ... Inquiry Officer Inquiry with the intent that the truth should not be discovered.'

In his written statement, Soldier C had told the Inquiry Officer Inquiry that he had seen Dad Mohammad with a radio and that the Afghan was tactically manoeuvring. He told that inquiry he had then shot and killed Dad Mohammad from 15 to 20 metres away. The inquiry officers had believed every word. But the footage broadcast by *Four Corners* undeniably showed Soldier C looming over the frightened and prone Afghan before killing him from almost point-blank range. The only thing in Dad Mohammad's hand was his set of red prayer beads.

One day I am contacted by one of the inquiry officers who back in 2012 investigated the raid that left Dad Mohammad dead. He tells me he had 'really felt proud' to be a member of the Australian Army.

'Now I feel dirty,' he says. 'When I saw ['Killing Field'] I felt sick and very angry. Very, very angry ... I just run through what would we do differently? What did we miss? I sort of say, "Well the bastards lied, that didn't help". But you feel like a schmuck.'

The inquiry team he was part of travelled to Afghanistan and later interviewed 3 Squadron SAS members on base in Perth about the Dad Mohammad killing. What he told me about their investigation perfectly fit the pattern of what the Brereton Report revealed: that inquiry officers were lied to; that inquiry officers were biased towards the accounts of SAS operators; that Afghan testimony was discounted or dismissed; and that inquiry officer reports invariably cleared special forces of any crimes or misdemeanours.

'We know [the SAS patrols] got onto helicopters at certain times, flew to a certain grid reference, were at that grid reference for a certain period of time, shot X number of people, got back on the helicopters, got back to [Tarin Kowt] at a certain time,' says the inquiry officer who was on the Dad Mohammad case. 'That's all in the operational reporting. That's all true. It's just the actual details of how the people were killed that obviously wasn't true.'

I ask him why no one could find evidence of a possible crime. Why did it take *Four Corners* to find the video that revealed what happened to Dad Mohammad in that wheat field?

'We asked for eye-in-the-sky and helmet cam and all that sort of stuff,' says the inquiry officer. 'It would seem that the eye-in-the-sky would turn away when the killing happened. And everyone swore on a stack of bibles that there was no helmet cam. That's been proved false.'

Again, the inquiry officers unquestioningly believed what they were told.

While they found that raid and the killing of Dad Mohammad to be lawful, the Brereton Report recommends further action be taken.

'There is a realistic prospect of a criminal investigation obtaining sufficient evidence to charge REDACTED with the war crime of murder,' the report concludes. 'The Inquiry recommends that the Chief of Defence Force refer the matter to the Australian Federal Police for criminal investigation.'

Under section 268.70 of the Commonwealth Criminal Code, someone found guilty of 'War crimes – murder' faces life in prison.

But the Brereton Report also recommends the other patrol member, presumably the dog handler, who was 'knowingly concerned' in the killing be investigated, saying there is enough evidence to charge him 'with aiding or abetting the war crime of murder'.

The killing of Dad Mohammad will also invoke the Pashtun tribal law of Pashtunwali and set a young man on the course of jihad with the Taliban.

'As you know that in our Pashtunwali, if someone kills another person the deceased's brother or son will take revenge,' says Dad Mohammad's younger brother Jamshid. 'Even if that killer is our relative, the revenge will still take place.'

Just a teenager when his brother was shot, Jamshid always believed his destiny lay with jihad. Now, revenge is also part of that destiny.

'I understood early that standing against [the foreigners] was my religious duty,' he says. 'Our religion teaches us that if my honour, property, dignity and religion are not safe from attackers I should revolt and protect them.'

Shortly after his brother's death, Jamshid goes to the Taliban and asks to join, but he is told he is too young and that he must wait. He waits a while and goes back. More than eight years after his brother's killing Jamshid is now a Taliban commander in Uruzgan.

'I am a *dagai masher* [head of his group],' he says. 'My group members are from my area. They are from our villages. I have 40 to 50 men ... I am their leader.'

Jamshid has now been shown the *Four Corners* footage of his brother's death, but he can't watch it all.

'It was too distressing,' he says. 'My message to the highest authority of Australia [is that] if something were done to your son or your brother, how would you punish the killer? I want the same justice for my brother.'

The Brereton Report contains redacted accounts of other killings I have investigated and reported. There are the deaths of Haji Sardar and Mirza Khan during the March 2012 raid by 3 Squadron SAS on Sarkhume. It accuses an unnamed soldier of providing a 'false narrative' that one of the Afghan victims was armed when he was killed. It says he did this 'in order to deflect and mislead any inquiry into the circumstances of his death.' The report states that something was placed on the body of the other victim 'in order to misrepresent that he had it on his person at the time he was killed'. We know from the botched Inquiry Officer Inquiry into the deaths of the two men four months after the raid that Haji Sardar's body was photographed with an AK-47 and Mirza Khan's body with a grenade. The Brereton Report alleges both were planted, and it recommends two SAS soldiers be referred to the Australian Federal Police. I know one of them to be Soldier B. Three of his own comrades have told me that they saw him take Haji Sardar away towards the mosque, before emerging to say that the elderly Afghan 'didn't make it'. The other is an SAS operator who also has a reputation for indiscriminate violence and is alleged to have shot and killed Mirza Khan as he was being mauled by an SAS dog.

'There is a realistic prospect of obtaining sufficient evidence' to charge both SAS soldiers with murder, the report concludes.

The next case detailed in the report is the 'village idiot' killing. Again, it says the unnamed Afghan victim (who I discovered was Ziauddin) was unarmed and was not participating in hostilities. The report describes how an SAS patrol member aided and abetted the crime by placing something 'that he carried in his backpack for use as a throw-down on the body of the deceased'. I know from Tom and Dusty, who both witnessed Soldier C kill Ziauddin, that this throwdown was a battle bra containing two AK-47 magazines. Like Sarkhume, the inquiry concludes that this was done to 'fraudulently misrepresent' that Ziauddin was a combatant. Again, it recommends a murder investigation by the AFP. But the patrol member who supplied the battle bra throwdown escapes investigation due to 'mitigating circumstances'.

After I had run my story about the 'village idiot' killing in May 2020, I had managed to track down an email address for the patrol 2-I-C, the soldier who was told to dress Ziauddin in the battle bra. I know he is still in the SAS, but I decide to write to him to ask if he will speak to me confidentially. I also tell him there are more stories to come and they involve members of his squadron. A few hours after I hit the send button my phone rings. It is not the 2-I-C. It is a contact within Defence.

'[He] reported your email. It has set off a wildfire,' the contact tells me. 'They are shitting themselves about what's coming next.'

As for Soldier C, in March 2021 I obtain his mobile number and call it. He answers using his first name and I introduce myself and ask if we could talk. Silence.

'Hello?' I ask after four long seconds. The phone goes dead. He has hung up. I then text him, telling him I am writing a book that covers his rotation to Afghanistan and that I want to talk or correspond with him or his legal representative. He never replies.

Inside the SAS, the *Four Corners* program starring Soldier C and the slow drip of subsequent stories like the 'village idiot' revelations are straining long-standing friendships. Some soldiers are saying that the 'bad apples' should have been dealt with years before, but the leadership turned a blind eye. Others are furious about how the stories are getting out, how their code of silence has been violated. One former operator tells me some of the wives have even stopped talking to each other. I wonder how they will react once the Brereton Report comes out. Now it has.

Inside the Defence theatrette, I read on. I recognise another case inside the Brereton Report. It is the killing of the bound prisoner from the Kuchi camp by the Wakunish soldier. Braden Chapman had told me that he saw Soldier A motion for the Waka to kill the man who was the target of the raid, an alleged bombmaker codenamed 'Yakuza Assassin'. He recounted how the Waka was confused, and how Soldier A motioned again to him to shoot the prisoner. Brereton's report describes the victim as 'unarmed and a person under control'. It states how an unnamed soldier 'directed, urged or encouraged' the killing. Again, a throwdown was placed on the body and a false operational report was made saying the dead man was 'an armed insurgent who tactically manoeuvred against the [SAS patrol] and who was then engaged and killed'. Not only is 'there a realistic prospect of a criminal investigation obtaining sufficient evidence to charge' Soldier A with the war crime of murder, the report also recommends that another SAS patrol member be investigated as an accessory after the fact to the war crime of murder.

The report also recommends Soldier A be investigated for the alleged killing of the Afghan that Braden Chapman calls 'the man in black'.

'It was almost like target practice for him,' Braden had told me. As the SAS patrol had converged on a compound, the Afghan in the black clothes had just walked out of it. When he had spotted the Australians, he had reached into his clothing, pulled out his phone, thrown it and put his hands in the air. Braden recounted seeing Soldier A approach the man, and as he reached him, raise his weapon to his hip and fire two rounds into the Afghan's chest. Then, as Soldier A had walked past, Braden said he had put another bullet into the man's head.

Brereton's report says the victim was 'not posing a threat, and in the course of surrendering' when he was unlawfully killed. Again, a throwdown was photographed with the body to 'fraudulently mis-represent' that the Afghan was a combatant and to deceive any future inquiries. And again, the report recommends the AFP conduct a war crimes investigation.

Then there is 'the tractor job', the December 2012 operation in northern Kandahar that left up to 11 civilians dead, including young Mohammad Zaher Shah who was believed to be only 13 years old. That was the raid in which Zulu 1 patrol had jumped from their chopper and begun firing wildly at the farmers who had been irri-gating and harvesting in their fields. Some of the farmers had tried to shelter behind a tractor.

'They were mass shooting,' farmer and survivor Abdul Qadus had told my fixer. 'They were practising their hunting.'

The shooting was started by the Zulu 1 patrol commander, Sergeant T. Then another trooper and Soldier C had joined in. Later, a farmer detained and cuffed by another operator had been shot dead after allegedly reaching for the operator's weapon.

Upon returning to base, Soldier C had confided in his former wife, Special Operations intelligence officer Captain Louise, who was on her first deployment to Afghanistan.

'He told me from his perspective what happened, which was that the patrol commander had accidentally shot one of these group of farmers,' recalled Louise. 'And then they made the decision that they couldn't leave anyone behind to tell [what happened]. So they decided to kill all of them.'

The day after this admission, Louise had checked the imagery from the operation on the database. There was a child among the dead. A boy who looked about 13 or 14 years old.

In the Brereton Report 'the tractor job' is Chapter 2.52. The inquiry accuses some of the Zulu 1 patrol members of planting throwdown weapons to fraudulently misrepresent that the farmers were combatants. It alleges the patrol commander misreported the engagement of one of the civilians as an armed insurgent who was 'tactically manoeuvring'. It says he also killed an unarmed civilian who was under control. This is the farmer who was detained and who supposedly went for the operator's gun. But the inquiry cannot rule out that the patrol commander did this in lawful self-defence in response to a 'perceived threat to a member of his patrol'. The Brereton Report recommends that three SAS operators in Zulu 1 – among them the patrol commander and Soldier C – be investigated for the war crime of murder. The so-called tractor job is the deadliest single atrocity investigated by the inquiry.

Not every incident that the inquiry recommends be investigated involves alleged unlawful killings. One chapter of the report details the 'cruel treatment' of a prisoner. It is the bashing of a detainee by Soldier B, the incident that left the Afghan with the worst broken nose medic Dusty Miller has ever seen.

Dusty had caught up to his patrol at a compound after being left behind, walking in to find Soldier B holding the Afghan prisoner up against a wall. Blood was running down his right leg and both arms. Dusty had shown me a photo of him treating the prisoner. The Afghan's nose wasn't just flat, it was bent inwards towards the man's face. Not only had Soldier B given the unfortunate man a pasting, but an SAS dog had ripped at his arms and legs.

'He went for my sidearm,' Soldier B had told Dusty at the time, explaining why he had bashed the Afghan.

The Brereton Report alleges that an unnamed soldier 'inflicted severe physical pain or suffering upon' the detainee while he was under control and not posing a threat. It states the soldier 'made a false report ... that [the prisoner] had attempted to grab his weapon and turn it against him, in order to fraudulently misrepresent that [the prisoner] had provoked the assault'.

'There is a realistic prospect of obtaining sufficient evidence to charge REDACTED with the war crime of cruel treatment', the report concludes. Under the Commonwealth Criminal Code, someone found guilty of 'War crime – cruel treatment' faces up to 25 years in prison.

The Brereton Report also includes a section by David Whetham of King's College London. A professor of Ethics and the Military Profession, he was appointed an Assistant Inspector-General of the Australian Defence Forces for the purposes of exploring why Special Forces knowingly committed clear acts of murder and why no one reported it.

Professor Whetham writes of a 'Dark Triad of Machiavellianism, narcissism and psychopathy' and of how one US study found that members of the military were twice as likely as the general public to have some sort of Antisocial Personality Disorder. He quotes an unnamed source as saying that Australian Special Forces soldiers in Afghanistan felt they were entitled to be treated almost as Roman gladiators, that they regarded themselves as exceptional and that they had a sense of entitlement. Professor Whetham also details how killing descended into a vile competition.

'There is clear evidence that some elements did keep score of the number of kills,' Whetham writes. 'A tally board total, and a desire to take it from 18 to 20 appears linked to the deaths of two prisoners who were shot following an explosive entry into a compound that didn't result in the expected outcome.'

'Guys just had this bloodlust. Psychos. Absolute psychos. And we bred them,' Whetham quotes one Special Forces insider as saying.

'No one's ever won in Afghanistan,' says former 3 Squadron operator Trooper Jim. 'We're fighting counterinsurgency. We're not going to win this on body counts.'

Professor Whetham also talks about the risks of blowing the whistle, how those like Braden Chapman put it all on the line.

332

'Some people clearly were fearful, for their own safety, their family's safety and for their career.'

For many soldiers who were put in impossible positions – people like Dusty Miller, Tom, Braden and Christina – that betrayal left them with a profound moral injury.

But as I sit in the theatrette at Defence headquarters in Canberra, one line in David Whetham's section of the report sums up almost everything about how and why some SAS soldiers killed unlawfully, indiscriminately, and, in some cases, gleefully in Afghanistan. It reveals just how easy it was.

'Given that no one was held accountable for these and other incidents, and these are just the ones that we actually know about, it is difficult not to conclude that some people were literally getting away with murder.'

I walk out of the dimly lit theatrette into a blinding hot November day in Canberra. The Defence Force Chief, Angus Campbell, has addressed the nation and taken all our questions. He is swallowing the shit sandwich that is the Brereton Report, the product of an inquiry that he signed off on as the Chief of Army nearly five years earlier. But he is doing it with as much dignity, patience and purpose as he can. Overall, I think he has done okay.

I look down at my phone and there is a missed call from Dusty Miller. I dial his number.

'G'day, mate,' he answers in his East Anglian brogue. 'Big day, isn't it?'

Dusty tells me he wants to speak, not just to me. He wants to do an interview and express how he feels now that the report is out. I suggest we do an interview for the ABC radio current affairs program *PM*. That way we can run it long and he can get whatever points across that he wants.

'The first feeling I thought was complete vindication,' he says once I get into the ABC Parliament House studio and hit the record button. 'It's all true. It happened. It's factual. It's not rumour.'

Rumours. That's what Paul Brereton and his team were first tasked with investigating. How do you start to investigate rumours about things that may have happened years ago in medieval villages and far-flung valleys in a country on the other side of the planet? In backwaters that are now largely in the control of a resurgent Taliban? How do you investigate a military unit whose specialty is secrecy and silence, and whose members are trained to deceive and to resist? How do you begin an investigation with not a single specific allegation or incident, and with only whispers of unsourced rumours? That is the task that confronted Brereton and his team.

It took incredible patience, persistence and dedication for the inquiry to penetrate the code of silence among the perpetrators of these crimes. But it also took time to break down the walls of fear in those who saw the killings and the cover ups. Winning the confidence of witnesses and whistleblowers often took months.

'It is often not the first, or even the second, interview at which the story, either full or in-part emerges; it takes time for trust to be established, and for the discloser's conscience to prevail over any impediments,' Brereton wrote.

At least one of those impediments in one case was broken down by the footage revealed in 'Killing Field'. Patrol members, including Soldier C, were hauled in and confronted about what was shown in the video. It was hard for them to argue against what their own helmet camera revealed.

After finding witnesses and breaking through their resistance, Brereton and his team were confronted with the challenge of uncovering corroborating evidence to turn rumours into allegations. Then they had to turn allegations into credible information that could underpin criminal investigations.

As I read the report, it was the final lines of the Executive Summary and Introduction that struck me most. It revealed both

334

the professionalism of the inquiry, and the growing despair that came with doing its work.

'We embarked on this Inquiry with the hope that we would be able to report that the rumours of war crimes were without substance. None of us desired the outcome to which we have come. We are all diminished by it.'

We are all diminished by it. That sentence hit me. It made perfect sense.

We elected successive governments who sent these soldiers back and back and back to Afghanistan. We pinned medals on them and sent them back again. The war broke them. And we sent them back again. Those governments, as always, escape the blame for conflicts like Afghanistan, for the civilian casualties, for the shattered lives of Afghans and Australians alike. The Brereton Inquiry's terms of reference could never extend to the role or responsibility of these successive governments in contributing to the conditions that turned some soldiers into murderers. Not a single former Defence Minister who was in office during the Afghanistan conflict stuck their head up in the wake of the Brereton Report's release. But the report does hint at government culpability for miring the Special Forces in a seemingly endless conflict and it slams a weak Defence leadership unwilling to push back against its political masters.

'It is a misuse of [Special Forces] capability to employ them on a long term basis to conduct what are essentially conventional military operations,' the report says. 'Doing this on a protracted basis in Afghanistan detracted from their intended role in the conduct of irregular and unconventional operations, and contributed to a wavering moral compass, and to declining psychological health.'

We, in the media, must also wear our share of blame. Sections of the media glorified the Special Forces, holding them up to be invulnerable superheroes they could never be. We wrote and broadcast puff pieces about valour and victory, about selflessness and sacrifice.

We extolled the virtues of a war that had long ago lost its strategic and moral imperative. I thought back to one of the helmet camera videos Braden Chapman had given me.

'We're definitely not trying to win the war anymore,' said one of the SAS operators in the footage. He had just been talking with his patrol mates about a fellow soldier bashing cunts, shooting cunts, executing prisoners. That didn't fit the narrative that we read in *The Daily Telegraph* or watched on Sky News or Channel Seven. In the media the war was winnable, and our soldiers were brave Diggers whose honour and courage were beyond reproach. To repudiate that narrative and to report on alleged war crimes by our Special Forces was to be unpatriotic or worse.

'Mark Willacy, you would be THE most treasonous Australian to ever walk the earth,' wrote *traitors@hotmail.com* in an email to me after the broadcast of one of my reports on alleged war crimes by the SAS. 'I hope you are kept awake for eternity in the knowledge that you are the most hated person in Australia ... you are a communist traitor to your country.'

'It's time to commit suicide, just like hitler [sic] ... you German nazi Kunt! [sic]' emailed 'Fixi'. 'Because you will hang for treason!'

'Every time I see the picture of the Aussie trooper pointing his gun at the idiot, bead-clutching goat-fucker lying in the grass, I wish it was me holding the gun,' emailed someone called Lawton, referring to Dad Mohammad in the 'Killing Field' footage. 'If it had been me, I would have used every round of ammo that I was carrying to turn the cunt into mincemeat.'

That attitude expressed by some members of the public – that only our elite soldiers understand the existential dangers of battle and that that bestows upon them a licence to kill indiscriminately – is not one shared by those who serve in the Australian Defence Force.

'This perception that we have that our Special Forces are these mouth breathers who say they should be just let off the leash, they should be allowed to do whatever they want, it's not only morally corrupt, it's militarily ignorant,' says former Army general Fergus McLachlan.

Those most damaged by the conflict in Afghanistan were people like Tom and Dusty Miller and Christina and Braden Chapman. They were not damaged through any actions of their own or moral failings on their part. They were diminished and broken because of the actions and moral failings of others. They were betrayed by those of their comrades who took away their choice to be good soldiers, by their colleagues who put them in impossibly immoral situations. They did it by taking Dusty's patient away from him and killing him. They did it by demanding Tom be part of a conspiracy of cover up after the 'village idiot' killing. They did it by making Braden go through the pockets of a freshly killed Afghan who he had just seen shot in cold blood. They did it by placing a hand on Christina's shoulder and by making her delete photos that were evidence of a war crime. These good soldiers were damaged psychologically, injured morally, and their careers were ruined.

Recording our chat for *PM*, I ask Dusty how his experiences in Afghanistan have affected him. He pauses.

'It ended my military career, which was a significant military career,' he says. 'It's ruined lives. The second, third order effects of these unlawful killings and what we witnessed has been so far reaching and so devastating to so many, so many people, so many serving members.'

I ask Dusty if some of his former comrades should go to jail for what they did.

'Yes, absolutely. They did the wrong thing,' he says. 'They did it thinking they would never ever have to answer for those crimes ... we crossed a very bad line, and we crossed it for a number of years. We need to pay that price now.'

The contents of the Brereton Report sparked enormous media coverage and shocked many Australians. The scale and seriousness of

the allegations of Special Forces war crimes dominated TV news bulletins and the front pages of newspapers.

But within days the media focus suddenly shifted from war
crimes and cover ups by SAS soldiers to what many regarded as a
tangential and somewhat irrelevant issue.

'Units live and fight as a team. The Report acknowledges, therefore, that there is also a collective responsibility for what is alleged to
have happened,' Defence Chief Angus Campbell had told us during
his press conference in the theatrette. 'With this in mind, I have
accepted the Inspector-General's recommendation and will write to the
Governor-General requesting he revoke the Meritorious Unit Citation
for Special Operations Task Groups who served in Afghanistan between
2007 and 2013.'

The Meritorious Unit Citation (MUC) is a collective award for
outstanding military service. It was awarded to about 3000 members
who served in those Special Operations Task Groups over more than
five years.

'The Task Force's outstanding performance against an unrelenting, cunning and ruthless enemy, in an unforgiving environment, was
achieved through the collective efforts of every member of the contin-
gent over the duration of the commitment,' part of the citation read
when it was awarded on Australia Day 2015.

By recommending the MUC be revoked, the Brereton Report
was saying that the thousands who had received it now had to hand
it back.

'It has to be said that what this Report discloses is disgraceful, not
meritorious,' the report states in its justification.

The decision to revoke the MUC caused outrage among many
who received it for their Afghanistan service, as well as the family
members of soldiers who died there.

'If [Angus Campbell] wants it back, he can come and collect
it himself from my son's gravestone,' Felix Solomon Sher told

The Australian newspaper. His son, Commando reservist Gregory Michael Sher, was killed during a Taliban rocket attack in 2009.

Predictably *The Daily Telegraph* jumped onboard with a 'Save Their Medals' campaign, arguing only soldiers convicted of a war crime should have to hand theirs back.

The newspaper even had an online poll, with the somewhat loaded and emotive question: 'Should the ADF reconsider stripping the bravery medals of our fallen war heroes?'

'I'm happy to hand mine in as long as the senior leadership – who all got distinguished service medals for their leadership – hand back their awards,' former New South Wales RSL president and Afghanistan veteran Glenn Kolomeitz told *The Australian*.

'When I see people arguing, "You should uphold the Meritorious Unit Citation" or "these poor Diggers", I don't know anyone who can actually sit there and read the Brereton [Report] and come away thinking that,' says Samantha Crompvoets. 'It's just overwhelming that things happened. Even though lots of [the report] is blacked out, it's so clear.'

The debate over the Brereton Report had been hijacked. Almost forgotten were the shocking allegations of war crimes – unlawful killings, the horrific ritual of blooding, and the systemic practice of cover ups. Instead, the media coverage had degenerated into a culture war about whether the revocation of a collective award bestowed on 3000 soldiers was a betrayal of their service.

Not surprisingly, the Prime Minister – who had not read the unredacted Brereton Report – moved quickly to effectively override the Chief of the Defence Force over the MUC. Then, a week before ANZAC Day in 2021, the new Defence Minister Peter Dutton announced that Special Forces veterans who served in Afghanistan would retain their MUCs unless convicted of war crimes or sacked for poor conduct. The minister dismissed the recommendation to strip the citation from all 3000 soldiers as a 'collective punishment'. The media campaign to save the citation had won.

To others with a greater knowledge and experience of military affairs than the Prime Minister and Defence Minister, the debate about citations ignored the gravity of Brereton's report and its revelations about Australian war crimes. It was a diversion that also undermined its aims and findings. To these veteran soldiers, the report's focus and value is in achieving justice for Afghans, punishing those who killed indiscriminately, and in shaping the moral and military ethics of future soldiers in the Australian Defence Force.

'I grew up as a young officer being educated about the My Lai Massacre in Vietnam,' says former Army general Fergus McLachlan. 'In my view, this must be taught the same way ... at its best the SAS has been one of the best units in the world. So if it can happen there, it can happen anywhere. Therefore, we need to actually embrace it as a stain.'

'I don't think [the Special Operations Task Groups] should be keeping the MUC. There are far too many allegations against the unit and fairly well proven cultural issues that weren't addressed,' says former Special Operations Task Group intelligence officer Captain Louise. 'It's a unit citation and doesn't belong to the individual.'

After the Brereton Report's release, I caught up with Christina for coffee. Conversation inevitably swung round to the outrage sparked by the proposal to revoke the MUC. Christina reached for her phone and began scrolling. She then handed it to me. On the screen was an email marked 2 November 2020, more than a fortnight before the release of the Brereton Report. Sent by Christina to Defence, the subject line read 'Defence Honours and Awards'.

'For my participation as part of Task Force 66 (TF66) Oct 2011 – Apr 2012 I was awarded a meritorious unit citation,' Christina wrote. 'I am deeply ashamed I served as part of TF66 and oppose the notion TF66 sustained outstanding service (for which the MUC is awarded). I therefore renounce this award and wish to both return it as well as have it expunged from my military record.'

I looked over at Christina.

'Look at their response,' she said.

I scrolled down. The email from Defence apologised for the delay in responding. The official then asked Christina for more time to get advice about her request. It was clear they were not used to people handing back their medals or awards.

A week later the same official emailed Christina back.

'Thank you for your patience. You may certainly return your Meritorious Unit Citation Insignia if you wish,' the official wrote. She then gave Christina a PO Box she could post the citation to.

A friend told Christina she should feel proud for standing up, for telling the Brereton Inquiry what she went through and what she witnessed. But there is too much pain for any pride. Christina is glad she has handed the MUC back. To her, it is tainted, just like her service.

'The question I asked myself is, can a unit still be deserving of praise for sustained outstanding service whilst also responsible for the most shameful conduct in ADF history?' she says. 'As a task force we failed to protect those who were unlawfully killed, and we failed to protect Australian soldiers who now live with profound mental scars as a result. The task force failed me; they betrayed the trust of the Australian people. Most importantly they failed the people of Afghanistan who are still waiting for justice.'

20

HOME

'When I got back from the war I couldn't wear any
of my old jeans and shirts. Those clothes belonged to
a stranger, someone I didn't know, even though they
still had my smell on them, or so my mother told me.
That person is gone, he doesn't exist any more'

Russian private who served in Afghanistan,
Boys in Zinc, **Svetlana Alexievich**

DUSTY

Dusty is up next on the stacker. He is in the bowels of his apartment
building, waiting to park his car again.

The stacker is always breaking down. And it only has two bays,
meaning Dusty often has to sit in line until it is his turn to drive his
car into it. He has been waiting for 15 minutes and it is his turn next.
He taps the steering wheel.

Dusty Miller has been back from Afghanistan for about a month.
It has been a nightmare of a time. Literally.

He dreads the night. That is when he sees Rahul again. He keeps
dreaming of the day the big Waka got killed at the mud igloo. In
some of his dreams, Dusty can't get to Rahul. He gets close, but he
just can't reach him. In others, he makes it to Rahul, who is alive.
But Dusty can't save him. The Waka dies in his arms, his brains
leaking onto the medic's lap. One eye open, the other with a bullet
through it.

Sometimes, when he isn't dreaming about Rahul, he dreams
of the death of Blaine Diddams. Again, he can't reach him or save him.

The dreams are so vivid. He wakes up agitated, sweating, unable to sleep for the rest of the night.

This is an awful way to live, he thinks. I'm a fucking nutter, an angry nutter. Never in his life has he felt such rage.

A lot of the time Dusty tackles it with booze, and that makes things worse. The vodka numbs, but only for a short time. Then the nightmares start again, and then sleeplessness grips him like its cursed twin.

In the dim light of his apartment basement, Dusty knows his life is unravelling. It isn't just what he saw in Afghanistan. It is what he was compelled to do. He was forced to cover, to lie, to keep quiet.

They have compromised me, he thinks. They have fucked with my moral compass. He feels like they have broken him as a man, a medic, and a soldier. Dusty Miller has been a soldier for 25 years, but he is no longer proud of his service. A son of ANZAC? What bullshit, he thinks.

Dusty puts his car into gear and readies to enter the stacker in the basement. With perfect timing, an old Commodore roars down the ramp and passes him in the waiting bay and takes his spot on the stacker. A murderous fury rises within Dusty Miller. He has been waiting his turn. He has been patient, and now this young fucker has just taken his spot.

Dusty flies out of his car and runs over to the Commodore and smacks on the window.

'Oi, fuckwit! Wait your turn. I was just about to go in there.'

The young man, all swagger and sneer, opens his door and gets out.

'Do you want to make something of it?'

'Fucking oath I do,' says Dusty.

And with that, fists fly. The younger man, bigger than the 40-something medic, connects with a glancing blow to the side of Dusty's face. But Dusty is white-hot with rage and won't be slowed or stopped. He fires a flurry of punches into the young man's head, and the car park thief falls on his backside on the concrete floor. Dusty squats over him and punches him again and again.

The fight is over. The young man stays down.

Dusty goes back to work with a black eye and two pins in his broken left hand. He is supposed to be a leader of men, a role model, a medic not a mauler.

Dusty's mentor, the SAS Regimental Medical Officer, Dan Pronk, has never seen this side of his friend.

Nice, professional, competent, a great sense of humour, is how Dan describes his mate. His Dusty is the 'fit-as-fuck' medic who smashed the record for Dan's 'Drip Mile' competition, he is the combat medic who went to Afghanistan and patched up civilians and soldiers alike.

Like others in the unit, Dan has heard that Dusty is losing his cool, that he has busted his hand in a brawl. Who is this Dusty Miller?

The fight at the car stacker is no one-off. One night in the throng at the pub a bloke bumps Dusty's girlfriend Rachel and spills her drink. Dusty fires up and punches are thrown. Once again, it is impossible to hide the latest war wound when he goes into work.

'Hey! What's with the black eye, Dusty?' asks one of the lads.

'Do as I say, and not as I do,' he replies. But again, Dusty knows he should be setting an example.

'Mate, we need to have a chat. What's going on?' says Dan.

'I'm good, Dan. Just get me back overseas. I'm good,' says Dusty. But Dan knows that is bullshit.

'I can say with authority that the soldier who left for war was not the same soldier who returned,' he says. 'He had a level of anxiety and anger and frustration that wasn't there before. That jovial, easy go lucky, fun Dusty wasn't there any longer.'

The two men talk about the most traumatic incident from Dusty's deployment – Sarkhume. The wounded Haji Sardar was his patient. He was in Dusty's care, and the medic let Soldier B take him away. Then Haji Sardar wound up dead.

'I wanted to kill myself,' says Dusty. 'I wish I fucking had said [to Soldier B] that you can't take him, he's my casualty ... that bothers me every single fucking day.'

Dan Pronk reassures Dusty that he did all he could.

'He did his role. He did it well. Then circumstances dictated that that individual was taken from him,' says Dan. 'I've had that chat with Dusty a number of times.'

Dusty goes to see the SAS psych. He must, if he wants to deploy again.

'I just wanted to get back overseas again. So I sort of just fucking lied to him and I told them what they needed to hear,' he says.

In 2013 he goes on another tour of Afghanistan, this time with the Commandos. Over in the 'Ghan, Dusty feels settled, like he has a purpose or a mission.

Back in Australia he posts out of the SAS to a reserve unit because he wants to return to his adopted hometown of Melbourne. Plus, his girlfriend Rachel has left him. She has had enough.

'I destroyed that relationship,' he says. 'She walked on me. It was all part of the carnage.'

He wants to get his life together, but despite the new start in Melbourne, the nightmares and the anger are back and getting worse.

Dusty throws himself into work. It is there in the reserve unit that a nurse catches his eye. Dusty and Megan become close. But Megan is a straight talker, and she confronts him about his problems. Why is he sleeping out on the lounge room floor? What are these nightmares about? Megan tells him if he doesn't sleep, he will plunge further into depression, that he must get help. His drinking is getting out of control. Megan gives Dusty an ultimatum.

'You either go [and see a doctor], or I am leaving. That was the ultimatum,' he says.

Dusty arranges to see a specialist he knows, and Megan goes with him.

'She knew I wouldn't fucking tell the truth. It wasn't because I'm a liar,' he says. 'I didn't want to lose my job.'

Dusty opens up for the first time about how he is feeling and what he has seen. It is cathartic. But the nightmares and the anger are still haunting his nights and days.

In 2017 Megan and Dusty get married. A couple of years later they head to Albury for a change of scenery. Dusty is posted to the Army School of Health as the Wing Sergeant Major. But he quickly comes to realise that the job is not what he had hoped it would be.

'Now I'm dealing with trainees that are sending inappropriate texts to one another and I'm having to discipline them. The wheels, they just fucking flew off the wagon,' he says. 'I just hit the vodka.'

Dusty is hanging by a thread, and one day at work the thread breaks. He goes to see the unit doctor.

'I just cracked one day at work. I knew I had to take myself off to medical. The doc assessed me and said, "You're very sick, mate". He put me straight away on leave.'

At home, he drinks some more. With every swig of vodka his thoughts become darker, his mood bleaker. Dusty decides that the only way he can beat the demons is to kill himself. He even plans how he will do it. He is going to gas himself in his car.

The day comes, and he says his usual goodbye to Megan as she heads off to work. He is acting as normal as he can. Once Megan has left, he pulls out a bottle of vodka and begins downing glass after glass. He is summoning up the courage to carry out his plan. He is blind drunk when Megan rings out of the blue. She knows Dusty and senses something is up. Dusty doesn't remember what he tells her, but he doesn't give his plan away.

After he hangs up, he staggers out into the backyard and lies down on the grass. After a while someone looms over him. It is Megan.

'What are you doing?' she says.

The next thing Dusty is in Ward 17. It is part of the Veterans Psychiatry Unit at the Heidelberg Repatriation Hospital.

This place is for fucking sick people. Why am I in the psych ward, he thinks.

Inside Ward 17, Dusty is surrounded by other veterans, and ambulance, police and fire brigade officers who have also experienced severe trauma. The doctors diagnose the combat medic with PTSD, anxiety and depression. He is given medication.

'I didn't even take Panadol. So the concept of even taking an anti-depressant, an anti-psychotic, I was really dead against it.'

The doctors also believe Dusty is suffering from moral injury.

'It's anguish. That's what it is, a constant anguish about you being involved in wrongdoing or not doing the right thing,' he says. 'That moral decision was taken away from you.'

The moral decision wasn't the only thing taken from Dusty. So too was Haji Sardar, his wounded patient in Sarkhume. He let Soldier B drag him away. You can't take him, you can't take him. That's what I should have said, thinks Dusty, over and over again.

I contact my fixers in Uruzgan and ask them to get in touch with Haji Sardar's younger son Hazratullah, who saw his father taken away that March day in 2012. Hazratullah had heard the cries from his father coming from inside the mosque. He had described finding Haji Sardar's body covered in big fat boot marks.

Hazratullah has already told Dusty via a video call that he had tried his best to patch up his father's leg wound. The young Afghan knows the medic feels a deep, welling guilt about what happened in Sarkhume.

'He provided dressing and treatment,' Hazratullah tells my fixer. 'We are thankful to him.'

'Should Dusty feel any shame or guilt about your father's death?' my fixer asks.

'Was he able to stop that person from taking my father?' says Hazratullah. 'If he had no authority or power to stop that person and his role was just as a medic, then he should not be blamed.'

But Dusty Miller does blame himself for some things that happened on that deployment. Like the time he took back the piece of the dead Taliban fighter's shattered tibia and the patrol commander dropped it on the desk of one of the intelligence guys. One of the 'computer fucking warriors' who sits in their safe office back on base.

'They were never on the ground,' Dusty says.

That is no excuse, and he knows it.

'That's a dead person and we fucked with a dead person. That's actually against the law,' he says. 'You just got caught up in this bullshit, this moral shift comes into play. I'm not proud of it.'

Dusty spends nine weeks in Ward 17. It spells the end of his career in the military.

'I had spoken to the doctor and told him I wanted to go back to work. And he said, "It's not your decision anymore",' he says. 'I still had a good ten years of work with Defence at least. And that's gone.'

Dusty is back in for more treatment in Ward 17 one day when he gets a call from the Inspector-General of the Australian Defence Force. He knows it is time to come clean, to put what he saw on the record. He does just that.

'There's that sentiment the SAS are untouchable, that these guys are the elite,' he says. 'Let's be honest and tell the truth ... we were no different to fucking Nazis really. Going into a country and then just killing innocent people, just because fucking what? I was still part of that deal.'

I go to visit Dusty on a winter's day in Melbourne. It is typically grey and frigid. As usual, his apartment is spotless, and everything is in its place.

He has a new baby boy, Thomas, named after Dusty's great uncle who was killed fighting the Germans in Europe during the

Second World War. Thomas is a little brother for Eliza, who has just turned two.

But Megan and the children don't live in the apartment. As a family they are still together, but Dusty lives on his own.

'We could live here together. We could, but it was too hard living with me. I've become quite obsessive and compulsive and she's found that really hard to live with,' he says. 'We're still very much together and that's only because Megan stuck by me ... I hope that Megan and I can live together, and we can have a proper family. I'd like that.'

But like many other families, this one has to cope with the ghosts of Afghanistan.

'There's things I'll never tell my wife. Never. I never will,' says Dusty. 'She asks me all the time. But I never will.'

One thing he certainly hasn't told her about is the day he saw two SAS operators kill an unarmed shepherd for no apparent reason. That incident has stuck in Dusty's head because it was so senseless and so random. We are sitting on Dusty's couch when I ask him to tell me the story.

It was in May 2012 and they had cleared a lot of compounds in 'the green', the fertile farming land that is nourished by the creeks and rivers that flow along the floors of Uruzgan's mountain-hemmed valleys. Dusty tells me how the operation involved several patrols from 3 Squadron, enough men to fill four Black Hawks. They had lain in wait for their prey, ambushing about six armed insurgents on motorcycles, killing all of them. After springing their trap, the men had walked out of the green and assembled on a plain, waiting to be picked up.

'Before we were picked up, there were lots of radio chatter,' recalls Dusty. 'There was a lot of smack talk from the Taliban on the radios. So we were sort of expecting [something] but nothing happened. We left.'

The choppers began their journey back to Tarin Kowt. But all of a sudden Dusty could feel his Black Hawk circling.

'We were like a few minutes into the flight and then suddenly we start doing a hard right bank. I'm looking out the window and I can see the other choppers were in a holding pattern. Then one peels off, lands. I can see some goats and shit. And then a herder.'

From his position high above Dusty could clearly see two operators jump out of the chopper and walk towards the shepherd.

'[They] moved towards him tactically, weapons up towards him. There was an exchange of words, I think. And then I just saw them shoot him dead.'

What range were the operators at, I ask him.

'Oh, it's fucking close. Within like three metres or four metres I'd say.'

Did the shepherd appear to be a threat?

'He definitely didn't have a weapon,' says Dusty. 'They sort of left the body there and then just jumped in the chopper, joined us and we all just fucking carried on back to base.'

Who were the operators?

'Got no idea,' he says. 'I could see enough to see what was going on, but not enough to identify anyone.'

The patrol report will say the young shepherd was a 'spotter' armed with an old rifle. But it does not mention he was carrying a radio, vital equipment for someone spotting for the insurgency.

I ask Dusty if this killing has haunted him over the years.

'Bloody oath it has,' he says. 'This kid wouldn't have been very old either.'

I leave Dusty and his spotless apartment, wondering who the shepherd was and why he was killed.

A month later I get an email from Afghanistan that I know will interest Dusty. It is from one of my fixers in Uruzgan, a brave journalist who helps me track down people throughout this untamed province, which is once again mostly controlled by the Taliban. He has found Mohammad Naim, the Shina villager who was badly mauled on the arm and groin by the SAS dog. Dusty had told me he was certain the Afghan would die from an infection caused by the horrific injury to his testicles. I had asked my fixer to see if he was alive.

It turned out Mohammad took Dusty's advice. He didn't go to the American Forward Operating Base for treatment but to Kandahar to buy antibiotics to prevent infection. Dusty's treatment and advice saved his life.

I read the email from my fixer. It says that after Dusty cleaned, treated and dressed Mohammad's wounds, the people of Shina took him home.

'He spent that day in the house and the next day he went for medication. He said two to three times he [had] gone for medication and it cost him 45,000 to 50,000 rupees.'

I text Dusty to give him the news that his patient lived, despite the odds. He texts back within minutes.

'You're kidding! Fuck, I'm better than I thought!!! That's at least a Nursing Cross!!'

Later over the phone Dusty tells me how happy he is hearing that Mohammad Naim survived.

'I always wondered what happened to him. I'm just really shocked that he's still alive, to be honest,' he says. 'I've got a lot of tiny scars and some big scars. I think it helps heal one of the tiny scars. That's the truth.'

CHRISTINA

It is just before 5 pm, nearly knock-off time, and Christina and her SAS colleagues are in the Special Recovery Operations room waiting to get their tasks for tomorrow. Sometimes Christina gets mapping requests, other times she has to help prepare intelligence reports or collect information about things like current and emerging IED threats. She has been back from Afghanistan for about four years and is nearing the end of her posting with the SAS in Perth.

Special Recovery Operations is her latest role. SRO can involve anything from planning and executing rescues of military personnel and Australian civilians from hostile environments to undertaking domestic counterterrorism operations.

Christina and the others look on as their boss, the SRO intelligence sergeant, writes everyone's task on the whiteboard. The sergeant gets to Christina's name.

K-I-L-L

What the fuck? The sergeant is still writing.

Y-O-U-R-S-E-L-F

Christina is dumbstruck. She looks again, but that is what it says.

KILL YOURSELF

A lump rises in Christina's throat and she fights back tears. Is this a joke? Or is it an order?

'That's a bit harsh,' says an intelligence analyst, a lance corporal.

The SRO sergeant doesn't seem to care. Christina and the sergeant do not get along. He releases everyone from duty for the day. The sergeant will later explain that he has scribbled KILL YOURSELF on the whiteboard as a prank, that it was supposed to be a 'dad joke' and that he didn't think it would upset Christina. He will later be disciplined and handed a 12-month good behaviour period.

But at this moment he doesn't know how badly Christina is struggling. He doesn't know that her mental health is so fragile she has been contemplating suicide.

Maybe I do deserve to die, she thinks.

She walks out of the office and the next day she goes AWOL for a while. Since returning from Afghanistan Christina has been struggling to sleep and has been unable at times to control her anger. In frustration she punches walls. Once she headbutted one, bruising her forehead.

Christina has been holding onto what she calls her enormous secret. It is, in fact, a series of secrets. These secrets consume her with guilt.

Christina knows she has embraced some of the more toxic aspects of SAS culture. There is the boozing, drinking until she passes out. She has partaken of Das Boot, the prosthetic leg taken off the dead Afghan and souvenired to be used as a novelty drinking vessel back at the SAS's Perth barracks.

'I wish I could take it back, but I can't,' she says about drinking from the leg.

Christina is troubled most of all by what she saw in Afghanistan as the Special Operations multi-media technician and imagery data base manager, the person tasked with handling all the photos and videos coming in from the field from the SAS and the Commandos.

There was the video of the Commando shooting what appeared to be a dead Afghan in the head. Christina reported that up the chain. The message came back down – delete it and don't talk about it again.

Then there was that hand on her shoulder, pushing her down in her chair. That powerful hand belonging to Soldier B.

'Go through the photos,' he had ordered.

He was talking about the photos from the Sarkhume operation. The raid in which Soldier B hauled away Haji Sardar, the old Afghan with the flesh wound who later ended up being found dead.

Soldier B had come into her office and held her down in her chair, his hand like a weight on her conscience. She can still feel his grip.

'Delete that one,' he had said.

It was a photo of a weapon they had planted to justify the killing. She deleted it.

'Delete that.'

It was the photo of a leering SAS engineer. He was carrying the wounded Haji Sardar. Was the old man alive in the photo? Or was he already dead? What does it matter? We know he had the life stomped out of him. He is dead, and now he is deleted.

'I have fucking nightmares about that shit,' says Christina of the photo of the engineer. 'He was smiling. That's fucking sickening.'

Christina feels that by deleting those images she has let down Dusty Miller. She has let herself down.

'I avoided introspection because to reflect on my deployment required me to come to terms [with the fact] that I participated in the cover up of war crimes,' she says. 'I came to the realisation that I was not the person I thought I was. When the chips were down, I failed to live up to the standards I expected of myself and of what others expected of me.'

This guilt gnaws at her. Back in Australia she has a two-pronged strategy for dealing with it. Distraction and suppression. Work and booze.

'I use alcohol to numb,' she says. 'I have difficulty sleeping almost all the time ... I've been diagnosed with PTSD, although I think it's probably more moral injury than it is PTSD. I've got depression.'

Then there is the sense of betrayal that has metastasised into paranoia. Christina doesn't trust anyone, not after what she went through in Afghanistan. The only other emotions she feels are anger and fear.

'I don't know the last time I was happy. I don't get excited by things or I don't feel happy or joyous,' she says. 'There's grief that I'm not going to get that back. I don't think it's ever going to come back. It's gone. It's gone forever.'

Christina's time at the SAS comes to an end and she is posted to the Army Learning Production Centre in Brisbane. From the military's most elite unit she is now with a team making training videos. She finds the work boring and pointless.

'Where I was working exceptionally long hours in Perth and dedicating most of my time to either working or drinking, a big part of that had sort of disappeared.'

She is still boozing, but her distraction at work has gone and her mental health is declining even more.

In 2017 Christina jumps at a chance to go to Melbourne's Simpson Barracks to do a course. But the course feels as pointless as her job and

Christina ends up drinking most of the time. The booze sends her deeper into despair. It no longer works at suppressing that cancerous guilt. Instead, the alcohol is now feeding it, and it engulfs her.

Back in her accommodation at Simpson Barracks she is drunk and inconsolable.

I should have reported all those things in Afghanistan higher up the chain, she thinks. I should have said, 'This is not right, this is not right'. Maybe if I had just jumped up and down and made a scene, the bad shit would not have happened. The throwdowns, Sarkhume, the cover ups, the deleting of evidence. But she knows it would not have made a jot of difference. They would have just labelled her a troublemaker and sent her home.

It is time to carry out that task, she thinks. The one written up on the whiteboard by the SAS intelligence sergeant. She is away from home, so neither her girlfriend nor her sister will be the ones to find her body.

She slips off her belt, loops it back through the buckle and fastens the long end to the doorknob in her room at Simpson Barracks. This is how her cousin's boyfriend killed himself. But it doesn't work for her. Another soldier hears strange sounds coming from Christina's room and forces his way in. Christina ends up in hospital.

Back in Brisbane she tries to put the suicide attempt behind her. She goes back to work. But the darkness keeps closing in on her. Christina again tries to take her life, this time during a visit to hospital. Once again she is found.

She is sent to the Soldier Recovery Centre at Brisbane's Gallipoli Barracks. It is for soldiers carrying the physical and mental scars of service. Christina is there for months. There are only two paths out of the Soldier Recovery Centre – rehabilitation and back into the military, or treatment and out into the civilian world. She is on the second trajectory.

In 2018, Christina is medically discharged from the Australian Defence Force. She buys a house in Brisbane and her girlfriend Deb moves in with her.

'I put Deb through hell,' says Christina. 'I was mentally ruined, and Deb did everything. I couldn't do anything for myself.'

But after a year in the house together Deb can no longer stand it. Christina is on the booze, she is paranoid. With Deb gone, she is now wrestling with her demons, alone.

——

My first contact with Christina came one night at home after the *Four Corners* 'Killing Field' has gone to air. I am lying on the couch when a Signal message flashes up on my phone. It is from a concealed number and the message is set to a timer to disappear after one minute. Down one column this anonymous correspondent has listed Soldier A, Soldier B and Soldier C. In the opposite column he has written their names. He has their pseudonyms, and their real names spot on. He, I assume, must be serving or former SAS. I write back.

'What more can you tell me?'

A message flashes up.

'Go and put a spoon on your head and take of photo of yourself.'

What the fuck? Then it dawns on me. He wants to be absolutely sure he is talking to me, and not someone pretending to be me. Paranoid perhaps. But I am intrigued, so I go to the kitchen and get a spoon, place it on my head and take a photo. I look like a dickhead, but I send it.

The person at the other end isn't a he, it's a she. It is Christina. She is paranoid, she tells me later. She thinks someone from Defence could be impersonating me to try to find out who is leaking to me. They could just get a picture of me from the internet and send that. But the photo of the spoon teetering on my head clinches her trust.

She agrees to meet me. Over the following months we end up spending a lot of time together, mostly on my back deck. Christina doesn't work anymore. But sometimes she goes in and helps out in a woodwork shop. One day she brings me a beautifully crafted box. The lid is made of jarrah, the sides of rock maple.

'I made this for you.'

I don't know what to say. The craftsmanship is precise, perfect in fact.

We sit on the deck and talk while sipping the terrible instant coffee I've brewed.

Many times her voice wavers, and the tears start. Sometimes she weeps, especially when we talk about Sarkhume and the anguish of Dusty Miller.

'That's one of the reasons I came forward. I've felt for a very long time that I was part of this incident [at Sarkhume]. And I know that he's been to psychiatric facilities, and did I have the evidence to help him at the time?' she says. Christina knows the answer to her own question. 'I deleted it from the system, and I feel fucking totally responsible for that.'

The guilt is always there, in her words, in her face, in the way she sits opposite me with her shoulders slumped. She is weeping now. There is nothing I can say to console her. I awkwardly pat her on the shoulder.

Christina is also damaged by the horrific images she has seen. She remembers processing a photo of a Special Forces raid in which a young boy was killed and two women were critically injured.

'[The women] actually refused medical attention because of the fear of what their husbands would do to them. So they actually chose to die rather than seek medical attention,' she says. 'At that point I was like, "What the fuck are we even doing here?"'

But it is the image of the little boy lying dead, his face torn by shrapnel, that stays with Christina after all these years.

'They don't have cameras over there. It is probably the first and only photo of that boy in existence,' she says. 'And the one photo is of him dead. That's why it's so upsetting for me.'

Christina has written to the Inspector-General of the Australian Defence Force to pass on everything she knows, to let go of her enormous secret. Christina tells me she feels like she, too, should be accountable for what she did.

'I'm at the point where I don't really care about what happens to me anymore. I care. But I am at the point where the truth is more important.'

I explain that the IGADF is probably not after people like her, soldiers ordered or compelled to cover for the trigger pullers. The IGADF is after those who killed prisoners or civilians, who murdered and bashed and forced others to shoot people.

But Christina's guilt has to be assuaged. A few weeks later she is interviewed by the IGADF Inquiry and tells them everything she knows.

One day we arrange to catch up on my deck for coffee. Christina arrives with some flat whites from a cafe up the road. Maybe it is a polite way of avoiding the awful instant coffee I usually serve up. She tells me she has been in hospital, that she hasn't been well. The guilt is getting to her. We talk books, about her dog and her family. We speculate about what the Inspector-General's inquiry will find.

The next morning I wake to a Signal message from Christina.

'I could have and should have done more. Speaking up may have minimised or prevented more unnecessary and unlawful deaths. I hold responsibility for my silence and inaction. I don't think I will ever overcome the guilt and shame I feel for failing to do more.'

ANGELA

Soldier B wants a party. It is his first birthday since returning from 3 Squadron's 2012 deployment to Afghanistan and he wants a proper bash. Why not? He will be turning 45.

Angela knows it is yet another excuse for a piss up, but she bakes him a cake and prepares some food for the guests.

Soldier B, Angela and her son Nick are still living in the 'marriage patch' next to Campbell Barracks in Perth and most of the invitees are the veteran operator's SAS comrades and their families.

Angela still struggles to grip things with her left hand. The ring finger has been permanently weakened from the break she sustained the night she fought to get Soldier B off Nick. The big SAS operator was pummelling the teenager, pissed and angry about Nick writing off Angela's car.

After being released by the police, Soldier B had broken down and sobbed and asked Angela for forgiveness. She had told him that her broken finger could symbolise the past and that they could change their relationship for the better.

'Let's just take it slow,' she had told him.

But first Soldier B had to beat the aggravated assault charges that would end his career in the Special Forces. So Angela and Nick wrote to the court to say that a conviction would bring disgrace to a man with a distinguished military career. They write that he is remorseful, that he has stopped drinking and he is attending counselling. But that isn't quite true.

'After the court case, and this letter was written and done, within a week he was drinking again,' says Angela.

He is also becoming verbally abusive again, blaming Angela for his arrest that night.

'You know it's your fucking fault I was taken from my bed naked by police,' he says.

'It's your fault you were ripped out of your bed,' she replies. 'So if I were you, I'd stop blaming me.'

With Angela and Nick refusing to testify against him, the charges against Soldier B are dismissed.

Two days later a Commendation for Gallantry is pinned on his broad chest at Government House in Perth. It is for acts of gallantry while a team commander on a tour of Afghanistan the year before. Angela sends me a photo of them after the ceremony. They are in Government House in front of a portrait of Queen Elizabeth II, Angela in a purple dress, her head on Soldier B's shoulder. He has his arm around her waist and the commendation on the lapel of his dress uniform.

After the assault, the SAS had sent people around to check on Angela. She thinks they were worried that if the case got to court she would air some of the Regiment's dirty linen. The crazy drinking up at The Gratto, the nudity and the punch ups, the men being out of their minds after deployment after deployment.

After the charges against Soldier B are dismissed Angela says the SAS never contacted her again about the incident.

'They thought, "Oh, they're going to be happy families now because I'm taking [him] back",' says Angela. 'And then they deploy him.'

In early 2012, just weeks after the court case is thrown out, Soldier B deploys yet again with 3 Squadron SAS to Afghanistan. It is the fateful tour that will result in him being accused of killing Haji Sardar at Sarkhume. He will also be accused of bashing a prisoner. He will be the subject of his comrades' mutterings out on patrol.

'His eyes rolled back like a shark,' one will say.

'Kill a kid, oh well, just keep shooting cunts,' says another. 'Bash more cunts.'

'Shoot a kid. Shoot some fucking grandparents.'

These men, battle-hardened operators of the SAS, are disgusted by Soldier B's behaviour. But they are too fearful to say anything.

I track down Angela after getting Soldier B's charge sheet and court records in Perth. She agrees to talk to me. She tells me about Soldier B's birthday party after the 2012 deployment. How it was going well, everyone seemed to be having fun, especially the birthday boy.

'He's intoxicated being the hero. He's carrying on about himself.'

Then neighbours down the road in the housing estate let off some firecrackers. No one thinks much of it until the police turn up.

'Because of the incident with [Soldier B] they're thinking gunshots,' says Angela.

One of the wives at the party explains to the cops that it was some kids down the road letting off firecrackers, that there is nothing to worry about and everyone at the party is having fun. The police leave. But minutes later someone tells Soldier B that the police have been by.

Angela watches as Soldier B marches over to Nick, who is sitting on the couch with his mate, the son of another SAS sergeant. She sees him waving his finger in the teenager's face. Nick is frozen, the colour has drained from his face and he is looking up at the big SAS operator in abject terror.

'Next time the fucking cops are at the door you fucking get me,' he yells at Nick.

Angela knows how quickly Soldier B's temper can explode, so she rushes over to the couch.

'Hey, what's going on?'

Angela has hold of Soldier B and has turned him around to face her.

'What the fuck is going on?' she asks again.

'Your son is a little fucking arsehole,' he says.

Everyone at the party is looking at them.

The woman who spoke to the police at the door comes over.

'I looked after it. It's fine,' she says to Soldier B.

But his temper won't be checked. Neither will Angela's.

'Nick, go to the bedroom.'

The sight of Soldier B threatening her son has triggered her fierce maternal instinct and she has had enough.

'If you've got a fucking issue with my kid, you talk to me,' she says.

Soldier B leans down, gets in her face. But Angela isn't intimidated.

'If you're going to kill me this time, make sure you kill me. Because if you don't, I will come for you,' she says.

Angela knows that, for his entire life, Nick has been bullied. By his biological father, by kids at school, and now by Soldier B. She thinks the time has come to put an end to all of it.

'You better do it,' she says to Soldier B, taunting him. 'You better do it.'

A few of the SAS guys at the party grab Soldier B and pull him away from Angela. But after seven years, she has had enough. She is going to end it.

'You are never coming near my son again,' she screams at him as he is taken from the house. 'You are finished. I gave you a chance. And you want to go this way ... you are finished.'

So, too, is Soldier B's birthday party. In the bedroom, Nick is in tears and is being hugged by the son of the SAS sergeant. The sergeant comes over and tells Angela he will deal with Soldier B.

Angela looks down at her son.

'It's never happening again,' she says. 'We can't live like this anymore. I'm not letting him do this anymore.'

The SAS sergeant comes back.

'Get your stuff. You're coming to my place,' he says. He is worried Soldier B will come back and there will be no one left to protect Angela.

But she is not budging. She has had enough of being abused. She has put up with this shit all her life and she is not running.

'The problem is that all of you people let him carry on the way he does,' she says to the sergeant. 'You just sit there and let him talk shit. You all bow down to him, but you can't stand him. He's getting away with what he's doing because you all allow him to do it.'

One of the operators and his wife stay the night with Angela in case Soldier B comes back.

Late the next morning Soldier B returns, and Angela is waiting.

'We're done. I'm too fucking good for you,' she says. 'I can't believe I wasted my life with you.'

Angela and Nick move back to the east coast.

'When I broke up with [Soldier B] I actually thought I was a different person. I thought I was coping, and that I'm new and I can do this, and he doesn't affect me,' Angela tells me. 'That's what I thought. And I started dating again.'

She meets a nice guy and eventually he moves in with Angela and Nick. But Soldier B is like a ghost that stalks her.

'I feel like he's still in my life. I still feel like he's there,' she says. 'I was having nightmares and reliving the incident of him and my son. But I was reliving it in scenarios, different rooms that we couldn't get out of. Or that he actually killed my son. It was constant that I was having breakdowns and crying all the time, and me and my partner now, we're just falling apart.'

One night Angela is watching commercial TV when a story comes on about Sarkhume. In the report Dusty Miller talks about his patient being taken away and killed.

'You know what? I reckon they're talking about [Soldier B],' she says to her partner.

'Oh, don't be stupid,' he says.

'My stomach is telling me, they're talking about [Soldier B]. I feel that is [him]. That is the person I think he is,' she says.

Eight years later I will tell Angela how Soldier B is under investigation by the Inspector-General of Defence over the brutal killing of Haji Sardar at Sarkhume.

'Wow! So he nearly went to jail for what he did to me. And then he goes and does this,' she says. 'I don't think they should have sent him [to Afghanistan]. If this incident happened after what happened to me and [Nick], they shouldn't have sent him away.'

Angela has not seen or heard from Soldier B since she and Nick left Perth, and despite eight years passing she still fears him.

'He is still in my head, you know. I don't know when and how to get rid of that.'

BRADEN

It is six months since Braden Chapman appeared on *Four Corners* and spoke about the killings he witnessed in Afghanistan. Half a year since his revelations stunned Defence and the SAS, and most of the country. He has no regrets. Why should he? Crimes were committed, and no one was held accountable. He kept his mouth shut for eight long years. But no longer.

Braden is in a Westfield shopping centre and is heading to JB Hi-Fi to look for some headphones. He is having a wander about, killing time after being put through his second ketamine session. It is the latest attempt to treat his anxiety and depression.

The doctor says of the 60 or so patients he has put through the treatment, all but a handful have responded well. Braden goes in and gets put on the ketamine drip.

'You trip out a bit,' he says.

What he sees while he is walking to JB Hi-Fi makes him wonder if he is still tripping. Strolling towards him is a man with a shaved head who is talking on the phone.

Jesus, I know that face, thinks Braden.

The man is looking straight ahead. As the distance between them closes, he glances at Braden. The man's gaze turns away for a split second before it swings back suddenly and his eyes lock once again on Braden.

It is those eyes. They are intense, they bore into Braden's. He knows that man. It is Soldier A.

Fuck me, thinks Braden. A jolt runs through him, his anxiety spikes. Keep walking, he tells himself.

Soldier A's expression does not change as he walks past Braden. But Braden knows that he has recognised him. Braden is the former soldier who has accused him of war crimes on television. But Soldier A is impassive, a walking statue.

Braden keeps walking too. He does not look back.

———

After his deployment with 3 Squadron SAS, Braden Chapman went back to Afghanistan a year later in 2013, but this time as an electronic warfare specialist attached to the US military. The Americans needed as many qualified Bears as they could get and the SAS was happy for him to go. Based at the massive Bagram airfield, his job was to track targets from inside special intelligence, surveillance and reconnaissance planes. Once the target or targets were found they were killed by strikes from unmanned drones, A-10 Warthog 'flying guns' or F-16 jet fighters.

Braden had no idea what the people he was finding had done, or what they were accused of. He didn't ask questions about that. His job was simply to find them so they could be killed.

'I don't even think once on that deployment I thought, "I wonder who this dude is?" It's just like, this target pops ... we found him. Let's blow him up.'

Braden got the targets off a device he was given and loaded onto his laptop. The targets weren't just Taliban commanders. The team Braden was working with was also finding and tracking high ranking al Qaeda operatives.

'Once they were on that list, they didn't need to be armed,' says Braden. 'If they got the approval to strike, they would.'

He remembers one strike on five people sleeping on the edge of a village.

'They just brought an A-10 in and they just strafed. We were watching it in infra-red, so it was just like "splash" as the heat was kicking up.'

The heat splashes were from the Warthog's lethal 30-millimetre canon rounds striking earth and human flesh.

'I just remember seeing the splash and then you could see half a body trying to move. And then the A-10 was going to come back. They wanted to hit it again. But by that stage women were running out towards the bodies. He would've been dead.'

It was video game warfare – remote, impersonal, grisly. There was no smell of burnt flesh or acrid gunpowder in this screen-based killing.

Braden didn't try to think too much about who was being torn apart by the Warthogs or the drone strikes. If they were on the target list, they must have been bad guys.

Back in Australia Braden returned to 4 Squadron, the SAS's secretive intelligence-focused unit. Out one night at a bar in Perth he meets Amanda, an electoral officer for a West Australian Liberal senator. Overcoming his shyness, he managed to get her number. At first, she ignored his invitations to dinner.

'A little while later he asked me out again. I went, "Okay he must be interested". It was pizza and a movie,' says Amanda. 'It wasn't anything over the top romantic. I don't think either of us do over the top romance. From that time onwards we were just together all the time.'

Amanda is petite, but she is tough. After meeting Braden, she changed careers, moving from her comfortable job working for the Senator to joining the police force as a rookie cop. She wanted to be an investigator, but like most police greenhorns she ended up on the front line, dealing with domestics, drug addicts, pub brawls and car accidents. On one job she became involved in a scuffle with a mental health patient who spat blood all over her.

'When we got to the hospital, they knew who she was. And they said, "You need to get yourself admitted because she's HIV positive",' she says.

After the all-clear she was back on the beat in central Perth.

Not long after they met in 2014, Braden had an accident during a squadron training exercise in a surveillance plane over Adelaide.

'I just had to walk up to the back of the plane to turn some equipment off as we were coming into land,' says Braden. 'We just went through turbulence and I just got picked up and thrown and bulged my disc in the lower back.'

He was in agony and had to have surgery to replace the disc. But the surgery did not relieve the sciatic nerve pain. Braden was forced off work for months.

'Suddenly I'm sitting around doing nothing. Then it's all starting to come out because you've got time to think.'

Anger and frustration came out. Braden's injury resulted in him being medically downgraded by the Regiment, meaning he could no longer deploy overseas or do training. His career was in the balance.

Amanda watched, powerless, as Braden struggled every day with that anger and frustration. She knew he was suffering from more than a back injury. She understood it was also trauma from Afghanistan, from incidents he would not speak about. She realised the trauma was not caused by gun battles with the Taliban, but rather it was sparked by guilt from being involved in what Braden had become to believe was an unjust war in which the Australians and their Coalition allies were the invaders.

'You try to look back at your career and be proud of it, but then you've got all these incidents. You see yourself as part of the bad guys,' says Braden. 'They're going to look back and see that we were the guys in there murdering and invading and not there to do something that is honourable.'

'He witnessed his own colleagues doing the traumatic things,' says Amanda. 'It was the person that he slept next to, trained with, worked with for the past couple of years.'

There was the hands up killing by Soldier A. Two in the chest, one in the head as Soldier A walked past the prone man.

Braden was ordered to go through the dead Afghan's pockets. He tried not to look at the man's head, all misshapen, his brain matter seeping out onto the ground. And that fucking dog coming over and chewing on his head. Braden pleaded with the handler to get the dog away.

'No, give him a taste,' replied the dog handler.

Fuck you, thought Braden. But he said nothing.

There was the execution by the Wakunish soldier on the insistence of Soldier A. That was just two days after the Waka's comrade, the ill-fated Rahul, was killed in the battle of the mud igloo. The bound prisoner was told to kneel, then there was a quick burst from the Waka's rifle and he was dead. The man was the target. But that didn't make it right.

They had already told headquarters that they had a 'Touchdown'. The target had been captured alive. He was secure, they were bringing him in. Except now he was dead.

For Braden, it was all flooding back. He was in pain, and all he could do was lie around and think. He needed relief from the agony and the memories.

'I was on OxyContin for like four months or something, zonking me out.'

One day in 2015 his military career came to an end. The injury was just too debilitating. Braden Chapman signed the discharge papers.

'One day the book just closed, and he's had to figure it out for himself from here on,' says Amanda.

Out of the military after more than a decade, Braden started to read more about the war in Afghanistan. In 2019 he saw my story about the 2012 SAS raid on Sarkhume on the internet and sent me the email that would spark the *Four Corners* 'Killing Field' program.

'I was like, "Oh fuck it. I'm just going to write everything and send it",' he says. 'Go do whatever you do.'

Braden thought once he sent me the email that would be the end of it, that I would use his information to track down leads or to confirm what I already had. But I wanted to talk to him, to meet him, to understand more. Our meetings would lead to the hours of helmet camera footage from 3 Squadron's 2012 deployment, and ultimately to Braden going on *Four Corners*. While he feared possible physical retribution from former comrades, Amanda was more concerned about blowback from the apparatus of the state.

'My issues were the legal ramifications, particularly if the AFP were to rock up at the front door and do a search warrant and raid the house. That was my main concern,' says Amanda. '[But] for him to want to be on TV, I saw that this is something that he really wants to do. So I'll support him.'

The story created a massive stir. Soldier C was suspended, and the AFP called in. But for Amanda the story was important for another reason.

'When the *Four Corners* [story] came up there were tiny bits of that where I'm like, "Wow, I didn't even know that he saw or experienced that". I learned something that day.'

Braden and Amanda now live in the high country. To get there I drive past blond hills flecked with grey tufts. They are sheep, rock still in the landscape. In the distance a gathering storm is creeping up from the south-west. Above my car two wedgetail eagles ride the thermal updrafts, their wings completely still as they swirl in these invisible whirlpools.

Sitting in his lounge room, Braden tells me he has joined the Rural Fire Service and is helping them with their radio communications. During the deadly 2020 bushfires he also helped rescue injured wildlife. He is now building a wombat enclosure in his backyard, next to the chook house.

'I was trying to do more things that were kind of compassionate. When you're at the Regiment everything you're trained for is to target people. So [I want] to get away from that mentality,' he says.

As we chat, rescued wombats Bert and Kal scurry around our feet. Wombats are nimbler than you think. They are both juveniles and playful. Bert wants his rump scratched. Kal wants to chew on my toes. Braden has nursed both back to health. Bert was found in the pouch of his dead mother who had been hit by a car. Kal was discovered during the bushfires badly injured after being attacked by something, possibly a dog.

As well as wombats Braden is also caring for a couple of eastern grey kangaroos and some redneck wallabies. He is also keeping busy studying aquaponics and permaculture.

But later, Amanda tells me that Braden still has his bad days.

'You don't choose to be depressed, you don't choose to have PTSD,' she says. '[Some days] he doesn't get out of bed. He'll sleep all the time and if I can get him out of bed it's sitting on the couch all day.'

On this day Braden and I are on his couch and we talk for hours, barring the occasional interruption from a wombat.

'You did really put them on a pedestal,' says Braden of his former SAS comrades. 'There's that myth about them, that they are the perfect soldiers.'

But a few of those perfect soldiers went rogue, and they fell from Braden Chapman's pedestal.

'It was a very toxic war,' he says. 'I heard guys say, "I don't give a fuck about this war, I'm just here to earn money and kill cunts." Guys were like, "I don't see them as people".'

One of those who Braden had idolised was Soldier A. When I had spoken to the SAS veteran, he was furious that the young Bear talked to *Four Corners* about what he had seen.

'You're making split second decisions which he'd never comprehend because he's always standing there with dinner plate eyes going, "What the hell is going on?"' Soldier A had told me.

But I believe Braden's lack of war fighting experience helped him see things more clearly. He was untainted by the corruption of the war

371

and not infected by the elitism and bullshit of some of the SAS operators. Braden was the only one with the guts to speak out publicly on *Four Corners*, to show his face while others hid. The greenhorn may have started the 2012 deployment imbued with some of the swagger of 3 Squadron but by the time the tour was over that bravado had all but evaporated. The gung-ho greenhorn was no more.

'I didn't fire my weapon at all, besides at the firing range,' he says of the deployment, without a hint of embarrassment.

Our talk turns to the Brereton Inquiry, and how – even though it went for more than four years – it is just the beginning of the process of achieving justice. Braden knows, because he is part of this process. He has already given multiple statements to the Australian Federal Police about what he saw on his deployment. About what he witnessed his comrades do.

'I'm just happy that I got to tell my story,' Braden says. 'And that people are actually listening.'

LOUISE

Louise is roused by something on the bed. It is the family dog Vasily.

That's not like him, she thinks. He usually sleeps on the sofa in the lounge room at the front of the house. He must need to go outside.

Louise checks the time. It is 3.15 am.

She gets up and leads Vasily to the back door of the house. But the dog refuses to go out. He seems spooked.

That's weird, thinks Louise. A bad feeling comes over her as she returns to the bedroom where her husband Ian now lies awake.

'I went to joke to [him], "I think we must have a ghost in the house",' she says.

But before she can get a word out there is a shattering noise. It tears through the house. Then there is another enormous crash. And another. What is going on?

Louise immediately runs to their one-year-old son who is in bed with them.

'Call the police! Call the police!' she screams to Ian.

He is out of bed, moving to the front of the house where the crashes have come from.

'I'm just going to see what's happening first,' he says.

He returns seconds later.

'Yes, call the police,' he says.

Louise dials triple-0 and the operator answers. Louise describes the shattering sounds at the front of their house. Then she tells the operator why she is so terrified.

'I'm a witness in a murder investigation. I'm concerned that it could be related.'

It is November 2020 and Louise is a key witness in an investigation into unlawful killings in Afghanistan. She has spoken to the Inspector-General of the ADF inquiry and to the Australian Federal Police about 'the tractor job'. After almost eight years the ADF intelligence officer and Afghanistan veteran has let go of this terrible secret. Louise has told them how Soldier C spoke to her just a few hours after returning from that job in December 2012. How he described the patrol commander accidentally shooting a farmer in northern Kandahar while out on the raid. How the patrol then made the decision not to leave any witnesses behind. How they then killed the rest of the civilians there near the tractor, including a boy of 13 or 14.

As a senior intelligence officer on that deployment, Louise had access to the reporting from that job. She later checked the photos that were brought back. Lots of head shots. One image showed what looked like a teenage boy. He too was dead.

Two months before this unwelcome 3.15 am wake up call Louise had given a statement to the AFP, setting out exactly what Soldier C had told her in the SAS Ready Room almost eight years earlier. Now she fears that someone has attacked their home because of it.

Ian has returned to the front of the house to make sure that no one tries to enter. Louise tells the triple-0 operator where they live. The police ineptitude that will follow is worthy of the Keystone Cops.

While she waits for the police, Louise goes to look at what has happened to the front of the house. She is confronted by smashed window and a sea of broken glass in the lounge room. Three large window panels, each with two panes of glass, have been shattered. But what stuns Louise is the force of whatever has shattered them. It has spread glass everywhere and even implanted it in the walls, ceilings and floor around the room.

'We had wooden floors. It had gouged the wooden floors underneath. It was embedded in the ceiling, over two and a half metres [away]. So it was embedded in the ceiling and embedded in the wall opposite,' says Louise. 'In some spots the glass was powder. So whatever they did required an awful lot of force.'

There is no doubt in her mind that if Vasily had stayed in the lounge room the dog would have been killed. But what mystifies Louise and Ian is that they can't see what has caused the windows to shatter and spread with such force.

'There was nothing thrown,' she says. 'So who knows what was used.'

The police still have not shown up. Louise calls again.

'They are there, at the address,' says the operator.

'They're definitely not here. We've been waiting all this time,' says Louise.

The police have gone to the wrong house.

'Look, I'm concerned because I am a witness in this investigation. I know that other witnesses have been threatened. And I don't know if it's related,' Louise tells the operator again.

Forty minutes after her initial call a police car pulls up out the front. The officers briefly survey the scene inside and then pop their heads into the lounge room.

'They walked into the room and back out again. They were in there for maybe 10 seconds,' says Louise. They have spotted one of her son's toys lying in the middle of the lounge room among the glass shards.

'That could have caused it,' says one of the police officers.

Louise can't believe it. They are not taking this at all seriously.

'Don't worry,' says one of the officers to Louise and Ian. 'We do keep a police presence here [in your suburb]. Cars drive by regularly.'

Then they leave.

The police will later apologise to Louise for their inept and tardy response. They admit they went to the wrong house and that the senior officer involved made a number of wrong 'assumptions'.

'The officer involved has indicated that he "dropped the ball" and stated he will do better in the future,' writes District Inspector Charles Hutchins in an apologetic email to Louise.

Louise isn't the only one concerned by the police response. The AFP officer who took Louise's statement about the tractor job is so concerned he goes into the local station and demands the police investigate the incident properly. But the police never get any leads on the case, let alone identify any suspects. That is despite a neighbour's CCTV camera picking up a figure heading to Louise's house in the early morning darkness.

'It did show someone walking around and it looked like they were looking specifically for an address. Because they were looking at street numbers before they came up to our house,' Louise says. 'We had security lights on outside. So they've actually stood directly under lights to do this as well. Everything lends itself to [us] probably being targeted.'

Defence also takes the incident extremely seriously. Louise is now a major and a senior intelligence officer based at Headquarters Joint Operations Command, which is responsible for the command and control of ADF operations around the world. Defence knows she is a witness who has given testimony about alleged war crimes to the IGADF inquiry and the AFP.

'We were put into emergency accommodation that day. [Defence] was amazing,' she says. 'They weren't certain that we were safe any longer in that house.'

But despite moving, Louise remains terrified after the attack on her house.

'If I wake up, and I do a lot and it's 3.30 in the morning, I get really frightened. I don't sleep well,' she says. 'I was diagnosed with PTSD, and this has made it a lot worse. Because I don't feel safe in my own home now ... I don't feel like I'm safe anywhere.'

Louise knows her post-traumatic stress has been caused largely by one thing – that secret she had been keeping for years. The secret her ex-husband, Soldier C, told her, about the tractor job and the slaughter of those Afghan civilians. The secret has been eating away inside her. She has been too afraid to come forward and tell anyone about it.

'I couldn't look at myself as myself anymore,' she says.

But then in March 2020 Louise sees the *Four Corners* story.

'I'll never forget. I was on maternity leave,' she tells me months after 'Killing Field' has gone to air. 'I'd gotten up early to watch it because I hadn't seen it the night before. I recognised Soldier C all through it. And then at the end I recognised his voice when he was asking permission [to kill the Afghan]. And it was shattering.'

Louise realises she can no longer keep the secret. She knows Paul Brereton is looking into allegations of Australian Special Forces war crimes for his Inspector-General of Defence inquiry.

'I've been carrying this for a long time and getting worse in myself with it,' she says. 'Especially once the Brereton [Inquiry] really started to kick off and knowing, "Here's your opportunity to say something and I'm making an active decision to not say anything". That sort of thing destroys you, and it has destroyed me.'

After watching the *Four Corners* program Louise contacts the Brereton Inquiry. Then the AFP gets in touch.

'It needs to be done,' she says. 'I think after having that happen to our house it makes me more certain that I want to see the right thing happen. Because I need to be able to look at my kids and say that I've done the right thing. But it is coming at great personal cost.'

Louise has not seen Soldier C since they caught up for coffee in Brisbane after the 2012–2013 deployment. She received an email from him in 2018. He was coming to town and wanted to catch up. Her response is brief. We will be out of town then, she writes. There are a couple of other emails from him but she doesn't write back.

'I just wanted to separate myself completely at that point,' she says.

Louise and Soldier C have known each other since they were 14. Started a relationship when they were 16. Were married at 20. She has known him for more than half her life. But she now avoids contact.

Before I met Louise for the first time, I had tried to talk to Soldier C. I call him, but he hangs up on me. I text him, but he doesn't respond.

But I know where he is and what he has been doing since being stood down from the military in response to the *Four Corners* story. I watch an online webinar he gives to a group of highly paid professionals. It is about leadership.

Soldier C, clean shaven in his dark jacket and business shirt, begins by giving the audience some background about himself.

'I made a career working in small teams in high-risk, high-stress environments in the military,' he tells them. He explains that he has done an MBA and that he is working towards a doctorate of public leadership. 'I've been looking at leading high-performance teams in strategically sensitive environments. Sample groups have included parts of the Australian Special Operations community, law enforcement,' he tells his online audience.

He then talks them through a series of PowerPoint slides with titles focusing on change, collaboration and leadership. There are colourful graphs that describe how to make these changes. He seems across all the management jargon too.

Soldier C hardly looks like the imposing SAS operator we see in the 'Killing Field' who is out in front of his patrol in his wraparound sunglasses and bandana and armed with an M4 assault rifle. Unlike in Afghanistan, the whiskers are gone, and the hair has been allowed to grow out a bit. He looks more like a middle management carpet stroller than a fearsome door kicker. He has reinvented himself.

Soldier C isn't the only one whose career in the military is over. When I catch up with Louise in April 2021, she has only been out of the ADF for a month. She has been medically discharged.

'It was 2018 that I started to think my career is coming to a pretty rapid end. Because that was when I really started to have a lot of issues, and my performance really went down. I'm not going to say I was super high performance, but I have always been okay. But I stopped being okay. It took me a long time. That was my identity for a very long time.'

Identity. I wonder about that as Louise and I sit and talk in the bland apartment I have rented. I ask her about some of the media coverage of the war crimes allegations. How some think what Soldier C and a few of his comrades did in Afghanistan was okay. This is war and shit happens, they argue.

'There's an easier truth to believe, isn't there, for the Australian public,' she replies. 'They don't want to believe that their heroes have done this. And they haven't. Only a very few did do this. It wasn't all of them. I think it's just such a testament to the guys who came forward that they have broken those cultural boundaries that they did in coming forward.'

'But they're not the heroes, are they?' I say.

'They're not. A lot of people will say that they're traitors,' says Louise.

And those who did commit the crimes?

'Wearing a uniform does not allow you to become a killer.'

This leads me on to a question I have to ask her. It is not an easy question. What about the prospect of taking the stand one day to testify against a man she has known since she was 14, a man she was married to?

'It's terrifying. It's terrifying. And it brings a lot of guilt as well,' she says. 'There's his mother and his sisters. His mother is someone I do actually still care about quite a bit. But I know that this is the end of having any relationship there.'

Louise pauses. I know this is an upsetting topic.

'I think that I'll probably be looked at as the vindictive ex-wife as well,' she says. 'You see that happen all the time, don't you? Which isn't the case. I'm just trying to do the right thing now and make sure the truth gets out there.'

'Do you think you're mentally prepared for that moment in the future looking at [Soldier C in court]?' I ask.

'No way. Not at all. I don't know how you prepare for something like that,' Louise says. 'I'm trying to still see him as a human. I think in some ways it would be easier to sort of dehumanise [him] and turn him into this big bad person, which I don't believe. I think he is someone who is probably really genuinely struggling with this now. But there are so many separate incidents. It's not just one thing.'

Louise is also struggling, despite unburdening herself and letting go of that terrible secret. The police now have an alert on her new address, should anything happen again. If it does, the AFP have told her that they may need to speak to their witness protection team. It is an awful, unthinkable prospect for Louise, Ian and their young child. To cope with the stress and the fear, Louise has developed a simple strategy.

'It works for me to focus on just being a mother. That is a nice way for me to just live my life,' she says.

But then.

'I don't know what I've brought onto my family. And that is a real fear for me.'

379

TOM

Someone has spat in Tom's locker again. The other day someone had left yet another opened condom in there.

This is schoolboy shit, thinks Tom.

But this juvenile spite is taking its toll on him. Tom thought that once 3 Squadron SAS had returned to Perth from the deployment the bullying would stop. Maybe they would lay off.

Tom is one of them, an SAS operator who has earned the sandy beret. He has three rotations of Afghanistan under his belt, he is supposed to be part of the brotherhood. But back at Campbell Barracks in Perth their nasty behaviour and petty pranks have ramped up.

'Tom is a poof', 'Tom sucks cock' is written on a whiteboard. They keep hiding his patrol pack. One day he finds it stuffed down behind his locker. They throw his webbing that he uses to carry his military gear on the ground, kick his boots all over the place.

Tom has had a gutful and goes to see the Squadron Sergeant Major about the bullying.

He is told that people who complain don't get far.

'You can always call the 1-800 number,' says the SSM. It is the Defence hotline for reporting abuse.

Once, Tom was prepared to die to be selected for the SAS. Now, after what he has seen in Afghanistan, he is wondering what the Regiment he strived so hard to join actually stands for.

'You have to come back and work with people here in Australia, and it's like, "Hang on a sec, mate, you should be in fucking jail",' he says. 'When I joined the SAS I thought it was going to be like the SAS and not the SS ... I didn't join the SAS to murder people. I wanted to help people.'

Like his friend Dusty, Tom is having nightmares about what he has witnessed in Afghanistan. They are fuelled by an unquenchable guilt.

'Because you're carrying all that shit round where you know what had occurred was wrong,' he says. 'I was implicated within the murder, within the "village idiot" killing.'

In his nightmares, Tom sees the disabled man running away in terror. He watches as Soldier C raises his weapon, and then there is the awful spectacle of the young Afghan's head exploding into a mist of blood and brain matter. Then there is the dead man being dressed in a battle bra and photographed.

'People view these things through the eyes of a Hollywood movie where the hero steps in and prevents that from happening. And in real life that doesn't really happen. It didn't really happen.'

Tom remembers helping to push that village car into the compound, the soldiers drenching it in fuel and lighting it up. The car is a pyre of flame and black smoke spirals into the sky. Pop, pop, go the tyres. The Afghans in the compound say nothing – they are too frightened.

Tom remembers the interpreter looking straight at him and asking, 'Why are you doing this?'

He has no answer to that. How can he put into words the deep well of shame within him?

'That was never in our SOP [Standard Operating Procedures]. That was never in our training,' he says.

There are other incidents that intrude on his thoughts, that have him waking up in a cold sweat.

Tom tells me about the time on his second deployment in 2011 when an SAS operator with a high-powered sniper rifle took out an insurgent running down an alley. It was the first time Tom had seen someone killed in combat. He remembers walking over and looking at the body.

'It sliced open his skull like a melon,' he says. 'He hit the ground and his brain was perfectly formed, sitting on the ground.'

An Afghan policeman strolled over to the body, picked up the brain and placed it gently on the dead man's lap.

'Here's this bloke just sitting there dead holding his own brain. It was just normal.'

Like Dusty, Tom is hitting the grog hard to try to make sense of this normal. People are noticing that something isn't right. One of them is Tom's girlfriend. She tries to talk to him, but he just doesn't respond. He is in another world.

'I was just disconnected. Just not being present, not having any emotional feeling,' he says. 'My mindset was taken up 99.9 per cent of the time of running scenarios through my head of what happened in Afghanistan.'

The relationship crumbles and his family is concerned.

'You don't seem yourself. Are you okay?'

'What's wrong?'

Bullying, breakdown, booze, a short fuse and disconnection. Tom goes to see a psych, who advises him to leave the SAS. But he sticks with it.

One day in Perth a driver cuts Tom off. Tom follows him, waits until the man pulls up at an intersection and then he jumps out. He drags the driver from his car and throws him on the ground. The man is terrified.

'Oh, mate, I'm sorry,' the driver stammers. 'I'm sorry.'

The sight of the man quaking on the ground snaps Tom out of his rage. Now he feels shame again.

'I'm so sorry,' Tom says. 'I'm sorry.'

He goes back to his car, pulls it to the side of the road, switches off the engine and hangs his head.

I am now acting like they were over in Afghanistan, he thinks. I am no fucking better than them.

Rage and shame, and a guilt that eats at him. Tom admits himself to a Perth clinic where he does a cognitive behavioural therapy course for anger management.

In 2013, he goes to see his Squadron Sergeant Major about transferring out of 3 Squadron. The SSM is glad to see the back end of Tom and shifts him to the boat squad.

'They transferred me out of an operational position, to the boat squad. This is not [an SAS] beret qualified position. It was a demotion,' says Tom.

He is not happy at the boat squad either, so he leaves and does a year of Indonesian language training. Then it is over to the dog squad. He is bouncing around the SAS with no clear career trajectory. Other junior soldiers, men who joined the Regiment years after Tom, are promoted above him.

In September 2016 Tom leaves the SAS. He has had enough.

Like other operators, his body has taken a beating from years of high tempo training and multiple deployments.

'I'd snapped my left leg – tibia, fibula – in a parachuting accident. I had degradation of discs in my lower back. A few other breaks and bits and pieces here and there. I could no longer run.'

But it is the psychological injuries that are the most debilitating for Tom. He is medically discharged. The now former operator looks back at an eight-year SAS career that promised so much but became a living nightmare.

He has been king hit and knocked out by a colleague in Afghanistan. He was left on the floor and no one came to his aid. He has been thrown out of his patrol over an argument with Dusty and shamed in front of his fellow operators by being put in with the support staff. He has had his possessions hidden, stolen and burned. He has had his sexuality questioned. He has been ostracised.

Dusty Miller calls it the worst case of bullying he has ever seen. Others agree.

'You could be a good soldier. But what defines you is not your soldiering,' says a 3 Squadron operator and friend of Tom's. 'It's whether you want to be one of the boys, be one of the cool kids.

383

And if the cool kids are the bullies and the tough guys and you want to be liked by them, then you've got to be like them.'

After leaving the SAS, Tom heads bush and disappears. He needs time to heal. He is suffering from PTSD, anxiety and moral injury. Tom doesn't answer phone calls or texts or open emails. He wants nothing to do with anyone, especially anyone from the Regiment.

Worried, civilian friends and old mates from the SAS call his parents.

'We can't get on to Tom,' they say. 'It's been six months. Where is he?'

'He's just taking some time out,' his parents tell everyone who calls.

Tom needs time to process what he has seen and experienced, time to wrestle with that fucking guilt.

'You think, "I should have said something, or I should have done something. I should have spoken up". And you run those scenarios through your mind a thousand times, a thousand different ways. "This person shouldn't have been killed. If I'd done this, they may still be alive".'

Up in the bush, Tom plants native trees and builds gardens around his new place. Six months stretches into a year. Dusty Miller is one of those who calls and leaves Tom a message.

Months later Tom calls back and the two old 3 Squadron mates catch up. Then, one night when they have had a fair few drinks, they call me. I catch up with them in Dusty's spotless Melbourne apartment. We talk about the concepts of guilt and moral injury, about the struggle to readjust after Afghanistan, about the 2012 deployment itself.

'The wrongs need to be righted,' says Tom. 'And that's one of the reasons why I'm chatting with you. Because I'm a big believer in justice. And the people in Afghanistan who were killed that shouldn't have been killed deserve a voice.'

Tom has been interviewed by the Inspector-General of the Australian Defence Force as part of the inquiry into 'rumours' of Special Forces war crimes in Afghanistan. He spends five and a half hours telling the investigators what he saw. After thinking it would be just another 'box-ticking' military inquiry, Tom leaves the interview feeling buoyant and unburdened.

'It was a cathartic process,' he says. 'It was like someone had stood off my chest.'

We get talking about ANZAC Day, about how it has reached mystical proportions, and about what this national commemoration means to these two Afghanistan veterans.

'It's a tough day for me,' says Dusty. 'People [say], "You're the sons of ANZAC". No, we're fucking not … we were a superior force. As far as technology went, we were far superior … and we did the wrong thing.'

That reminds me that I have brought along some photos of the ANZAC Day ceremony at the SAS base at Tarin Kowt in 2012 when Dusty and Tom were there. I tell Tom he was a member of the catafalque party that day, one of the sentries given the task of guarding the ANZAC cross at the Tarin Kowt barracks.

'No,' he says. 'You've mixed me up with someone else. I didn't do that.'

I tell him he did do it, I have the photos here.

'Not me, mate,' he says.

I find the photos on my laptop. The men of 3 Squadron are in rows paying their respects to the fallen. Tom is out in front of them. He is in his camouflage uniform and his sandy beret, his head bowed, weapon slung over his shoulder, and hands crossed in front of him. He is one of four soldiers standing guard around a white cross inscribed with 'Lest We Forget'. Tom looks like a poster boy for the SAS. Muscular, clean-cut, respectful and resolute. He reminds me of one of those bronze statues of a chiselled Digger in big city parks or at intersections in country towns.

Tom looks at the photo. I can see he is straining to remember.

'That's you, mate,' says Dusty, shaking his head and laughing.

Tom leans in again, his hair unkempt and his three-day-old growth flecked with grey. He concentrates hard on the image. You can see he is straining to recognise the man in the photo.

I tell him that's definitely him.

'Fuck. That is me,' he says.

The chiselled Digger is no longer. The erect, clean-cut SAS operator in the photo never left Afghanistan.

ACKNOWLEDGEMENTS

The vast majority of those who helped me with this book cannot be publicly acknowledged. There are many reasons for this. Some are still serving in the Special Forces and are not supposed to talk to journalists. Some have family and careers they want to protect. Others simply fear that if they are identified there will be reprisals. In this, they are not exaggerating. Several people I spoke to have been threatened. Many took a great risk speaking to me, even anonymously. I thank them for their candour, their courage and their patience. They spent many hours talking me through events and incidents. They explained how the hierarchy of the Special Forces works and how these units operate both at home and on deployment. They told me of things they saw in Afghanistan, of events they were reluctantly drawn into. They were generous also with contacts.

To me, the true heroes of this book are the men and women who told me their stories despite the pain and trauma my questioning dredged up within them. People like Dusty Miller, Braden Chapman and Tom, who allowed me into their homes and who showed remarkable tolerance by answering every single question I put to them, often over days of journalistic interrogation. People like Christina, who sat with me day after day reliving events that caused her deep distress. Every time I would suggest a break, she would insist we plough on. I do owe Christina a sincere apology, not only for my relentless and often upsetting questioning but also for the almost undrinkable instant coffee I served her on my back deck every time she came over.

I want to thank Angela for telling me about another battleground, that of her home life with Soldier B. Her trauma springs from a different theatre but is no less serious or debilitating than the trauma inflicted on our soldiers in Afghanistan. Domestic violence, like

Afghanistan itself, was another secret war, one endured by some of the women hitched to the Regiment.

I am indebted also to Captain Louise for reliving her life with Soldier C and of her deployment to Afghanistan where she had inflicted upon her that terrible secret of slaughter. Like many I have mentioned, her battle is not over. It will stretch on for years should these men accused of war crimes be charged and brought to trial. This will test these courageous people like Captain Louise once again, on the battlefield of truth. None of us should underestimate how historic the day will be when an Australian soldier is brought into an Australian court to answer charges of war crimes. That the process must be fair and the defendants entitled to the presumption of innocence is beyond question. But what also must be recognised is the steadfast bravery of the whistleblowers who have risked all to speak out, not to mention the terrible suffering this moral courage has caused them.

Thanks also to Fergus McLachlan, Dan Pronk, Samantha Crompvoets, Andrew Hastie, Jeremy Ross and Neil Greenberg who were interviewed (most of them multiple times) for this book.

The genesis of this book arose from a series of stories about alleged Special Forces war crimes in Afghanistan that I did for the ABC over two years. Unlike the soldiers of the SAS, I did not put my hand up for selection. I was drafted into this onerous mission by the editor of ABC Investigations, my boss Jo Puccini. A multi Walkley Award-winning journalist and a veteran of the investigative reporting trenches, Jo knew that getting to the heart of this story would mean months of slog, and she has been unrelenting in her support of this journalistic deployment from the beginning. But I must admit that I was a latecomer to the Afghanistan war crimes story, years behind the likes of Chris Masters, Nick McKenzie, Dan Oakes, Sam Clark and Andrew Greene. All of these fine journalists forged a path by breaking important stories, and despite the often hyper-competitiveness of our trade, they have been generous with their counsel, contacts and support. Rory Callinan, Wayne Harley, Sally Neighbour and Morag Ramsay were also key players in getting the *Four Corners* 'Killing Field' program to air, a broadcast that made me realise that there was so much more of this story to tell. Thanks also to John Lyons and to producer Alexandra Blucher who has been my journalistic partner in crime for five years now.

Thank you to Nicki Webber, Ian Altschwager and Michael Brissenden who read the draft manuscript and offered sage and constructive advice. I am indebted also to Dan Ruffino, Michelle Swainson, Deonie Fiford, Anna O'Grady and the indomitable Fiona Henderson from Simon & Schuster who saw something in this book from the very beginning and backed it to the hilt. Of course, my agent Grace Heifetz was also central to getting it off the ground, as was Emily Martin who acted as my Praetorian Guard on the legal front.

My wife Suzie, and our daughters Nina, Kate and Eva, must be acknowledged for putting up with an absent husband and father as he traipsed around the country for weeks on end assembling the components of this work. They tolerated these absences whether I was on the road, locked away in my study, or a world away in my head. These wonderful women understood that I needed to write this book, despite it taking me away from them.

Finally, I want to acknowledge the Afghans who appear in these pages. Too often ignored or dismissed by the Australian military and sections of the media, their testimony is central to the story of Australian war crimes in Afghanistan. I am lucky that I work for this country's best news organisation, a public broadcaster with both the resources and the drive to get to the bottom of a complicated and controversial story. That has allowed me to reach the Afghans who witnessed or were victims of these crimes, and to tell their stories on the ABC. Those stories have been fleshed out in the pages of this book. These accounts would not have been accessible without the courage, industry, and journalistic commitment of my Afghan fixers.

These incredible people braved Taliban insurgents and local warlords and battled potholed goat tracks and extreme weather to get to the people I needed to hear from. More than once they were accosted or threatened for doing this journalism. Thankfully, they were not harmed. And thankfully, they always insisted on going back, trying a different road or track, or bringing people in to Tarin Kowt or Kandahar for interviews. I cannot thank them by name, because to do that would put them in danger. They know who they are. They are the bravest of journalists.

GLOSSARY

353s: nickname for SAS operators. Refers to the Army's Employment Category Number for SAS operators

Australian Defence Force (ADF): referred to commonly as Defence

Australian Defence Force Academy (ADFA): Academy that provides military and academic education for junior ADF officers

Australian Defence Force Investigative Service (ADFIS): the investigative arm of the ADF responsible for major disciplinary and criminal investigations involving the ADF and its members

Australian Secret Intelligence Service (ASIS): Australia's overseas secret intelligence agency

Bear: Nickname for Electronic Warfare Operator in an SAS patrol, troop or squadron

Cat: Nickname for SAS operators

Catafalque party: guard, often four soldiers, that stands watch over a monument. Used for commemoration services such as ANZAC Day

CIVCAS: civilian casualties

18 Deltas: Special Forces medics in the US military

Explosive Ordnance Disposal tech: specialist soldiers who defuse bombs such as IEDs

EKIA: enemy killed in action

Exfiltration: to remove or withdraw someone clandestinely from an enemy-held area

Forward Operating Base (FOB): a secured forward military position, usually a base, often located in hostile or enemy territory

Fusion and Targeting Cell (FATC): a cell of intelligence specialists tasked in identifying insurgent leaders, bombmakers, and senior fighters to be targeted for killing or capture

frag out: throwing a fragmentation grenade

Hazara: Persian-speaking ethnic group from central Afghanistan

Hellfire missile: air-to-ground precision missile mostly used to destroy high-value targets

High Value Target (HVT): a person or resource that an enemy commander requires to complete a mission

ICOM: a personal radio communication device, often a two-way radio

Improvised Explosive Device (IED): a makeshift bomb often employed in terrorist actions or in unconventional warfare by insurgents

India: troop call sign used by 3 Squadron SAS during its 2012 rotation

Inquiry Officer Inquiry: a type of inquiry, headed by or conducted by officers, initiated by the ADF

Inspector-General of the Australian Defence Force (IGADF): statutory officer holder that conducts reviews and inquiries. Appointed by the Minister for Defence and independent of the ADF chain-of-command

International Security Assistance Force (ISAF): NATO-led military mission in Afghanistan whose main purpose was to train Afghan security forces and to confront the Taliban insurgency

Joint Prioritised Effects List (JPEL): the official register of enemies marked for capture or assassination.

Joint Terminal Attack Controller (JTAC): directs combat aircraft and fire onto targets

M4 [carbine]: 5.56x45mm, air-cooled, magazine-fed, short-barrelled, light weight assault rifle used by SAS operators

Magazine (as in firearm): an ammunition storage and feeding device for a firearm

MP5 [machine pistol]: a German-designed submachine gun used by law enforcement and military units

NCO: Non-commissioned officer. A soldier who has not earned a commission and who gains their position of authority by promotion through the enlisted ranks

Objective (as in person): a goal for a particular military operation, usually a target person. For example, Objective Oberon (senior insurgent leader whose real name is Nek Mohammad)

Operator: an SAS soldier who has passed the Regiment's selection course and reinforcement cycle and has earned the sandy beret

Patrol Advanced First Aiders (PAFA): soldiers trained in advanced first aid, like civilian paramedics.

Person under confinement/control (PUC): People detained or captured by Australian forces.

Raouza: Pashto for 'come out'

Rat line: an escape route or a way of moving people clandestinely through an area

Returned to Unit (RTU): What happens when a candidate fails or withdraws from SAS selection

Rules of Engagement: rules setting out the circumstances in which military forces can engage in combat with opposing forces. In this case, rules issued by the ADF

SAS: a military regiment trained to conduct special operations. Its traditional role has been to conduct long-range reconnaissance and surveillance in small teams in enemy-controlled territory

Secured Compartmentalised Intelligence Facility (SCIF): an enclosed area in a military base or facility that is used to process sensitive and classified information

Secure Electronic Enrolment Kit (SEEK machine): a biometric machine used to capture and match forensic-quality fingerprints and iris and facial scans

security detachment (SECDET) team: troops that provide security to diplomats and VIPs at facilities, events and in convoys in hazardous environments

sensitive site exploitation (SSE): the forensic collection of material and information from a site or person to extract as much potential intelligence as possible

SLR: self-loading rifle

Special Operations Commander Australia (SOCAUST): Commander of the SAS, the Commandos, the Special Operations Engineer Regiment, the Special Operations Logistics Squadron, and all Special Forces training. SOCAUST also runs the Special Forces' domestic counterterrorism deployments

Special Operations Engineer Regiment: Formed in 2002 to respond to chemical, biological, nuclear and explosive incidents. The regiment is part of the Special Operations Command

Special Recovery Operations (SRO): Element of the SAS charged with planning and executing rescues of military personnel and Australian civilians from hostile environments and undertaking domestic counterterrorism operations

Standard Operating Procedures (SOP): a set of directions compiled to help soldiers carry out operations

Squirter: an Afghan presumed to be an enemy trying to escape or take up a better tactical position

Thermobaric grenade: a grenade whose explosion uses oxygen from the surrounding air to generate a high-temperature blast

Throwdowns: a weapon or item, such as an ICOM or mobile phone, planted on the body of an Afghan to justify their killing

Unmanned Aerial Vehicles (UAVs): commonly known as a drone, a UAV is an aircraft without any human pilot, crew or passengers on board. Can be used to strike at enemy personnel and positions and to capture video footage of operations

USP pistol: a semi-automatic pistol developed by German firm Heckler & Koch

Waka: Australian SAS slang for Wakunish, the Afghan police special forces. Partner force to the SAS on the 2012 rotation

Withdrawal at Own Request: a form a candidate can use to withdraw from the SAS selection course. If used, the candidate is barred from ever applying for SAS selection again

ENDNOTES

CHAPTER 1: KILO

1. 'Even the air of this country has a story to tell about warfare. It is possible here to lift a piece of bread from a plate and following it back to its origins, collect a dozen stories concerning war – how it affected the hand that pulled it out of the oven, the hand that kneaded the dough, how war impinged upon the field where wheat was grown', from Nadeem Aslam, *The Wasted Vigil*, Faber & Faber, 2009, p. 59.
2. The information about Uruzgan's life expectancy and literacy is based on a December 2010 report by the Australian Government development agency AusAID entitled 'Aghanisation Strategic Approach 2010'.
3. A secret cable leaked on wikileaks based on Afghan intelligence from the US Ambassador to Afghanistan, Karl Eikenberry, suggested up to half of the Taliban are Kuchis.
4. The information that the enemy killed in action included the target plus three younger boys, most likely suicide bombers who'd come straight out of a training camp in Pakistan, is sourced from Mark Donaldson, *The Crossroad*, Pan Macmillan, Sydney, 2014, p. 568.

CHAPTER 2: BEAR

The information about 4 Squadron operatives and their activities is sourced from an article by Rafael Epstein and Dylan Welch, 'Secret Squadron: SAS elite operate at large as spies in Africa', *The Sydney Morning Herald*, 13 March 2012.

CHAPTER 3: ANGELA

The quote about Paddy Mayne is from Ben Macintyre, *SAS: Rogue Heroes*, Penguin, 2017, p. 37.

CHAPTER 4: GIVE HIM A TASTE

1. 'Now you see how it is here. Somewhere in the war there's supposed to be honour. Where's the honour here?', statement from fictional Afghan Mujahedeen leader 'Masoud' in *Rambo III*, Carolco Pictures.

2. The figures of the US spending USD $1.5 million per day, and the Taliban making USD $200 million per year are from a report by Justin Rowlatt, 'How the US military's opium war in Afghanistan was lost', *BBC News*, 25 April 2019.

CHAPTER 5: KING HIT

'Sitting in Saigon was like sitting inside the folded petals of a poisonous flower, the poison history, fucked in its root no matter how far back you wanted to run your trace', from Michael Herr, *Dispatches*, Picador, 2004, p. 41.

CHAPTER 6: SARKHUME

The quotes from Special Operations commander in Uruzgan, Jon Hawkins, that 'People who have not been in combat have no idea' and 'It is just absolute chaos yet [the Australian Defence Force Investigative Service] treat war as if it is a clinical event. It is not a clinical event. It is a complete and utter mess' are both from Chris Masters, *No Front Line: Australia's Special Forces at War in Afghanistan*, Allen & Unwin, Australia, 2017, p. 456.

CHAPTER 7: KILLING FIELD

1. 'It's one thing to say don't commit atrocities on the battlefield. It's another thing to say don't get caught doing atrocities', disgraced former US Marine Corps Lieutenant-Colonel Oliver North, Frontline interview, PBS, 9 October 2000. Oliver North was a member of the US National Security Council in the late 1980s when he became caught up in the so-called Iran-Contra affair, which involved re-directing funds from the illegal sale of weapons to the Khomeini regime in Tehran to support the Contra rebel groups in Nicaragua.
2. 'Australia's Special Operations Commander, Adam Findlay, hauls in all the SAS squadrons. He makes the extraordinary admission that war crimes by the Special Forces in Afghanistan may have been covered up. He blames the war crimes on "one common cause", from an article by Nick McKenzie & Chris Masters, 'Special forces chief acknowledges war crimes, blames "poor moral leadership", *The Age*, 28 June 2020.

CHAPTER 8: IN CASE OF WAR, BREAK GLASS
The lines that open the chapter are from Rudyard Kipling's 'The Young British Soldier'. According the Kipling Society, this was one of the first group of poems of *Barrack Room Ballads* published after Kipling came back to England in 1889 and was 'sung or recited by an experienced soldier to half-trained men who have just arrived in India and are misbehaving in a foolish and dangerous manner'.

CHAPTER 9: SHINA
John Nagl, a counterinsurgency adviser to top American general David Petraeus, famously describing the JPEL as 'an almost industrial-scale counterterrorism killing machine' is quoted from a report by Gretchen Gavett on 'Frontline', Public Broadcasting Service, 17 June 2011.

CHAPTER 10: THE WELL
The Winston Churchill quote 'But who in war will not have his laugh amid the skulls' is from an article by James Wood, 'Unseen Churchill letter reveals for first time how brazen Lord Mountbatten nearly shot dead RAF chief at secret WWII conference', *The Daily Mail*, 27 September 2018.

CHAPTER 11: THE CASE OF ALEXANDER BLACKMAN
1. 'For in that sleep of death, what dreams may come, When we have shuffled off this mortal coil', William Shakespeare, *Hamlet*, Cambridge University Press, 2005.
2. 'If you ask your men to go into hell, you ask them to give you their unswerving loyalty. When they come back out, those that do, you give them your unswerving loyalty in return', quoted from an article by Frederick Forsyth, 'A "rigged" trial and a hero betrayed by the top brass: Frederick Forsyth asks what happened to loyalty and honour in the treatment of Marine Alex Blackman', *The Daily Mail*, 27 October 2015.
3. '... they saw severed limbs of dead mates hung from the trees to taunt them, found the flayed-alive body of a soldier taken alive by the Taliban, carried their colleagues with severed legs to the "casevac" helicopters, some alive, some dead', from an article by Frederick Forsyth, 'Marine A: The shambles that shamed us', *The Spectator*, 30 March 2017.

4. A comrade describes Blackman as 'a husk of his former self', from an article by Haroon Siddique, 'Marine who killed Afghan prisoner was "John Wayne" type, court hears', *The Guardian*, 7 February 2017.

CHAPTER 12: STIRRERS

1. 'Recruits tended to be unusual to the point of eccentricity, people who did not slot easily into the ranks of the regular army, misfits and reprobates with an instinct for covert war and little time for convention, part soldiers and part spies, rogue warriors', from Ben Macintyre, *SAS: Rogue Heroes*, Penguin, 2017, p. xv (Author's Note).

2. 'Nine Newspapers reported that SAS members who witnessed what happened were prepared to testify that Roberts-Smith, then an SAS corporal, had unlawfully killed the man', quoted from an article by Nick McKenzie & Chris Masters, 'Police launch second war crimes investigation into Ben Roberts-Smith', *The Age*, 16 December 2019.

CHAPTER 13: THE DEATH OF DIDDAMS

1. 'Every day and every night that our soldiers continue to fight in Afghanistan, every day that we have troops overseas in harm's way, you hope the family will not be receiving some fateful news – but they do. That is the thankless reality of war', Prime Minister Julia Gillard speaking in Parliament on a condolence motion regarding the death of Sergeant Blaine Diddams, 14 August 2012.

2. '3 Squadron SAS is just a few days away from heading home. It has been a busy rotation. Some say it has been the most successful of any of the 17 Special Forces deployments so far. More drugs seized by the Commandos, more enemy fighters killed or captured by the SAS, and more weapons and explosives seized or destroyed than on any other rotation', from Chris Masters, *No Front Line: Australia's Special Forces at war in Afghanistan*, Allen & Unwin, Australia, 2017, p. 471.

3. 'Donaldson hears Diddams shout "Frag out!" over the radio' … 'Didds is hit, he's down' … 'Blaine Diddams has been hit by a round that has passed through his clavicle and hit his aorta', from Mark Donaldson, *The Crossroad*, Pan Macmillan, 2013, p. 596.

4. 'He was behind a small rock wall and had risen to fire at the Taliban fighters when he was struck above his chest plate', from Chris Masters, *No Front Line: Australia's Special Forces at war in Afghanistan*, Allen & Unwin, Australia, 2017, p. 474.
5. 'Donaldson hears that Diddams has been loaded onto an aeromedical evacuation chopper, and he is just minutes away from the Role 2 medical facility at Camp Russell', from Mark Donaldson, *The Crossroad*, Pan Macmillan, 2013, p. 597.

CHAPTER 14: THE TRACTOR JOB

'It was terrible. They were slaughtering villagers like so many sheep.' Sgt Lawrence LaCroix, squad leader 1st Platoon, Charlie Company, United States 1st Battalion, 20th Infantry after the My Lai massacre, Vietnam 16 March 1968, quoted from the Mai Lai trials entry, Professor Douglas O. Linder, 'Famous Trials' website, https://www.famous-trials.com/mylaicourts/1649-ridenhour-ltr

CHAPTER 15: THE GOAT FUCKER

1. 'A medevac helicopter was called to take the dog back to the hospital on base for urgent treatment. But Fax was declared dead on arrival' and 'It was an excellent example of the courage and determination required of a [Combat Assault Dog] in the SASR', from 'Australian War Dogs Combat Profiles', www.aussiewardogs.org.
2. 'The [Australians] allowed themselves to be used by local allies, who competed with each other for Western military resources to empower themselves as tribal leaders. Some then used those resources to target their rivals', from an article by Amanda Hodge, 'Afghan henchman "used ADF troops", says Dutch journalist', *The Australian*, 29 January 2021.
3. 'The warlord is very generous to his friends, and as revealed by the ABC in early 2021, he regularly presented Rado watches worth more than $1000 to Australian Special Forces soldiers in Uruzgan', from an article by Andrew Greene, 'Afghan militia leader Matiullah Khan gave gold watches to Australian Special Forces commanders', *ABC Online*, 5 February, 2021.

CHAPTER 16: CIRCLE OF FRIENDS

1. 'Let me remind you that you must never think of yourselves as an elite ... No, you are not an elite force. You are something more distinguished', quote by David Stirling, founder of the British SAS, from Ben Macintyre, *SAS: Rogue Heroes*, Penguin, 2017, p. 317.
2. 'The SAS is convinced Rapier exists. To them he is "the white whale", their extant and abiding obsession that is seemingly always one step ahead' ... 'By the time the SAS regrouped, Rapier was gone' ... 'Later that year, Rapier was said to have escaped again, slipping through a Dutch cordon disguised as a woman', from Chris Masters, *No Front Line: Australia's Special Forces at war in Afghanistan*, Allen & Unwin, Australia, 2017, p. 244, 187, 292.
3. 'The mission is described in detail by veteran journalist and author Chris Masters in his book, *No Front Line*. It recounts how four alleged Afghan insurgents were killed in the raid, and how a "shit storm" will soon erupt'. Chris Masters, *No Front Line: Australia's Special Forces at war in Afghanistan*, Allen & Unwin, Australia, 2017, p. 517.
4. 'One SAS trooper will later claim that the experts described the removal of hands as the "gold plate solution",' from an article by Dan Oakes & Sam Clark, '"What the f**k are you doing": Chaos over severed hands', *ABC Online*, 11 July 2017.
5. 'Another said someone asked, "So you're sweet with us bringing back a hand?" The reply reportedly went, "Yes ... you've got to do what you've got to do on the battlefield"' ... 'The ADFIS sergeant leaves the meeting thinking the SAS members now regard the severing of hands as legitimate. "That's all they were focused on," he would say later', quoted from an article by Dan Oakes & Sam Clark, '"What the f**k are you doing": Chaos over severed hands', *ABC Online*, 11 July 2017

CHAPTER 17: THE GOOD SOLDIER

'Every soldier thinks something of the moral aspects of what he is doing. But all war is immoral and if you let that bother you, you're not a good soldier' US Air Force General Curtis Le May, quoted from Henry Steele Commager & Donald L. Miller, *The Story of World War II*, Simon & Schuster, 2010, p. 459.

CHAPTER 18: WHERE OTHERS FEAR TO TREAD

1. 'A war begun for no wise purpose, carried on with a strange mixture of rashness and timidity, brought to a close after suffering and disaster, without much glory attached either to the government which directed, or the great body of troops which waged it. Not one benefit, political or military, was acquired with this war', British Army Chaplain George R. Gleig on the First Anglo-Afghan War of 1839–1842, from William Dalrymple, *Return of a King: The Battle for Afghanistan*, Bloomsbury, 2014, p. 489.

2. 'What's going on? Back in those early days, these weren't stories about war crimes', quoted from 'Character is the Foundation: Major General Jeff Sengelman', *No Limitations Podcast Episode 61*, 3 December 2020.

3. 'I reached the point as a leader when I knew that if I couldn't elicit from my own soldiers the truth, and if I didn't have a relationship with them that believed enough in me to at least tell me their stories about what they thought was going on, then actually the very foundations of my position as SOCAUST, my unwritten contract as a leader, would be held in some doubt. I knew I had to try something different', from 'Character is the Foundation: Major General Jeff Sengelman', *No Limitations Podcast Episode 61*, 3 December 2020.

4. 'I brought in the bulk of the members of the Regiment in a single room and I asked them to tell me their stories. But I asked them in a way that encouraged them to believe in me. So I expressed my concern about what was going on and why. I invited them to each write me a letter to tell me honestly what was going on in their own words', From 'Character is the Foundation: Major General Jeff Sengelman', *No Limitations Podcast Episode 61*, 3 December 2020.

5. 'It was people from within Special Operations who told the stories, not outsiders. People inside. Our own people came forward and shared those stories,' Sengelman says. From 'Character is the Foundation: Major General Jeff Sengelman', *No Limitations Podcast Episode 61*, 3 December 2020.

6. 'All were shot and bayonetted to put them out of their misery,' Captain Brereton told those gathered in the jury-rigged courtroom. 'I submit the act was a deliberate, calculated, cold blooded murder', from Tony

Cunneen, 'Russell Le Gay Brereton (Dooley) and the War Crimes Trials in Labuan in 1945', *Barnews: The Journal of the NSW Bar Association Summer 2020*.

7. 'Sergeant Major Tsuruo Sugino was today sentenced to death for having massacred 46 Allied prisoners ... He was found guilty after 15 minutes' consideration ... he is the first Japanese to be sentenced for crimes against humanity', from 'Death Sentence for Jap Officer', *The Courier Mail*, 6 December 1945.

8. 'I feel like a parent who's had to take their loved son or daughter down to the police station because you realise they've done something really wrong. Doing the right thing can sometimes feel really tough, mate', from 'Character is the Foundation: Major General Jeff Sengelman', *No Limitations Podcast Episode 61*, 3 December 2020.

CHAPTER 19: LORD OF THE FLIES

1. The observation by General Sir John Hackett that opens this chapter is part of this longer quote: 'What a society gets in its armed services is exactly what it asks for, no more and no less. What it asks for tends to be a reflection of what it is. When a country looks at its fighting forces it is looking in a mirror: if the mirror is a true one, the face that it sees there will be its own', from *The Profession of Arms*, by General Sir John Hackett, Macmillan, 1983

2. '"He hasn't got shit", boasted one SAS soldier at a barbecue in Perth the year after Brereton's inquiry began', from an article by Nick McKenzie, Chris Masters & Anthony Galloway, 'How a determined judge cracked the SAS code of silence', *The Age*, 22 November 2020.

CHAPTER 20: HOME

'When I got back from the war I couldn't wear any of my old jeans and shirts. Those clothes belonged to a stranger, someone I didn't know, even though they still had my smell on them, or so my mother told me. That person is gone, he doesn't exist any more', Russian private who served in Afghanistan, from Svetlana Alexievich, *Boys in Zinc,* Penguin, 2017, p. 51.

ABOUT THE AUTHOR

Mark Willacy has been a journalist for more than 25 years and has reported for the ABC from more than 30 countries. Mark is a seven-time Walkley Award winner and in 2020 he was awarded Australia's highest honour in journalism, the Gold Walkley, for exposing alleged Australian SAS war crimes in Afghanistan. His winning *Four Corners* report 'Killing Field' made headlines around the world and sparked a federal police war crimes investigation. As the ABC's Middle East correspondent for four years, Mark reported on the ground from the Israeli-Palestinian conflict and the 2003 war in Iraq. He was also the Japan correspondent in 2011 when the country was hit by its most powerful earthquake in more than a thousand years. Mark has twice been named Queensland Journalist of the Year and in 2019 he won a Logie Award for his *Four Corners* world exclusive on the Thai cave rescue. Mark lives in Brisbane.